riva specht
ACSW

grace j. craig
University of Massachusetts

HUMAN DEVELOPMENT
a social work perspective

prentice-hall, inc., englewood cliffs, new jersey 07632

Library of Congress Cataloging in Publication Data

SPECHT, RIVA.
   Human development.

   "Based on Grace Craig's successful text, Human
development"—Pref.
   Bibliography.
   Includes index.
   1.–Developmental psychology.   2.–Social
psychology.   3.–Social service.   I.–Craig, Grace J.
II.–Title.
BF713.S68   1982   155   81-8479
ISBN 0-13-444778-6   AACR2

Printed in the United States of Amercia

10   9   8   7   6   5   4   3   2

Editorial/production and interior design: Jeanne Hoeting
Cover design: Diane Saxe
Cover Photograph: United Nations, Photo by Marcia Weinstein (NJ)
Manufacturing Buyer: John Hall

Prentice-Hall International, Inc., *London*
Prentice-Hall of Australia Pty. Limited, *Sydney*
Prentice-Hall of Canada, Ltd., *Toronto*
Prentice-Hall of India Private Limited, *New Delhi*
Prentice-Hall of Japan, Inc., *Tokyo*
Prentice-Hall of Southeast Asia Pte. Ltd., *Singapore*
Whitehall Books Limited, *Wellington, New Zealand*

CONTENTS

chapter four

THE PRESCHOOL CHILD
ages two to six 99

chapter six

ADOLESCENCE
the search for identity 182

PREFACE

The purpose of this text is to present a multi-dimensional view of human development to students interested in the field of social work. Following the introduction, chapters are chronologically arranged and discuss development from conception to death.

We draw upon theory and research from many disciplines, and each chapter includes a discussion of the physical, cognitive, and emotional changes that occur at a particular stage of life. We discuss individual growth in the context of the family and the larger society, so students will see the relationships between social institutions and individual or group behavior.

Descriptions of different theoretical perspectives on development are integrated into the text. These perspectives are based on sociobiological, psychoanalytic, cognitive, learning, and humanistic theories.

Presentations of theory and research are followed by illustrations of how this knowledge is utilized by social workers in a variety of settings, including public welfare agencies, mental health programs, schools, hospitals, community centers, and planning agencies. Special emphasis is placed on demonstrating the relevance of the subject matter to the practice of social work with low-income populations and minority groups.

In addition to the case illustrations offered throughout the text, chapters 2 through 9 conclude with a few detailed case examples drawn from social work practice. A list of suggested readings follows each chapter.

Throughout the text, the words set in **boldface** have been defined in the Glossary beginning on page 319.

The introductory chapter includes a discussion of the importance of theory in understanding the biological and social factors affecting human development, a perspective on social work as a developing profession, and an introduction to some basic concepts that will help the student understand the research studies described throughout the text.

The structure and content of the book is based on Grace Craig's successful text, "Human Development," now in its second edition. The present text, coauthored by a social worker, includes revisions and additions that make it specifically applicable to social work students.

A great deal of appreciation is owed to the numerous individuals who offered information and helpful advice. Special thanks are offered to Sandra Bemesderfer, who shared in developing the outline for the text, to Harry Specht for his painstaking editing of the completed manuscript, and to Ronnie London for her expert typing.

HUMAN DEVELOPMENT

chapter one

Marc Anderson

INTRODUCTION
an approach
to human development

outline

A STUDY OF THE LIFE SPAN

Biological and environmental influences

Theories of human behavior

The universal and the particular

THE SOCIAL WORK PROFESSION

Attributes of a profession

Fields and methods

RESEARCH METHODOLOGY

Developing a hypothesis

Designing a study

Interpreting the results

Ethical issues

MILLIONS OF FRAGILE and microscopic sperm swim against great odds to reach the egg cell; only one unites with it to begin a new person. Infants form bonds with those close to them, and as their physical, intellectual, and emotional needs are met, they learn to trust others. Toddlers touch, taste, pull, and climb as they discover the nature of the world and their own powers. Preschoolers learn intricate verbal sequences as they engage others by inquiring, persuading, commanding, and teasing. Schoolchildren conform to peer group rules to gain acceptance. Adolescents explore different roles as they gain independence from their parents. Youths, adults, and the aged explore a variety of relationships as a continuing part of human development.

This text will introduce the social work student to theories of human growth and development and will illustrate the relevance of theory and research for the social work practitioner. In this first chapter we will introduce three topics that will help the student to understand the material that follows: first, the *theoretical framework* used in discussing stages of the life cycle; second, a brief discussion of the *social work profession*, its fields of practice, and methods of intervention; and third, several concepts of *research methodology*, to help the student understand the research findings presented throughout the text. In each of the remaining chapters we will present a single stage of development, integrating broad theoretical concepts that cut across the entire life span.

A STUDY OF THE LIFE SPAN

The process of human development is complex and rich, blending biological and cultural factors and integrating thought and feeling. It begins with conception and continues through old age. This text will examine developmental processes during eight stages of the life span.

Our goal in studying human development is to gain greater understanding of human behavior by observing some consistent common processes amid all the complexities. We begin with observations and descriptions of human growth and behavior and progress to hypotheses that can be tested. In the course of studying behavior it is important to examine those developmental processes and experiences of childhood that may contribute to adult behavior. It is also instructive to look ahead at the physical and psychological characteristics of the mature stage of development the child is moving toward (Neugarten 1969). For example, we value self-awareness and goal orientation in adults, but we often overlook the behavioral cues in children that signal the appearance of these characteristics. We can be more sensitive to the significance of developmental changes in children when we view them in the context of the entire life span (Montada and Filipp 1976).

Biological and environmental influences

The processes by which change takes place are of major interest to developmental psychologists. No clear agreement exists on precisely how children acquire a nearly complete language structure by age five, or why reminiscing seems to be an essential part of aging, or how children learn to express love, grief, and hostility. Nevertheless, as psychologists and others investigate and debate the issues, they rely on carefully defined common terms and concepts.

Development refers to the changes over time in the structure, thought, and behavior of a person. These changes are usually progressive and cumulative, and they result in enlarged body size, increasingly complex activity, and greater integration of functions. For example, motor development seems to progress from an infant's random waving of arms and legs to purposeful reaching, grasping, creeping, and walking. The development of thinking proceeds from the recognition of concrete objects in infancy to the formation of abstract thought in adolescence.

Some development is primarily biological, such as prenatal growth. Other changes, such as learning family language patterns, are strongly influenced by the environment. However, most development cannot be neatly categorized as either biological or environmental, because it involves an interaction of both elements.

All living organisms develop according to a **genetic code** or plan. Insects follow a precise plan that allows for little behavioral alteration compared to the flexibility of human development. When psychologists refer to the process of growth based on genetic determinants, they use the term **maturation.** Physical structures and motor capabilities mature at different rates. **Growth** usually refers to the increase in size, function, and complexity to the point of optimal maturity; **aging** refers to the biological changes occurring beyond that optimal point.

We are constantly subject to *environmental influences* that can either stunt or promote our growth. For example, personal and impersonal forces may enable us to meet our biological and psychological needs by providing us with food, physical safety, and loving relationships. War and famine, on the other hand, create a very different climate for human development.

Learning is the basic developmental process by which behavior changes in response to experience. We learn to avoid touching hot toasters, to factor algebraic equations, to choose a mate, and to express our angry feelings. We learn skills and knowledge, but we also learn attitudes, values, and patterns of thought. Some important learning theories are presented throughout the text; we shall discuss conditioning, modeling, imitation, verbal mediation, and hypothesis testing. We shall also consider the role of insight and discovery in human development.

Socialization is the general process by which the individual becomes a member of a social group such as a family, a religious group, and a community. It involves learning all the attitudes, beliefs, customs, values, and role expectations of the particular social group. It is a lifelong process that helps individuals live comfortably and participate fully in their society (Goslin 1969). A young girl's behavior in a single day may reflect the following roles: pupil, neighbor, older sister, daughter, Catholic, team member, and best friend. When she reaches her teens, she will acquire new roles that require her to learn new behaviors and values. This socialization process occurs in all stages of life.

In the past researchers theorized that the behavior of children depended almost entirely on how parents and teachers behaved toward them. However, recent studies have focused on how parents and children mutually influence each other's behavior (Gewirtz and Boyd 1976; Lewis and Rosenblum 1974; Martin 1975). Infants are socialized by their experience within the family, but at the same time the presence of the infant also forces others in the family to learn new roles.

How much of our behavior is due to maturation and how much to learning? There are no definitive answers. An infant sits, then stands, then walks, primarily because of maturational processes. Yet even this behavior may be affected by such environmental factors as cultural expectations, diet, disease, and emotional stress. Children are born with the capacity for speech, but they must *learn* a language. Infants spontaneously show emotions such as anger or distress, but they must *learn* how to handle such feelings (Hebb 1966). An inherited susceptibility to a disease such as asthma or diabetes can be triggered by environmental factors (Anastasi 1958); the disease, in turn, may affect socialization and intellectual development if it interferes with school attendance. And inherited physical characteristics such as body type, skin color, and height, also affect a person's self-concept and social status.

Social workers learn to see an individual as not only the product of past maturation and learning but also as part of a social system with which the person continues to interact. For example, one child may belong to a family that adheres to the cultural traditions of upper-class Mexican society and another to a family from the particular subculture of the American Appalachian Mountains. Both families would interact with the educational system and would be affected by the extent to which their labor is rewarded by the economic system. Individuals and families may also interact with the social welfare system. As social workers encounter clients and attempt to diagnose the nature of their problems, they draw on one or more theories about human behavior.

Theories of human behavior

What is basic to human nature? Are we primarily rational and goal-oriented, or are we driven mainly by passions? Do we learn by discovery and insight or by small sequential steps of increasing complexity? Are we motivated by reward, pain, curiosity, or inner drives? What is a *conscience* and how does it develop? When we turn to developmental psychology to seek answers to these basic questions, we find that the answers differ according to particular theories of human development and the corresponding sets of assumptions about behavior on which these theories are based.

Social scientists use theories to help formulate significant questions, to select and organize their data, and to understand the data within a larger framework. Without theories, we would be overwhelmed by enormous quantities of unusable data. In testing a theory, a researcher attempts to test the predictions it makes about human behavior.

Each of us probably has our own "theories" about the issues discussed in the text. We lean toward one explanation of a problem over another, probably because of our underlying assumptions about behavior. For example, you may view juvenile delinquents either as responsible for their actions or as victims of their environment and early training. You may believe that six-year-olds can decide for themselves what they should study in school, or you may think that children cannot be expected to know what they want. These views are probably part of a broader package of general assumptions about the degree to which individuals are responsible for their behavior and the degree to which human rationality can be relied on to direct human actions wisely.

Social workers' actions reflect the theories they accept as well as their personal characteristics and their agency settings. These theories offer explanations of why people behave as they do, how the environment affects their behavior, and what is likely to be the result of particular social work interventions (Specht and Vickery 1977). It is important that we understand a number of theories, as each may explain a different aspect of behavior or be applicable to different populations. It is always worthwhile to examine behavior through another "pair of glasses" that presents reality in a different frame of reference from the familiar one.

This text will give particular attention to concepts of sociobiology, learning and cognitive theories, and the viewpoints of the schools of psychoanalysis and humanistic psychology. Various therapies are based on these and other theories of behavior, but we shall not discuss therapies as such. The social work practitioner employs a number of theories to devise the strategies of intervention most likely to succeed in dealing with the client's problems; individual counseling is one of these forms of intervention.

The universal and the particular

Given the fact that individual behavior is the product of so many interacting factors, how are we to ever generalize about human development? Given the wide range of differences in the perceptions, values, and child-rearing practices of different cultures, do we need a separate book on human development for each ethnic subculture? Our approach is that each individual is in some ways *completely unique;* in other ways *similar to others* in behavior and values; and in still other respects *like all other human beings* (Kluckhohn and Murray 1948).

We have already presented the idea that genetic and environmental factors interact to influence each individual in a completely unique fashion. One child may have a genetically based disability, and a sibling may have an extremely placid temperament. Each characteristic will elicit different reactions from other family members. Throughout the text we shall present examples of factors that cause unique differences among individuals.

We shall also generalize about particular ethnic, racial, and social-class groups, pointing out cultural differences in child rearing, cognitive training, and family structure. These generalizations will usually be based on research studies indicating that people in one group are more likely to exhibit certain characteristics than people in another. We shall also point out how various subcultures are affected by the socioeconomic structure of the larger society, through overt discriminatory practices and by differential opportunities and rewards. However, as we shall see later in the chapter, knowing the high probability that members of a certain group are alike in certain characteristics does not tell us whether any *particular* group member will exhibit those characteristics.

Social workers must have a comprehensive understanding of the cultures of the groups with which they work. They will frequently need to supplement what they learn in school by reading the professional literature on the subject, by familiarizing themselves with ethnic newspapers, and by talking with knowledgeable members of the community. Ethnic agencies offer additional assistance in bridging the gap between the ethnic community and the social work bureaucracy (Jenkins 1980). Researchers have often studied white middle-class populations exclusively, and this imbalance needs correcting. However, we must also guard against overgeneralizing about minority groups. Not only is each individual unique, but there are also significant differences based on socioeconomic status within ethnic groups—for example, differences in child-rearing practices between middle-class and lower-class black families.

Finally, some human characteristics appear more or less universally, just as we find some similarities between humans and other primates. In reading the literature on other cultures and historical periods, we continually find statements of the human condition that strike a common chord with our own responses. American college students in the 1970s found relevance in the teachings of ancient Buddhist philosophers. We can still understand the dreams of a Don Quixote whose creator lived in sixteenth-century Spain and be moved by the pain in the face of a starving child from a distant African tribe.

Social workers must learn about individuals in the context of both the universal and the particular. A Mexican-American youth's behavior may be understood in terms of ethnic identification, social-class membership, family relationships, inherited characteristics, and the interaction of these and other factors with social institutions during the youth's unique life experiences. A disabled child should be seen as a unique individual, as a member of a group needing special services, and as a child who will experience the same developmental issues as other children. In the next section we shall discuss some ways in which professionals analyze problems and develop plans for dealing with them. Social workers must continually supplement their general knowledge with an inquiry into the individual and social forces impinging on the particular situation. To help the student to better understand the relationship between knowledge about human development and social work practice, we turn now to a brief description of the social work profession.

THE SOCIAL WORK PROFESSION

Social work has been defined as a "social institutional method of helping people to enhance their social functioning and to resolve their social problems" (Siporin 1975, p. 27). It is a *profession with a dual purpose:* to assist individuals and groups whose needs are not adequately met and to help change institutions so that they are more responsive to individual and group needs (Gilbert and Specht 1976). It is but one of several professions that service the institution of *social welfare*. Social welfare programs are concerned with housing, education, health, and corrections, as well as social services. Social workers are most frequently involved in providing voluntary and public *social services* such as child welfare, family counseling, information and referral, protective services, and services to the elderly (Gilbert, Miller, and Specht 1980).

In this section we shall present some of the characteristics that make social work a profession; we shall then identify the fields and methods of social work practice.

Attributes of a profession

We have referred to social work as a profession. What does this mean and why do we use the label? We do so because one of the major attributes of a profession is its use of knowledge and skill based on a systematic body of theory (Greenwood 1957). The purpose of this text is to present part of that body of knowledge and to help the student appreciate the importance of continuing research in the area of human development. In the last section of this chapter, we shall discuss research methods and how they are used to add to our knowledge.

Another attribute of a profession is that its authority is based on community sanctions for practice, which may include state licensing of social workers. A profession is also regulated by a code of ethics and has an organizational structure that supports its professional interests (Greenwood 1957). The ethics of the social work profession will be illustrated by case examples throughout the text. The code of ethics includes: respect for the dignity of clients and for their rights to self-determination; a nonjudgmental and unbiased attitude toward clients; avoidance of discriminatory practices; maintenance of the client's interest as the primary concern; confidential treatment of information about the client; and a commitment to work toward improving the general social welfare (National Association of Social Workers 1979). The code also states that social workers must be responsible for basing their practice on existing relevant knowledge. Increasingly, professional ethics dictate that the worker maintain allegiance to these values rather than offering automatic allegiance to the values and practices of their employing agencies (Bartlett 1970). Gordon Hamilton, another pioneer in the development of social casework, stated the situation clearly when she said that "the characteristic method of social work incorporates within its processes both scientific knowledge and social values" (Hamilton 1951, p. 3).

We shall turn now to a discussion of some settings in which social work is practiced and the methods that social workers use in applying knowledge to practice.

Fields and methods

Each chapter of the text contains illustrations of how social workers use knowledge about human development in a variety of **settings.** The settings include medical and psychiatric facilities, schools, juvenile courts, and family and child welfare agencies. In some of these settings the social worker acts as the bridge between the client's needs and institutional needs. For example, the worker can serve as a go-between when school policies affect a particular individual unfairly.

The **services** offered in these settings include the following: individual and family counseling, information and referral, children's protective services, case management of physical disability, foster home placement, group work with children and adults, consultation, and community planning. As mentioned before, there is increasing awareness that people of all income groups rely to some extent on the public availability of these services. We shall see how family crises, child abuse, and physical and mental disability create serious dislocations for middle-income families as well as for the poor.

The traditional **social work methods** of helping people are **casework, group work,** and **community organization;** all three are referred to throughout the text in illustrating social workers' use of theory and knowledge about human development. Social workers also intervene to bring about change through planning and administering services and take part in the development of social policy (Siporin 1975). The illustrations we present often describe the social worker in a particular setting, using one major social work method such as casework or group work. However, at times we offer a *generalist approach* to the delivery of services, based on social systems theory. This means that the social worker assesses a particular problem at the *individual, group,* and *institutional* levels. The crucial factor in using the generalist approach successfully is the ability of both practitioners and researchers to determine which problems respond best to intervention through casework with an individual client, which to work with the entire family, which to community programs, and which to changes in social institutions. Traditional casework has often been criticized for being ineffective when actually it was simply the wrong approach to the problem at hand (Wood 1978). For example, casework is particularly appropriate when an individual or family seeks to strengthen its ability to handle a crisis. But casework may be ineffective with involuntary clients sent by the probation department. When dealing with interpersonal problems among elementary schoolchildren, group work can be very effective, but when working with a delinquency-prone gang group work could strengthen their cohesiveness and thus increase the extent of their illegal behavior. On the other hand, providing well-paid jobs to gang members might be an effective way to reduce delinquency. In our examples of how social workers respond to human needs at each stage of the life cycle, we shall discuss economic concerns as well as psychological needs and interventions. Students who plan to use any of the direct service methods or to work in research, program planning, and administration should be aware of the range of human needs and the varied forms of social interventions.

As part of this social systems approach, we shall place primary emphasis on the individual's physical, cognitive, and emotional development. In addition, we shall point out ways in which the individual interacts with family, peers, and other social groups and institutions. We turn now to a discussion of how research adds to our body of knowledge and examine some of the methods used by researchers.

RESEARCH METHODOLOGY

Establishing reliable facts about human behavior is a challenging task. Both researchers and practitioners must decide what constitutes "reliable" evidence and when "enough" evidence has been gathered to support a theory. Personal experience and common sense are useful, and many new scientific theories have been stimulated by astute observations of an event. Someone observes something different, asks questions about it, continues to observe it, tests its limits, and arrives at a basis for a new generalization and prediction.

We all use observations to help us predict the behavior we can expect from others. In this section we shall discuss how researchers state their predictions about behavior and relationships in a form that allows the predictions to be tested and proven right or wrong. Although absolutely certain proofs are seldom possible, enough convincing evidence can be amassed so that reasonable people will accept the conclusions. Unfortunately, much available research and many of the studies we shall cite as evidence for a particular **hypothesis** are based on methodology that does not easily allow one to generalize about how all people will behave. This section will examine the relationship between theory and methods of research so that we can better understand how researchers can reach different—and sometimes contradictory—conclusions about human behavior. We shall discuss how hypotheses are developed, how evidence is gathered, and how conclusions are drawn from the data. Finally, we shall consider some ethical problems in conducting research.

Our knowledge of human development is constantly expanding as researchers add new information and theories are revised to accommodate the new information. Frustrating as this may be to those who seek definitive answers, this dynamic intellectual process is a necessary part of scientific methodology.

Developing a hypothesis

A research study starts with a hypothesis that makes a prediction about the relationship among two or more **variables** that can be proved or disproved. For example, one may hypothesize that the higher-than-average infant death rate among Hispanics is related to a lack of bilingual facilities. This statement is based on certain known facts about the proportionately higher infant death rates among minority populations and on certain theories about the relationship of culture and language to the use of available services. From these facts and theories we might develop a number of hypotheses that test different variables related to being Hispanic and having higher than average infant mortality. In this way we seek to explain whether the high mortality rate is related to a higher proportion of Hispanics being poor, to their lacking access to facilities offering prenatal medical care, to their lacking access to services in Spanish, or to some combination of these and other factors. If we know which of these variables are most responsible for the undesired result, we can plan programs that are more likely to correct the situation.

The researcher must also take care to define the terms used in a hypothesis; some hypotheses are more carefully drawn than others. In our example, the term *Hispanic* is but one of the terms that must be given an **operational definition.** We need to establish the criteria for who will be included in this category. Will it be a Spanish surname, exclusive use of the Spanish language, a measurable degree of bilingualism, or some other criterion? The definition of terms is crucial in determining what interpretation can be drawn from the study's results. The task of providing operational definitions for terms becomes even more complex when we must define and measure such phenomena as "feelings" in order to determine whether certain programs result in an increased level of "happiness" or "satisfaction."

Some studies will be based on more specific and carefully drawn hypotheses than others. Some researchers will conduct a more thorough review of the existing literature than others; their theories will be based on a more informed understanding of the problem. Some hypotheses also seek to explain more complex behaviors than others do. We turn now to a discussion of some issues involved in designing a study to test a hypothesis.

Designing a study

We have indicated that the purpose of a research study is to test a hypothesis. Most of our references to research will mention only the study results, but the original research paper should present the results in a form that indicates their predictive value. Some studies use statistical measures that indicate the likelihood that the results are not just due to chance. The smaller the research sample, the greater the chance that studies of different samples of that population might yield different results, and therefore we should exercise caution in generalizing from a small study group to the entire population. However, even when an entire population is studied, caution is still called for, since it is possible to obtain results that do not significantly differ from those obtainable by chance.

Research settings range from highly controlled laboratory settings to natural locations such as playgrounds, schools, and hospitals. The researchers' control over subjects and conditions will vary dramatically with the setting, but it is impossible to maintain complete control over the research environment and eliminate all extraneous outside influences. Some researchers cited in the text use the *participant-observer method* of field research. This technique is often used by anthropologists, who temporarily join the group to be studied in order to observe their behavior. We shall also cite *survey research* studies in which standard questions are used either in face-to-face interviews or in mail or telephone surveys and polls. Some studies use census statistics, health department records, and other existing *documentary evidence*.

Descriptive studies usually deal with phenomena about which relatively little is known. For example, most of the recent research on battered wives (a relatively unresearched problem) is concerned with gathering descriptive information about the age, race, and social class of the victims and documenting the extent to which incidents are reported and the way in which they are handled. Once sufficient information about a problem has been gathered, researchers begin to develop hypotheses about relationships and to engage in *analytic research*. For example, they may seek to test the hypothesis that the incidence of violence against wives is related to the age of the couple.

An *experimental design* is the most scientific means of testing theories: Researchers systematically introduce an **independent variable,** then observe the resulting outcome, which is called the **dependent variable.** Although it is impossible to eliminate all other factors that might influence the outcome, the researcher tries to control them as much as possible. For example, in studying the effect of race (independent variable) on IQ scores (dependent variable), a researcher would test different racial groups that are as similar as possible in other factors most likely to influence the outcome, such as socioeconomic status and education. Or, a researcher might compare the use of prenatal medical services (dependent variable) by members of an ethnic group who are alike in most ways but differ in their knowledge of English (independent variable).

Interpreting the results

Social workers generally read about research after the results have been published in professional journals or in the mass media. Their major concern, therefore, is how to interpret the results and whether to accept the explanation of human behavior that is offered. The following discussion will briefly introduce some of the concepts involved in evaluating the results of research, in hopes that the student will be motivated to study the subject further.

First, we shall consider the concept of **reliability,** or the extent to which we can expect the same results by repeating a study. One way in which reliability is adversely affected is by observer or interviewer bias. For example, an interviewer who has predetermined expectations may fail to notice behavior that differs from the expected pattern. Such an interviewer may record different responses than another person interviewing the same respondents, causing the study to lack reliability.

A study may be reliable but lack another important quality: validity. **Validity** refers to how well the study measures what it sets out to test. For example, once a study defines "intelligence," it must show that the tests it uses on subjects really measure those qualities. One might question, for example, whether standardized IQ tests offer a valid measure of intelligence. Or a study may seek to determine the effects of foster home placement on child development. It therefore includes observations and tests of children both before and two years after placement. It is probable that such a study is measuring not only the effects of placement but also maturational changes that occur in all children over a two-year time period. Unless the study controls for this intervening factor, one might question its validity. Still another study might lack validity because the results reflect the study population's response to the interest shown in them by the researchers rather than their response to the variable being studied.

One of the research projects cited in Chapter 7, "Young Adulthood," bases its conclusions on an intensive study of Harvard University students

(Vaillant 1977). While we indicate how the study furthers knowledge, we also point out that the unrepresentative nature of those studied limits the extent to which these findings can be applied to all young adults. The theories tested in this study will either be confirmed or disproved by additional research, and our total store of knowledge will gradually be increased. However, we must remember not to transfer findings automatically from one population or set of conditions to another. Research from an Israeli kibbutz offers valuable information that may help us to design programs for American children. However, because American children grow up in a very different social system and are subject to different cultural values, we must test theories about collective child rearing in an American setting to see whether the results are the same.

We shall often use terms such as **probability,** or "greater incidence of" in describing research results. Why do studies so frequently qualify their answers in this manner, and why do we speak of the "probability" of an occurrence rather than predicting an occurrence? The distinction is crucial. Research can only inform us about probabilities; it cannot provide absolute certainties. A positive outcome is one in which there is a high probability of the occurrence of the expected relationship. For example, the Sutton-Smith and Rosenberg (1970) study cited in Chapter 5 states that the firstborn child is *more likely* to be achievement oriented than are later children. We already know that, by chance factors alone, half of first children will be more achievement oriented than their siblings. Therefore, the study must be able to show a statistically higher probability of firstborn children developing this characteristic. Even then, the results do not mean that *every* first child will develop in this way, only that they are more likely to do so. This is one reason why individual behavior continues to surprise us with its unpredictability. However, we are able to plan many beneficial social programs based on the knowledge that certain factors are highly related, even though we cannot say with certainty that the relationship will exist in any particular case. An example of this is programs that can reduce the incidence of infant problems by reducing the incidence of prematurity, even though not every premature infant develops symptoms of distress.

Another frequent source of confusion involves the difference between **correlation** and **causality.** There are many statistically significant correlations, or variables, that are related to one another to a much greater degree than would occur merely by chance. However, a correlation between two variables does not necessarily indicate that one variable causes the other. For example, there may be a significant correlation between prematurity at birth and subsequent learning disabilities. But one cannot state that prematurity "causes" learning disabilities. Poverty is also highly correlated with both prematurity and learning disability, and the causal factor may be related in some way to poverty. Fortunately, the development of computer technology simplifies the statistical techniques for analyzing the effects of more than one experimental variable.

Ethical issues

During the 1970s governmental regulations aimed at protecting the rights of research subjects increased markedly. (This has been paralleled by increased concern for the individual rights of clients of social agencies.) The basic premise is that research should neither knowingly harm anyone nor violate any basic individual rights. Abuses have been particularly flagrant in cases of research on dependent groups such as children, the mentally ill, and prisoners, some of whom may feel constrained to participate in a study. In this section we shall discuss the following issues: *informed consent, confidentiality,* and the right to *protection from harm.* Some of these issues are more complex than they appear, and most professional organizations have set guidelines for the conduct of research with human participants. The National Association of Social Worker's Code of Ethics includes a section on research.

Professional organizations generally hold that people should participate in research voluntarily and should be fully informed of the nature and possible consequences of their participation. Problems arise when young children are studied and the researcher must rely on parents' consent, or when the subjects' ability to give informed consent is questionable because they do not fully understand the issues.

Subjects also have a right to expect researchers to hold in confidence any information about private lives and thoughts. Furthermore, inappropriate use of research data by those outside of the project must be prevented so that information that categorizes individuals as "predelinquent," "dull," or "impulsive" does not reach parents, teachers, and employers, who may easily misinterpret and misuse the information.

Everyone agrees that researchers should never knowingly harm a subject. Yet it is often difficult to determine in advance what will be harmful. For example, in studying obedience, is it reasonable to give children orders just to see if they will follow them? In studying response to novelty, is it reasonable to expose infants to increasingly novel items for long periods of time? Another example concerns test failure: Cognitive researchers sometimes design experiments in which they know that some children will repeatedly experience failure. It is difficult to know how much anxiety and failure a research subject can experience without being harmed to some extent. Some researchers feel that they have a responsibility to protect people's rights to self-esteem and want to expose subjects only to test situations that will enhance their self-concepts. The rights of participants in research are still being explored and defined; many studies considered permissible only two decades ago are no longer considered ethical.

Research is important to the profession of social work, providing a means for developing new knowledge and questioning old assumptions. Scientific investigation of a subject requires careful observation, guarded generalization and prediction, and further observation and testing. This is a painstaking process, but it is necessary if professional practice is to be based on scientific knowledge.

chapter two

Erika, Photo Researchers

THE BEGINNINGS OF HUMAN LIFE
pregnancy and childbirth

outline

ELAINE AND BILL are in their mid-thirties and after twelve years of marriage are eagerly expecting their first child. They both wanted to become financially and professionally established before starting a family. Elaine has applied for a three-month maternity leave, but is unsure whether she will then return to full-time employment or seek a less demanding job until the baby is a little older. Elaine has regular prenatal checkups, watches her diet carefully, and attends classes on natural childbirth with Bill.

Helen and Robert have also been married for twelve years, but they are expecting their sixth child. They are overburdened with financial concerns, and cannot afford to move from their crowded three-bedroom apartment. Although Helen has high blood pressure, she often feels unable to mobilize herself and the three youngest children to make the long bus trip to the prenatal clinic. Her doctor has offered to "tie her tubes" to prevent another pregnancy—a suggestion that she finds unacceptable at present. Having a cigarette and a cup of coffee are among her few forms of relaxation.

THE SOCIAL CONTEXT OF PREGNANCY

Attitudes about having children vary considerably among individuals and groups in our heterogeneous culture. Children may be desired to maintain family traditions, or they may represent fulfillment of their parents' personal needs. Parents may see childbearing as a duty or as a blessed event. They may believe that children are an inevitable part of life about which one does not make conscious decisions, or they may plan carefully for each birth.

During the prenatal period the impending birth affects the entire family. Their views of the pregnancy may be influenced by family income, health, housing, age, religious beliefs, and marital status. We shall discuss attitudes toward having children in greater detail in Chapters 7 and 8, which cover the adolescent and young adult years.

Whether or not a woman will use available prenatal medical and social services will depend in part on her attitude toward the pregnancy. If the pregnancy is unwanted, a woman may refuse to see a doctor in the vain hope that the "problem" will go away if it is not medically confirmed. Another woman may look forward to personal involvement in each stage of a pregnancy and seek health services early. Economic and social factors are also strong determinants of whether available health services will be used (Watkins and Johnson 1979). Those who must rely on public transportation may find health facilities relatively inaccessible. Other women may feel that health care providers are insensitive to their income and ethnic differences. Advice about prenatal care is more likely to be followed if it reflects the family's cultural patterns. For example, the diets suggested for pregnant women should be tailored to their individual and cultural tastes—whether Mexican dishes, "soul food," or vegetarian fare.

Not all pregnant women react in the same way to the major physiological changes they are experiencing. Some women feel a unique sense of personal fulfillment during pregnancy and maintain a positive self-image despite great physical discomfort. Others may experience only minor discomfort during the period of increased weight gain and reduced mobility. The way in which the woman perceives her new body image and the way in which others respond to her will affect her attitude toward the new child.

Thus, the child does not begin life with a "clean slate." Almost from the moment of conception, a child is part of a social and psychological context. Later in this chapter we shall give closer attention to some of the environmental influences that have a direct impact on the developing fetus. First, however, we shall discuss the biological and maturational processes that take place during the prenatal period, from conception to birth. Prenatal development is one of the most dramatic examples of maturation— the unfolding of inherited potential. Prenatal maturation of human infants occurs within the highly controlled environment of the uterus and follows a predictable sequence. An understanding of this process is of particular importance to social workers. The prenatal period is of great consequence in family life, and problems during this time may call for crisis intervention as well as preventive social planning. Social workers may be called upon to help teen-agers or very young mothers understand prenatal development. Social workers must also be knowledgeable in order to participate effectively in formulating public policies regarding family planning and abortion.

PRENATAL DEVELOPMENT

Conception

Human development begins at the moment of conception, with the joining of a single sperm and a single egg cell, each containing half of the hereditary potential of the individual. This fertilized egg, which can hardly be seen by the naked eye, will then carry all the genetic information needed for the development of the new organism.

The process of fertilization begins when an **ovum,** an egg cell that has developed in one of the woman's two ovaries, is stimulated by hormones and enters a sudden period of growth. This results in **ovulation,** whereby the ovum is released to begin its journey down one of the two Fallopian tubes. In many women ovulation occurs about the fourteenth day after the onset of menstruation, but the exact time of monthly ovulation may vary even for the same individual. The mature ovum survives for only two to three days. A man's **sperm,** deposited in a woman's vagina during inter-course, can survive for as long as three days. Hence, there is a range of possible days in the menstrual cycle during which conception may occur. It takes only one of the approximately 300 million spermatozoa deposited in the vagina to move up through the uterus to the Fallopian tube and fertilize the ovum during this critical period. Otherwise, the ovum continues down the tube to the uterus, where it disintegrates and is flushed from the body during menstruation. For the microscopic sperm cells, the trip to the ovum is long and difficult.

There is continuing research being conducted on problems of infer-tility and interest in learning more about the differences between sperm bearing the male and the female chromosome that determine the sex of the unborn child. Social workers may be involved in the work of Planned Parenthood clinics, which serve as a resource for couples having difficulty conceiving a child as well as for those wanting to prevent conception. Some-times ignorance about the nature of conception and infertility will increase the emotional distress people feel when they experience a delay in attaining a hoped-for pregnancy.

Infertility affects approximately 10 percent of married couples. The problem is more frequent among older couples trying to conceive a first child (Guttmacher 1973). Medical specialists have diagnostic tests that can often identify the causes of infertility, and couples who are having difficulty conceiving can also be helped to pinpoint the exact time of ovulation through use of body temperature charts. Artificial insemination is some-times a possibility, and still other alternatives are being explored by re-searchers. Meanwhile, adoption has become increasingly difficult for many couples since fewer healthy infants are placed for adoption. There are also many less white babies available for adoption than formerly.

Social workers sometimes see women who are very upset by symptoms indicating the possibility of an unwanted pregnancy. The first symptom is usually a missed menstrual period. However, a missed period can also be caused by illness, malnutrition, sudden weight loss from extreme dieting, or psychological distress. Conversely, brief menstruation can occur during the early months of pregnancy.

Although a doctor can make a tentative diagnosis during the sixth week of pregnancy (eight weeks after the last period), and a firm diagnosis based on physical signs of pregnancy between the twelfth and twentieth weeks, special pregnancy tests are available that give reliable answers as early as two weeks after a missed period (Guttmacher 1973). These tests take only a few minutes to perform and can give almost instant relief from the great anxiety of "not knowing."

Embryonic development

The process of continuous cell division begins just a few hours after fertilization. In some cases the first division results in two identical cells, which then separate and develop into identical twins. Therefore, identical twins are always the same sex and share the same inherited traits. Sometimes two ova released at approximately the same time are fertilized by two sperm cells; the resulting fraternal twins may be as different or as similar as other brothers and sisters.

The **embryonic period** begins near the end of the first week, with the completion of the fertilized ovum's journey down the Fallopian tube and the implantation of the developing organism in the uterine wall. This period lasts about seven weeks, during which the crucial structural development of the embryo takes place. Although the internal organ systems are not yet functional, all organs and features of the embryo are already beginning to develop at this time. The embryo has arms, legs, fingers, toes, and a heartbeat before the mother is even aware that she is pregnant.

Miscarriages, or spontaneous abortions, are most likely to occur during this crucial period. They are often caused by inadequate development of the embryo, placenta, or umbilical cord. The placenta is an organ which develops as a means of nourishing the embryo, providing for a continuous exchange of nutrients and waste materials between the mother and the embryo. The developing child receives these nutrients through the mother's placenta, which is connected to the circulatory system of the embryo by the umbilical cord.

When spontaneous abortions are caused by defects in fetal development, the mother can usually deliver a normal child subsequently without medical intervention. Indeed, medication to prevent early miscarriages may increase the chances of having a defective child. Nonetheless, miscarriages are often upsetting for the parents, particularly if they have had difficulty conceiving. Ideally the medical consultant should be sensitive to the potential of emotional distress and refer the patient for counseling as needed.

The fetal period

The **fetal period** lasts from the beginning of the third month until birth. During this period the organs, limbs, muscles, and systems of the fetus become functional. We shall mention only a few of the developmental highlights, in order to indicate the rapid pace of fetal growth. Students planning to work with new parents or infants will want to study this fascinating stage of development in greater detail.

During the third month, the first external signs of sex differentiation become apparent. All the nerves needed to connect the eye to the brain are now in place, and teeth, eyes, and nails begin to form. The liver begins to function, and the lungs and stomach begin to respond. At this point the fetus is only about three inches long and weighs about half an ounce.

During the second trimester (fourth through sixth month) there is a continuation of all the processes described above. By the fifth month the mother feels the fetus as it moves around during its waking periods. By the sixth month the fetus has grown to about twelve inches and weighs approximately one and a half pounds. The end of this second trimester marks the critical point at which the fetus usually becomes viable—that is, able to survive outside the mother's body if it were placed in an incubator and given special care.

The 1973 Supreme Court decision striking down restrictive abortion laws differentiates between the trimesters by giving unrestricted legal rights to an abortion during the first trimester, imposing some restrictions during the second, and prohibiting abortion during the last trimester unless continuation of the pregnancy represents a threat to the mother's life or health. In 1977 the Court held that the government is not required to fund elective abortions for the financially needy, but debate about this question continues.

At seven months the fetus is sensitive to touch and can feel pain. Its nervous system is mature enough to control breathing and swallowing. The fetus will startle at a very loud sound, but more moderate noises are drowned out by the loud, rhythmic sounds caused by the surges of blood in the uterine walls, sounds that correspond to the mother's heartbeat (Walker, Grimwade, and Wood 1971).

Researchers have determined that the fetus is a reactive organism capable of responding to touch and sound; it is even thought to experience needs such as hunger and thirst. If this is true, the movements that the fetus makes may be more than just random reflexes. Facial expressions of the fetus may indicate pleasure and displeasure, and the turning and kicking may be purposeful movements that make the fetus more comfortable in the womb (Carmichael 1970).

Infants born after eight months have a survival rate of 70 percent, but they do face risks (Rugh and Shettles 1971) that often dictate their placement in incubators until a fuller assessment of their condition can be made. We will go into more detail about some of the problems resulting from prematurity later in the chapter when we discuss neonatal risk.

During the ninth month the fetus continues to grow and begins to turn to a head-down position in preparation for the trip through the birth canal. Immunities to disease pass from the mother to the fetus and supplement the fetus' own developing immune reactions. Approximately one to two weeks before birth, the baby "drops" as the uterus settles lower into the pelvic area. The weight gain of the fetus slows, the mother's muscles and uterus begin sporadic, painless contractions, the cells of the placenta begin to degenerate—all is ready for birth. Birth occurs after an average **gestation** period of 266 days.

GENETIC INFLUENCES

We can rarely ascribe a personality or behavioral trait to a specific hereditary factor, and social work practice is based on the belief that genetics and environment interact to shape an individual. Although social workers place much importance on family life style and child-rearing practices, they must also be aware of the principles of genetics and their social applications. We shall examine in this section the mechanisms of inheritance, then briefly describe a few of the genetic defects that social workers are apt to encounter in their practice. Finally, we shall make reference to the relatively new field of genetic counseling.

Principles of inheritance

Cells, chromosomes, genes, DNA and *RNA* are all familiar terms. Nevertheless, a brief review of their significance will be helpful before we discuss the processes of inheritance.

Human life begins with a single ovum penetrated by a single sperm cell. Within hours the pronuclei of the two cells, each containing half the normal forty-six **chromosomes,** have joined to form the **zygote.** The zygote, or fertilized cell, now has the twenty-three pairs of chromosomes required to develop a normal human baby.

Thousands of **genes** are strung out in chainlike fashion on each of these chromosomes. Some estimate that there are close to 1 million genes on all forty-six chromosomes (Winchester 1979). These genes are made up of **DNA** (deoxyribonucleic acid) molecules that contain the genetic code or "blueprint" regulating the functioning and development of the organism. Locked in the nucleus of the cell, they control the "what and when" of development.

RNA (ribonucleic acid) is a substance formed from DNA that acts as a messenger to the rest of the cell. RNA moves freely within the cell and serves as catalyst for the formation of new tissue.

Once the two reproductive cells combine to form the zygote, the process of cell division begins. In the process of **mitosis,** or ordinary cell division, cells duplicate themselves exactly. First the DNA of each gene replicates itself, then each chromosome splits and reproduces the chromosomal arrangement so that each of the new cells is exactly like the original cell. The process that creates reproductive cells **(meiosis)** differs in that each new cell will have only half the genetic material of the parent cell. A reproductive cell (either an ovum or a sperm) will have only twenty-three chromosomes, one from each pair of the parent cell. The rearrangement of genes and chromosomes resulting from meiosis is like the shuffling and dealing of cards; the chance that any two siblings may receive the same assortment of chromosomes is about 1 in 281 trillion.

When the fertilization of an ovum takes place, the sex of the resulting organism is determined by the sperm. All ova carry an X chromosome, whereas sperm have an equal probability of carrying either an X or a Y chromosome. When an X and a Y chromosome are paired, the child will be a male. The XX combination is female.

Nearly all of a person's tens of thousands of genes occur in pairs, one inherited from the mother and the other from the father. Alternate forms of the same gene pair are called **alleles.** In order to understand the inheritance of genetic defects, it is necessary to review some basic principles of dominant and recessive traits. Some hereditary traits, such as eye color, are carried by a single gene pair. For example, a child may inherit an allele for brown eyes (B) from the father and an allele for blue eyes (b) from the mother. The child's **genotype,** or gene pattern, for eye color will therefore be Bb, and the child's eyes will be brown. This is because the allele for brown eyes (B) is dominant and the one for blue eyes (b) is recessive. When a gene is dominant, its presence in a gene pair will cause that particular trait to be expressed. Thus an individual with either the genotype Bb or BB has brown eyes. The expressed trait, brown eyes, is called the **phenotype.**

Let us now assume that the father's genotype is Bb (brown eyes) and the mother has blue eyes (which must be the genotype bb). All of their children will inherit a recessive gene for blue eyes from the mother. From the father, however, they may inherit either the dominant gene for brown eyes (B) or the recessive gene for blue eyes (b). Therefore, the children will be either blue-eyed (bb) or brown-eyed (Bb). Thus, if we know the genotypes of the parents, we can determine all the possibilities of genotypes and phenotypes, and the probabilities of each for their children.

Most traits do not usually result from a single gene pair, but from a combination of many gene pairs that interact in various ways. For the characteristic of height, for example, several genes or gene pairs seem to combine in an additive fashion to create larger or smaller people, with larger or smaller limbs and other parts. Gene pairs may also interact in such a way that one gene pair either allows or inhibits the expression of another gene pair. These various types of interactions frequently give rise to phenotypes that differ markedly from those of either parent.

Genetic defects

A gross chromosomal abnormality such as a missing or an extra chromosome is usually lethal to the fetus. Other genetic abnormalities result in a characteristic pattern of impaired development. One example is **Down's**

syndrome, or mongolism. These individuals have an extra chromosome that causes improper physical and mental development. Down's syndrome occurs in approximately two to three births per one thousand (Hunter, Schucman, and Friedlander 1972), with the risk of occurrence increasing with maternal age at time of conception. For example, mothers under thirty years old have a risk of under one in one thousand of having a child with Down's syndrome; the risk increases to one in one hundred for forty-year-old women, and to one in forty-five for those over forty-five years old. We do not yet know why risk increases with age (Guttmacher 1973). Diagnosis at birth is made by noting distinctive characteristics such as short fingers and slanting eyes. We shall discuss the possibility of prenatal diagnosis of this condition in the later section on genetic counseling.

A variation of Down's syndrome is known as "mosaic" Down's syndrome. Children with this genotype have both normal cells and cells with a Down's syndrome pattern of an extra chromosome. The extent to which their learning ability is impaired and they show other mongoloid characteristics depends on the number of abnormal cells produced; this in turn depends on how early in the gestation period the developmental error occurred (Sarason and Doris 1953). Some people may be severely retarded and only respond to simple training tasks such as feeding and dressing themselves; they will need a highly protected environment throughout their lives. Others may be only moderately retarded (IQ range about 40–54) and trainable in simple communication and manual skills. Although they need supervision, they can benefit from living in the community and government funding is increasingly available to provide them with community care rather than hospitalization. There is also an increasing awareness that the extent to which anyone's behavior is functionally impaired is influenced by early environment as well as by genetic inheritance.

Other types of abnormalities may occur because of the arrangement of the sex chromosomes. For example, some individuals have an extra X chromosome, yielding an XXY arrangement. This phenotype usually results in sterility, small external male sex organs, and mental retardation. Other types of abnormalities result when a chromosome breaks at some point and the broken portion is lost in subsequent cell divisions or becomes attached to another chromosome. The effects of chromosome breaks are not yet fully understood, but breakages early in the development of an organism may have a very marked effect on later growth.

Hemophilia, or bleeder's disease, is probably the most dramatic example of a sex-linked genetic abnormality. In hemophilia an element of the blood plasma needed for normal clotting is deficient, and hemophiliacs may bleed for hours from a small wound that would normally clot within five minutes. Internal bleeding is particularly dangerous as it may go unnoticed and cause death. Hemophilia is carried as a recessive gene on the X chromosome, but because the Y chromosome is much shorter than the X chromosome there is no corresponding gene to pair with it on the Y chromosome. The traits that are related to these single genes on the X chromosome are called sex-linked traits, and males will express all such unmatched traits, whether they are dominant or recessive in nature. Females, as was pointed out earlier, have two matching X chromosomes.

However, the vast majority of inherited traits are carried not on the sex chromosomes but on the other twenty-two pairs. Some are carried by a single recessive gene. These include *sickle-cell anemia, cystic fibrosis,* and *Tay-Sachs disease.* For these disorders to be expressed, a child must inherit the recessive genes from both parents—that is, both parents must be carriers of the traits. When both parents carry these genes, approximately 25 percent of the children will inherit the disorder, 50 percent will be carriers, and another 25 percent will not inherit the recessive genes at all.

An interesting characteristic of these particular disorders is that they occur almost solely within a specific nationality, race, or ethnic group. For example, Tay-Sachs disease occurs primarily among Eastern European Jews; cystic fibrosis is most common among Caucasians; and sickle cell anemia is found among Africans, American blacks, and some Mediterranean populations.

Some abnormalities are carried by dominant genes instead of by the pairing of recessives. In other words, some abnormalities may be caused only by one gene inherited from one parent. One such abnormality is *Huntington's chorea,* a disorder that causes progressive and severe deterioration of mental and motor functioning, and that does not appear until the victims reach middle age or later, after the childbearing years. Those who eventually develop this disease may produce children who also inherit the dominant gene before the parents are aware that they are carrying the defect.

The discovery that one is carrying a so-called "bad" gene is a frightening experience. It has a great impact on decisions about marriage and childbearing. Most people never know what genes they carry, although we all probably harbor a number of potentially lethal genes. Most recessive and nonsex-linked genes will probably never be expressed. Still, should the need arise, much information about our own genetic inheritance and that of a potential partner can be obtained.

Genetic counseling

Once we know the dangers inherent in certain types of gene pairings and the tragic consequences of various chromosomal abnormalities, what can we do to avoid them? Genetic counseling is a newly available resource that can help people evaluate genetic risks in childbearing and assist them in making intelligent decisions.

Social workers engaged in family planning, adoptions, and services to the physically or mentally handicapped see many clients who might benefit from genetic counseling. Yet current estimates show that less than

5 percent of the population that might benefit actually receive such services (Schild 1977). Most people have great difficulty making decisions that involve genetic defects, particularly when they can learn only the statistical probability of a particular defect occurring in their children.

Among the techniques that allow for early prenatal diagnosis of potential problems are **amniocentesis, ultrasound pictures,** and use of **fetoscopes.** In amniocentesis, the primary technique, a small amount of amniotic fluid is withdrawn by means of a long, thin needle with syringe attachment. Fetal cells in the fluid can then be examined for various genetic defects. Pictures produced by ultrasound mapping reveal the location of the placenta, size of the fetal skull, position of the fetus, and characteristics of the fetal heartbeat. A fetoscope, a long hollow needle with a small lens and a light source at its end, enables the doctor to observe the developing fetus.

Medical geneticists agree that pregnant women over thirty-five or forty years of age should consider amniocentesis, as should those with a family history of chromosomal abnormality. This is particularly important for X-linked recessive conditions that lead to severe defects (Reilly 1977). However, this type of prenatal diagnosis has not gained widespread acceptance and is primarily used by middle-class and better-educated women (NICHHD 1976).

A genetic counselor is able to prepare a pedigree of the prospective parents and their relatives, as well as a family health history that can assist in pointing out the risks of abnormality in prospective offspring. Sometimes the counselor's findings may be fairly certain, as when amniocentesis reveals an abnormal chromosome arrangement in a developing fetus. On the positive side, the counselor's evaluation may reassure parents who have had an abnormal child that the problem was not of genetic origin and that risks to future children are minimal.

If analysis shows a high risk or certainty of abnormality, parents may need counseling to help them with the difficult task of deciding whether to abort the fetus. It is difficult for parents to accurately anticipate their reaction to raising a handicapped child. Amniocentesis also reveals the sex of the unborn child, thus potentially providing the parent with an option of whether to have a child of a particular sex.

Although it is now technically possible to prevent the birth of many fetuses known to be defective, the social worker dealing with programs of genetic screening or counseling must recognize the complex factors to be considered in the development of public policies dealing with the prevention of genetic defects. The least controversial programs are those calling for low-cost, low-risk mass screening to prevent defects in the newborn that might otherwise require costly institutionalization (as, for example, the compulsory screening in almost all states for the PKU factor—phenylketonuria). More complex—and controversial—is whether amniocentesis should be made compulsory in order to decrease by abortion the number of children born with Down's syndrome or other defects. Another complex issue is the development of policies regarding sterilization of the severely mentally retarded.

Phillip Reilly (1977) presents a number of fascinating case histories attesting to the often incompetent public efforts to prevent sickle cell anemia. Some of the early state laws, which required mandatory screening, failed to specify that diagnosis of sickle cell anemia differs from the diagnosis of being a carrier of the trait. Other laws ignored the fact that children with sickle cell anemia can live healthy lives for a relatively long time before the disease becomes manifest. These confusions sometimes led to public misunderstanding and even job discrimination against those identified as having this type of problem. Therefore the reaction to compulsory screening was understandably negative, especially because the only possible recommendation to many of those at risk was that they avoid having children. As a result of experiences with poorly written state laws mandating screening for blacks only, the 1972 National Sickle Cell Anemia Control Act called for voluntary participation in community screening programs and confidentiality of results. Reilly also points out that most states that mandate genetic screening do not also mandate the costly adjunct of genetic counseling for the parents involved.

As technology increases the options, social workers dealing with high-risk populations should be involved in the development of policies and programs aimed at resolving the conflicting interests sometimes involved in genetic screening and counseling. For example, consideration should be given to the rights of the individual newborn, the rights of the family, the financial costs to the community of lifetime care for the severely disabled, and the potential impact on future generations. In addition, there are broad questions of how society regards its "defective members" and how it decides whether defects are so serious that we may wish to prevent them. The two extreme responses are either to offer a eugenics program that empowers some people to sterilize those whom they consider to be "unfit," or to provide a broad range of social services, in the belief that all people are entitled to quality care regardless of the cost. Our current public policies fall somewhere between those two extremes. Social workers, who often work with those using public and private social services, can make a significant contribution to the difficult task of establishing and monitoring these policies.

Although hospitals can now test for many genetic defects through amniocentesis and blood analysis, corrective gene therapy (the manipulation of individual genes to correct certain defects) is still in its infancy. Sophisticated techniques in genetic research already allow scientists to transplant genetic material from one species into a cell of another species, resulting in a new hybrid with the characteristics of both donors. Scientists can now use this gene-splicing technique to create a strain of bacteria that will produce the human growth hormone (Baxter et al. 1979).

These exciting advances in basic genetic engineering have also created new problems for society. Scientists may unlock the mysteries of genetic diseases such as sickle-cell anemia, diabetes, and cystic fibrosis by splitting and recombining genes. But widespread use of recombinant-DNA techniques brings with it the potential for laboratory accidents. Because of public concern that powerful new strains of bacteria that are immune to antibiotics might be released, the government is developing guidelines to minimize these risks.

New techniques may help us to predict certain genetic characteristics, but we still cannot predict the total development of any given individual. A child's potential also depends on environmental influences both before and after birth. We shall now look at some prenatal environmental influences.

PRENATAL ENVIRONMENTAL INFLUENCES

Every year, some 5 to 8 percent of babies born in the United States have some type of birth defect. Only a small proportion of these can be attributed to inherited factors; most are caused by environmental influences during the prenatal period or during childbirth, or by the interaction of heredity and environmental influences.

The study of developmental abnormalities is called **teratology,** and a teratogen is the specific agent that disturbs the development of the fetus, such as a virus or a chemical. Old wives' tales notwithstanding, a mother's momentary thoughts will not affect the fetus. If a woman "thinks bad thoughts" her baby will not suffer a psychic burden, and if she is frightened by a snake, the child will not begin life with a defect. However, prolonged and intense emotional stress during pregnancy can cause chemical changes and muscular tensions that affect the environment of the developing child (Montagu 1950). Furthermore, prolonged stress may cause an expectant mother to also neglect her diet, become frail or physically ill, ignore medical advice, or take harmful drugs. Certain viruses, foods, and drugs also influence the development of the unborn child, as they pass directly through the placenta to the growing organism.

Critical and sensitive periods

Environmental factors may influence prenatal development in different ways, depending on when they are introduced. This is true for prenatal hormones, most teratogens, and deficiency states such as malnutrition.

Sensitive periods are all those times in which an organism is acutely receptive to a particular influence. **Critical periods** are the *only* times when an organ, structure, or system is sensitive to a particular influence. Although most experimental studies concerning these periods have been conducted with laboratory animals, enough evidence exists to indicate that humans also go through such periods.

For example, rubella (German measles) can sometimes cause blindness, heart defects, brain damage, or other deformities in a fetus; the nature of the damage depends on the point in the developmental sequence that the mother contracts the disease. Unfortunately, most environmental factors have maximal impact during the first trimester of pregnancy, often before a woman is even aware of her condition. Therefore, the most effective method of preventing defects due to rubella is to vaccinate children, thus protecting women in the earliest stage of pregnancy by eliminating the disease in the general population.

The existence of prenatal critical periods is tragically illustrated by the story of the "thalidomide babies" (Taussig 1962). During the late 1950s and early 1960s, a large number of European children were born with stunted or missing arms and legs, large disfiguring birthmarks, and a variety of internal defects. Physicians and other researchers traced the disasters to the mothers' ingestion of sedatives containing the drug thalidomide. In every case, the mother had taken the drug sometime between the thirtieth and fiftieth day after the onset of her last menstrual period. When the mother took the drug only later in pregnancy, abnormalities did not appear.

Only through strong opposition to the drug by a Federal Drug Administration (FDA) employee, Dr. Frances Kelsey, were the American rights to market thalidomide denied to the drug company involved. Dr. Kelsey doubted the adequacy of the documentation submitted to prove that thalidomide produced no harmful effects. Had the FDA authorized the drug, many more deformed babies would have been born in the United States.

There is also a critical prenatal period for sexual differentiation, or formation of gender. Every embryo possesses a pair of undifferentiated glands that may become either testes or ovaries and two sets of tissues that are the precursors of male and female sex organs. At some point during the seventh or eighth week, the sex chromosomes affect development in such a way that the glands of genetic males develop into testes and those of genetic females into ovaries. Thereafter, the development of male or female body type and sex organs depends entirely on the hormone balance in the prenatal environment.

Normally, the testes of a genetic male soon begin to secrete a "masculinizing" mixture of hormones that triggers the further development of male sex organs and inhibits the development of female sex organs. If for some reason the testes do not produce an adequate amount of masculinizing hormones, the embryo will develop a female body despite its being a genetic male. In other words, all embryos, genetic males as well as genetic females, will develop female sex organs and body types if not enough masculinizing hormones are present at the right time to promote the full development of genetic males (Money 1977). Professionals engaged in sexual counseling will need to know more about the complex determinants of the biological basis for sexual identity.

Nutrition and maternal health

The most important element in the prenatal environment is nutrition. The effects of improper nutrition can extend throughout an individual's entire life span, causing stunted brain development and diminished mental capacity (Rosenfeld 1974).

H.G. Birch and J.D. Gussow (1970) cite a range of studies showing that carefully controlled "nourishment programs" for expectant mothers resulted in full-term, healthy babies. Malnourished pregnant women, however, often have spontaneous abortions, give birth prematurely, or lose their babies shortly after birth. Even less severe nutritional deficiencies can cause problems that last a lifetime.

Among women who live in extreme poverty, a host of factors such as malnutrition, poor health, high disease rates, and intense stress increase the risk of prenatal damage. Analysis of public health statistics clearly shows the relationship of race and economic status to the incidence of health risks to mother and fetus, with more nonwhites suffering disadvantages at birth because they are disproportionately represented among those with the lowest incomes (Birch and Gussow 1970). Most of our resources for research and care of the mentally retarded are spent in helping the most severely impaired (a population that is more evenly spread among all social classes), yet the possibilities of prevention are much better for the milder forms of retardation because they are more often environmentally caused and therefore amenable to environmental intervention (Mandelbaum 1977).

Drugs

In considering the whole range of drugs recognized as teratogenic agents, we must keep in mind that a drug that has one effect on the mother may have quite a different effect on the embryo or fetus. Developing structures are usually more vulnerable to drugs than fully developed ones. Furthermore, fetal systems may not be able to handle a drug as efficiently as the maternal system can. A drug that has been found "safe" for use by adults is not necessarily safe for the tiny organism that lives in the environment provided by that adult. We have already noted the drastic effects of sedatives containing thalidomide.

Babies born to narcotics users generally suffer serious distress, with the severity of the symptoms depending on the extent of the mother's addiction, the size of the doses, and how close to the time of delivery the last dose was taken (Burnham 1972; Ananth 1976). Babies of addicts tend to have low birth weight and to suffer withdrawal symptoms such as extreme irritability, vomiting, shaking, and faulty temperature control. Many continue to suffer from disturbed sleep, poor appetite, and lack of weight gain (Restak 1979). Because their physical problems are often compounded by the mother's being in prison or otherwise unable to care for the child, social workers may be called upon to assist in finding special foster homes that can offer appropriate parenting to these extremely difficult infants.

Hormones taken by pregnant women can cause special problems. A recent example is the discovery that women who had been given the synthetic hormone diethylstilbestrol (DES) in order to reduce the risk of miscarriage were unknowingly increasing the risk of vaginal cancer in daughters born of such pregnancies (Winchester 1979).

Although babies born of mothers who drink alcoholic beverages in moderation show no marked or prolonged adverse effects, babies born to alcoholic mothers sometimes are mentally retarded, are underweight, and suffer from other physical abnormalities (Warner and Rosett 1975; Segal 1973).

The inhaled products of cigarette smoke also cross the placenta, and each time the mother smokes a cigarette the fetal heart beats more quickly (Simpson 1957). Babies born to heavy smokers tend to weigh less at birth than those of nonsmokers (Smith 1975).

Radiation

Excessive radiation in early pregnancy from repeated X-rays, radium treatment for cancer, or high levels of radiation in the atmosphere (nuclear explosions, for example) have produced marked effects on prenatal development (Sternglass 1963). Statistics kept by the U.S. Public Health Service will allow later analysis of the risks to unborn children of nuclear accidents such as the leakage resulting from the accident at the Three Mile Island nuclear plant in 1979.

Further research is needed on the effects of low-level radiation, but there is growing public awareness that, as with the use of drugs, the pregnant woman is better off with as little radiation exposure as possible. There is no way to completely eliminate all potential hazards from our environment; the public debate is over the costs and benefits of programs to eliminate specific agents known to be teratogenic.

Other maternal conditions

We have already noted the effects of maternal health and of specific viruses such as rubella on the unborn child. *Venereal diseases* can also cause the unborn child to suffer mental deficiency, blindness, or deafness. We shall mention a few of the other maternal conditions that affect the developing child.

The *Rh factor* is an example of a formerly dangerous situation that is now easily identified and controlled. The Rh factor is found in almost all blacks but in only 85 percent of whites. Its presence makes a person's blood "Rh positive," rather than "Rh negative." Rh type is genetically inherited and incompatibility occurs only if the mother is Rh negative and her baby is Rh positive. In such cases trouble begins when some of the baby's blood "leaks" into the mother's system, causing the mother's body to build up antibodies that leak back into the baby's system and attack its blood cells. No danger exists for the mother, only for the unborn child. Furthermore, the antibodies usually do not build up quickly enough to affect the firstborn, only those born subsequently.

CHILDBIRTH

We shall now turn from the prenatal period to childbirth and the **neonate.** A new branch of medicine, **perinatology,** considers childbirth as beginning with conception and extending through the prenatal period and delivery to the first few years of life. Social workers may be part of a team of geneticists, obstetricians, biochemists, pediatricians, and others involved with the multifaceted health problems of this crucial period in human development. Social workers can contribute a special awareness of the impact of medical problems on the family and community and can recommend and implement the social programs needed to assist families in coping with difficulties and to prevent problems from occurring in the future.

Neither researchers nor parents agree entirely on the best way to deliver a child or on the kinds of first experiences mothers and newborns should have together. We shall therefore present a general discussion of the birth process and the psychological aspects of childbirth as they affect the infant and the family.

Sequence of childbirth

Although attitudes toward pregnancy and childbirth vary from culture to culture, the birth of a child always follows the same biological sequence. We usually describe the process as occurring in three stages: *labor, birth,* and *afterbirth.*

Labor, the first stage, is the period during which the cervix of the uterus dilates to allow for the passage of the baby. Although labor can last from a few minutes to over thirty hours, the modal time (that is, the most frequently observed among a range of observations) from onset of pain through expulsion of the afterbirth appears to be about ten hours for first births and six hours for subsequent deliveries (Guttmacher 1973). Labor is somewhat longer for women whose first birth occurs after age thirty-five. Labor begins with mild uterine contractions, usually spaced fifteen to twenty minutes apart. The contractions then increase both in frequency and in intensity until they are only three to five minutes apart. The muscular contractions of labor are involuntary, and the mother can best help herself by trying to relax during this period.

The second stage of childbirth is the birth of the baby. Birth is usually distinguished as the period between the time that the cervix is fully dilated and the time when the baby is free of the mother's body. This stage may last from twenty minutes to two hours; as with labor, it tends to last longer for a first birth.

Generally, between ten and twenty contractions occur during birth. These contractions occur regularly every two to three minutes, and they are of greater intensity and longer duration than labor contractions. Each birth contraction lasts about one minute. The mother can actively assist in the birth by bearing down with her abdominal muscles during each contraction.

Normally, the head of the baby emerges first from the birth canal. It emerges more and more with each contraction until it can be grasped. The tissue of the mother's perineum (the region between the vagina and the rectum) must stretch considerably to allow the baby's head to emerge. The attending doctor often makes an incision, called an episiotomy, to enlarge the vaginal opening; this can heal more neatly than the jagged tear that might occur naturally.

In most normal births the baby is born head first. There is more difficulty when the baby is positioned in a breech presentation (buttocks first) or a posterior presentation (facing toward the mother's abdomen instead of toward her back). In each of these cases, the baby is usually assisted to prevent unnecessary injury to the mother or itself.

The third stage of childbirth is the afterbirth, when the placenta and related tissues are expelled. This stage is virtually painless and generally occurs within twenty minutes of the delivery. Again, the mother can help the process by bearing down. After the expulsion, the placenta and umbilical cord are checked for imperfections that might signal damage to the newborn.

Delivery of the baby

Anesthetics were not used to relieve childbirth pains until the middle of the nineteenth century, although they were used elsewhere in medical practice. Three major types of medication came into use at this time: analgesics, such as Demerol or Valium, which diminish the sense of pain; amnesics, which are sometimes used concurrently to wipe out the memory of events; and general or local anesthetics, which eliminate all sensation in the affected areas (Guttmacher 1973). In the past few decades there has been increased concern about the dangers resulting from these procedures.

Researchers and physicians have long known that when drugs reduce the mother's level of awareness and sensitivity, they also affect the infant's alertness and responsiveness at birth. The extent to which these are only temporary effects is still unclear. However, if drugs lengthen the birth process, they increase the danger of an insufficient amount of oxygen reaching the baby's brain. Therefore, medication during childbirth should be used with caution and to the least degree found necessary. The dangers of drugs given during pregnancy and childbirth were noted by Grantly Dick-Read (1953) and later by others.

Findings such as these supported the wishes of many mothers to experience their child's birth in an atmosphere free from the unnecessary impositions of the hospital regime. The **natural childbirth** movement pointed out that hospitals treat all patients as sick, but that childbirth is not an illness. The term *natural childbirth* implies maternal preparation, limited medication, and participation. Grantly Dick-Read felt that the key was preparation, because women in Western society had often come to anticipate childbirth with exaggerated fear based on limited knowledge. Their fear created a muscular tension that made labor more painful than necessary. Dick-Read proposed to teach the mother about the birth process so that she could participate in each stage, be more relaxed during labor, experience less pain, and therefore need little or no medication. This last point is important, because it is overly simplistic to think that medication need *never* be used if one is properly prepared. This leaves mothers with an unnecessary sense of failure if they require anesthesia because of a complicated delivery. For most couples, however, participating in natural childbirth produces the twin rewards of having a more alert and responsive newborn (Grimm 1967) and having been awake to participate in the satisfying efforts of hard labor rather than being the passive receiver of frightening pain or being unconscious throughout the birth experience. It is important for doctors to be open to a variety of childbirth options, and to give consideration to parental preferences.

Natural childbirth classes, some using techniques developed by *Fernand Lamaze* (1970), usually involve both parents. Parents attend from six to eight classes in which they learn about the birth process. The expectant mother is taught exercises for relaxation, breathing, and muscle strengthening. Increasingly, fathers are being allowed into the labor room and even in the delivery room, but some hospitals are still resistant to these changes in procedures.

As noted above, birth complications are unpredictable, and in approximately 5 percent of births, delivery through the birth canal may be a problem. A fetus may be too large to pass through the mother's pelvic bones, the mother may have diabetes or some other illness that will put too much stress on the fetus, or the cervix may not dilate and the prolonged stress of a lengthy labor may affect mother and fetus adversely. Conditions such as these usually lead to a recommendation for a *Caesarean section*. This is a surgical procedure used to remove the baby and the placenta from the uterus. After a woman has had one Caesarean delivery, future deliveries are often, but not always, done in the same manner.

Psychological aspects of childbirth

It is generally recognized that during childbirth both mother and child undergo very powerful experiences; less attention has been paid to the father's relationship to his wife and newborn child during the birth processes. However, we still do not know how infants experience birth and whether they have enough sensitivity in the first day of life to experience birth as an ordeal. Otto Rank (1929), a follower of Freud, proposed that the dramatic expulsion from the safe, all-satisfying uterine environment creates the first basic trauma of life. He believed that this trauma establishes a basic anxiety that underlies neuroses.

Frederick Leboyer, a French obstetrician, has developed a method of childbirth that tries to avoid this trauma. In *Birth Without Violence* (1976), he agrees with Rank's description of the birth ordeal and proposes a re-organization of hospital procedures. He suggests that infants be born in a quiet, dimly lit room, placed immediately on the mother's abdomen, and only later bathed in warm water. While parents who choose a particular type of birthing experience usually find it satisfying, social workers should avoid proselytizing for any particular alternative birth experience based on their own life style and experience. For example, home delivery and use of midwives may be admirably suited to those who wish to experience the birth of the child in familiar surroundings, unhampered by hospital sched-ules. Parents choosing this alternative, however, should have the resources and motivation to obtain prenatal care that detects any high-risk conditions that would preclude a home delivery. A prospective mother should also have an emergency plan, should hospitalization be required at the last minute. Although midwives commonly deliver babies in Sweden, Finland, Holland, and Japan, where the infant mortality rate is lower than in the United States (Barnett 1977), it is well to remember that nurse-midwives in these countries are often highly trained graduate nurses (Guttmacher 1973). For many years, poor rural Americans had their children at home but did not receive high-quality prenatal and obstetrical care. Such home delivery was associated with a high infant mortality rate and failure to detect or deal with emergencies such as jaundice or respiratory distress.

Other less controversial innovations that can make the hospital more like a "normal" environment for childbirth include *alternative birth centers,* where family members are included in the total birthing experience, and *rooming in,* an arrangement where the infant stays in the same room with the mother rather than being housed in a separate hospital nursery. Rooming in provides mothers with an opportunity for demand-feeding of the infant and lets them become familiar with their babies before leaving the hospital. Again, some mothers may choose not to avail themselves of these options, particularly if they have felt overburdened by numerous births and are "looking forward to a few days rest." One compromise procedure is to have the baby with the mother during the day but removed to the nursery at night.

THE NEONATE

During the first month of life, a new baby is known as a neonate. This very special period in a baby's life is distinguished from the rest of infancy. It is the time the baby must adjust to leaving the closed, protected environment of the mother's womb for the outside world. Unlike many other animals, humans need a continued period of protection and nourishment after birth. The first month is a period of both recovery from the birth process and adjustment of vital functions such as respiration, circulation, digestion, and body-heat regulation. This earliest period should be of special concern to social workers, who must understand the problems of prematurity and early infant death in order to design effective preventive programs.

At birth, the average full-term baby weighs between five-and-a-half and nine-and-a-half pounds and is between nineteen and twenty-two inches long. The baby's skin may be covered with fine facial and body hairs that drop off during the first month. The newborn's head may look temporarily misshapen, as a result of the squeezing together of the soft bony plate of the skull in the birth canal. The general appearance of the newborn may even be a bit of a shock to new parents who expect to see the plump, smooth, three- to four-month-old infant shown in advertisements.

Neonatal assessment

Not all neonates are equally well equipped to adjust to the abrupt changes brought about by birth, and it is important to detect problems at the earliest possible moment. Great advances have been made in this area in recent years. At one time, babies were considered healthy if they merely "looked OK." Then, in 1953, Virginia Apgar devised a standard scoring system and hospitals were able to evaluate an infant's condition quickly by observing the pulse, breathing, muscle tone, general reflex response, and color of the skin (or for nonwhite babies the mucous membranes, palms, and soles).

In the first few days after birth, most hospitals provide a much more extensive evaluation of the newborn, often including a neurological examination and a behavioral assessment. As mentioned earlier, most states now require mass screening for PKU since prompt introduction of a special diet can prevent retardation.

The question that comes to mind at this point is why, with all these advances in technology, the United States in 1973 was sixteenth among the nations in respect to rate of infant mortality and why 1974 statistics show that in the first year of life the death rate of nonwhites was 55 percent higher than for whites (National Conference for Health Statistics, 1976). In addition, when there is a high infant mortality rate one may also expect a high risk of developmental defects in infants who survive. Some of these questions have been addressed in the section on prenatal environment, and we will consider them again when we discuss prematurity and the special risks it presents.

Meanwhile, it is helpful to have a somewhat fuller description of the normal newborn. One interesting aspect of behavior in newborns is the presence of a number of complex reflexes and combinations of reflexes, most of which disappear after three or four months. These are instinctive patterns, not learned behavior, and a few deserve special mention. When newborns are startled, they react first by extending both arms to the side, with fingers outstretched as if to catch onto someone or something. The grasping reflex allows infants to close their fingers over any object, such as a pencil or finger, placed on their palm. Some neonates can grasp with such strength that they support their full weight for up to a minute (Taft and Cohen 1967).

A very useful reflex is the rooting reflex. When one cheek is touched, babies "root," or move the mouth toward the stimulus, seeking the nipple. A mother who is unfamiliar with this response may try to push the infant's head toward the nipple. The baby will then move toward the stimulus of the hand, thus seeming to reject the breast.

The sucking reflex, like the rooting reflex, is clearly necessary for infant survival. Like some other reflexes, sucking begins in the uterus. Many other reflexes govern the behavior of the newborn. Some, like sneezing or coughing, are necessary for survival. Others seem to be related to the behavior patterns of our primate ancestors. Still others are not yet understood.

Until about twenty years ago, psychologists thought that neonates were incapable of organized, self-directed behavior and did not use the higher centers of the brain until they were almost one year old. Early behavior was considered to be almost entirely reflexive. We now know that neonates are organized beings capable of predictable responses and more complex mental activity than was once thought. They have definite preferences and show a striking ability to learn (Stone, Smith, and Murphy 1973).

Vision has been by far the most investigated sense, with hearing a distant second and the other senses trailing well behind. From the first moments, newborns' eyes are sensitive to brightness, and they can visually track an object such as a doctor's penlight or a face that moves within their field of vision. However, they are able to focus only on close objects, usually seven to twenty inches away, and distant objects appear blurred.

Individual variations

From the moment of birth, infants demonstrate their uniqueness and variability. Parents with more than one child are quite aware of differences in their children's personalities, even though their children were all "brought up" in more or less the same way. These differences can frequently be noted even before a child is born. One fetus may kick actively; another may shift position gently or cautiously. Newborns differ also in their responses to new, prolonged, or slightly annoying stimuli. Some are able to detect, attend to, and then grow accustomed to changes in their environment. Others may be less responsive, or they may be overly responsive and too easily irritated to adapt easily to changes.

How profound are these differences in temperament among neonates? What are the dynamics of interaction between the baby's personality and the parents', and what are their effects? The individuality of the newborn has been the subject of many recent studies. Brazelton (1969), using broad descriptions, identified three general temperamental types: the average baby, the active baby, and the quiet baby. In 1973 he developed the *Neonatal Behavioral Assessment Scale* in an attempt to assess the future personality and social development of infants.

In a study of 136 children, Chess (1967) identified nine criteria to differentiate neonatal behavior. Like Brazelton, she found that children can be divided into three basic types. She also determined that qualities seen as early as two or three months of age can be traced throughout childhood. The largest of Chess's three groups is the "easy children," babies (and later children) who are biologically regular and rhythmical. The easy child sleeps and eats on schedule, accepts new food and new people, and is not easily frustrated. The "difficult children" form a smaller group. They withdraw from new stimuli and adapt slowly to change; their mood is often negative. The third type is the "slow-to-warm-up child." Children in this group withdraw from activities quietly, whereas difficult children do so actively and noisily. This last group will show interest in new situations only if they are allowed to do so gradually, without pressure. Chess found no evidence that these temperamental types were influenced by parental behavior. On the contrary, children's temperaments seemed to be as much a part of them as the inherited color of their eyes.

Although the basis of newborn individuality is not entirely understood, researchers generally agree that widely different behavioral styles are apparent at birth and that these differences increase over the first few months of life. During this same early period, infants and parents will establish relationships that are based on their own unique personalities (Lewis and Rosenblum 1974). Many studies suggest that infants' temperaments and behavioral styles influence parental behavior and partially determine the quality of early interactions.

Researchers regularly find that babies differ greatly in the amount of attention they evoke from their parents, with irritable infants receiving more parental stimulation than overly placid ones. Such attentiveness, however, may be accompanied by feelings of anger, bewilderment, or self-pity in the caregiver as numerous efforts to soothe the baby fail. Conversely, parents of babies who have regular sleeping and eating patterns and who are easily quieted may feel more competent and satisfied in their caregiving.

Crying is the one infant state that causes caregivers the most worry; it challenges them to find the cause and then invent ways to stop it. Of the many techniques used to soothe babies, three stand out in their effectiveness: picking them up, providing constant rhythmic movement, and for some, reducing the amount of stimulation that they get from their own bodies by swaddling them in blankets. Parents have often sensed that babies sleep best when wrapped in a blanket and taken for a ride in the carriage (or the car).

Newborns differ greatly in how easily they can be soothed and in which methods work best. The most important factor is whether the parents' technique for soothing the baby matches the baby's "soothability." When the match is wrong, awkward, or nonexistent, both mother and child may get themselves into behavioral patterns that may be difficult to change.

Mild personality differences between parent and infant are fairly common, and even the most willing and enthusiastic parent needs time and patience to become acquainted with the infant's unique personality. The development of mutuality, reciprocity, and a "symbiotic relationship" between parent and infant is certainly not automatic or instinctive, as we shall see later in the chapter on infancy.

Prematurity and neonatal risk

So far we have discussed only the development of full-term babies. A substantial number of newborns are considered to be premature, a condition that can pose serious problems for infants and caregivers alike. In fact, it is the chief cause of neonatal deaths.

Two indicators of prematurity are frequently confused. The first is gestation time. The infant born after a gestation period of less than thirty-seven weeks is considered premature. The second indicator is low birth weight; because the average birth weight is seven and a half pounds, an infant who weighs less than five and a half pounds is usually classified as premature or in need of special attention, although only half of such infants have a gestation period of less than thirty-seven weeks. Low-birth-weight babies, even when full term, often have problems resulting from fetal malnutrition, for example. Therefore, both the above indicators are used in classifying babies as premature (Babson and Benson 1966).

Prematurity may occur for a number of reasons. The most common is a multiple birth, when two or more infants are born at the same time. In this country, multiple births occur more often among blacks than whites, and among mothers between thirty-five and forty-five years old. Approximately one pregnancy in ninety results in twins. Chances of a multiple birth have recently been increased by the introduction of hormones from the human pituitary, prescribed as a remedy for nonovulating women. These hormones often cause multiple ovulation and have resulted in multiple births ranging from twins to octuplets (Guttmacher 1973).

Prematurity and its resultant problems are likely to come to the attention of social workers dealing with some of the disorders of childhood. For example, there is a significantly larger incidence of prematurity and birth complications in the history of people suffering from cerebral palsy, epilepsy, mental deficiency, and behavior disorders than there is in the rest of the population. Birch and Gussow (1970) point out that it is the young, black mother, pregnant for the first time, economically impoverished, and receiving poor prenatal care, who is the most likely to have a premature infant. They further note that while very young mothers are at the least risk of death during childbirth, their infants are at greater risk, a situation that is compounded by the occurrence of very closely spaced births.

Premature infants usually have greater difficulty in making adjustments than do full-term babies, starting immediately after birth. Their adaptation to the basic processes of circulation, respiration, and temperature control is more complicated. Because they have difficulty maintaining body heat, premature newborns are usually put into incubators immediately after birth. Feeding is also a problem, since it seems almost impossible to replicate the nutritional conditions of the late fetal period so as to produce a comparable growth rate outside the uterus.

Although many defects that appear later in life have been shown to be associated with prematurity, one must be very careful in interpreting the meaning of the findings. For example, poor maternal health or crowding in the uterus also may cause a number of problems in the newborn. Similarly, it is difficult to prove whether the lack of good prenatal and delivery services causes children to be at greater risk, even though the two sets of factors are correlated (that is, occur together more frequently than would happen merely by chance). It may be that factors associated with being poor are the cause of both poor prenatal care and high risk of problems at birth. Birch and Gussow (1970) aptly point out, however, that even a conservative reading of the research leads to the conclusion that one can improve the chances of having healthier babies by improving health care delivery systems. The problem of nonutilization of existing medical services has not yet been remedied, nor have we provided services in every geographic area. In 1960, 40 percent of nonwhite mothers in New York City received very late prenatal care or none at all. By comparison, only 15 percent of white mothers received late or no prenatal care (Baumgartner 1965). It is a challenge to social workers to discover the reasons for these differences and to devise better means for delivering prenatal services, such as neighborhood outreach programs.

Some of the problems premature infants experience may also arise from their treatment during the first few weeks of life. Because they are kept in incubators and protected from harmful microorganisms, they have little of the normal contact of touching and closeness that most newborns experience. Some are unable to suck at all for the first few weeks, and few are even held while being bottle-fed. Moreover, the social isolation of the premature child may persist if the parents become so accustomed to protecting the child that they carry on a restrictive regime long after it is necessary.

Some of the potentially detrimental effects of prematurity may be offset by an enriched environment during the first year of life. Zeskind and Ramey (1978) ran a pilot program for infants born prematurely because of fetal malnourishment. These infants were provided with full-service day care in addition to the necessary medical and nutritional services. Most of them reached normal performance levels by eighteen months. A matched group of fetally malnourished infants received the same medical and nutritional services but were cared for at home, not in the day-care program. These infants were slower to reach normal performance levels, and deficits in their performance were still apparent at two years. Zeskind and Ramey's study suggests that with proper medical care, nutrition, and care giving during their early development, premature infants need not be seriously disadvantaged by the conditions of their birth.

CASE ILLUSTRATIONS

To illustrate the practical applications of the material in this chapter, we shall examine the hypothetical case of a social worker in the prenatal clinic of a metropolitan hospital. Located in an area known to have the highest infant mortality rate in the city, the hospital introduced a special preventive program in an attempt to lower this rate. The multidisciplinary staff of the project includes a social worker assigned the following tasks: to take social histories of new clinic registrants, to work with mothers defined as high-risk in regard to potential maternal or neonatal problems, and to develop a neighborhood outreach program to locate mothers who have not contacted the clinic for prenatal assessment. Among the cases the worker deals with are the following:

Mrs. Jones

A pregnant woman whose family medical history indicates the presence of sickle cell anemia, Mrs. Jones is afraid to be tested to see if she is the carrier of the trait. After her initial appointment with the doctor, she was confused about the purpose of the tests. She is also likely to drop out of the clinic since she understands that the father will need to be seen, and she no longer wants to have anything to do with him after a recent and violent fight.

It is only after the social worker listens to her concerns, which are about other matters, that Mrs. Jones is able to understand a simple explanation of sickle cell anemia. She then agrees to return for future appointments.

Tests reveal that Mrs. Jones is the carrier of the sickle cell trait, although she herself will not get the disease. Since the father's genetic history is not available, the social worker has to outline several sets of probabilities for risk of the child's inheriting the disease. The worker privately agrees with Mrs. Jones' decision to go ahead with the birth, remembering other times when she had to separate her own views favoring termination of a pregnancy from those of a client intent on having her baby in spite of highly unfavorable circumstances. The social worker's task is to help people obtain information and explore their own feelings so that they are better able to handle crises in their own way. However, it is often difficult to refrain from telling people what to do when they ask for help.

By being helpful but not overly intrusive, the worker establishes the basis for a relationship that Mrs. Jones can safely draw on for later help. This relationship led to Mrs. Jones' later use of the pediatric clinic to provide follow-up care for her child, who did develop sickle cell anemia.

Juanita

The worker is also assigned to visit a nearby housing project to try convincing Juanita, a pregnant adolescent, to register at the clinic. She knows about Juanita because the special project staff meets monthly with representatives of the local high school in an effort to reach pregnant young teens who are unlikely to come to the clinic for prenatal care. The social workers and a public health nurse have been giving a minicourse at the high school to educate young teens about the importance of prenatal care and to allay some of their fears about using the clinic.

Feedback from class members has helped the worker to realize that Juanita's family comes from a rural area where "people only go to the hospital to die." She arranges for Juanita's club group to be given a special tour of the hospital, which Juanita had never seen before.

After talking with several teen-agers who were very reluctant to register at the clinic, the social worker meets with the project director to revise the proposal for the project's second year, recommending an office for the public health nurse at the popular local teen recreation center. The director agrees to this suggestion, after first determining that teen-agers do, in fact, continue using the recreation center after they become pregnant. The director also adds an evaluation section to the proposal, to properly assess whether this approach will effectively increase the use of prenatal services by high-risk pregnant women.

Mrs. Williams

In contrast to Juanita, Mrs. Williams knew she had a diabetic condition and has come to the prenatal clinic regularly in order to obtain the best care possible. In spite of receiving excellent care, Mrs. Williams' baby was born blind. The worker's present task is to transfer the case, which she carried during the prenatal phase, to the pediatrics unit of the clinic. She will present a summary of the medical and social history of the family to the pediatric staff who will be seeing the family. In this way the new staff will know that Mr. and Mrs. Williams both attach great value to having a male child, that Mrs. Williams was rejected by her own parents for having made a "bad marriage," and that to some extent she feels that the child's handicap is a punishment for having defied her family. This will help them plan a support system with Mrs. Williams that may or may not include help from extended family. In addition, the staff will be informed of Mrs. Williams' present dependence on her husband for all crucial decisions so that they will arrange to meet with both parents together to help them plan how to enable their son to develop to his fullest potential.

The Agency

Social workers do not spend all of their time meeting with clients. They must also participate in setting agency policies. In dealing with individuals facing crises, the social worker has access to clients' medical records and to considerable information about their private lives. The 1980 *Code of Ethics of the National Association of Social Workers* includes a section on the client's right to have this information treated in a confidential manner. Generally, if information about a client is to be shared with others, the client is entitled to know "with whom" and "why." It is becoming standard practice for agencies to require prior written consent before sending out confidential material to other agencies.

The social worker also has an obligation to share information with the client, with increasing emphasis being placed on the client's "right to know." Agency practices vary, but right-to-know issues are of particular importance to workers dealing with problems of neonatal assessment. Because recording of infant medical conditions at birth can help in making a sound diagnosis of later developmental problems, the social worker must be as honest as possible in presenting the contents of the medical record to the parents. This is a difficult task—the prognosis and even the diagnosis may be very tentative since frequently not enough is known to "predict the future."

Many changes have been made in the ways agencies deal with these issues, and social workers will help to formulate continuing changes in policy. One issue that is still characterized by heated debate is the question of how much information adopted children are entitled to have about their natural parents. Their "real" birth records are often sealed by law and unavailable to them, although information about family's medical history may be necessary if questions arise later about genetic defects. An understanding of some of the questions raised in this chapter should assist practitioners in making sound judgments when dealing with requests for information about these very early days of life.

SUMMARY

Human development begins with the fertilization of the ovum, when the genetic material of the egg unites with the genetic material of a single sperm cell. From this zygote a process of continuous cell division produces first the embryo and then the fetus. The embryo develops within the amniotic sac and receives oxygen and nourishment through the placenta. By the time the fetus is ready for birth all its organs and systems have become functional, and it can react to touch and sound.

Genetic inheritance and cultural environment interact in shaping the individual. Inheritance is determined by both orderly principles of dominant and recessive traits among paired genes and accidental occurrences. Inheritance is transmitted through the pairing of twenty-three chromosomes from each parent. Each chromosome carries thousands of genes that in turn are composed of DNA molecules.

The study of birth defects is called teratology. Genetic counseling can assist parents in understanding and dealing with genetic risks. Mental retardation is one outcome of chromosomal abnormality. Some defects are sex-linked; some are dominant, and others are recessive.

Most of the harmful disturbances in fetal development are caused by various environmental influences, such as poor maternal health or nutrition, venereal disease, drugs, or radiation. These factors have their greatest impact at sensitive and critical periods. These periods usually occur during the first trimester, when the pregnancy may not yet have been detected.

This prenatal period also has psychological and social significance for the family, and adjustments made at this time will have an impact on the new family member.

Childbirth consists of a period of labor during which the involuntary contractions of the uterus work to ready the mother for the later birth contractions, which expel the baby through the dilated cervix. This is followed by a brief afterbirth, during which the placenta is expelled.

Anesthesia or drugs may be used to relieve pain during childbirth, "natural" childbirth may be experienced, or a combination of the two methods may be used. Since childbirth may sometimes have unexpected complications, midwives should be used only if they are trained to detect emergencies.

Infants are called *neonates* during the first month after birth. The first week after birth is a period of high risk, especially for those born prematurely. The Apgar score provides a quick neonatal assessment.

Although the neonate has a large repertoire of reflexes, recent studies show that a good deal of learning also takes place at this time. Individual differences in infant temperament are increasingly being recognized. Investigators find a reciprocal relationship between infant behavior and attitudes of the caregiver to the infant. These often establish patterns for the future.

Prematurity is a chief cause of neonatal deaths; premature babies also have a higher risk of developing problems later. Multiple births and poverty are among the factors associated with a high degree of prematurity.

Social workers dealing with problems such as infertility, unwanted pregnancy, and birth defects will find a knowledge of this early phase of human development especially relevant. A familiarity with statistical data on neonatal problems may also be helpful to social workers concerned with the special needs of low-income communities.

SUGGESTED READINGS

Birch, H.G., & Gussow, J.D. *Disadvantaged Children: Health, Nutrition and School Failure.* New York: Harcourt Brace Jovanovich, 1970. An excellent and readable discussion of research findings on the effects of prenatal environment on infant and maternal death rates is included in the presentation of the relationships between poverty and learning disabilities.

Dick-Read, G. *Childbirth Without Fear.* New York: Harper & Row, 1953. A classic presentation of the theory and practice of one approach to "natural" childbirth.

Guttmacher, A. *Pregnancy, Birth, and Family Planning.* New York: Viking, 1973. A medical pioneer in education for the layman offers concise answers to typical concerns about the topics covered. The author shows understanding of the social context within which these events occur.

Leboyer, F. *Birth Without Violence.* New York: Knopf, 1976. Portrays birth procedures radically different from those normally used in hospitals. Contains many compelling photographs.

Mandelbaum, A. Mental Health and Retardation. In *Encyclopedia of Social Work.* Washington, D.C.: National Association of Social Workers, 1977. This ten-page summary offers a description of types of retardation and discusses the factors associated with its occurrence. There is also a review of social work services to the retarded.

Rugh, R., & Shettles, L. *From Conception to Birth: The Drama of Life's Beginnings.* New York: Harper & Row, 1971. The processes of prenatal development and childbirth are clearly and fully described in a manner appropriate for new parents as well as teachers and nurses.

chapter three

Doris Pinney, Photo Researchers, Inc.

INFANCY
developing competencies
and relationships

outline

AGES AND STAGES: AN OVERVIEW

> *Age four months*
>
> *Age eight months*
>
> *Age twelve months*
>
> *Age eighteen months*
>
> *Age twenty-four months*

COGNITIVE DEVELOPMENT

> *The sensorimotor period*
>
> *Memory and symbolic representation*
>
> *Environmental influences*

ATTACHMENT: DEVELOPING RELATIONSHIPS

> *Sociobiology: Theories of bonding*
>
> *Mutuality*
>
> *The handicapped infant*
>
> *Separation anxiety*
>
> *Maternal deprivation*
>
> *Separation and loss*

MOTHERS AND CAREGIVERS

> *Working mothers*
>
> *Infant day care*
>
> *Fathers and infants*

THE PSYCHOANALYTIC TRADITION

> *Freud: Oral and anal stages*
>
> *Erikson: Trust and autonomy*

CHILD REARING AND PERSONALITY DEVELOPMENT

Trust and nurturance

Autonomy and discipline

Self-awareness

CASE ILLUSTRATIONS

SUMMARY

SUGGESTED READINGS

DAN ALWAYS SEEMED FUSSY, from the day of his birth. He slept irregularly and was given to long crying spells. At eight months he began to have temper tantrums when things did not go his way. He knew at an early age which toys, food, and people he preferred. At twelve months he was very active and independent. He had been walking for a month and disliked being restrained from moving about. By eighteen months his active temperament became even more distinct. He continued to disturb his parents' sleep occasionally with his sudden waking and howling. His expressions of surprise, joy, and anger were always intense, which puzzled his parents, who were quiet, calm people.

Paul, on the other hand, developed in a different way. By the end of twelve months, he was quiet, placid, and still content to sit in his playpen for long periods of time. He showed no signs of temper and rarely cried. At eighteen months he continued to be easy-going and gentle. He lost his earlier fear of strangers and became more outgoing and friendly. His eating and sleeping habits were quite regular.

During the period from birth until two years of age, children develop rapidly. They become aware of themselves and the world around them. They learn to manipulate objects, themselves, and other people. They learn to communicate and to represent things symbolically. They begin to discriminate among people, places, tastes, and sounds.

Although norms of growth and behavior have been established for children at various ages and stages of development, great variations exist in individual temperament and personality (Brazelton 1969). These different styles will persist throughout the life span. Such individuality is apparent in the two children described above and becomes even more obvious as children grow older.

In the first part of this chapter we describe the motor and cognitive development of infants. We then examine the parent-child relationship and its importance to the emotional development of the child. Two different theoretical perspectives on this early attachment will be presented, the sociobiological and psychoanalytic. In real life, the cognitive and emotional development of infants is interrelated; they are not discrete areas of development. Professionals who work with families of infants must be aware of the effects of genetic and environmental influences on both cognitive and emotional development.

AGES AND STAGES: AN OVERVIEW

Developmental psychologists have made many careful descriptive studies comparing the infant, the child, and the adolescent at various ages. Arnold Gesell and his colleagues reported their studies in a series of books: *The First Five Years of Life* (1940), *The Child from Five to Ten* (1946), and *Youth: The Years from Ten to Sixteen* (1956). Gesell compared hundreds of children to determine the ages at which they were able to perform such actions as walking, running, picking up a small pellet, cutting with scissors, and drawing the human figure. From the resulting data, he then determined the capabilities of "average" children at various ages.

Gesell believes that physical, cognitive, and personality development follow an orderly **sequence of maturation.** His view is that development unfolds in an innate pattern, given a reasonably normal environment. This pattern of behavior functions in spiral fashion, with a child at one age exhibiting expansive, outgoing, vigorous behavior, which becomes consolidated and better controlled in the next age. The child is then ready for the next developmental spurt.

There are weaknesses in Gesell's theory and method. First, he describes when developmental phenomena occur, but he does not explain why they occur. He implies, but gives no evidence, that maturation *causes* the observed behavioral changes. Second, the children studied by Gesell came from one socioeconomic class in one community, and he does not examine the extent to which the similarity of environment may have resulted in similar behaviors.

Based on the norms established by Gesell, many have tended to equate chronological age with a specific developmental stage. This hasty reading of Gesell's ideas has produced such oversimplified concepts as "the terrible twos," "the trusting threes," and "the frustrating fours." Because of these weaknesses, it can be misleading to use Gesell as the arbiter of the normality of a particular child's behavior. For example, he describes the four-year-old child as tending to "go out of bounds" in many ways—in social behavior, in speech, and in motor activity (1940). Parents and caregivers of four-year-olds may begin to wonder whether something is wrong with their children if they do not attempt to exceed parental restrictions. However, some cultural subgroups emphasize conformity more than others, and children in these families will tend not to behave in the manner that Gesell describes.

Nevertheless, Gesell's contribution remains a substantial one if we use his descriptive material cautiously. We should keep in mind that they reflect the middle 50 percent and not those children who are nearer the two extremes of the developmental scale. Therefore, the age-level descriptions that follow are not intended to serve as measures of what *each* infant should be doing at a particular age, but rather as a useful picture of the expected sequence of development and as a baseline from which to examine the range of individual differences. In this spirit, we present a summary description of some milestones in the development of infants.

Age four months

At the age of four months, most infants resemble the chubby children seen in magazine advertisements. They have nearly doubled in weight since birth and have probably grown four or more inches in length. Their skin has lost the newborn look, and their fine birth hair is being replaced by new growth. Their heads are not growing as rapidly as the rest of their bodies, so that they are better proportioned than at birth.

The first tooth erupts at four or five months in some children, although the average age for this is closer to six or seven months. Many bones are still soft cartilage; they tend to be pliable under stress and rarely break. Muscles, however, may pull and become injured easily. Occasionally, well-meaning adults discover this when hoisting infants up by the arms and swinging them in play (Stone, Smith, and Murphy 1973).

When four-month-olds are placed on their stomachs, they can generally hold up their heads and chests. They can hold their heads steady from a sitting position and carefully observe everything that goes on. Average infants of this age can roll over from stomach to back and from back to stomach (Stone, Smith, and Murphy 1973). Most can reach for and grasp an object (Frankenburg and Dodds 1967).

Self-discovery usually begins about this time. Infants discover their hands and fingers and may spend periods of several minutes studying their movements, bringing them together and grasping one hand with the other (Church 1966). Some four-month-olds also discover their feet and manipulate them in much the same way (Brazelton 1969).

At four months, nearly all babies smile, laugh, and coo quite selectively. They will react with a wide range of emotional responses to persons or events. Many babies also begin to engage in elementary social games in which they enjoy having adults mimic their vocalization. At this age, adults have to imitate the baby's sounds, not the other way around. Much to the delight of parents and caregivers, the average baby begins to settle into the family routine and sleep through the night.

Age eight months

At eight months, babies have gained another four or five pounds and have grown about three more inches in length, but their general appearance does not differ dramatically from that of four-month-olds. They probably have at least one tooth, and their hair is thicker and longer. Their legs are oriented so that the soles of their feet no longer face each other.

Most eight-month-olds can get themselves into a sitting position, and nearly all can sit without support once they are placed in position (Stone, Smith, and Murphy 1973). About half of the eight-month-olds can pull themselves into a standing position, and a few may even begin to sidestep around the crib or playpen while holding on; some babies may walk by using furniture for support.

Although an occasional baby does take a few steps alone, it is generally too early for free walking (Stone, Smith, and Murphy 1973). The age at which walking begins varies widely, depending on both individual abilities and cultural factors (Hindley et al. 1966). Meanwhile, babies usually develop some method of crawling that enables them to explore the world around them.

Most eight-month-old babies are able to pass objects from hand to hand, and may delight in filling both hands with objects. They are usually able to bang two objects together—a feat they often demonstrate endlessly. They are also able to coordinate their actions by reaching out, grasping an object, and bringing it to their mouths. Such successful reaching requires a number of different abilities: accurate depth perception, voluntary control of grasping, voluntary control of arm movements, and the ability to organize these behaviors in a sequence (Bruner 1973). In the visually guided reach, infants functionally integrate many pieces of behavior and subordinate them to the general pattern. This is in sharp contrast to the behavior of the one-month-old infants, who respond to the sight of an attractive object in an uncoordinated manner by staring intently, then waving their arms while opening their mouths as if about to suck the object.

The infant begins to pay more attention to speech at eight months, turning toward a voice and even imitating some speech sounds. Most infants will repeat a few sounds or words, such as *mamma, dada,* or *bye-bye,* even though they usually will not know what the words mean. The sounds in infant babbling are much more complex and varied at eight months than at four months. Infants possess a seemingly inborn ability to differentiate between speech and nonspeech sounds. This ability to recognize speech sounds and to analyze them phonetically is basic to learning a language (Eimas 1975). Infants' sensitivity to speech and their ability to recognize familiar voices also strengthens the bonds of attachment to their parents or other caregivers. This, in turn, encourages further cognitive development.

Age twelve months

At twelve months, most infants are about three times heavier than they were at birth, and they have grown about nine or ten inches in length; girls tend to weigh slightly less than boys. After the first year, the dramatic rate of earlier weight increase slows significantly.

Many babies are now walking alone or can walk while holding onto furniture. They are often able to stand alone in one place, and some can even stoop and then recover their balance. However, as we mentioned earlier, normal children may vary from this timetable.

Twelve-month-olds actively manipulate the environment. They are able to undo latches, open cabinets, pull toys, and twist lamp cords. Their newly developed pincer grasp—with the thumb opposing the forefinger—allows them to pick up grass, hairs, cigarette butts, and dead insects. They can turn on the television set and the stove, and they can explore electrical outlets and bottles of cleaning fluid. While children this age are busy exploring their environment, caregivers must set limits on these explorations. Adults have to strike a balance between too much restriction and sufficient control to keep the baby safe. Sensible persons will "baby-proof" the house by placing fragile and dangerous objects out of the infant's reach, thus minimizing some of the stresses of this period. It should be evident that children of this age require careful and constant supervision, and that staffing ratios for day-care services must reflect this requirement.

This propensity for exploration, which develops before the infant has a concept of safe versus unsafe objects, places a great strain on parents—particularly those who lack an understanding of the maturational value of these explorations and those who become easily frustrated when their orders are "disobeyed." Social workers find that parents who physically abuse infants when they misbehave sometimes misinterpret the child's failure to respond as a personal rejection of them.

As they enter the second year, children are often able to play games. A favorite game is to "hide" from someone by covering their eyes; another is to roll a ball back and forth with an adult. Many are also beginning to feed themselves, using a spoon and a cup.

Most infants are on the verge of language at this time. They also become aware of themselves as individuals separate from their mothers or caregivers. They begin to exercise choices, and may suddenly protest loudly about bedtime or refuse a food that they have always liked. Formerly trouble-free events, such as being placed in a high chair may now be the occasion for a "battle of the wills."

Age eighteen months

The eighteen-month-old is usually referred to as a "toddler." This is an imprecisely defined stage during which the child has a somewhat top-heavy stance and a gait that is neither solidly balanced nor smoothly coordinated. However, almost all children at this age are walking alone, usually pushing or pulling something with them. They may not be able to climb stairs yet, and most lack sufficient balance to stand on one foot in order to kick a ball.

Children at this age can sometimes stack blocks to build a tower and scribble with crayons or pencil. They have improved their ability to feed themselves and may be able to partly undress themselves. Many of their actions are imitative of those going on around them—"reading" a magazine, sweeping the floor, or chattering on a toy telephone.

Most eighteen-month-olds have made great strides in language and may have a vocabulary of several words and phrases. They can point to and name body parts, and some have begun to combine words effectively.

Age twenty-four months

Two-year-olds have not been as available for studies by research psychologists as have children of other ages because they are no longer seen monthly by pediatricians and are usually not yet in nursery school. This is particularly unfortunate, as the two-year-old is a fascinating creature, just beginning to break through into new areas of skill and accomplishment.

Children of this age not only walk and run, but they can usually pedal a tricycle, jump in place on both feet, balance briefly on one foot, and accomplish a fairly good overhand throw. They crawl into, under, around and over objects and furniture; they manipulate, carry, push, or pull anything they see. They put things into and take things out of large containers. They pour water, mold clay, stretch the stretchable, and bend the bendable. They explore, test, and probe. All this exploration provides a vital learning experience, teaching them about the nature and possibilities of their physical world. It also plays an important part in their cognitive development. In their play with objects, they demonstrate a memory for repeated events, match their actions appropriately to various objects, and develop their understanding of the social world through pretending and imitation.

The language development of most two-year-olds shows some marked gains. They are able to follow simple directions and use three or more words in combination. Given a crayon or pencil, they may create scribbles and be briefly fascinated with the magical markings. Their spontaneous block play shows matching of shapes and symmetry. If they are willing, they can take off most of their own clothing and even put on some items.

It is now time to stop and ask ourselves how social workers can make use of this information about infant development. We have already cautioned against using it to determine when all normal children should sit, walk, or begin to speak. This is not the sort of checklist that a worker would wish parents to post as a handy reference for judging whether their youngster "measures up" to norms each month. Nonetheless, it is a good general guide to the sequence of infant maturation, and the descriptions can provide a useful baseline from which to view an infant's general rate of development. For example, an infant who is still not sitting independently at one year will also be late in walking and possibly be slow in many aspects of maturation.

Some parents are needlessly concerned about a child who, though developing normally, may be slower in physical development than a sibling, or a neighbor's child, or the statistical average. However, there is cause for concern if a child shows a *significant* lag in one or all aspects of maturation. A social worker noting such a situation might refer the family or the child to the community resource providing the most competent evaluation and testing services for infants. A thorough evaluation will explore the possibility of genetic or birth defects, and investigate the physical and emotional environment in which the infant currently lives.

Social workers may become involved in evaluating the family environment when infants fail to thrive or to develop normally. Infants at risk may first be identified when parents bring them to hospital clinics suffering from acute physical distress, such as a recurrent respiratory infection or an injury that might be the result of child abuse. Doctors examining such infants may then notice other symptoms, such as failure to gain weight and seriously retarded motor and language development. These judgments are based on information on average norms for infant development, such as those presented in this chapter.

In extreme circumstances, infants may be neglected or even abandoned. Some infants whose development has been impaired by neglect are able to express their normal maturational potential once they are placed in a normal environment; others may have additional organic reasons for their problems. As yet we have no clear-cut answers to questions about critical periods for development. We do not know whether children must develop certain capacities by a particular age or lose the potential for full development. However, in extreme cases when the family environment is considered harmful to the normal development of the child, the court may order the family to be placed under the supervision of a social worker in the county agency dealing with children's protective services.

Social workers involved with the placement of infants either in foster homes or with adoptive families must be familiar with general developmental guidelines. Infants needing placement have often been subject to a great deal of environmental stress, and some have been neglected or abused. Any evidence of developmental lags should therefore be carefully evaluated before a permanent placement plan is made.

COGNITIVE DEVELOPMENT

The sensorimotor period

The first period of cognitive development is called the **sensorimotor period** because infant intelligence relies on the senses and on bodily motions for equilibration. It is a practical intelligence, which enables the infant to become aware that an object exists in time and space, independent of the infant's own perception of it. According to Piaget, **object permanence** is the primary accomplishment of this period, and infants do not develop the full set of object concepts until they are about eighteen months old. We shall present a more complete view of Piaget's cognitive theories in Chapter 4.

To understand how infants develop the idea of object permanence, Piaget (1952) and other researchers investigated infant search behavior. They found that most infants under eighteen months do not sustain a successful search for an object that they have just seen. They form an idea of their mother's permanence, but they do not generalize this insight to other external objects. During the first year, "out of sight, out of mind" seems literally true of them. Thus, they will show no interest in a covered toy they cannot see, even if they are holding it under the cover.

The development of object permanence involves a series of accomplishments. First, infants must develop the ability to recognize familiar objects. Some do this as early as two months; they become excited at the sight of a bottle. Second, infants about two months old can watch a moving object disappear behind one edge of a screen and then shift their eyes to the other edge to see if it reappears. Their visual tracking is excellent and well timed, and they are surprised if something does not reappear. However, they do not seem to mind when a completely different object appears from behind the screen (Bower 1971).

We have already mentioned that infants do form the concept of person permanence somewhat before object permanence, but the developmental processes are similar. Bower (1971) arranged mirrors so that infants would see multiple images of their mothers. He found that most infants less than five months old were not disturbed at seeing more than one mother; in fact, they were delighted. However, infants older than five months had learned that they had only one mother and were very disturbed at seeing the double image.

Infants do not reach a full concept of object permanence until they begin to search for hidden objects (Gratch 1972; Gratch and Landers 1971; Piaget 1954). Searching behavior proceeds through a predictable sequence of development. Infants younger than five months, as we have noted, seem to forget about an object once it is hidden. Somewhere between five and eight months, they start to enjoy hiding and finding games; they like covering their eyes with their hands and having the world reappear when they take their hands away.

There are still some irregularities in the hunting behavior of one-year-olds. If a toy is hidden in place A and they are accustomed to finding it there, they will continue looking for it at place A, even when they have seen it hidden in place B (Piaget 1952). Infants of this age seem to have two memories, and the memory of finding the object seems to be stronger than the memory of seeing the object.

The final attainment of object permanence occurs at about eighteen months and seems dependent on locomotive ability. Once infants can crawl and walk, they are able to pursue their guesses and hypotheses more actively. If a ball rolls away, they may follow it. If mother is out of sight, they may go and find her. In this way, they test the properties of the world around them through their own actions.

Memory and symbolic representation

Most of the sensorimotor abilities discussed so far require some form of memory. Four-month-old infants prefer to look at new objects, showing that they have already established some memory for the familiar (Cohen and Gelber 1975). The imitation seen so often in the play of infants requires that they be able to remember the sounds and actions of the other person. Infants also enjoy searching for a toy that they remember seeing someone hide in a particular location. Although sensorimotor abilities have been thoroughly studied, little attention has been given to the role that memory plays in the development of these abilities.

Imitating, finding hidden objects, and pretending are all part of an underlying process of symbolic representation. Pretending behavior develops over several stages (Fein et al. 1975). At first, infants perform actions that are merely the simplest forerunners of symbolic representation—the ability to represent something not physically present. For example, infants may smack their lips before the bottle reaches their mouths, or they may continue to make eating motions after feeding time is over.

Between six and twelve months, children begin actively pretending—that is, using actions to represent objects, events, or ideas. For example, they may represent the idea of sleeping by putting their heads down on their hands. By about twelve months, most children can pretend to eat, drink, or sleep. By eighteen months, they may include another person in their pretending play; they may pretend to feed someone.

Toward the end of the second year, children are able to use objects appropriately in symbolic play. For example, they may use a shoe box to represent a truck, with a doll for its driver. Such pretending behavior shows that children of this age can create symbols by pretending that an object represents something other than its original meaning. Such forms of pretending represent a further step in cognitive development. By noting the rough similarities between a shoe box and a truck, children combine a distant concept with a familiar one and thus establish a symbolic relationship between the two. Language, of course, is the ultimate system of symbolic relationships, as we shall see in the next chapter.

Environmental influences

Optimal physical and cognitive development during the first two years always depends on more than just the natural processes of maturation. We turn now to a discussion of two of the most important environmental factors affecting the infant's physical and cognitive development: adequate diet and appropriate environmental stimulation.

We have already mentioned the effects of the mother's diet on the child during the prenatal period. The quality of diet during the first two years will also affect the infant's rate of growth, muscular development, tooth and bone formation, and mental abilities. Six-month-old infants need twice as many calories and five times as much protein as an adult requires for each unit of body weight. A two-year-old needs three times as much protein as an adult for each unit of body weight (Calder 1966). Such large amounts of protein and other nutrients are necessary because young children are in a critical period of the growth cycle. *Acute malnutrition* and *chronic subnutrition* can permanently retard growth of the brain and the nervous system (Cravioto and Robles 1965; Perkins 1977). A number of studies have shown that this retardation of brain cell development is irreversible (Coursin 1972; Winick and Brasel 1977; Wyden 1971). It may result in impaired ability to give close attention to mental tasks, as well as defective ability to process information that is given (Birch 1972). Poor nutrition also affects cognitive development by placing the infant at greater risk of infection and serious illness.

There are two kinds of malnutrition—one due to an insufficient quantity of food, the other to an insufficiency of the proper kinds of food. The latter type is more prevalent in the United States. Ours may be considered the best-fed nation in the world, but many still suffer from nutritional deficiencies. One study of infants from poor families in Tennessee (Hutcheson 1968) found that 20 percent suffered from severe anemia (a red blood cell deficiency caused by a lack of iron in the diet), and another 30 percent suffered from moderate anemia. The diets of the poor most often lack iron and vitamins A and C. One survey, conducted in 1965, reported that 18 percent of American families with a yearly income of less than $3,000 had diets that were deficient in one or more essential ingredients (Birch 1972).

Many people cannot afford to buy animal proteins, and they receive inadequate amounts of proteins from other sources. Others who can afford a good diet may consume too many "empty calories" in the form of food high in carbohydrates but low in proteins, vitamins, and minerals. The adequacy of a family diet is related to both income and level of education.

Authorities disagree as to what types of social welfare programs are best able to remedy problems of malnutrition in very young children. Children in school or child-care programs can be given nourishing meals directly. Infants living in the family home are not as easily reached. There are welfare programs such as Women's, Infants' and Children's Supplementary Food Program (WIC) and the food stamp program for low-income individuals and families. These income-transfer programs are intended to ensure that benefit payments are spent on food rather than other items. But aside from feeding children directly or heavily subsidizing items such as milk, government programs cannot monitor the nutritional adequacy of foods offered in the family home.

Some critics argue against any program that cannot guarantee that recipients will use the extra money or vouchers to improve the quality of their diet. They prefer programs that distribute nutritional foods directly to the poor, allowing them no choice as to which foods they prefer to purchase. In the past, food distribution by the Department of Agriculture was governed more by the needs of farmers who had surplus commodities than by the needs or wishes of low-income consumers. Moreover, such programs rarely reflect the ingrained dietary preferences of different racial and ethnic groups.

One of the first decisions that a new mother must make is whether to *breast-feed* or to *bottle-feed* her infant. The breast milk of a reasonably well-fed mother contains a remarkably well-balanced combination of nutrients as well as antibodies that protect the infant from some diseases. Breast-fed infants also are less likely to develop milk allergies (Heiner, Wilson, and Lahey 1964). Yet mothers in both the developed and the less developed countries have shifted in recent years to bottle-feeding with infant formula. While this shift has caused no hardship or nutritional problems for the great majority of infants in developed countries, it has resulted in widespread malnutrition and high infant mortality in poorer countries. Malnutrition occurs when people lack the money to buy expensive infant formulas; in addition, many babies die when the commercial formula is diluted with contaminated water, thereby transmitting intestinal diseases to the infants. For these reasons, concerned groups have campaigned against corporations that encourage widespread marketing of these products in third world countries.

Mollie and Russell Smart (1973) report a number of studies, both in the United States and England, that show a reversal of the earlier association of breast feeding with a low-income population. Today, middle-class, upper-class, and better-educated women are more likely than other women to breast feed their infants.

At the beginning of this section, we spoke of the importance of an adequate diet and appropriate environmental stimulation as prerequisites for optimal cognitive development. Most **environmental stimulation** comes from the primary caregiver who forms a close attachment to the infant. The remainder of this chapter describes the crucial effects of this relationship on the emotional development of the infant. However, we shall first describe the impact of the environment on cognitive development during this period.

The mother who cuddles her child and sings to it is offering a range of stimulating experiences to the infant—touch sensations as she strokes its skin, muscle sensations and inner ear stimulation as the baby is moved from one position to another, and visual and auditory experiences (Smart and Smart 1973). In contrast, studies of infants raised in institutions have pointed to the negative effects of lack of exposure to environmental stimulation. Of course, not every institutional environment is as deprived as one setting described, in which babies were kept in cribs with covered sides and were rarely spoken to or even picked up for their feedings (Dennis and Najarian 1957). The infants observed in this study had no opportunity to practice skills such as sitting, standing, and walking, and this caused severe retardation in all aspects of their development.

Most institutions do not offer infants the same variety of objects and situations as they would receive in most family environments. Studies show that babies raised in institutions tend to show less exploratory behavior (Collard 1971). As we pointed out earlier, sensorimotor exploration is the primary way in which infants learn about the world around them.

Collard (1971) also compared infants from middle-class and low-income homes and found that the former group had developed more complex mental structures than the latter. This finding may be due to the fact that the middle-class babies in the study had all been exposed to block play, and most came from families with fewer children and more opportunities for the adult to play with each child. Those babies who had adults play with them did better than babies who played only by themselves.

Studies on infant development have important implications for educators seeking greater equality of educational achievement among school-age children from different socioeconomic backgrounds. Bronfenbrenner (1974) presents evidence that education for cognitive development starts with the play experiences of infants; therefore, corrective interventions must involve the total family environment. He points out that basic environmental requirements for optimal child development include adequate housing, health care, nutrition, and employment for all families.

There are some educational programs for infants already in operation. In addition to establishing a caring relationship with each child, these programs also offer a variety of stimulating objects and experiences appropriate to the child's developmental stage. Such programs have reported that participants made substantial gains in cognitive skills as compared to control groups (Smart and Smart 1973, pp. 161–162).

An optimal amount of environmental stimulation can be provided without a vast assortment of toys or a massively enriched environment (Yarrow et al. 1972). In fact, some of the best toys for infants are pots and pot covers, wooden spoons, boxes filled with objects that can be safely manipulated, and sturdy toys that can be pulled on a string. A pail, shovel, pile of sand, and container of water can provide the basis for skill development. Expensive equipment is not needed.

Educators and social workers concerned about the cognitive development of infants might want to read about the Russian approach to environmental stimulation of infants. Rosenham (1969), in comparing the American and Soviet approaches, cites Dr. Spock's advice to parents as evidence of the American belief that children will be better off if we do not push their cognitive development but merely offer an environment that facilitates the natural unfolding of their maturational potential. In contrast, he cites a Soviet manual that emphasizes how teachers are to make use of their relationship with each infant in the nursery to provide constant environmental stimulation. The Soviets believe that systematically exposing infants to certain experiences will lead to their developing the proper physical, cognitive, and social skills later in life.

Americans are more concerned than the Soviets with individualized programs of infant care. Psychologists and social workers believe that it is possible to overwhelm an infant with too much stimulation. Sometimes parents or other caregivers overstimulate a child out of their needs to have the baby respond to them. For example, they may be unable to recognize and respond appropriately to cues that an infant needs to be put to sleep in a quiet place. Instead, they may respond to the irritable crying of an overly tired child by offering more toys to play with or more interaction with adults. Social workers are often able to help parents respond more appropriately to behavioral cues from their infants. Parents should recognize that they provide a constant source of stimulation in the course of feeding, diapering, bathing, and dressing the infant. This stimulation can be helpful or not, depending on the "fit" between parental and infant needs.

We have shown that babies come into the world with certain response styles. Some are more sensitive to light or to sudden loud sounds than others. Some are fussy and react quickly to discomfort, and others are placid and adapt easily to new stimuli. We have also noted that infants gradually become aware of themselves as individuals able to control their own bodies and interact with their environment.

Now we shall focus on infants' first relationships and the extent to which the caregiving adult is able to perceive and respond adequately to their basic needs and response styles. We shall examine how personality develops within the context of these relationships and how infants perceive the environment as responsive or unresponsive to their needs. Two different theoretical perspectives on infant attachment will be presented: sociobiological theories of bonding, and psychoanalytic theories about early relationships.

ATTACHMENT: DEVELOPING RELATIONSHIPS

In the course of a lifetime, most individuals develop a number of significant interpersonal relationships. The first and undoubtedly most influential bond is the one that immediately begins to grow between the infant and the mother or caregiver. This bond becomes firmly established by eight or nine months of age and establishes patterns for future relationships and for the acquisition of basic attitudes, expectations, and behavior. Since the mid-1960s, many psychologists have applied the term **attachment** to the process involved in forming this first relationship. It is characterized by strong interdependence, intense mutual feelings, and vital emotional ties.

Significant attachments, losses, and separations occur throughout life. The process starts in infancy as the child develops trust and confidence in the caregiver. Later, a characteristic sequence of events takes place in reaction to the loss of this intense first relationship. This early response to attachment and loss lays the foundation for later relationships, whether with peers, relatives, or other adults. Hence, this infant–caregiver bond is called a *prototypical relationship.*

All animal babies seek close and continued contact with one or two caregivers of their own species, and each species develops characteristic patterns of behavior that serve to create this bond, or attachment (Ainsworth 1973). Human attachment behavior includes behavior such as crying, smiling, vocalizing, and actively approaching and embracing the other person. The significant aspect of this theory of attachment is that it views the infant as the initiator of behavior that invites nurturant responses from the caregiver. The attachment process is seen as a mutual system: The infant's behavior prompts the caregiver to act in certain ways, and the caregiver's actions set off responses in the baby.

Sociobiology: Theories of bonding

Why does attachment occur? Is it a conditioned response, or is there an innate need to establish a relationship? For a long while, developmental psychologists thought that babies formed attachments only because caregivers fulfilled infants' primary needs. It was thought that children *learned* to associate the caregiver's nearness with the satisfaction of primary drives, such as hunger (Sears 1963). However, researchers in the field of **sociobiology** have reminded us that the human infant is helpless at birth, and therefore must become attached to others in order to receive the care and protection necessary for survival. We turn now to a brief look at some theories of sociobiology, followed by a description of some specific applications of imprinting and bonding in human infants.

Sociobiology is a relatively new discipline. It seeks to integrate biological theories of the fixed limits of our biological nature with social science theories about the cultural organization of human life (Hampshire 1978). Sociobiologists claim that many complex patterns of social behavior are genetically determined (Wilson 1975). They cite evidence to show that many human behavior patterns expressing dominance, territoriality, mating, and aggression reflect but a thin veneer of cultural learning superimposed on a genetically inherited base.

For example, *Konrad Lorenz* (1967), an Austrian zoologist, views all animal aggression as instinctual, with functional origins in the need to preserve the species. He concludes that this instinct in humans must constantly be redirected by the culture, as it cannot be eliminated.

Similarly, Strayer and Strayer (1976), in analyzing patterns of social interaction among children, observed a dominance hierarchy that seems to serve the function of lessening the amount of intergroup conflict. Sociobiologists point to hierarchical patterns among other primates that serve a similar function.

Recently, developmental psychologists have become interested in studies showing the similarity of human responses to environmental stimuli to the innate behavioral adaptations of other species. They have also used biological methods of observation in order to study humans in their natural settings rather than in contrived laboratory situations.

Most psychologists still believe that human social behavior is primarily learned. They generally look at situational and historical causes of behavior. The sociobiologists focus on the adaptive function of behavior that assists in the preservation of the individual or the species. For example, when a baby cries the situational cause may be that the baby is in pain. The historical cause may be that the baby has been rewarded by care after crying in the past. The functional or adaptive cause is that it alerts the mother and "triggers" her nurturance. In this sense, crying is an innate and functional behavior pattern, directed toward the specific target of nurturance and based in the innate immobility of the human infant (Hess 1970).

We can better understand infants' first relationships with their caregivers if we look at the maternal relationships of some other animals. These relationships have been studied extensively in ducks and geese by Konrad Lorenz. He observed that goslings began to follow their mother almost immediately after hatching. This bond between goslings and parent was important in helping the mother protect and train her offspring. Interestingly enough, Dr. Lorenz found that when he nurtured orphaned graylings during their first twenty-four hours, they developed a pattern of following *him*, rather than another goose. This pattern was relatively permanent. (It was sometimes annoyingly persistent, as when Lorenz's geese preferred to spend the night in his bedroom rather than on the banks of the Danube River [Lorenz 1952].)

Imprinting refers to the process by which newly hatched birds form a relatively permanent bond with the parent in a comparatively brief period of time. A critical period exists for imprinting; it must occur after hatching, when the gosling is strong enough to get up and move around, but before it has developed a strong fear of large moving objects. If imprinting is delayed, the gosling will either fear the model or simply give up and grow limp, tired, and listless.

Baby birds may be imprinted to various objects that differ greatly from the mother. In a laboratory setting, for example, ducks have been imprinted to duck decoys, flashing lights, windup toys, and even to a checkerboard wall (Hess 1972). The strength of this bond varies, however, and seems to depend on the activity of the duckling and the type of stimulus. A stronger bond is formed when the imprinting stimulus is a large, moving object.

Biologists who study imprinting are concerned with **triggering,** or the release of particular kinds of behaviors by the presence of target stimuli. A large moving object may be all that is necessary to release the behaviors of following and vocalizing and thus begin the process of imprinting. In a natural setting this triggering process is mutual. The mother's clucking releases peeping, visual scanning, and following behaviors in the duckling. Similarly, the duckling's peeping triggers the mother's vocalizations (Hess 1972).

Researchers disagree about the role that imprinting plays in human behavior. Do particular aspects of the caregiver trigger certain behaviors in the infant? Newborns clearly prefer the sight of a human face, as noted at the beginning of this chapter. The human face seems to trigger a smile, and human caregivers are also able to draw babies into a stream of mutual vocalization. With ducklings, vocalization and following behavior lead to a bond with the caregiver. Does the human infant's behavior work in somewhat the same way? Human infants can signal by crying, smiling, and vocalizing. They can visually scan, and later they can physically follow the caregiver. All of these seem to be possible "imprinting" behaviors.

However, no clear evidence exists for a critical imprinting period in humans. Some researchers suggest that caregiver and infant are highly receptive to cues from each other during the first few days after birth and that these earliest interactions are the major determinants of their future relationships (Kennel, Trause, and Klaus 1975). Most researchers believe that human behavior is highly adaptable during an initial period of several months. John Bowlby's studies (1969) lead him to conclude that infant attachment begins between three and six months of age and that it becomes increasingly difficult for the infant to make an attachment past that period of time.

Other researchers note changes in mother-infant interactions that seem to indicate a lengthy trial-and-error process during which both parties seek to establish a mutually satisfactory style of signal and response. Judith Dunn (1976) observed seventy-seven mother-child pairs within a period of five years and detailed several important shifts in their interaction. For example, she concluded that the mothers' responsiveness to infant crying was at least partly dependent upon the infants' developing behavior and was not completely predetermined by earlier interactions.

Further support for this flexible and adaptive view of mother-infant bonds comes from studies of premature babies, who are often isolated from their mothers in incubators for as much as several weeks. One study indicates that this isolation does not have a devastating impact on future relationships between mothers and children (Field 1977).

In summary, there is still some question about the existence of a critical period in infancy similar to the imprinting period of goslings. A period of heightened receptivity may well exist during the first few days of life, but relationships established at this early stage also seem to be affected by later influences.

Mary Ainsworth (1973) has described what she considers to be the three major stages in the gradual process by which human infants develop attachments; these are based on her extensive observations of infants in both this country and Uganda. The first stage is marked by increasing *social responsiveness*. During the first two or three months of life, infants use signaling and orienting behaviors (crying, vocalizing, visual following) to establish contact with others. However, infants at this stage do not distinguish between primary caregivers and other people and react to everyone in the same way. Later, they begin to recognize familiar figures and to direct their attention more toward significant caregivers than toward strangers. This is an intellectual achievement marking the development of a scheme for "mother" or "caregiver" and a sensitivity to discrepant elements.

Ainsworth's second stage, *active proximity seeking*, begins at about seven months and extends through the second year. At this stage, infants become capable of some form of locomotion and begin to play a much more voluntary and active role in the attachment. They hold out their arms to be picked up, they cling to or clamber onto a person, and they call out to greet someone.

Both Bowlby (1969) and Ainsworth (1973) suggest that this attachment continues to develop beyond infancy, and enters a third stage of *partnership behavior* when children are about three years old. In this stage, children become aware of the caregiver as a separate and important person who acts and reacts with them in a relatively understandable environment. They can develop a satisfactory give-and-take relationship with the caregiver, modifying their behavior in order to meet the expectations of others and thus further the attainment of their own goals.

Mutuality

We have presented the view of some researchers that mother and child establish a dialogue during the first few months through a process of trial and error. This emphasis on mutual influencing between mother and infant represents a new conceptual approach. In the past, many psychologists considered maternal behavior to be the sole cause of infant behavior. Today, most theorists believe that babies strongly influence the parent-child relationship from the very first days. A responsive baby supports and maintains the interaction; a rejecting baby interrupts the give-and-take.

Schaffer (1977) has investigated the way in which mutuality between infant and caregiver is achieved. Films of mothers face-to-face with their three-month-old infants revealed a pattern of mutual approach and withdrawal; both took turns looking and turning, touching and responding, vocalizing and answering. Schaffer observed that most infant behavior followed an alternating pattern. For example, in visually exploring new objects, babies stared and then looked away. Some caregivers responded to these patterns with more skill than others.

Caregivers do not respond merely to the behavioral rhythms of the child. They also change the pace and nature of the dialogue by a variety of techniques. They may introduce a new object or imitate and elaborate on the infant's sounds and actions. By monitoring the baby's responses, caregivers gradually learn when the child is most receptive to new cues. For example, a mother who is attuned to her child's signs of fatigue will not seek to introduce a new behavior until the child is alert and rested.

This process of mutual responsiveness takes many months to develop fully. However, some techniques have been found to be particularly effective (Field 1977; Paulby 1977). Field studied *three different maternal behaviors: the mother's spontaneous behavior, her deliberate attempts to catch and hold the child's attention, and her imitation of the child.* The infants were most responsive to the mother's imitative behavior. This may be due to the slower and more exaggerated nature of imitative action. The greater the similarity between maternal and infant behavior, the less babies have to deal with discrepancies and the more attentive they will be. Furthermore, the mother engaged in imitative behavior must carefully observe her infant's cut-off, or gaze-away, point. Field suggests that respect for the child's need for a pause is one of the earliest rules of "conversation" that a caregiver must learn.

Early mutuality and signaling provide the foundation for long-term patterns of interaction. This has been illustrated in studies of maternal responses to crying. Mothers who respond promptly and consistently to infant crying in the first few months are most likely to have infants who cry less by the end of the first year. A quick response gives babies confidence in the effectiveness of their communications and encourages them to continue developing ways of signaling their mothers (Bell and Ainsworth 1972). When maternal care is inconsistent, infants fail to develop confidence and become either insistent or less responsive.

Mutuality continues to develop into the second year of life. Some toddlers exhibit spontaneous sharing behavior with parents and other children—showing a new toy, placing it in someone's lap, or using it to invite another child to play. Such behavior indicates toddlers' interests in the properties of toys, their delight in sharing, and their realization that others will respond to their actions in a positive manner. Children apply skills acquired in the mother-child dialogue to a wider social context, suggesting that some toddlers are not as egocentric as Piaget believes (Rheingold, Hay, and West 1976).

Matas, Arend, and Sroufe (1978) measured attachment in eighteen-month-old babies, dividing them into three categories: securely attached, avoidant, and ambivalent. Behavior was measured again six months later, and the results are striking. Children who had strong attachment relationships at eighteen months had grown more enthusiastic, persistent, and cooperative. They were also more effective than the children in the other two categories in coping with tools, in social interaction with other children, and in the spontaneity of imaginative or symbolic play. A secure attachment with the caregiver supports active exploration and an early mastery of object play and the social environment. It also gives the child a firm base from which to establish other competencies.

Because of the great importance of the mother-child dialogue in laying the foundation for a child's future development, social workers should be alert for signs of disturbance in this process of mutuality and seek early corrective interventions. Sometimes all that is needed is to educate the parent on the infant's needs and how to interpret behavioral cues more effectively. At other times, the infant may have special problems that require further care and continued support for the parents. The situation posing the most threat to the infant is when lack of mutuality results from a state of serious depression or other emotional disturbance in the caregiver.

The handicapped infant

Infant handicaps often cause severe stresses in mutuality. Blind infants cannot search out caregivers' faces or smile back at them, deaf babies may appear to be disobedient, and infants with other severe handicaps are unable to respond to signals as normal babies do. Handicaps that are evident from birth, such as Down's syndrome and cerebral palsy, are certain to create serious adjustment problems for all family members. Until recently, we often ignored the effect that the infant has on the caregiver, concentrating only on the impact of the caregiver's behavior on the child. In the last decade, researchers have begun to devote more attention to the former situation. When we study how infants' behaviors influence the adults around them, we begin to notice all the subtle ways in which infants contribute to the fundamental links that are so essential to their later socialization.

We have shown how visual communication between caregiver and child is prominent in establishing attachment relationships. The visual-perceptual system is one of the normal infant's best resources for learning. Babies particularly like to look at human faces, and caregivers depend heavily on subtle responses from their infants to maintain and support their own behavior. Blind infants, who cannot observe the subtle changes in their caregivers' facial expressions or follow their movements, fail to receive much of the information that sighted babies use in formulating their responses; therefore, caregivers may unconsciously feel that a blind infant is unresponsive. It is essential for both parent and child that a mutually intelligible communication system be established to overcome this handicap.

The first few months of life are extremely difficult for both the blind infant and the parent. The child's seeming lack of responsiveness can be emotionally devastating for caregivers, and supportive counseling may be necessary during this crucial period. Otherwise there is a danger that communication and mutuality will break down, and the caregiver will start to avoid the child (Fraiberg 1974).

Although blind babies do not develop a smile-language as early as sighted children and have fewer facial expressions, they do develop an expressive vocabulary of hand signals. They eventually learn to transfer these signals from caregivers to other unseen people. If parents and caregivers are trained to watch for and interpret hand signals, they can be helped to establish parent-child dialogue, attachment behavior, and further the socialization of the blind infant (Fraiberg 1974).

The developmental difficulties of deaf infants differ from the pattern just described. Their well-developed visual responsiveness generally compensates for their deafness in the first few months of life. However, after about six months, communication between parents and infants begins to break down. The child's responses fail to meet parents' expectations. Often parents do not discover the child's deafness until the second year, and by this time the child has already missed a good deal of communication. One of the first indications of deafness in one-year-olds is seeming disobedience. The child may also show a startled reaction when people approach unexpectedly. By the second year, the deaf child may be having temper tantrums and showing signs of frequent disobedience and severe withdrawal. The child will probably fail to develop normal expectations about the environment. The diagnosis of deafness may come as a shock to parents who have been "talking to my child all along." As with parents of blind children, they may need special training and counseling to help their children to develop fully. Without careful attention during infancy, deaf children will have problems communicating during the preschool years and develop severe social, intellectual, and psychological deficits later in life (Meadow 1975).

When children have severe handicaps—these and other developmental disabilities such as cerebral palsy, autism, and retardation—there is a high risk of maternal rejection, withdrawal, and depression. A severely handicapped infant may strain marital ties and trigger a variety of disturbances in other children in the family. Social workers usually will be able to refer families to special agencies for the handicapped and well-established programs for the blind or the deaf are often available.

The increasing trend against institutionalization of the handicapped child places a greater burden on community facilities to provide the services needed by the child and family. As we have indicated, assistance should begin in the very early stages of life if the child is to be ready to participate in the mainstream of educational and community life in later years. One of the more serious gaps in service is the paucity of child-care facilities for the handicapped child. While these facilities need not be limited to the handicapped, they should provide the extra attention necessary in order to assure the development of attachment and mutuality between handicapped infant and caregiver.

Separation anxiety

One of the developmental landmarks of the attachment relationship is the appearance of both **stranger anxiety** and **separation anxiety.** Pediatricians and psychologists often make no distinction between the two, as both appear around seven to nine months of age. Suddenly, babies who have been smiling and friendly become shy and fearful in the presence of strangers. They also become extremely upset at the prospect of being left alone in a strange place, even for one minute. No traumatic event, sudden separation, or frightening encounter is necessary to trigger this behavior. Children at this stage will cling to their mothers and look at a stranger only after being reassured of the parental attachment.

If no specific event is necessary to trigger such anxiety, why does it occur in most children at about the same age? Most psychologists see stranger and separation anxieties as a normal sign of intellectual development in infants. As infants' cognitive processes mature, they develop schemes for the familiar and become aware of anything that is not familiar. They can distinguish caregivers from strangers, and they become keenly aware of the absence of the primary caregiver. They experience anxiety when they detect a departure from the expected (Ainsworth 1967); this is known as the **discrepancy hypothesis.**

The infant is now aware that the caregiver's presence is an assurance of safety. Things seem secure when familiar caregivers are around and uncertain when they are not. Recall the description of Bower's study of infants' responses to multiple mother images, at the beginning of this chapter. Before twenty weeks, two or three images are more stimulating than one image; after that age, infants find the multiple images very disturbing. Thus, a seven-month's anxiety can be viewed as a demonstration of the infant's more complex and sophisticated expectations.

Stranger anxiety is also a milestone of social development. When children learn to identify the mother as a source of comfort and security, they feel free to explore new objects in her presence. Children who may not feel such a secure attachment will prefer to hover near their mothers and miss out on opportunities for new learning. Children under stressful

conditions may regress to needing constant closeness and reassurance before moving out on their own again. On the other hand, some infants are
too readily comforted by strangers or show wariness when returned to their
mothers. This is a different kind of social maladjustment, indicating uncertainty about the caregiver's ability to protect them (Sroufe 1977). These
children may suffer from a more pervasive and unresolved anxiety that
will interfere with further development. In still another type of situation,
the mother has a strong emotional need to keep the infant tied to her in
a symbiotic relationship. Such parents will not allow the infant to experience
the sense of mastering separation anxiety that is necessary for future autonomous development.

Infants from a variety of cultures usually form a basic attachment
within the first year of life. Although development of this relationship
follows a fairly consistent pattern, the intensity of the bonding and separation anxiety during this period varies with the child-rearing practices of
the culture and the specific relationship of parent and child. Infants who
have had a relatively exclusive relationship with a parent or caregiver tend
to exhibit more intense separation anxieties and show them at an earlier
age than infants whose relationship has not been that exclusive (Ainsworth
1967). A child who is constantly with the parent, sleeps in the same room
at night, and is carried in a sling on the parent's back during the day
experiences a dramatic and intense separation reaction. On the other hand,
the child who has experienced a number of different caregivers from birth
tends to accept strangers or separation with less anxiety (Maccoby and
Feldman 1972).

In some Israeli kibbutzim, for example, children are reared collec-
tively, spending only limited amounts of time with their parents. These
children clearly view their parents as special people and seek attachments
with them as do children reared at home. However, their attachment behaviors and anxiety reactions are less intense than those of home-reared
children (Maccoby and Feldman 1972; Spiro 1965). Applying the discrepancy hypothesis, we would expect that these children would not become
as anxious on seeing new faces because the familiar environment already
includes a variety of faces.

Maternal deprivation

We have just described the function of separation anxiety in the normal development of the infant. Most children learn to master these temporary separations effectively, but social workers sometimes see older children who, under emotional stress, return to this stage and again need a
temporary period of closeness and parental reassurance. Sometimes play
therapy is helpful in enabling the child to master the fears that have threatened an existing equilibrium. This is particularly evident in children who

are hospitalized and face sudden separation from parents at a time when they are very frightened.

Thus far we have discussed only temporary separation and infants' methods of coping with it. However, social workers often must deal with family situations where there has been either maternal deprivation or more severe types of separation and loss of the maternal figure or caregiver.

If the attachment relationship is an essential part of normal development, what happens to the child who does not have such a relationship or whose progress toward attachment is interrupted? What happens to the infant who is brought up in an orphanage and is handled by numerous, changing caregivers during the first few years? What happens to the infant who must spend a prolonged time in a hospital when the primary attachment is just becoming established?

Harry Harlow (1959) conducted an important series of studies on social deprivation in monkeys. Because monkeys are biologically similar to humans, Harlow studied their conceptual development in a laboratory experiment that controlled for the effects of the mothers' teaching. Having removed the mothers from the cage, Harlow stumbled upon the fact that separation from the mother had a disastrous effect on the young monkeys. Some died, others were frightened, irritable, and reluctant to eat or play. Baby monkeys obviously required something more than regular feeding to thrive and develop. Harlow then experimented with surrogate monkey mothers made from wire forms that could hold a bottle (Harlow and Harlow 1962). Some of the surrogates were covered with soft cloth, others were bare wire. Regardless of which surrogate supplied the food, all the young monkeys showed a distinct preference for the cloth form, clinging and vocalizing to it, especially when frightened. The infant monkeys developed bonds with their cloth surrogates and would not accept substitutes. The object they looked at and clung to was the focus of their psychological attachment, regardless of food source.

The results showed that monkeys with cloth surrogates did not exhibit the extremely fearful, neurotic behavior of the completely orphaned monkeys, but they still failed to develop normally. As adults, they had difficulty establishing peer relationships and engaging in normal sexual activity. More recent studies (Coster 1962) in this series have indicated that peer contact among infant monkeys at least partially makes up for the deprivation of the infant-adult attachment. Infant monkeys who are raised with surrogate mothers and who have adequate opportunity to play with others develop reasonably normal social behavior.

Research on human infants tends to bear out these observations of monkeys. We have already seen that prolonged institutionalization in an unstimulating environment retards the development of cognitive and sensorimotor competencies in infants. Social deprivation can have even more dramatic and devastating results on the emotional development of the infant. A child who is handled by continuously changing caregivers who meet only his most basic physical needs will be unable to develop an attachment relationship. For such a relationship to develop, there must be consistent mutual responses between the child and the primary caregiver, and the social interaction must permit the expression of emotion (Bowlby 1969; Dennis 1973; Spitz and Cobliner 1966). Otherwise the result is profound apathy, withdrawal, and generally depressed functioning. Ultimately, these babies come to regard people as interchangeable, and they lack the ability to fully love another person (Fraiberg 1977). They become the most difficult adult clients that social workers will see. Social workers often rely on their "relationship" with the client to help the person learn new behavior. Workers must use other modes of intervention when dealing with adults who have a severely limited capacity to trust others or care about their feelings. In Chapter 5 we shall discuss learning theory and behavioral techniques appropriate for work with persons who are severely limited in emotional responsiveness.

In a review of the research literature on the effects of maternal deprivation on infants in institutional care, Urie Bronfenbrenner (1979) notes that these infants usually suffer from both maternal deprivation and an insufficiently stimulating environment. Both impede healthy development, and it is difficult to study their effects independently. Bronfenbrenner concludes that the earlier an infant is separated from the parent figure, the greater the chance of long-term negative consequences. However, these effects can be averted or reversed by placing the child with caregivers who can form relationships and interact with the child in a stimulating physical environment. Other studies show that infants can improve when they are placed in foster family homes that provide greater interaction between adult and child. However, these children continue to suffer to some degree from a lessened capacity for relationships, their responses remain less flexible, and their play is less imaginative than other children (Provence and Lipton 1962). There is a great need for further research to determine the long-term effects of early institutional care, as there is little data comparing adults who were reared at home with those who were institutionalized at an early age.

Separation and loss

We turn now to the child who has already begun to establish a close relationship and then is suddenly separated from the primary caregiver. This situation differs from that of the child who has never established such a relationship. The "attached" child goes through a series of rather dramatic reactions to both brief and prolonged separation. Freud and Burlingham (1943), in their study of children evacuated during the World War II "blitz" of England, documented the fact that children abruptly separated from their parents were more adversely affected emotionally than were children who lived through the bombings together with their families.

John Bowlby (1960) studied the separation reactions of hospitalized toddlers, and divided them into three stages: *protest, despair,* and *detachment.* During the protest stage children refuse to accept separation from the attachment figure. They may cry, kick, bang their heads against their beds, and refuse to respond to anyone who tries to care for them.

During the second stage, which may follow anywhere from a few hours to several days after the initial reaction, the children appear to lose all hope. They withdraw and become very quiet. If they cry they do so in a monotonous and despairing tone rather than with the anger exhibited earlier.

Eventually, separated children begin to accept attention from the people around them and appear to recover from their misery. When visited by the primary caregiver, they usually react with detachment or disinterest. The following description illustrates the child's reaction to a separation that extends far beyond the limits of the brief separation experiences described earlier, in which the child learns to master the anxiety that results from recognizing differences between the familiar and the unfamiliar.

> A child living in an institution or hospital who has reached this state will no longer be upset when nurses change or leave. He will cease to show feelings when his parents come and go on visiting day; and it may cause them pain when they realize that, although he has an avid interest in the presents they bring, he has little interest in them as special people. He will appear cheerful and adpated to his unusual situation and apparently easy and unafraid of anyone. But this sociability is superficial; he appears no longer to care for anyone (Bowlby 1960, p. 143).

When faced with the first two stages of a child's separation reaction, well-meaning adults often try to inhibit what they see as inappropriate behavior. But such adults underestimate the complexity of young children's reactions and do them a disservice by forcing them to suppress fears of abandonment. In fact, young children need to "work through" these emotional reactions in order to come to terms with the inevitable separations that occur throughout life. The child's response is a prototype of behavior later in life when there are other experiences of separation and loss.

Some hospitals have made it possible for parents to room-in with very young children. Social workers have been vigorous advocates for these programs that attempt to reduce the psychological traumas faced by hospitalized infants. Play therapy has also been used to help young children express and achieve mastery of feelings that might otherwise be overwhelming. In the world of make-believe the child can be the aggressor rather than the victim and therefore feel less helpless and anxious.

When an infant is permanently removed from the primary caregiver, the infant usually experiences more serious and long-term disturbances (Yarrow 1964). Nonetheless, placement of infants and young children has often been made without concern for the emotional impact of the sudden and permanent separation from their caregivers. Too often, social workers have acted as if a young child could instantly "forget" the parent or former caregiver. The research evidence from developmental psychology does not support this view and points to the need for special concern with infants' feelings of loss when a close relationship is suddenly severed. Special assistance should be given to all members of the family during a transitional period, and visits should be arranged to allow the infant to gradually become familiar with new surroundings. Evidence also points to the benefits of a foster child's maintaining continued contact with the natural parent once a relationship has been established, even if the mother is currently unable to care for the child. Obviously, the easiest time for the child to make a transition to a new caregiver is within the first six months. This knowledge is the basis of current attempts to achieve permanent placements for children when they are still very young.

There is increasing concern in our society about the present structure of child welfare services where large numbers of children drift from foster home to foster home, without opportunities to form close attachments to substitute caregivers, and yet essentially without ties to their natural families (Keniston and Carnegie Council on Children 1977; Kadushin 1977). The current reform movement strives to enable more families to keep their children at home by offering such services as homemakers, respite care, day care, and counseling. There is a simultaneous shift toward keeping the natural parent as involved as possible when the child must go into temporary foster care, in an attempt to avoid a drift into a lifetime of foster care because of a lack of continued meaningful contact with the parent. Any systematic public policy that aims at keeping families together must, of course, provide an adequate income base for all families. Family breakdown related to poverty has been of special concern to those working in minority communities. Although most children living in poverty are white, the proportion of children in poverty is higher in minority communities (Kadushin 1978).

The other side of the reform movement is an increased inclination to free the child for permanent placement if the family situation does not improve sufficiently within a limited time. Even if greater resources were available to support the family unit, some parents would still be abusive and neglectful; others are unable to provide even minimal care for their children because of physical or mental illness (Kadushin 1978).

When greater emphasis is placed on children's rights to a permanent home, there will be a corresponding interest in programs that terminate some parental rights. Such programs must be based on a definition of what constitutes a family environment so detrimental to the child's developmental needs that the courts will order permanent removal from the home.

Such programs also require public financing that can provide those coordinated services that enable families to cope with their parenting problems
adequately enough to keep the child at home. Many thorny legal entan-
glements are encountered in terminating parental rights. Unfortunately,
workers in child protective service units are well aware of cases in which
judges make decisions based on their own biases rather than on the needs
of the child. This may result in a child's being placed in a foster home less
nurturing than the home judged unfit or in an infant's not being removed
from a home so abusive that it is a threat to life.

Despite these problems, programs are being devised that increase
children's chances of growing up with permanent rather than ever-chang-
ing caregivers. Some new programs and policies require that placement
agencies work with natural parents in situations that call for short-term
placement, and that clear decision-making processes be established to determine whether long-term placement is indicated. Regulations are also
being changed to allow foster parents to adopt children who have been
placed with them and then become available for adoption. Additional re-
forms provide opportunities for foster parents to assume legal guardian-
ship of children needing long-term care who are not free for adoption and
allow adoptions to be subsidized in order to increase the ability of low-
income minority families to adopt nonwhite infants. Finally, there are increasingly successful efforts to find adoptive homes for handicapped infants
(Kadushin 1977).

MOTHERS AND CAREGIVERS

The terms *mother* and *caregiver* have been used interchangeably in this
chapter in order to indicate that the primary relationship of the infant may
be with a person other than the mother or with persons in addition to the
mother. However, the evidence presented thus far on attachment, separation, placement, and maternal deprivation should make it equally clear
that not every caregiver provides the close primary relationship necessary
for infant development. In this section, we shall examine some of the special
problems working mothers have in finding good substitute caregivers for
infants and the changing roles of fathers in the family.

Working mothers

In 1974, 31 percent of *married* women in the United States with children under three and 46 percent of *unmarried* women with children under
that age worked outside of the home; in 1976, 6.5 million children under
six years of age had mothers who worked (Authier 1979). From 1960 to
1974 labor force participation rates of married women with children under
three years old increased 15 percent, and the rates continue to increase

(Kreps and Clark 1975). We can expect that one of the central issues of the eighties will be the provision of child-care services for both married and unmarried working mothers, and the adequacy of that care in meeting the developmental needs of very young children.

Working mothers must adjust their traditional role as nurturer in order to accommodate new occupational and professional tasks. If unmarried and living alone, they may lack support in dealing with these pressures on a daily basis. If married, the shifting of some child-care and household responsibilities from wife to husband may add to marital stress. However, one of the greatest problems facing all working mothers is the critical shortage of adequate infant day care. Even when facilities do exist, many women must take considerable time away from their jobs to care for the newborn and tend sick children. Today's nuclear family rarely includes a grandmother to share child-rearing tasks, and it is no longer common for unmarried women to live with their families as the "maiden aunt" who formerly served as surrogate parent.

Infant day care

Most American families are no longer of the storybook variety, with one breadwinner and one caregiver who stays home to raise the children. Some mothers must return to work almost immediately after giving birth because they cannot afford to forego their salaries and do not wish to receive public assistance payments. Others have demanding, challenging careers they do not want to abandon. These mothers face the difficult task of arranging safe and reliable supervision for their children while they work. Even mothers who can afford to hire a reliable sitter or who have a relative willing to take on this responsibility often have problems of employee turnover. However, low-income mothers whose options are more limited experience the greatest difficulties.

There are some federally subsidized day-care programs for low-income parents but not nearly enough to meet the need. Many parents must turn to proprietary family day-care homes, most of which operate outside the state licensing structure. The quality of services within each of these alternatives varies widely; some day-care homes or centers are far superior to some individual baby sitters, and vice versa.

Several studies present evidence that children ranging in age from three and a half months to thirty months develop at least as well in a good group-care situation as children of similar backgrounds reared at home (Keister 1970). Belsky and Steinberg (1978) conclude that good day care has neither positive nor negative effects on a child's intellectual development and that the mother-child bond is not seriously disrupted by group care. Children in day-care centers do form close attachments to their teachers, but usually prefer their mothers if given a choice (Fauren and Ramey 1977; Kagan, Kearsley, and Zelazo 1978).

However, most research studies of infant day care are carried out under ideal conditions in university laboratory schools. Similarly, studies from countries such as Sweden, which show the positive results of day care (Cochran 1977), reflect an environment in which day care is popular and publicly supported to a greater degree than in the United States. Bronfenbrenner (1979) confirms the fact that *good* day-care programs in this country tend to promote cognitive and intellectual development among disadvantaged populations. However, there are great difficulties in conducting research with matched groups that are sufficiently alike in their characteristics so that variations in behavior over time can truly be attributed to differences in child-rearing settings. In addition, very few studies compare different types of settings. Because poorly run day-care centers rarely admit researchers, we have insufficient data on the effects of inferior facilities (Belsky and Steinberg 1978). Frequently, children are moved from facility to facility as mothers seek a suitable arrangement.

Day-care centers in the United States are often hampered by inadequate funding and untrained staffs. Selma Fraiberg (1977) paints a bleak picture of the ability of private facilities to meet the needs of infants for nurturing relationships. Although the recommended federal standards are for a one to three staff ratio for infant care, the average ratio in the United States in 1971 was ten to one (Lansburgh 1977). Many facilities keep their rates at a level low-income mothers can afford by using few and poorly trained caregivers. Federally subsidized programs are able to operate on a higher budget but are under political pressures to keep costs down and expand the number of children served.

Fathers and infants

Most research on child development has focused on the relationship between mother and child, paying little attention to the father's role in child rearing. Evidence shows that infants form strong early attachments to fathers as well as to mothers, particularly when they have had regular and frequent contact from birth. The stronger the early attachment, the more influence the father will have on later socialization. As the child grows older, the father becomes an important role model. He may also become an admirer and advocate of the child's achievements. There seems to be a strong continuity between paternal interaction in infancy and interaction in later childhood. Fathers who are inaccessible to their infants may find it difficult to establish strong emotional ties later.

Although the father is most often a secondary caregiver in our culture, he plays an important part in the complex system of family interaction. The system cannot be understood by studying the two-way interaction between mother-infant and father-infant, since all three affect one another's behavior. Clarke-Stewart (1978), in her study of the three-way pattern in families, found that the mother's influence on the child is usually direct, whereas the father's is often indirect, operating through the mother. In contrast, the child usually influences both parents quite directly.

Other studies indicate a distinct difference between maternal and paternal styles of interaction with the baby. Fathers are more often physical and spontaneous. Play between fathers and infants occurs in cycles with peaks of high excitement and attention followed by periods of minimal activity. Fathers tend toward unusual, vigorous, and unpredictable games that infants find highly exciting (Lamb and Lamb 1976).

In many families, mothers seem to be more "naturally" responsive to their children than fathers. Several reasons for this are possible. One may be that women have inherited nurturant traits from our mammalian ancestors. Another may be the strong emotions aroused by breast-feeding. A third may be the way in which women are socialized. In any case, some fathers have to learn to be responsive to their infants (Rossi 1977).

When the father is the primary caregiver in our society, he tends to act more as mothers do. These fathers smile more at their infants, imitate their facial expressions, and vocalize with them more than secondary fathers do (Field 1978). Field suggests that the more imitative behavior of primary caregivers (whether mother or father) may occur for an even simpler reason than the possibilities we have mentioned, and that is because they are more familiar with the infant's behavior. They know that the baby enjoys and responds to imitation.

THE PSYCHOANALYTIC TRADITION

We shall briefly introduce a few major concepts of the psychoanalytic tradition, founded by Sigmund Freud. It has had a tremendous influence on our views of early childhood and the development of personality. This will be followed by a concluding section on the effects of child-rearing practices on personality development during infancy.

Freud: Oral and anal stages

The theories of Freud, the neo-Freudians, and the ego psychologists form what we call the *psychoanalytic tradition*. The source of data for these theories has been primarily clinical case-study material. Freud's philosophy of human nature is a *deterministic* one, as is that of the learning theorists; however, he emphasizes the determinism of **innate drives** rather than the determinism of the environment. According to psychoanalytic theory, human beings are constantly trying to redirect or channel potent instinctual forces. These forces are evident from childhood and are expressed in different ways as the individual personality matures. Neo-Freudians no longer see instinctual drives as the sole basis for human behavior, but they still draw heavily from the analytic tradition.

Sigmund Freud (1856–1939) grew up during the Victorian era, and many of his views were in reaction to the repressive sexual attitudes of that society. Freud asserted that humans are biologically directed and that biological drives such as sex and aggression are the primary forces behind human behavior. Freud also acknowledged that parental responses to these drives are crucial factors in the development of personality, and he was well aware of the effects of society on the expression of instinctual drives.

According to Freud, the personality develops in several psychosexual stages. During the first three stages, which occur well before puberty, children's pleasurable feelings are focused in different areas of the body called **erogenous zones.** During the **oral stage,** the child's mouth becomes the center of sensual stimulation and pleasure, and the tension of hunger is relieved through the mother's provision of both food and oral gratification. Infants also receive pleasure from sucking their thumbs, and from objects such as toys and pacifiers. The Freudians regard adult use of alochol, cigarettes, and gum as carry-overs of this infantile method of receiving gratification.

If children experience too much frustration or too much gratification at any psychosexual stage, they may become **fixated** on the major needs of that stage and continue to focus on them inappropriately in later life. For example, the infant that is breast-fed, or held closely when bottle-fed, receives oral gratification while learning that the mother is the source of the pleasurable feeling. This lays the basis for the sense that the world is a gratifying place. On the other hand, social requirements dictate that the bottle eventually be relinquished. This shift is made most easily when the infant's oral needs have lessened in intensity. Freud attached great importance to the oral stage because he believed that humans ultimately learn to modify their instincts in order to maintain the love that they have experienced early in life (Miller and Swanson 1966).

The next stage in Freud's framework is the **anal period,** in which the child experiences pleasure in the bodily functions of elimination and learns to control these functions in order to maintain parental approval. Again, what is crucial for personality development is the manner in which infants are directed to modify this instinctive pleasure. We shall discuss toilet training again in the section of this chapter on child rearing, and explain Freud's subsequent stages (phallic, latency, and genital) as they occur in the developmental sequence.

Erikson: Trust and autonomy

Erik Erikson's theory of personality development has much in common with Freud's theory of stages, but his model is *psychosocial* rather than *psychosexual.*

Erikson expands on the way in which the child's innate drives are met by parents, and he places greater emphasis on the development of individual capacities for dealing with the social environment. Parental attitudes and the social milieu both affect the way the individual handles developmental conflicts. Erikson's model expands on Freud's in another important way, in that his eight stages of development encompass all ages of human life, rather than ending at puberty.

Erikson's book *Childhood and Society* (1963) presents his model of the eight stages of human development. He points out that adjustment made at each stage can be altered or reversed later on. For example, children who are denied affection in infancy can grow to normal adulthood if they are given extra attention at a later time. Specific developmental conflicts become critical at particular times in the life cycle, but the conflicts are present throughout life, and adjustments made at one stage affect the handling of subsequent conflicts. For example, autonomy needs are especially important to toddlers, but people continually test the resolutions made at that stage as they move on to new relationships throughout life.

The first stage Erikson describes is *trust versus mistrust*. From early caregiving, infants learn about the basic trustworthiness of the environment. If their needs are met and they receive attention and affection in a reasonably consistent manner, they form a general impression of a trustworthy and secure world. But if their world is inconsistent, painful, and threatening, they come to believe that life is unpredictable and that people are not to be trusted.

The second stage, corresponding to Freud's anal period, is *autonomy versus shame or doubt*. Toddlers discover their own bodies and how to control them. They explore feeding, dressing, toileting, and many new ways of moving about. When they succeed in doing things for themselves, they gain a sense of self-confidence and self-control. But if they are continually punished for failure or labeled as messy, inadequate, or bad, they learn to feel shame and self-doubt. We shall come back to Erikson's theories as his stages occur at other times in the life cycle.

The psychoanalytic tradition continues to make an important contribution to the understanding of human behavior. Its basic strength lies in the richness of its approach to the whole individual, including both conscious and unconscious mental processes. Many other traditions barely touch the influence of the unconscious on human behavior. The psychoanalytic approach also provides an integrated set of theories about the nature of basic relationships between child and parent.

The weakness of this approach is inseparable from its strength. The theory deals with the complex structure of personality, yet this is precisely the area that is almost impossible to define or validate by experiment. The result is a theory that is often vague and unscientific. There are no clear behavioral referrants that can be used to validate the theory because either the presence or the absence of an expected behavior can be interpreted so as to allow the theory to remain intact. This will be seen more clearly in

Chapter 4, when we describe defense mechanisms. An additional problem with psychoanalytic theory is that it draws much of its data from case studies of adults in treatment who subjectively reconstruct their childhood.

At one time social casework relied heavily on Freudian theory to teach about the emotional development of children and adults. Today, psychoanalytic theories are still taught in schools of social work, but teachers and practitioners also tend to utilize techniques based on other theoretical frameworks. Some social workers reject Freudian theory entirely, basing their practice on learning theory and empirical evidence of measurable changes in behavior. Other social workers prefer theories that emphasize interpersonal relationships but do not examine the historical causes of emotional problems.

CHILD REARING AND PERSONALITY DEVELOPMENT

Both parents and researchers often ask the wrong questions about child rearing. Their questions are very specific: whether to breast-feed or to bottle-feed, when or how to wean, whether or not to pick up crying babies immediately, when and how to toilet-train. If we look at each of these questions separately, we fail to understand that mothers can and do vary widely in specific child-rearing practices without harming their children.

However, general child-rearing patterns do have an enormous influence on later personality development. It is through child rearing that we transmit personality characteristics valued by the culture. We constantly teach children attitudes and values about the degree of physical closeness that is desirable, the amount of dependency allowed, the acceptability of self-stimulation, and the goodness or badness of both their behavior and their basic nature as human beings.

There are many studies describing widely divergent patterns of child rearing in other cultures and their effect on personality. Anthropologists such as Ruth Benedict and Margaret Mead have made important contributions to this literature. Differences in child-rearing patterns have also been noted among ethnic and social groupings in the United States, but the research studies in this area are often fragmentary. Although social workers should be aware of child-rearing differences among ethnic groups, they must also guard against assuming that all minority families necessarily follow particular cultural patterns without first examining the specific family's socioeconomic status, religious identification, and degree of assimilation into the majority culture (Boulette 1978; Sena-Rivera 1979). For example, middle-class blacks in urban areas raise their children in much the same way as middle-class whites; they do not tend to rear their children in the same way as poor blacks (Scanzoni 1971). Similarly, some people with Spanish surnames, while usually retaining a strong sense of family ties, may be similar to their middle-class Anglo neighbors in other respects; they will be puzzled by a social worker who expects to understand them from having read about the life style of migrant farm laborers.

Trust and nurturance

With these warnings about the need to accurately describe each individual's degree of attachment to a particular cultural tradition, it is useful to look at a few cross-cultural studies of child-rearing patterns. These patterns not only direct the expression of the instinctual drives described by the Freudians but also tend to support personality characteristics valued by the particular culture. For example, a study of the different attitudes of American and Japanese mothers toward their infants (Caudill and Weinstein 1969) found that the American mother viewed her infant as passive and dependent, and her goal was to raise the child to be independent. In contrast, the average Japanese mother saw her child as an independent organism who needed to be brought into a dependency relationship within the family in order to learn to function in a society that values conformity. These differences in attitude result in different styles of child rearing. American infants are ideally put in cribs in their own rooms, whereas Japanese infants traditionally share a bedroom with their parents. The Japanese mothers in the study group tried to respond quickly when their babies cried, and infants were fed on demand. The American mothers tended to let their babies cry for a short while, in the hope of establishing a more regular feeding schedule.

In some cultures, the transitional period between the infant's birth and separation from the mother lasts for at least three years, with breast-feeding as an integral part of this relationship (Mead and Newton 1967). Some African children may sleep close to their mothers, be carried around in a sling during most of the first year, and be breast-fed until the age of three (Goldberg 1972). In the American culture, infants are usually given separate beds and placed in separate rooms almost immediately, unless families are unable to afford the extra living space or have recently immigrated from societies where such separation is neither possible nor considered to be desirable.

Weaning the child from breast or bottle is a crucial part of the feeding pattern. The way in which it is accomplished has an impact on personality development because it represents a major change in the degree of physical closeness between parent and child. Some cultures allow the child to be completely dependent on the mother for nurturance for several years and then abruptly break the bond by sending the children away to live with relatives (Goldberg 1972). In other cultures, weaning may take place over an extended period of time, even years. American families in the 1930s were advised by the experts to adhere to a feeding schedule that would be seen today as evidence of extreme parental rigidity.

Social workers sometimes question parents about how they weaned their children in order to learn more about the child's earliest experiences of losing a source of pleasure: Was it an abrupt or a gradual transition? Did the child accept the change easily or show signs of stress? Was the parent angry or casual about the child's continued use of the bottle? This material must be evaluated within the context of the cultural norm for each particular family.

Middle-class attitudes toward sucking as a means of infant gratification have become more accepting over the years. Thumb sucking was once regarded as a dirty habit, and elaborate devices and vile-tasting applications were often used to break the habit. Parents should recognize that infants vary widely in the strength of their need to suck and the length of time that sucking remains important to them.

When parents live in a heterogeneous society such as ours, they may find that what they think is the proper response to the child conflicts with what their parents, in-laws, and neighbors think. Social workers must look at many factors if they are to assist parents who are experiencing conflicts over child-rearing practices. Today, most Americans tolerate their children sucking on a thumb or pacifier to some degree, knowing the need for sucking will lessen over time. The current theory is that children who continue to seek comfort by sucking past the preschool years are not having their other needs met sufficiently to be able to relinquish these more infantile means of satisfaction.

Autonomy and discipline

By the time infants are one year old, they have usually learned some guidelines for acceptable behavior regarding their needs for dependency and closeness. In the second year, parents and caregivers must cope with a diversity of issues arising from the toddler's growing desire for independence and autonomy. In order to appreciate some of these problems, let us review a few aspects of toddlers' behaviors that were presented at the beginning of the chapter.

> Ruth, age two, explores the qualities and possibilities of almost everything in her environment, including the delights of endlessly pulling on the roll of toilet paper. She enjoys picking up crumbs, cigarette butts, and other small objects, which she puts in her mouth. She may alternate between clinging dependence and daring exploration within the space of a few minutes. She has learned to say "no."

This description graphically illustrates the extent to which two-year-olds experience increased needs for autonomy while retaining needs for dependence because of limited skills. The resulting ambivalent behavior was noted by Margaret Mahler and her colleagues (1975). They observed an intense renewal of separation anxiety as toddlers were torn between a desire to stay close to their mothers and a wish to be independent. Their new sense of being separate beings seemed to frighten them, and they sometimes tried to deny it by acting as if their mothers were extensions of themselves. For example, a child might pull the mother's hand in an effort to have her pick up an object that the child desired.

How do caregivers deal with the challenging behavior of toddlers? Should they set limits on the seemingly constant attempts of children to test the limits of authority? If parents are too strict, will the child develop a frustrated, anxious, or overly submissive personality? If they overindulge the child, are they in danger of producing a willful personality, unresponsive to the needs and rights of others? Today's social workers might generally agree that caregivers should allow a great deal of childhood explorations, provide a safe environment, and set clear limits that will enable the child to gradually adapt to the social requirements of the environment. The worker would probably also place a high value on the caregiver's explaining the reasons for limits when the child develops the capacity to understand the explanation. The emphasis would be on providing growth and increasing independence. Children raised in this way tend to become self-reliant and able to tolerate reasonable limits. Soviet educators place greater emphasis on compliance with routines rather than autonomy, and on cooperative rather than aggressive behavior toward peers (Smart and Smart 1973, p. 230).

Obviously, guidelines must be tempered with common sense and must consider a child's need for safety as well as for independence and creative experience. Children permitted to run, jump, and climb can also be taught to walk quietly, to hold someone's hand, and to allow themselves to be carried in public places. Children who have developed a strong attachment relationship and whose needs are met through loving interaction with an adult are neither spoiled by lots of attention nor frightened and threatened by reasonable limits. They are stronger and more confident because they have a trustworthy basic relationship from which to venture forth into independence.

The social worker will encounter many variations from the middle-class expectation of autonomy and self-discipline described earlier. For example, studies of working-class families show that they tend to do less talking and explaining with their children and use more physical methods of discipline than middle-class families. They also demand a greater degree of compliance from their children (Miller and Swanson 1959). One explanation for these differences lies in the middle-class concern that children learn behaviors that will be most effective in the bureaucratic and technological world they will be entering. Middle-class parents pass on the verbal and negotiating skills that they value highly themselves and that they anticipate will be rewarding for their children.

American Indian children are generally disciplined in nonverbal fashion, by a stern look or occasional teasing (Miller 1979). Black children in some communities learn that it is dangerous to openly challenge white authority or ask too many questions. Researchers also note *social-class differences* in child rearing within specific minority communities (Kamii and Radin 1967; Boulette 1978; Scanzoni 1971).

When assessing family child-rearing practices, social workers must also take into account the extent to which adults in the household must keep fairly flexible timetables and the number of other children and caregivers in the home. It may be difficult to schedule individualized sleeping schedules for young children in an overcrowded home, and working mothers may require an infant to adapt quickly to a caregiver's schedule.

Finally, a parent's or caregiver's personality can make scheduling and setting of limits either effortless or highly stressful. Caseworkers have seen parents who describe their toddler in terms that suggest a powerful monster who cannot be limited, and yet the worker finds the youngster active but very amenable to effective parenting. On occasion a parent will ask for help in handling an "impossible" child, and the worker discovers that the parent is really unwilling to have the toddler relinquish the aggressive behavior because it satisfies the needs of one of the adults in the family. At times, one child may become the family member who acts out the problems of others, and therapeutic efforts need to be directed at the interaction within the family system.

Although Freudian theory led to an emphasis on methods of toilet training, recent studies view toilet training as but one part of a cluster of child-rearing issues. Social workers tend to look at the range of adult attitudes toward children's explorations of their bodies and toward their need for autonomy. Parents who are severe and harsh in toilet training are usually strict about other behaviors requiring self-mastery and independence, such as feeding, dressing, and general exploration. Some adults demand that a child have early and total control of bowel and bladder; they regard "accidents" as intolerable and dirty. Such people are likely to be severe when children break a plate, play in the dirt, explore new places and objects, and attempt to feed themselves.

Although some studies have shown that children are ready for training between the ages of one and a half and two years, the timing is not that crucial (Mead and Calas 1955). Some children appear to be trained earlier; however, it is usually the mothers who are trained to anticipate the children's functions and then rush them to the bathroom at the appropriate time. Other children are not toilet trained until the age of three. The important point is to encourage children to achieve autonomy and independence when they are ready. This means waiting until they are physically able to control bladder and bowels, to communicate their needs, and to wait briefly after signaling those needs. Ideally, this should be done without threat of punishment and with as little fuss and bother as possible.

Self-awareness

At the beginning of this chapter, we described how infants gradually develop the ability to distinguish between themselves and the world around them. By the end of the second year they are aware of sex roles and some of the cultural expectations about these roles (Goldberg and Lewis 1969). Parental attitudes about sex roles and about infants' natural exploration of their genitals vary widely. Many mothers try to prevent exploration of this part of the body; others permit infants to discover the pleasures of masturbation.

By the end of the second year the child's language has considerable self-reference. Children know their names and often describe their needs and feelings in the third person: "Terry wants water." The words *me* and *mine* assume new importance in their vocabulary, and the concept of ownership is clearly and strongly acted out. Even in families where sharing is emphasized and ownership is minimized, toddlers show fairly extensive evidence of possessiveness. It may be that they need to establish a concept of ownership in order to round out their definition of self. Sharing and cooperation come more easily once toddlers are confident about what is theirs.

Self-awareness is a result of self-exploration, cognitive maturity, and reflections about self. Toddlers can often be heard talking to and admonishing themselves ("No, Lee, don't touch") and rewarding themselves ("Me good girl!"). They incorporate cultural and social expectations into their reflections as well as their behavior, and begin to judge themselves and others in light of these expectations. If they enjoy consistently loving interactions with the caregiver in an environment that they are free to explore and can begin to control, they learn to make valid predictions about the world around them. Gradually, they establish a perception of themselves, ideally as acceptable, competent individuals.

CASE ILLUSTRATIONS

Ms. Edwards

Ms. Edwards is a social work consultant to a publicly subsidized day-care center that serves infants from six months to two years old. She knows that the high staff ratio, availability of staff training, and stimulating physical environment make it one of the best resources for infant care in the city. There is a long waiting list for admission, and many mothers do not qualify because their income is too high for the eligibility standards. Some infants have already had a succession of sitters and caregivers by the time they enter the program. Since she began work at the center, Ms. Edwards has introduced the practice of assigning staff members to particular infants rather than having the staff rotate among the entire group.

George is a twenty-month-old youngster who has just entered the program, and Ms. Edwards is concerned about his slow development in several areas. She referred him for testing, and no physical problems were found. His muscular coordination and perceptual abilities are excellent. However, he has no vocabulary, and his play consists largely of aimless running around. He never plays with toys in a purposeful way and he often seems too distracted to follow simple instructions, although he understands the meaning of the words. He points to what he wants and often has temper tantrums if he does not get it immediately. However, he responds to being picked up and carried around, and the social worker feels he has the ability to form a relationship with an adult. But he seems unready for a group experience, and she decides to obtain further information in order to explore alternative forms of care.

George's mother, Wilma Johnson, is a friendly young woman, barely nineteen years old. Eight months ago, she left the small, poverty-stricken rural area in Georgia where she grew up to make a new start for herself. She could offer little information about George's early development, since from birth he had been raised by his grandmother and aunt while Wilma completed high school. Her main recollection was that he was a good baby, but she disapproved of what she thought was "spoiling him" by giving in to him whenever he cried. However, at that time she was battling her mother for her own independence and so relinquished any claim to control over how George was being raised. Later, after living on her own for six months, finding a boyfriend, and enrolling in a community college training program, she sent for George to live with her. The initial period of reunion was marred by George's continual crying for his grandmother. He couldn't understand the loss of the person he had known as "Mama."

Wilma seems very unsure about her attachment to George and whether he really belongs to her or his grandmother. George's grief at the loss of his grandmother has intensified her feeling that she "never really got close to George." Her present goals are almost entirely focused on her own developmental needs, and she is not ready to give George the time and attention he needs at this stage. Although group day care is appropriate for some twenty-month-olds, it is not adequate to meet George's present needs for an intimate individual relationship, similar to that needed by a much younger infant.

Ultimately, Wilma decides to send George back to her mother, where he feels more secure. She also decides that he will enter a half-day nursery program when he is two years old, in order to further his cognitive development and help him mature socially.

Mr. Frank

Mr. Frank works at a parental stress unit connected with a children's hospital. He has just received a referral from a doctor who suspects that parental abuse is responsible for an infant's injuries—large bruises and bone fractures have been observed on several occasions. The doctor has reported his suspicions to the county children's protective services unit, and after an initial evaluation it was decided that no charges would be filed if the parents took part in counseling and no further incidents were reported.

While interviewing the Ferguson family, Mr. Frank discovers that many of his assumptions about child abuse are incorrect and that abusive parents are found among all social classes. The father in this family is a graduate student and the mother is also well educated. However, they have no close friends or relatives they can turn to for emotional support.

The Fergusons admit that they have beaten their infant daughter when they could no longer tolerate her continued crying. Their baby had many digestive problems from birth and still cries more than most infants. At six months, she is frequently awake for several hours during the night. Marital battles ensue when Mr. Ferguson claims that his studies are suffering because of this badly behaved child. He was raised by very strict parents and believes that children of all ages will behave properly if their mothers raise them properly. He is not prepared to deal with crying that can not be rationally diagnosed and immediately remedied. Mrs. Ferguson had wanted to have a baby immediately in order to have "someone who would always love me." Now, she interprets her child's crying to mean that she is not loved.

If their first baby had been easier from birth, with a more mature digestive system and a different sleeping pattern, the Fergusons might not have responded in this fashion. However, through group conseling they are able to gain enough understanding of their mistaken notions about the needs of infants to modify their own behavior. They are given a phone number to call whenever they feel overwhelmed by stress. They are also encouraged to join a babysitting group so they can get out more often and also so they can share their frustrating experiences with other parents of infants. Not all cases are as amenable to change as the Fergusons.

Ms. Fernandez

Ms. Fernandez is a foster-care worker for a public agency, in charge of supervising a large number of foster children. She knows that many of the foster homes are less than ideal, but she must constantly weigh these against the disadvantages of the child's natural family. Joe is a nine-month-old infant who is in care because his mother was involved in drug dealing. A number of violent incidents at the home lead to her eventual arrest. Joe's earlier history indicated maternal neglect, lack of adequate diet and medical care, and little stimulation from his environment. In many respects his developmental level now resembles that of a six-month-old, and it is hard to know his real developmental potential.

There are no other family members able to care for Joe. At present, the worker's major goals are (1) to keep as much contact between Joe and his mother as possible, and (2) to continue to assess the mother's potential for offering an environment that will not endanger Joe's development. Ms. Fernandez's supervisor feels strongly that a decision as to whether Joe can return home should be made within a year. If he cannot, the supervisor favors going to court to have him relinquished for adoption.

Ms. Fernandez is distressed over these options, as she would like to have more time in which to work with the probation officer in offering supportive services to Joe's mother. She knows that there is a distinction between a deviant life style and an environment in which drugs and weapons continue to be present, but she would like to keep the option for Joe to return home, should the family situation change.

Meanwhile, the available foster homes cannot offer the sense of permanency that Joe needs. Ms. Fernandez knows that he needs a permanent home, but she is not yet sure of the best way to achieve this.

SUMMARY

Although predictable changes occur in physical and cognitive development during the first two years of life, infants vary greatly in their rates of development. Arnold Gesell described the physical, cognitive, and personality development of children at various ages; he viewed development as dependent on maturational processes. However, the physical and emotional aspects of the environment can significantly influence the course of maturation.

The first two years is a critical period of growth. Given optimum conditions, an infant's motor and perceptual abilities mature rapidly during the first year. The senses function independently at birth and require about a year to become fully coordinated. Toward the end of the second year, infants are usually walking alone, feeding themselves, imitating some adult actions, and speaking a few words.

Intellectual development begins during what Piaget calls the sensorimotor period. During the first two years, infants acquire concepts about the uses of familiar objects and develop the ability to imitate. They come to understand object permanence and can use memory and symbolic representation. These abilities are seen in their play and in their growing use of language.

The environment has a powerful effect on the development of infant competencies. Lack of stimulation, poor diet, and an unresponsive environment will retard children's sensorimotor and cognitive development. Social workers often see infants who fail to thrive because of adverse environmental conditions.

Personality development begins with the first relationship between infant and caregiver. Psychologists are not sure exactly how this happens, but they find parallels in animal behavior. For example, geese have a critical period during which a process called imprinting forms the basis for an attachment. In several species, this bond is initiated as a result of the infant's own activities such as following, vocalizing, and clinging behavior. Faulty attachment results in abnormal behavior that is only partially relieved by substitute contact with peers. Sociobiologists see these as examples of the genetically determined and instinctual nature of many aspects of human behavior, which are rooted in their value for the survival of the species.

Researchers disagree about how closely the animal model applies to human attachment. There is evidence that the mother-child dialogue is affected by influences beyond those of the first few days. The early pattern of mutuality between infant and caregiver develops more gradually, but it does establish a pattern for future relationships and does depend on infant responses to the caregiver. Handicapped infants present special problems in regard to establishing mutuality.

A secure attachment provides a base that allows a child to explore new people and things. Separation anxiety occurs at about seven months and is part of normal cognitive development in that the infant becomes able to detect discrepancies between the familiar caregiver and strangers. However, maternal deprivation, or loss of an attachment that has already been established, will have serious consequences for the infant's personality development. A child who is not given the opportunity to develop a pattern of consistent mutual response with the primary caregiver will be unable to develop an attachment relationship. Institutionalized infants often suffer from both maternal deprivation and an insufficiently stimulating environment. Studies show that such infants can improve when placed in a better environment, but the long-term effects of such early deprivation are not fully understood. Social workers often see people whose emotional capacities are impaired because of early deprivation or loss of a significant relationship.

When a child must be removed from the mother or primary caregiver, attention should be given to the effect on the child. Some hospitals have developed more responsive regulations regarding parental visiting of children. Child welfare workers are trying to place more emphasis on permanence of placement for children. Placement is a complex issue, involving the rights of both parents and children.

An increasing percentage of mothers of infants work outside the home. They face a severe shortage of adequate day-care facilities. Good day care can be a positive experience for the child, but high child-staff ratios and inadequate caregivers can cause emotional problems for the infant. Fathers are playing an increasingly important role in the care of the child, even during infancy.

Sigmund Freud was especially interested in the early development of the child. His theory of human nature is deterministic; personality develops as parents respond to the child's innate drives. The oral stage is a time when the infant's mouth is the center of sensual stimulation and pleasure. The tension of hunger and the need to suck are both relieved through the provision of food, and the infant learns whether to expect that his basic needs will be satisfied. Later, in the anal stage, the infant must learn to control other urges in order to maintain parental approval.

Erikson later broadened these theories to emphasize psychosocial rather than the psychosexual interaction. He also believed that the developmental conflicts of these early stages—trust versus mistrust and autonomy versus shame—may be reworked and more satisfactorily resolved later in life.

Child-rearing practices vary greatly from one culture to another and result in distinctly different personality types. Parental attitudes toward feeding, weaning, and toilet training convey fundamental messages to children about their goodness, their ability to depend on themselves, and the nature of their bodies. Patterns of handling dependence and autonomy needs have particularly pervasive effects. From the sum total of their social experiences and growing cognitive skills, children develop attitudes about themselves.

The case illustrations indicate some of the ways that social workers use these concepts in day care and in child welfare settings concerned with child abuse and foster care.

SUGGESTED READINGS

Brazelton, T.B. *Toddlers and Parents: A Declaration of Independence.* New York: Dellacorte, 1974. A colorful description of the phases of development during the second year, with suggestions to parents on how to manage their children's behavior.

Caplan, F. *The First 12 Months of Life.* New York: Grosset & Dunlap, 1973. Written in a style appropriate for parents, this book supplies much practical information drawn from the Princeton Center for Infancy and Early Childhood.

Fraiberg, S. *Every Child's Birthright: In Defense of Mothering.* New York: Basic Books, 1977. A presentation of the inadequacies of most substitute caregiver arrangements, and the detrimental effects on infants who will not experience the close, consistent attachments they need in order to develop into loving adults.

Smart, M.S., & Smart, R.C. *Infants: Development and Relationships.* New York: Macmillan, 1973. An excellent and comprehensive selection of readings on the cognitive and emotional development of infants. There is a good integration of theory and practical research findings.

Spock, B. *Baby and Child Care.* Washington, D.C.: Department of Health, Education and Welfare, 1957. This "bible" of child care in American society needs no introduction.

U.S. Department of Health, Education and Welfare. *Child Welfare Strategy in the Coming Years.* H.E.W. Publication No. (OHDS) 78–30158, 1978. An excellent set of readings illustrating how social workers deal with some of the developmental issues raised in this chapter. Included are articles on the special concerns of Spanish-speaking and other minority children.

chapter four

VISTA, Christiansburg, Va., Bartlett

THE PRESCHOOL CHILD
ages two to six

outline

AT TWO YEARS OF AGE, Nina was constantly pulling her mother's skirts and demanding attention. Her favorite expressions were "no" and "Mommy see." She howled with frustration if her mother was inattentive, and was apt to respond to unexpected delays in having promises fulfilled by lying on the floor and kicking her feet.

By six years of age, Nina can explain many of her feelings of loss and frustration and has developed into a more thoughtful child. She now makes up stories in which she is the most powerful person and accepts the fact that she cannot always control real-life situations. She sometimes spanks her teddy bear for "being bad" but rarely hits other people when she becomes angry.

In this chapter we shall discuss the rapid development of physical-motor competence, language usage, and symbolic thought processes that occur during the period of early childhood, emphasizing the cognitive theories of Piaget. We shall then turn to issues of personality development.

In real life, these are not discrete categories but rather interacting influences on the growth of the child that occur in a social context. The physical-motor development of preschool children cannot be separated from their perceptual and cognitive growth. Children's understanding of the world depends on the information that they receive from their perceptions, their motor activity, and their thoughts about themselves. In turn, their explorations of the world contribute to their future motor skills, their cognitive processes, and their social and emotional development. A girl walking on a log is not just learning to balance but is also grasping the concept "narrow," and increasing her sense of self-confidence. Many aspects of development, including complex thought, proceed from a physical-motor base.

Some developmental sequences are continuous, as in the natural progression from scribbling to writing. Others seem somewhat discontinuous. Children may randomly explore different textures of material with their fingers and eyes before they are ready to classify or compare the materials. Other developmental sequences involve functional subordination. For example, there is an initial value in the child's random scribbling with crayon and paper. Later, merely placing marks on paper becomes functionally subordinated to more complex skills, such as writing, drawing, and creating designs.

PHYSICAL-MOTOR DEVELOPMENT

In this section we shall describe several aspects of physical development in the preschool child: maturational processes, or the unfolding of the child's natural potential for increased skill development; the process of teaching and learning new skills; and the implications of these skills for cognitive learning.

Maturation

Compared to infants, two-year-olds are amazingly competent creatures who can walk, run, and manipulate objects. However, when compared with four- or five-year-olds, they are quite limited. Although they can climb, push, pull, and hang by their hands, two-year-olds have little endurance. They are also inclined to use both arms or both legs when only one is required (Woodcock 1941), and are likely to extend both feet when they want a single shoe tied.

By the age of three, children no longer need to keep a constant check on what their feet are doing (Cratty 1970). They run, turn, and stop more smoothly than they did formerly, although their ankles and wrists are not as flexible as they will be in a year or two (Woodcock 1941). Three-year-olds are already likely to extend only one hand to receive one item, and they begin to show a preference for either the right or left hand.

Four-year-olds are able to vary the rhythm of their running, and many can skip rather awkwardly and execute a running jump (Gesell 1940). The average child of four can probably use a crayon to draw lines, circles, and simple faces.

Five-year-olds can skip smoothly, walk a balance beam confidently, stand on one foot for several seconds, and imitate dance steps (Gesell 1940). They manage buttons and zippers and may be able to tie shoelaces. They can throw a ball overhand and catch a large ball that is thrown to them (Cratty 1970).

Whereas three-year-olds may push a doll carriage or a large truck for the fun of pushing it, four-year-olds have functionally subordinated their pushing into a fantasy of doll play or a game involving trucks. By the age of four much of children's play involves the acting out of complex roles or the purposeful construction of objects and games.

Learning new skills

Preschool children usually learn physical-motor skills in the course of everyday activities such as feeding and dressing themselves, drawing, skipping, and jumping. However, as we have noted in the last chapter, Soviet educators disagree with this casual approach and believe in teaching specific skills at as early an age as possible. Lisina and Neverovich (1971) report that Soviet preschool children are drilled in gymnastics and music, and they cite the award-winning performances of nine-year-old gymnasts as evidence of the efficacy of this early training. Although American psychologists generally believe that young children learn best with a minimum of training and a maximum of free exploration, there is a growing interest in the physical training given to children in other countries. Some American community centers now offer Kinder-gym programs and swimming for preschoolers. These programs may involve parents and children as participants in the same class.

Both Soviet and American psychologists have identified these important conditions for physical-motor learning: *readiness, motivation, activity, attention,* and *feedback.* We shall examine each in turn.

The first requisite for learning a new skill is an appropriate state of **readiness;** this consists of a certain degree of maturation, some prior learning, and the mastery of the necessary preliminary skills. Myrtle McGraw's classic study of twins (1935) demonstrates that early training in the normal motor skills may result in only a temporary acceleration in the rate of skill acquisition. In this study, one twin was offered a concentrated and enriched training program; the other received no special help. Contrary to their expectations, researchers found that training was advantageous only until the twins reached the normal stage of readiness for the task involved. At that point, the untrained twin quickly caught up with the trained one. There were no long-term advantages to the training given before the appropriate maturation point had been reached.

It is difficult for parents and teachers to know exactly when children have reached this readiness point. Yet this knowledge is a key factor in deciding when to introduce new physical-motor learning. At the optimal point of readiness, children learn quickly and easily with little training because they want to learn, enjoy practicing, and are pleased about their performance (Lisina and Neverovich 1971). Sometimes they provide clues by starting to imitate particular skills that they observe in others.

Competence motivation is another powerful factor influencing the acquisition of motor skills (White 1959). Children like to try things out, perfect their skills, and test their ability. They run, jump, climb, and skip because these activities offer satisfaction; this is called **intrinsic motivation. Extrinsic motivation** comes from parental demands or encouragement and also plays an important part in skill development.

Activity is essential to motor development. Children cannot master stair climbing or learn to throw a ball unless they have practiced these activities. Children who are raised in limited and restricted environments show a lag in the development of their physical-motor skills. If they are raised in crowded surroundings they often show a delay in the development of large muscle skills and lack strength, coordination, and flexibility. Children must have some objects to play with, places to explore, tools to use, and a few people to imitate in these activities.

When given these opportunities children will imitate and repeat a task endlessly, setting their own pace for learning. They will discover ways to make shapes as they stack blocks. They will pour water repeatedly from one container to another and thus discover the concepts of *full* and *empty*, *fast* and *slow*. These self-paced schedules of learning are often more efficient than some adult-programmed lessons (Karlson 1972). Playing is the way in which toddlers learn; in a sense it is their "work."

Social workers can be helpful in interpreting the benefits of play to parents whose children are spending inordinate amounts of time watching television. Parents who did not play with formal toys when they were children may be helped to understand that they had many natural opportunities to develop these skills by participating at an early age in the life of the household, aiding the adults in chores at home, and also at work. Such tasks provide the environmental challenges we have outlined as necessary for the learning of physical-motor skills.

Learning during the late preschool period is also enhanced by concern for the quality of the child's **attention** (Zaporozlets and Elkonin 1971). Two- and three-year-olds tend to learn in a passive way that does not require them to pay much attention to the activity; they can learn to play patty-cake if someone moves their hands for them and makes them attend to the activity. In contrast, children past three years of age have the mental alertness to actively attend to and imitate an activity. Increased learning results from this focus on active imitation of an adult or peer model. By the time children are five or six years old they can attend closely when only verbal instructions are given (Zaporozlets and Elkonin 1971).

Feedback is another significant factor influencing the learning of motor skills. Extrinsic feedback comes in the form of rewards such as cookies or praise given for a task well done. The anticipation of such rewards provides the extrinsic motivation previously discussed. Intrinsic feedback occurs when children discover that their actions have certain consequences. These may act as stronger motivators than an arbitrary form of extrinsic feedback. Children may derive great pleasure from the feeling of tension in their muscles when they climb a jungle gym or from the pleasure of seeing a panoramic view when they are high off the ground. If they feel a bit "wobbly," this feedback is intrinsic to the task and usually more effective in making children aware of their need to stabilize themselves than their being told by an adult to "be careful."

Implications for cognitive development

We have already seen that children who are given ordinary opportunities for practice will develop a multitude of useful skills involving physical strength, endurance, control, and coordination. However, theorists differ about whether these skills also form the basis for cognitive learning. For example, some researchers believe that children begin to conceptualize ideas of equivalence in mathematics when they balance their bodies and observe their own bodily symmetry (Forman 1972). Others believe that children first work out the basic notions underlying speed, numbers, time, and spatial relations physically, long before they are ready to deal with them intellectually. Kephart (1966) holds the view that adequate motor experiences are necessary prerequisites to learning related mathematical and scientific concepts. Others have questioned this view, pointing out that many children with cerebral palsy or other severe physical handicaps eventually develop considerable facility with complex concepts. Although some preschool programs provide special physical experiences in the belief that they are necessary to later cognitive development, the research evidence about this relationship is still unclear.

LANGUAGE

By approximately four and a half years of age, most children have developed amazing verbal competence. Their vocabulary may be limited and their grammar far from perfect, but their unconscious grasp of language structure is remarkable. They not only use words to designate things and communicate thoughts, but they also exhibit a sophisticated understanding of the rules governing language. They speak in full sentences with phrases, clauses, and appropriate grammatical constructions. This is a startling cognitive achievement when we think of the enormous complexity of the underlying rules of syntax and semantics. A child must first master basic cognitive concepts in order to manipulate the elaborate system of symbols that constitutes a language. Sometimes a child's grammatical errors help us to understand these logical processes. For example, Tommy may never have heard his parents say "amn't I," and yet he has arrived at this form by following his own rules of logic. Indeed, nothing is wrong with his logic. The form just happens to be considered incorrect.

Thus far, we have described language as a cognitive development. Language is also the way in which children learn cultural values and social roles. Language intersects both cognitive and social development; it is also a bridge between infancy and childhood. Once children can understand and communicate their needs and observations, they can interact with the world around them in a much more complex fashion than formerly.

Perhaps more than any other single accomplishment, the acquisition of language illustrates the incredible complexity and unlimited potential of the human organism. During the preschool period, children progress from single words to brief sentences to complex grammatical structures. This development follows a regular and predictable sequence in every language. Slobin (1972) and his colleagues studied the acquisition of language in many countries and discovered remarkably consistent patterns from culture to culture. We turn now to an examination of how and why this occurs.

Acquiring language

In recent years, a great deal of research has been devoted to the question of how humans progress from crying—to babbling—to speaking adult language. There has been much controversy and little agreement as to precisely how the process works, but it is possible to divide the numerous theories into four major groups, each emphasizing one of the processes: *imitation, reinforcement, innate language structure,* and *cognitive development.* All four approaches probably have some validity, and will be presented below.

Imitation plays a large part in language learning. The first words that we speak are obviously learned by hearing and imitation; we would not be understood if we invented all our own words. However, the imitation theory of language cannot account for the child's development of an original syntax and a grammatical structure. Forms such as "amn't I" and "all gone bottle" are clearly original, and children tend to use these structures rather consistently, even when they are corrected by adults.

Reinforcement is another of the processes by which language is acquired. Children are influenced by the reactions to their speech and are likely to repeat words that bring favorable results such as smiles, hugs, and increased attention. But this theory also fails to explain the acquisition of syntax. Nor is it possible to reinforce all correct forms and extinguish all incorrect ones. When children first begin to talk, adults tend to reinforce any form of speech, however incorrect. Even when adults become more discriminating, they are more likely to respond to content than to form. The child who says "I eated my peas," will probably be praised if the statement is true or called to task if the vegetables remain on the plate.

Noam Chomsky (1959), a prominent contemporary linguist, rejects both the above theories. He believes that every human being is born with an **innate mental structure** for acquiring language. This structure enables children to formulate a grammar and to process linguistic data selectively from their environment. Thus, children unconsciously induce rules when they hear people talk, and they then form their language according to these rules. This process follows a developmental sequence; children can assimilate certain data before others. But, according to Chomsky, at least some of the basics of language are preprogrammed into the human organism.

This theory has considerable merit. For one thing, it takes into account the incredible complexity of human language. For another, it points out the inadequacy of simple imitation and reinforcement theories. However,

Chomsky's argument does not really explain the process of language learning. In a sense he claims that we learn language because we are programmed to learn language.

The fourth major theory of language acquisition—**cognitive development**—explains the phenomenon in terms of the development of concepts and relationships. This view is supported by the fact that basic grammatical structures are not present in earliest speech but develop progressively. This leads some theorists to conclude that at any given time children can only express linguistically what they have already mastered conceptually (Bloom 1970).

At present, no one of these theories of language acquisition seems adequate. But each presents a point of view that has merit as an explanation for certain aspects of the process by which we acquire a language.

We turn now to the relationship between language and the transmission of cultural behavior from one generation to the next.

Language and culture

Suppose, for a moment, that you are traveling in Mexico for the first time. You have studied Spanish in school for four years and have learned to read it reasonably well. You have no trouble with menus or street signs and can even enter into a limited conversation. But you feel socially inept because you know that you will always sound like an American. To behave and feel like a Mexican you would have to master thousands of behavioral details, such as knowing what form of address to use, what tone of voice to adopt, and what is considered rude or polite.

Every culture defines the appropriate social uses of speech, just as it dictates pronunciation, syntax, and vocabulary. For example, politeness is esteemed in many Asian cultures and therefore children learn polite forms of expression at a very early age. In Java, a child's first word may well be "njuwun," meaning "I humbly beg for it."

Many American children must cope with the demands of two different languages and cultures at the same time. Each year, many non-English-speaking children enter our schools, but only recently have attempts been made to start instruction in their native tongue while teaching English as a second language. Today the enrollment of a single urban school may include children who speak Chinese, Spanish, Japanese, Vietnamese, Tagalog, or Russian. These children will be learning new cultural forms along with a new language. Spanish-speaking children, for example, may find that their parents monitor their speech for the proper expression of respect for adults while their teachers evaluate their speech for its analytical and problem-solving qualities (Hertzig et al. 1968). The way in which schools help children to make language transitions is important. The goal should be to enable children to maintain self-esteem and pride in their own family culture while acquiring a new language and its attendant cultural forms.

Language usage is very dependent on the social relationship between the speaker and the listener. We show our awareness of another person's status by our tone of voice, grammar, and mode of address. For example, the speech of a domineering father will usually convey his expectations of obedience and respect from his children. His children, in turn, may express their deference to his authority by modulating their voices and using polite forms of address. In general, children are quick to perceive degrees of status and to adapt their speech to conform to the requirements of a wide variety of social settings.

A recent study (Anderson 1979) examined how children between four and seven years old learn to speak in ways appropriate to the topic, listener, and situation. Anderson found that even the youngest children had a clear understanding of social context and power relationships and that they adjusted their vocabulary and speech accordingly. Four-year-olds expressed their understanding of social position by varying the pitch and loudness of their speech. Those who played the role of authority figures such as fathers and physicians stretched out their vowels and talked at a lower pitch than those who played lower-status figures. It is important for social workers to recognize the many ways in which language usage varies according to different cultural norms and different views about status relationships. Otherwise, a family caseworker might attempt to change communication patterns in a manner that makes no sense to the participants.

Status and role awareness are not the only social influences on a person's speech. Social class and ethnic identification are also determinants of the structure and content of language. In the next chapter we shall discuss the controversial issue of language diversity and its implications for teachers, students, and parents. Meanwhile, we shall present several theories about the nature of social class and ethnic language differences among English-speaking children. Perhaps we can clarify the issues by first presenting evidence of cultural differences in language usage and then considering the value judgments that are made about these differences.

The social science literature cites many examples of the relationship between socioeconomic status and language style, although there is considerable difference of opinion about the nature and the implications of these relationships. The most common view is that middle-class parents consciously use language to initiate questioning of cause and effect in their children, whereas working-class parents tend to give commands that will control behavior and spend less time explaining rules and reasons to their children (Olim, Hess, and Shipmen 1965 a, b, 1967). Scanzoni (1971) cites evidence that working-class parents tend to want their children to conform to authority whereas middle-class parents tend to want their children to think for themselves. Scanzoni's research shows that black middle-class families follow the dominant middle-class pattern of child-rearing practices that further individualism and achievement, even though black children are more likely to be frustrated in achieving their goals because of racial discrimination.

A review of some recent articles by Hispanic professionals indicates their view that Hispanic cultures emphasize an orientation toward persons rather than abstractions and a concern for familial values rather than individual competitiveness and independent learning styles (Dieppa and Montiel 1978; Gallegos and Valdez 1979). Black, Asian, and Hispanic researchers point out that their cultures emphasize helping relationships within the extended kinship network, in contrast to the more individualistic values of the predominant American culture.

Bernstein (1966) distinguishes between a lower-class restricted language code and a middle-class elaborated code. In describing the difference, he finds the middle-class code to be more complex and to offer children a wider choice of syntax to express themselves and greater opportunities to develop more flexible and creative speech patterns.

Labov (1970) is critical of this theory of *language deficiency*. He cites the richness and complexity of black English as evidence that nonstandard English is no less complicated in structure than middle-class English. The work of Labov and other recent researchers has led many educators to recognize black English as an ordered and syntactically consistent dialect rather than a collection of careless errors (Baratz 1970).

This leads us to the heart of the controversy, which is the extent to which value judgments are made about language differences. Until recently, working-class language and cognitive styles were often considered to be among the deficiencies that caused continued poverty and unemployment among particular groups in the population. Such theorizing has been called "blaming the victim." Today, many social workers believe that the structure of our social and economic institutions is largely responsible for inequality and poverty, including our heritage of institutional racism.

However, even social scientists and practitioners who hold to the above philosophy are not in complete agreement. There is some dissatisfaction with theories that might in any way connote the superiority of one set of values over another or that might imply that acculturation is always necessary. Labov criticizes the position that working-class language is "deficient" even though Bernstein describes the deficiencies as stemming from social factors rather than personal limitations. A number of black and Hispanic researchers strongly reject theories implying that child-rearing practices of minority cultures are in any way the cause of low academic achievement or low economic status (Billingsley 1968; Leigh and Green 1979; Gallegos and Valdez 1979). But there does seem to be grounds for a future consensus in Gallegos' suggestion that college students should be helped to become bicognitive as well as bilingual and bicultural, thus ensuring that the benefits of both cultures are offered to the individual. We shall discuss these issues further in the next chapter, which is concerned with the school-age child.

Language and thought

Just as there are conflicting theories about the relationship between language and culture, there are also conflicting theories about the relationship between language and cognitive development. However, these differences are based more on lack of conclusive research evidence than on opposing values or philosophy.

Piaget presents the following sequence for the development of thought: Actions come first; these lead to the development of structures for logical thinking; language follows later as the symbolic expression of these thought processes. He cites the studies of Furth (1966), which show that cognitive development still proceeds through the normal sequences of stages, even when children are deaf and cannot speak.

Luria (1961) takes a stand directly opposite to Piaget's. He believes that language plays a key role in the organization of the child's activity and that this role increases as children grow older and can use labels to identify the common features of things. Language thus plays a part in shaping our concepts of reality. Although the evidence is mixed, it does seem safe to conclude that language facilitates many kinds of learning but that the absence of certain linguistic structures does not necessarily prevent intellectual growth.

Feldman and Shen (1969) have provided an interesting illustration of the relationship between language and thought by comparing the cognitive abilities of bilingual five-year-olds. Far from being the handicap it was once thought to be, the experimenters found that the bilingual children performed significantly better than monolingual children in certain tests of cognitive development such as naming objects and using these names in sentences.

COGNITIVE DEVELOPMENT

The cognitive abilities of children increase dramatically between the ages of two and five. Very young children have "magical" ways of thinking about the world. They may believe that they were born before their mothers or that their fathers once were girls. They may fear that the toilet will swallow them or that the train's noise indicates anger. What are some of the aspects of these thought processes that, by adult standards, seem so confused?

Cognitive theories provide a conceptual framework for viewing the development of human intelligence. Anyone seeking to understand human growth should learn about Piaget's work on the stages of mental development. *Cognitive theorists* are a relatively recent addition to the American psychological scene, but their roots in European tradition are very old. The tradition of European rationalism has always been concerned with discovering principles of mental organization.

The learning theorists, whom we shall discuss in Chapter 5, tend to have a mechanistic view of the individual as being acted upon and responding to the environment. In contrast, cognitive theorists see people as competent not merely to receive information but also to process it. Furthermore, they see each person as innately motivated to master problems. People are curious, they discover, and they create relationships. They not only respond to stimuli but they also create structure and meaning.

Cognitive theories: Piaget

Jean Piaget, a Swiss psychologist born in 1896, has woven a complex integrative theory about mental development that has sparked the interest of researchers. He was one of the most influential and prolific of twentieth-century psychologists. As a young man he was interested in biology and epistemology, the branch of philosophy that seeks to define human knowledge. In his life-long effort to understand human knowledge, Piaget restored the use of a biological model to the study of psychology. To Piaget, the mind does not simply respond to stimuli; it also changes and adapts to the world. The cognitive psychologists have been called *structuralists* because they are concerned with how the mind processes information (Gardner 1973). The major cognitive theorists are Piaget, Jerome Bruner, and Heinz Werner.

In his early years Piaget worked with the Binet intelligence (IQ) test. While testing children, he became interested in the patterns underlying their incorrect answers, as these seemed to provide a clue to the way thought processes develop. He theorized that the mental differences between children and adults were qualitative and not merely a question of adults having a greater quantity of information than children. (A recent study of Mexican-American children, DeAvila and Havassy 1975, suggests that Piagetian measures of cognitive development may be much freer of cultural bias than the traditional intelligence tests.)

Piaget began to see that the mind is not a blank slate on which knowledge is written, nor is it a mirror that reflects what it perceives. If new information, perception, and experience is understood, then it is *assimilated.*

If the perception does not fit, the mind either rejects it, or the mind changes itself in order to *accommodate* the information or experience. Piaget uses the word **scheme** to designate these mental structures for processing information; schemes change and become more complex as the individual matures. Infants use a mouthing scheme to explore any objects that can be grasped and brought to the mouth. As they grow and discover more and more objects that do not fit this scheme, they change to another scheme; they learn to explore with their hands.

This is essentially a biological model for describing the processes by which our minds adapt to the world. For example, an animal adapts to the intake of food by the production of enzymes in the digestive system and by the muscular activity of peristalsis. The body also assimilates the food, making it part of itself. Piaget proposes that we gain intelligence in the same way. We adjust our existing schemes to accommodate new information, but at the same time we assimilate this new learning into the structure of the mind. On seeing a new object for the first time, we try to fit it into what we already know. Is it a weapon, a grooming tool, or a cooking implement? If we cannot assimilate it into our present scheme, we may have to accommodate by changing our conceptual framework.

We have presented the view that humans develop progressively complex schemes to organize information about the outside world. Piaget divided this development into four discrete and qualitatively different stages: the **sensorimotor period,** which takes place during infancy; the **preoperational period,** from about two to seven years of age; the stage of **concrete operations,** from ages seven to eleven; and the final stage of **formal operations,** which usually begins after age twelve. We shall consider only the second stage at this time and will refer to the others as appropriate in the chronological presentation of the life span.

Preoperational thought

The preoperational period is divided into two parts: the *preconceptual stage,* from about two to four years of age; and the *intuitive or transitional stage,* from about five to seven years of age.

The preconceptual stage is characterized by an increased use of symbols and symbolic play. Children develop the ability to think about something not immediately present, which gives them greater mental flexibility. Similarly, words now have the power to communicate, even in the absence of the objects they refer to. However, preconceptual children still have difficulty distinguishing between mental, physical, and social reality. They think that all moving things are alive, even the moon and the clouds. They also expect the inanimate world to obey their commands; partly from their egocentricity, which leads them to an exaggerated view of their powers.

At approximately age five, children enter the intuitive stage. They begin to separate mental from physical reality and to understand mechanical causation as separate from social norms. For example, they no longer believe that everything was created by their parents or some other adult. They begin to understand multiple points of view. However, they have only a partial comprehension of how things may be arranged by size and number, and they are unable to perform many basic mental operations.

The most significant part of the preoperational stage is the development of **symbolic representation.** Without this ability, there can be no symbolic play, no language, not even a basic understanding of multiple points of view. Once children develop the ability to use words and images to represent events or experiences, their thought processes become progressively more complex (Piaget 1950; 1951).

By adult standards, the thought processes of this period are still quite limited, and preoperational children have a long way to go before they become logical thinkers. Their thinking is concrete, they cannot deal with abstractions, and they are only concerned with physical things that they can easily represent. They think of events and relationships as irreversible, and they cannot imagine how things can be returned to their original state.

Another characteristic of this developmental stage is that thinking is egocentric. Preoperational children concentrate on their own perceptions and assume that everyone else's outlook is the same (Piaget 1954). Their thinking tends to be centered on only one aspect of an object or situation at a time. They also have a relatively short memory and attention span, and this causes difficulty in organizing action. A child may forget why he is putting things together before he has finished the first part of the task.

Phillips (1969, p. 61) cites this example of a preoperational child's thinking. A four-year-old subject is asked if he has a brother. He replies "yes" and states that his brother's name is Jim. He then is asked if Jim has a brother and the answer is "no." Our subject is unable to grasp the notion that *having* a brother necessarily involves *being* a brother to someone else.

Preoperational children judge things according to their appearance rather than speculating on how they came to be that way. They also have very little appreciation of time sequences. A three-year-old does not really understand the meaning of "Grandma will come to visit next week," and a child waking from a nap may not even know whether it is the same day as it was before the nap. With only a limited time sense, it is difficult for children of this age to grasp the notion of cause and effect. In fact, their early use of the words *cause* and *because* may have nothing to do with the usual adult understanding of these terms.

Several of these preoperational limitations can be observed by following one of Piaget's classic experiments on the concept of the **conservation of matter.** In the experiment a child is presented with two identical balls of clay. As the child watches, one ball of clay is transformed into various shapes while the other remains untouched. At each transformation, the child is asked which has more clay, the untouched ball or the one that has been rolled into a sausage, or several small balls, or a pancake. The child might say that the untouched ball has more clay because it is fatter, or that the sausage has more because it is longer. The child might choose the smaller balls because there are more of them, or the pancake because it is all spread out. At no time does the child understand that the two are identical. Preoperational children focus on the *current state* of an object rather than on the *process of transformation*. Their thinking is concrete and is based on direct experience in the here and now. Piaget concludes that they do not have the cognitive ability to understand the principle of the conservation of matter.

However, other researchers claim that preschoolers are able to solve such problems if the tasks are simplified (Gelman 1978). If one modifies some of Piaget's classic tasks, by using fewer objects or simplifying the directions, the subjects will achieve a measure of success (McGarrigle, Grieve, and Hughes 1978). Piaget (1968) himself has reconsidered the preoperational period and feels that children can understand one-to-one relationships. In other words, they seem to know that if, for example, a cord is pulled, the window shade will come down; the lowered shade is seen as a function of the act of pulling the cord. Piaget calls this the *logic of functions.*

Knowledge of the preschool child's thought processes has important implications for helping children to learn and for testing the level of conceptual development in children whose behavior appears inappropriate. Most educators now believe that children begin to develop concepts of sequence, time, classification, and space by interacting with the environment—moving, manipulating, watching, and verbalizing. Their cognitive development is best stimulated at this stage by exposing them to a wide variety of experiences and providing them with opportunities to deal with concrete objects. Only then can children learn to conceptualize *how many, how much,* and *what kind.* Children do not learn concepts such as relative time or classification of objects by learning the words for these relationships. Teachers must proceed at the proper pace, taking into account the level of cognitive skills present and also the limitations at a particular stage of development.

Social workers dealing with this age group should also be aware of the relationships between thought processes and the level of play in which the child engages. Later in this chapter we shall see how emotional development is dependent on the level of cognitive ability. In addition, educational psychologists use concepts of cognitive development in offering appropriate prescriptions for remedial teaching. For example, a child may need more experience with concrete operations such as sorting out objects according to size before progressing on to more abstract tasks. The theory behind such a prescription is that by returning to an earlier stage that was not properly mastered, children can progress past a learning block.

Another application of these ideas is in psychological testing of children with suspected psychoses. It may be important to know whether an older child thinks about cause and effect on a preschool level, or thinks that events are irreversible, or has an egocentric view of reality. We still know very little about the causal relationship between cognitive organization and mental illness. Cognitive theories are concerned mainly with intellectual development and have not been as successful in exploring the individual's potential for dependence, aggression, and sexuality.

Memory

The ability to remember is a fundamental aspect of cognitive development. It allows a person to perceive selectively, to classify, to reason, and to form complex concepts. Some psychologists have used the computer as a model for explaining the memory functions of the human brain. The brain has storage capacity for information and an array of "associational switches" that gives access to what is stored; this system of switches allows the individual to put new items into the memory and take them out in a particular order.

Information theorists think of memory as having three parts: a **sensory register** that records information; a **short-term memory** that holds what the mind is conscious of at the moment; and a **long-term memory** that holds items for as long as a lifetime. When information comes into the system, it makes contact with the sensory register, which holds it for a very brief period of less than one second. This is sometimes called the "very short-term memory." The information is then either lost or transferred to the short-term memory, often described as the "working memory." The short-term memory holds the information that the person is consciously aware of at any one time, but this lasts only so long as it is the focus of concentrated attention.

Long-term memory provides storage of information for periods of up to a lifetime. Some theorists believe that nothing in the long-term memory is ever lost, except by damage to the brain. This information constitutes a person's permanent knowledge base and includes such necessary information as one's social security number and birth date (Atkinson and Shiffrin 1971; Hagen, Longeward, and Kail 1975).

Researchers often refer to a visual memory, a motor memory, and a verbal memory. The visual memory is the first to develop and is evident during infancy. Adults are usually unable to remember much about the period before the age of three. Some people may recall very early memories while in psychotherapy or under hypnosis. These memories tend to be pictorial and difficult to describe verbally. However, events that occur after the ages of four to six years have usually been verbally coded before being stored, and therefore we are able to talk about these memories. Social workers, as well as psychotherapists, often use play situations involving symbolic objects that children can manipulate to act out feelings and memories that they are unable to put into words.

Studies of the memory of preschool children focus on the dual skills of recognition and recall. **Recognition** refers to the ability to select the familiar from pictures, objects, or events. **Recall** refers to the ability to retrieve information about objects or events from the short- or long-term memory. For example, a child is recalling information if he can anticipate the next picture when looking through a familiar book.

Myers and Perlmutter (1978) found that preschool children perform better on recognition than on recall tasks. However, both forms of memory improve between the ages of two and five. After a single viewing of a number of objects, even two-year-olds could correctly recognize 81 percent of them, and the five-year-olds remembered 92 percent. Most children showed considerable proficiency in the recognition skills necessary to code and retain substantial amounts of information. However, their recall was much poorer; the three-year-olds in the study could only recall 22 percent of the items and the four-year-olds only 40 percent.

Preschool children are clearly better at recognition than at recall. Their recall difficulties are generally assumed to be related to their limited strategies for coding and retrieval (Flavell 1977; Myers and Perlmutter 1978). If adults are given a list to memorize, such as "cat, chair, airplane, dog, desk, car," they might first classify the items as "animals," "furniture," and "vehicles" and then rehearse the words quietly before being asked to recall the list. Adults use the strategies of organization and rehearsal. Both adults and children over the age of six can improve their ability to recall information if they are taught these memory strategies. However, younger children have great difficulty in learning to organize and rehearse information.

Some researchers conclude that these limitations indicate that young children have no memory strategies at all. Yet preschool children do remember a great many things ranging from TV advertising slogans to stories and folksongs. They remember things that have structure, sequence, and interrelationships; only recently have psychologists included such elements in their laboratory memory tasks. Some recent studies (Sheingold and Tenney 1978) have tested preschool children's memories for events and found that they have a format for remembering. Children between the ages of three and five are aware that a birthday party has a beginning, a middle, and an end. They can tell the researcher who came to the party and the order of events. They can also recall a wealth of detail about critical events, such as what Mommy and the new baby were wearing when they first brought the newborn home from the hospital. Preschoolers perform better on recall related to these important events than they do on unrelated laboratory test items.

SOCIALIZATION

We shall describe the processes of child rearing in this section: *reward and punishment, modeling,* and *identification.* As we noted at the end of the last chapter, child rearing is the major way in which the personality characteristics valued by a particular culture are transmitted to children. Besides integrating the child into the family unit, parents or caregivers are the first people to interpret cultural requirements to the child, and these are conveyed at an early stage in the child's life. In a cohesive society, other people constantly reinforce and expand parental teaching, and there is little contradiction between the family's way of doing things and the customs of the community at large. However, in our complex and multiethnic society there are many different cultural traditions and individual preferences. Parents may take measures to inculcate their own values so that their children will not become assimilated into the majority culture. Sometimes these minority values are sociopolitical, ethical, or representative of a particular ethnic culture. These values may be expressed to children by the parents' approach to daily routines such as food and clothing, by their advocacy of a particular style of discipline and education, and by continued use of their native language.

Parental influences are just one element in the overall process of socialization. Socialization is the lifelong process by which individuals learn to become members of a social group. Americans generally have membership in many groups and must develop the ability to deal with many different social expectations. Family members, peers, teachers, and employers are but a few of the socialization agents who determine what is learned, how well it is learned, and how tense or anxiety-provoking the learning process will be.

Depending on their familial culture, children can become predominantly passive or aggressive, dependent or independent, vegetarian or meat-eating. The behavior that they adopt is the behavior that their family's social, ethnic, religious, or other group considers appropriate. Let us now consider some child-rearing practices by which caregivers ensure that their children will become fully participating members of society.

Child-rearing practices

Parents often believe that children learn to behave because of a system of rewards and punishments. **Rewards** do commonly produce or reinforce behavior patterns; children who receive attention when they whine are very likely to become chronic whiners. They are motivated to repeat a desired behavior if they are rewarded for that behavior.

On the other hand, the effects of **punishment** are not so easily interpreted, as the word is used to refer to a wide range of practices. For example, parental disapproval can be conveyed by any of the following actions: stern looks, demands that the child leave the room until there is evidence of "improved" behavior, demands that the child be isolated for a long period of time in a room that is locked or unlocked and with or without toys, withholding of privileges for a short time or a long time, and mild or severe spanking either immediately or sometime after the misbehavior occurred. In the next chapter, we shall discuss the learning theorists, who focus on parental interventions as either positive or negative reinforcers of behavior. However, at this point we should recognize that if punishment is to further the process of socialization, then it must lead to the child's eventually being able to internalize the desired standards of behavior.

It is difficult to define abusive behavior toward children without a knowledge of the relevant community standards. Historically, there have been culturally accepted reasons for treating children in ways that are now considered to be shocking and brutal. These actions have been taken in the name of education, discipline, religion, and the economic demand for child labor. Children have been viewed as the property of their parents, and it was taken for granted that parents might punish them as they saw fit. Furthermore, certain forms of physical cruelty such as foot binding and ritual scarring represent customs that have deep symbolic meaning in other societies. Practices such as infanticide or abandonment have been the time-honored measures desperate adults have used to cope with illegitimacy, disease, and other traumas. The Calvinists of the sixteenth century believed that children had an evil nature, and some of the early American colonies went so far as to enact a death penalty for youthful disobedience (Radbill 1974).

Modeling, or imitation, is another way in which socialization occurs. From early childhood on we observe and imitate the actions of those around us, sometimes copying behavior patterns down to the most minute detail. As many an embarrassed parent will testify, young children have a remarkable talent for capturing Mommy's or Daddy's actions, words, and mannerisms and then mimicking them publicly. Modeling is also practiced by adults in the following of fads and fashions in thoughts and actions.

The influence of modeling on learning has been extensively studied, and research shows that certain models are more influential than others. The three most important characteristics that encourage imitation are *power, nurturance,* and *perceived similarity* (Bandura 1969). Power is the ability to control desirable resources and to exert influence over others. Studies reveal that a child is more likely to imitate a relatively powerful adult than a relatively powerless one (Bandura, Ross, and Ross 1963). Nurturance, or affectionate care and attention, also plays a part in learning. Children are more likely to imitate a nurturing, rewarding model than a cold, punitive one. The third significant factor in the effectiveness of modeling is the degree of perceived similarity with the model. Boys tend to model other boys or men; blacks tend to model other blacks; muscular, athletic children tend to imitate athletes; quiet, pensive children tend to select reserved or reflective models. Modeling continues throughout the entire life span. An adolescent may wear faded jeans because they are in fashion, then put them aside for tweeds after graduation from law school.

While training and modeling are responsible for a large portion of social learning, they cannot explain certain complex behavioral phenomena that develop over time. Many theorists find the concept of identification most useful in explaining complex developmental patterns.

Although **identification** has been defined in a wide variety of theoretical contexts, we shall use the term to refer to the process of internalizing, or incorporating within oneself, the values, attitudes, and behavior patterns of another. This can occur at any age, but it is most important in personality development during the preschool years. We shall be referring to this process later as we discuss the ways in which preschool children cope with feelings and develop a sense of sexual identification and the beginnings of conscience. Through the processes of modeling and identification, we begin to form a sense of self and a way of thinking about who and what we are.

Coping with feelings

Between the ages of two and six, all children go through a process of learning how to deal with their emotions; they develop characteristic coping strategies that may last a lifetime.

One little boy had particularly impressed his teacher by his obedient and cooperative attitude during the first few weeks of school. He arrived each day neatly dressed, and he never argued with the teacher or got into fights with the other children. The teacher was delighted with this industrious "model child."

One day, the little boy was drawing in the dirt with a stick during the play period. A cat came into the playground and walked across the drawing the boy was making. The child stiffened and suddenly grabbed the cat by the tail and flung it against a tree trunk with all his might.

How can we explain such apparently unprovoked behavior? This six-year-old boy had learned the specific behaviors expected of him but had not been able to cope with his angry feelings. His "model" behavior provided no acceptable outlet for the emotions he had learned to reject. The result was that his usually calm behavior was periodically interrupted by such bizarre actions. Although this is an extreme case, it illustrates the tremendous effect of the way in which young children are trained to deal with their feelings. In this case, the parental child-rearing practices had been unusually rigid, but one cannot always predict specific behaviors such as the outburst just described from specific types of training. As we have already noted, there are a number of factors influencing children and how they eventually cope with particular conflicts.

During these early years children learn to handle a wide range of feelings such as joy, affection, sensuality, anger, fear, jealousy, and frustration. Parents play a major role in determining the ways in which two-year-olds gradually learn to achieve a balance between the desire for immediate satisfaction of impulses and the demands for social control. Parents must help children with the difficult task of finding outlets for feelings of affection, sensuality, anger, and jealousy that will be acceptable to both parent and child.

Children must learn appropriate ways to express positive as well as negative feelings. For example, some cultures tend to welcome the expression of affection and playfulness among children and adults; others frown on open displays of affection. Cultures that are restrictive about displays of joy and affection may create special circumstances such as celebrations, rituals, and games that call for emotional expression considered inappropriate for everyday life. Children must learn all these social norms. They must also learn norms about masturbation and sex play, as they discover that some pleasurable activities are frowned upon to a greater or lesser degree.

In our heterogeneous society there are many models of child rearing. This can be problematic for social workers unless they recognize their own particular biases and respect those of other groups. For example, American social workers should realize that free expression of children's anger toward adults is considered terribly insulting by some groups, and that open displays of affection and physical closeness are considered more desirable by some groups than others.

All children appear to experience some conflict at this stage of development between their own impulses and societal prohibitions. However, the degree of anxiety experienced during the process of socialization can vary, from a tolerable degree of tension that leads to new learning to a crippling amount of anxiety. Anxious children experience a vague and generalized feeling of apprehension without knowing its precise origin. The indirect cause of these anxieties may be a sudden change in parental expectations, such as the beginning of toilet training, or a move to a new neighborhood.

Parents are most helpful if they are not overly strict in setting limits and are patient in allowing the child sufficient time to learn behavioral controls. They should convey temporary disapproval of a particular behavior and never rejection of the whole child. The dangers inherent in overly strict punishment are that it may produce undesired effects. For example, if children are routinely punished for all forms of aggressive or dependent behavior, they may learn to feel anxious about all angry or dependent feelings. Or, if children learn that the world is a fearful and dangerous place, they may become excessively aggressive adults who always attack first to avoid being attacked.

Caregivers who use physical punishment to discipline their children actually serve as aggressive models. Their children may learn to imitate the aggression even if they stop the behavior that provoked the punishment (Parke 1972). It is also possible that aggressive children force their parents to resort to spanking and slapping, thus enabling the wrongdoer to feel guilt-free, since the score has now been evened. Physical punishment does not lead to the growth of an internalized sense of conscience that can operate independently later in life (Fraiberg 1959).

Children may become excessively anxious if parents are perceived as unable to set limits or to protect children from becoming overwhelmed by their impulsive feelings. Nor is it helpful for children to grow up unaware of the norms of the community in which they live. As we have already mentioned, children experience a certain amount of anxiety in the normal course of growing up; psychoanalytically oriented theorists believe that they learn to handle guilty feelings and fear of punishment by incorporating the attitudes and rules of behavior of the powerful authority. We feel ourselves less helpless as we become more like the authority figure. This concept will be discussed later in the chapter under the heading, "Identification."

Aside from the fear of anticipated punishment, the preschooler must deal with many other sources of anxiety and fear. Irrational thinking, full of fantasy and magical happenings, is normal at this age. Toddlers face many unpredictable and confusing situations and lack the knowledge base that will later assist them in coping rationally with the world around them. Some fears are necessary for their survival, such as the fear of being hit by a moving car. However, young children imagine terrible monsters that personify their fear about their own feelings and their uncertainty about the responses of others.

Sometimes it is difficult to trace the source of a particular fear. Children's fear of the dark may be more related to fantasies and internal conflicts than to any real events in their lives. When fears and anxieties continue, even after parents are sympathetic and encouraging, it may be necessary to seek professional help in order to locate the source of the anxiety. It is never desirable to use force or ridicule to overcome children's fears.

Defense mechanisms

It is difficult to do experimental studies of the fears discussed above because by the age of five or six years children have learned many ways to hide or disguise their feelings. Anna Freud (1946) described a number of these **defense mechanisms,** or ways in which we all learn to cope with our feelings. Some of these strategies for reducing tension are considered more acceptable by one culture than others; some are considered normal in preschool children but only minimally acceptable in adults, who are expected to be more rational in their thinking.

Withdrawal is a very common defense mechanism in young children. It is the most direct defense possible: The child simply runs away (either physically or mentally) from a difficult situation. This defense is useful in some circumstances but problematic if used excessively. Children need to develop a variety of coping mechanisms that will be useful later in life.

Denial is the refusal to admit that a situation exists or that an event has happened. Children may react to a situation such as the death of a pet by pretending that the pet is still living in the house, eating in the kitchen, and sleeping in the child's room at night. Children will often resort to denial when they first begin to develop a sense of conscience. The child who recognizes that it is best to deny having spilled soap powder all over the floor may be taking the first step toward eventual self-control. It is best to recognize and encourage the child's wish that the untoward action could be "undone," rather than to emphasize the evils of lying. However, when denial is used as a major coping mechanism, children may never learn to deal realistically with difficult situations. A consistent distortion of reality can become emotionally crippling and require therapeutic help.

Repression is an extreme form of denial in which a frightening event or circumstance is erased from consciousness. Adults in therapy are sometimes able to recall these earlier experiences and recognize how they still affect their thoughts and feelings. Analytically oriented therapists believe that once these experiences become conscious, the painful conflicts can be resolved more rationally, thus reducing the intensity of the symptoms. However, repression can also serve useful functions and the extent to which it leads to future problems depends very much on the surrounding circumstances.

Regression is a way of coping with stress by returning to an earlier or more infantile form of behavior. Examples are a child's return to thumb sucking or drinking from a bottle when a new baby joins the family or to bedwetting when a child is overwhelmed at the prospect of starting school. Temporary forms of regression can be expected in the normal course of development, but massive or prolonged regression is a sign that the child and parent need help in identifying the source of the tension.

Reaction formation occurs when children have thoughts or desires that make them anxious, and they react by adopting the opposite form of behavior. For example, children may want to be messy but react because they fear that being messy will result in loss of parental love. They then become extraordinarily neat and clean. Or they may behave with an exaggerated independence and assertiveness when they would like to cling to their mothers. This defense is more common as children get older.

Projection involves a distortion of reality in which children may actually be confused in their own minds about what really happened. Their real thoughts and actions are undesirable, so they attribute them to someone else. "He did it, not me" is a common statement of projection. Although it is acceptable for preschool children to project blame onto a teddy-bear, we would consider it psychotic if an adult believed that a teddy bear was causing all the accidents in the house. On the other hand, there are culturally sanctioned forms of projected blame that allow the individual to escape feelings of guilt without being labeled as deviant. This is true not only of cultures that believe in evil spirits; in our own society there are extreme social movements that attract people who cope with their feelings by projecting blame onto minority groups.

Rationalization is a very common adult defense mechanism. Children use it less frequently, since it requires verbal skills and knowledge of social rules. Rationalization involves inventing a socially acceptable explanation for unacceptable behavior or thoughts. For example, a child might say "I had to hit my baby sister because she was being bad," when in fact the baby had not misbehaved.

Displacement occurs when an individual expresses emotional reactions toward a substitute person or object, rather than at the real source of the feeling. For example, a boy may be angry at his father but be unable to admit this fully to himself because he also loves and depends upon his father. He therefore displaces the anger onto a safer target of aggression such as a sibling.

When interests are channeled into more socially acceptable forms it is called **sublimation;** an example of this is the child turning to mud pies and finger painting at a time when playing with feces may be attractive but forbidden.

Identification is generally a more positive defense mechanism than many we have mentioned. It is the process of incorporating into oneself the values, attitudes, and beliefs of others. However, sometimes children or adults will feel such a high degree of anxiety and helplessness that they will identify with powerful figures who are harmful to them. This is called *identification with the aggressor* and has been offered as an explanation for the positive attitudes people sometimes adopt toward their captors after they have been held hostage for a long period of time.

As we noted in Chapter 3, critics of psychoanalytic theories point to the difficulty of empirically verifying concepts such as defense mechanisms that make inferences about motivation. Some social workers find these concepts useful for understanding behavior; others prefer to deal only with conscious and measurable behavior.

AGGRESSION AND PROSOCIAL BEHAVIOR

We have described some of the ways in which children learn to deal with other people and to handle their own emotions. These interactions can produce both affectionate and aggressive responses. At one point children may seek to please and be close to another person, and a short time later they may become angry and hostile. We have also described the Freudian view of defense mechanisms as ways in which children learn to deal with anxiety.

Now we shall describe in greater detail how children are socialized to channel aggressive feelings in acceptable ways and are taught positive behaviors such as helping and sharing.

Aggressive behavior may be verbal or physical, it may be directed at people, or it may be displaced toward objects. Social psychologists generally refer to aggression as behavior intended to hurt or destroy, reserving the term **assertive** for behavior that is not intended to injure others. Assertive behavior, in this sense, refers to direct acts such as calmly but effectively stating one's rights or initiating vigorous action toward some goal. Freudian theorists, however, claim that these are examples of socially acceptable ways of expressing aggressive feelings.

Prosocial behavior is another broad, culturally relative term that must be carefully defined. Mussen and Eisenberg-Berg (1977) describe prosocial behavior as actions intended to benefit others, taken without the anticipation of external reward. These actions often entail some cost or risk to the individual. Generosity, helping, sharing, and sympathy are examples of prosocial behavior. People tend to exhibit these behaviors when they feel happy and secure.

Socially appropriate behavior is always situationally and culturally defined. Aggressive behavior is obviously considered desirable for combat troops. And a constantly altruistic person, who is always unselfishly concerned about our welfare, may be considered annoyingly intrusive. Considerable research has been devoted to both aggressive and prosocial behaviors in an attempt to find out how each originates and what factors control them. We shall present some of these explanations.

Frustration and aggression

Psychologists with several different perspectives have hypothesized a direct relationship between feelings of frustration at the blocking of a desired goal and acts of aggression. Some suggest that all aggression is derived from frustration, and that all frustration results in direct or disguised forms of aggression (Dollard et al. 1939). The aggression might be directed physically or verbally at the source of frustration, or it might be displaced onto another person or object. It might also be disguised and channeled outward through constructive activities or turned inward, as with self-destructive behavior. Nevertheless, it is believed to be evident somewhere, if only one looks for it carefully enough.

One well-known study (Barker, Dembo, and Lewin 1943) recorded the behavior of preschool children during a frustrating play situation. The children were given a number of attractive toys, which were then removed and placed behind a wire screen where they were visible but unattainable. The children reacted in different ways to the frustrations they felt. Some were aggressive toward their peers, some toward the investigators, and some toward the wire screen. Others tried to escape from the room or regressed to earlier behaviors such as thumb sucking. Some just patiently waited or turned their attention to something else. The experiment seems to reveal that overt aggression is by no means the only or even the dominant reaction to frustration. However, some theorists consider regressive behaviors as a disguised form of aggression.

Other studies (Dollard and Miller 1950) indicate that aggression is not the only response to frustration, and that sometimes aggression is simply imitative behavior. For example, soldiers are trained to act aggressively whether or not they feel angry or frustrated.

Rewards, punishment, and modeling

If frustration does not always cause aggression and empathy does not always result in helping or sharing, what other explanation might account for prosocial and aggressive behavior? Recently, some important studies have dealt with the effects of direct reward and punishment and the observation of role models. These influences were noted earlier as examples of child-rearing practices by which children are socialized.

Our culture offers different models and systems of reward and punishment to different segments of society. For example, the models and rewards available to boys differ from those offered to girls. Although both sexes are equally adept at understanding how another person feels, females are more apt to express their concern for the feelings of others than males are (Hoffman 1977) because our culture encourages this differentiation. Similarly, children who live in neighborhoods where their peers are highly aggressive are more likely to be rewarded for aggressive behavior than those who do not have to "fight for their rights."

We have already noted that modeling occurs more completely when the model is perceived as powerful, has characteristics similar to those of the child, and has a nurturing or close relationship with the child. For example, a girl may model herself after her father because he seems powerful, or because she and her father have a strong nurturant relationship, or because other people comment on the fact that they have similar temperaments.

One study found that children are most likely to imitate other children who have "dominant" personalities. These are children who are the most powerful and who engage in the most useful and interesting activities (Abramovitch and Grusec 1978). However, dominance is not the same as aggression, and another study shows that preschool children spontaneously dislike overly aggressive playmates, preferring those with whom they share common activities and who play well with them (Hayes 1978).

Keeping these variables in mind, we can observe certain patterns in the way that modeling and reward and punishment influence behavior. Children behave more aggressively after observing an aggressive model and after they have been directly rewarded for such behavior (Cowan and Walters 1963; Lováss 1961). This positive reinforcement can take either of two forms. It can be an extrinsic reward, such as a gift or an expression of approval, or it can be the intrinsic pleasure of achieving success. If aggression "works" for the child, this acts as a powerful reward.

Although research indicates that rewards will encourage aggression, we have already noted the lack of agreement about the effectiveness of punishment in discouraging such behavior. Children who are punished for aggressive acts are very likely to inhibit the behavior, at least in the presence of the punisher. But they will probably channel their aggressive feelings and acts into other outlets. They may turn to less physical forms of aggressive behavior, such as angry fantasies, name calling, and tattling, or they may direct their aggression toward inanimate objects such as dolls. Punishment may even backfire and produce the opposite of the desired effect. Anyone who uses physical punishment to curb a child's aggression may be encouraging it by actually serving as a model for aggressive behavior. It seems reasonable to conclude that punishment is effective only if it results in strengthening the child's ability to eventually achieve self-control.

Social workers should be alert to the possibility that parents will often use the word *punishment* in the general sense of any attempt to "discipline" the child, or curb undesired behavior. For example, a parent who denies television privileges to a child for hitting a younger brother while watching a program may consider this to be "punishment," while a behaviorally oriented worker may consider it to be an appropriate withdrawal of a "positive reinforcer." In situations such as this, the social worker must be clear about the specific meaning of terms, especially when advice is being offered about "punishing the child less." Otherwise, parents are apt to feel increasingly helpless and often angry.

Studies show that modeling also influences prosocial behavior. In a typical modeling experiment, children observe a person performing a pro-social act, such as donating prizes to needy children. A similar control group watches a model who does not exhibit the prosocial behavior. Each child is then given the opportunity to denote something that he or she won. The researchers usually find that children who witness another person's generosity become more generous in their own behavior (Mussen and Eisenberg-Berg 1977).

Although researchers have found that rewards and punishment affect aggression, there is no conclusive evidence that helping and sharing are increased by rewards and decreased by punishment (Rushton 1976). Sharing is found to increase after rewards are offered, but it is difficult to rule out the effects of modeling (Aronfreed 1968; Aelfand et al. 1975). When the experimenter gives a reward, he or she is also modeling "giving."

The child-rearing practices of parents or caregivers play a large part in the aggressive and altruistic behavior that children learn. However, even the most careful parents cannot shelter a child completely from opportunities to imitate negative behavior, and many psychologists and sociologists feel that the omnipresent television provides children in our society with a clear model for aggressive behavior. It is only recently that studies have attempted to show the effects of television on prosocial behavior.

Impact of television

Television is a major socializing force in our society. Many have concluded that by exposing children to a large amount of casual violence on the screen, we teach them to think of aggression as a commonplace and acceptable outlet for their own frustrations. According to Gerbner (1972), children's cartoons are among the most violent fare on television. We have seen how the presence of aggressive models increases the likelihood of aggression in the observer, and we know that many children spend hours in front of the TV each day, watching cartoons, violent westerns, and sometimes adult programs featuring assault and murder.

According to one theory, viewing violent acts on television has a "purifying" effect (Feshbach and Singer 1971). Television stimulates violent fantasies, and these fantasies act as substitutes for overt aggression. This theory is appealing, but research evidence overwhelmingly refutes it (Liebert, Neale, and Davidson 1973). Actually, observation of television violence has been shown to result in increased rather than decreased aggression by viewers (Friedrich and Stein 1973; Leifer and Roberts 1972).

An additional factor to be considered is the extent to which programs can be clearly identified by children as part of the world of make-believe. Television often seems more real to children than stories in picture books, and this makes it harder for them to sort out fantasy from representations of the real world. This is a particular problem when children watch adult programs; cartoons are easier to identify as make-believe.

One should also take into account the *content* of the cartoon or drama. A Mickey Mouse cartoon, for example, shows a tiny mouse managing to somehow outwit the big bullies of the world. Mr. McGoo may be blind and bungling, but he comes through every adventure unscathed. Violence in the service of such simple themes does very little damage to most children. Those who are the most adversely affected by seemingly casual violence are children with limited real-life models and those who already have serious emotional problems. Unfortunately, many of the children seen by social workers have such characteristics, and many also live in homes where they are allowed unlimited television watching and where other recreational outlets are limited.

Still, television does have the potential to teach children many forms of prosocial behavior, as research has shown. Carefully designed children's programs are able to portray themes such as cooperation, affection, control of aggression, and coping with frustration. There is evidence that children who have seen these programs for even relatively short periods of time become more cooperative, sympathetic, and nurturant (Stein and Friedrich 1975). Again, the child's perception of the model will determine the amount of prosocial influence. The most effective television models are those who resemble parents and teachers who have the ability to demand certain behaviors and impose sanctions if children do not comply.

In sum, research seems to suggest that television is a potent socializer that can influence children's behavior in either positive or negative ways. However, social workers should also look at the total amount of time a child devotes to watching television. A child may be deprived of many educational play experiences because caregivers are allowing or encouraging too much passive television viewing. Throughout this chapter, we have referred to the role of play in furthering the child's development. Play promotes the growth of sensory capacities and physical skills, it provides endless opportunities to exercise and expand new-found intellectual and language skills, and it provides a structured and safe avenue for expressing a wide range of feelings. A child who spends most of the day actively engaged in pursuits such as playing a game with peers, making up spontaneous rhymes, seesawing with another child, pretending to be an astronaut, drawing a dragon, or constructing a bridge out of blocks is having an entirely different life experience than the child who spends many hours passively in front of the television set.

DEVELOPMENTAL ISSUES

We have described some of the difficulties young children face as they learn to express their feelings in a socially acceptable form. Preschoolers also deal with a number of developmental issues. One pressing issue is achieving a balance between the continued need for dependency and the growing need for autonomy, mastery, and competence. During this time children also begin to develop a sense of self-esteem. Growth during the preschool years occurs through the processes of identification and the learning of sex roles and a sense of conscience.

Dependency and autonomy

Dependency refers to our wishes and needs to be aided, nurtured, and protected by others. It implies an emotional closeness and acceptance by another person. It is a normal need in people of every age, despite the connotation of weakness or inadequacy that it often carries in American society. It is also necessary for the very survival of infants and young children, who must look to adults for the satisfaction of both their physical and psychological needs.

Toddlers show their dependency by demanding close physical contact with adults. However, by age four or five, children develop more indirect ways of showing their need for others. They become verbal and seek attention by asking questions, by offering to help, and by showing off. A study by Craig and Garney (1972) traced this developmental trend by observing the ways in which children at ages two, two and a half, and three maintain contact with their mothers in strange situations. The two-year-olds spent most of their time physically close to their mothers, looking up frequently to make sure that their mothers were still there. The two-and-a-half-year-olds and three-year-olds did not stay as close to their mothers as the younger children, and they did not check as often to see if their mothers were still present. Older children were able to maintain verbal contact instead of relying solely on physical contact. This study also found evidence of a wide range of individual differences within each age group, confirming the findings of other research.

Although dependence and independence are commonly considered opposite types of behavior, dependent behavior in young children does not necessarily lead to their becoming dependent adults. In fact, children who have strong and satisfying dependency relationships in their early years often become the most self-reliant adults (Sears, Rau, and Alpert 1965).

Children may also alternately display dependent and independent behaviors, especially when independence is measured in terms of self-reliance and striving for achievement (Beller 1955; Heathers 1955). They may display dependence by showing affection and seeking attention and at the same time show independence by initiating their own play activities. Parents can help by praising efforts toward independence while simultaneously tolerating dependent behaviors.

As discussed in Chapter 3, the second stage in Erikson's theory of personality development is characterized by the drive for autonomy. This drive is seen throughout life and is closely related to the need for mastery and a sense of competence. Toddlers gain a sense of self-confidence as they learn to control their bodies and experience doing things for themselves. If their efforts at autonomy are frustrated by criticism or punishment, they feel a sense of failure and shame (Erikson 1963; Murphy 1962; White 1959).

Most people derive satisfaction from the ability to change the environment to suit themselves. Toddlers may express their need for autonomy by crayoning on a forbidden wall. Unfortunately, a little boy's mastery over a white wall, or the discovery that he can "improve" the vacuum cleaner by filling its tubes with clay, does not always fit in with his mother's need to keep the house clean. These opposing needs produce genuine conflicts between parent and child and within the child.

All children have a need to master the environment and to feel competent and successful. What happens when their attempts meet with constant failure or frustration? What happens when they have little or no opportunity for independent activity, or when their environment is so chaotic that they cannot see the consequences of their acts? If their efforts at mastery become too problematic, they may give up and adopt a passive approach to life. Erikson characterizes this as the *need for initiative versus the sense of guilt* that results from being constantly punished for independent activity. Several studies show that such children fail to develop an active, exploratory, self-confident approach to learning (White and Watts 1973). School social workers may see this reaction in some children with learning problems—they lack the confidence or assertiveness to "tackle a problem." Children whose parents discourage or frighten them whenever they venture into new activities may become anxious and learn to deny, minimize, or disguise their autonomy needs. Such induced anxiety about autonomy is especially common among young girls in our culture.

Children who are physically or mentally disabled or who experience a prolonged illness have less opportunity to test their skills in mastering the environment. Social workers can help in such situations by showing others how these children can achieve a sense of mastery in alternative ways and by helping to design an environment that lets them play and explore safely. Fortunately, today handicapped children have increasingly positive role models, such as people in wheelchairs in various forms of employment. These models are especially important in helping parents see that even permanent physical disability need not lead to excessive psychological dependency. In the next chapter, we shall consider the special problems schools face in enabling disabled students to fulfill their potential.

During the preschool years, children's notions about themselves expand as they develop competence and mastery of the world about them. We have seen infants begin to make the distinction between self and others. Later, children begin to develop a sense of psychological uniqueness, a process that continues throughout life. This self-evaluation by preschool children is often a direct reflection of what other people think about them. If a girl's parents tell her that she is a troublemaker, she may soon come to believe it. These early attitudes eventually become basic elements of the individual's self-concept, but they are often difficult to explore in adulthood because they were partially learned at a nonverbal level. Later, unless there has been severe damage to the self-concept, children learn to measure themselves against their own ideals of what they think they should be.

When children compare themselves with their parents and others, they are also discovering what they are like as separate individuals. One study suggests that activity is the most important factor in preschool children's development of a self-image. The children tested defined themselves primarily in terms of statements such as "I go to school," "I can pick up things," and "I wash my hair myself" (Ketter et al. 1978). Since children are constructing a relatively consistent view about themselves we can see how essential it is that they develop a positive sense of themselves as active and capable forces in their world. People tend to act in systematic ways, and they will try to bring their behavior in line with these developing beliefs and attitudes about themselves. Parents provide the strongest influence on children's developing self-image because parents are the most significant evaluators of children's actions. They also provide the child with definitions of right and wrong and serve as models of behavior.

Children who are abused by their parents tend to develop low self-esteem and often have difficulty in adequately integrating their needs for dependency and autonomy. Psychologists know that a large number of abusive parents were themselves abused as children (Parke and Collmer 1975). Although it is not entirely clear why child abuse tends to occur from one generation to the next, it is possible that children who learn that dependency needs are unacceptable will follow this model when they themselves become parents.

Identification: Developing a conscience

We have already described the processes of socialization, during which children learn to incorporate the values and moral standards of the society in which they live. We use the term *conscience* to refer to an internalized set of morals, values, and standards of behavior (Hoffman 1970). Some cognitive theorists contend that conscience is primarily the result of learning to reason. However, most psychologists think that the process is more complicated and that it begins even in the prelogical child. When Mary says "No, no, no!" as she crayons on the wall, she is showing the beginnings of self-restraint at the same time that she is following her whim. In a few years, she will have developed enough self-control to arrest such impulses as soon as they reach her consciousness.

The internalization of some values is necessary for the survival of societies. If people did not develop an internal sense of right and wrong, no law would be strong enough to control their impulses. How does this internalization occur? How does a two-year-old who feels nothing but fascination at banging a sibling on the head come to develop both self-restraint and genuine feelings of remorse by age five or six? While modeling, reinforcement, and punishment are important agents of socialization, many theorists believe that the process of internalizing standards and controls is the result of the more complicated process of identification.

Identification is the process by which the values, attitudes, and behavior of others are incorporated into the self. It is the primary means by which children develop sex roles and a conscience. The identification process requires the learning of not just one specific act but of a whole complex of attitudes and behaviors.

There are three characteristics of identification as a learning process: It occurs very early in life, it seems to happen spontaneously, and it involves behaviors and attitudes that become basic parts of the individual's personality (Sears, Rau, and Alpert 1965). As in modeling, children may identify with a parent or teacher, with older siblings, or with other models. At first glance, identification and modeling seem to be much the same, but many theorists believe that identification is an infinitely more complicated process. A two-year-old boy may want to be just like Daddy, and therefore mimic all Daddy's actions. But by the time he is five, these simple imitated attitudes and patterns of behavior become deeply imbedded in his personality as a well-established set of expectations and behaviors. In other words, certain attitudes and behavior patterns have become internalized and are now a part of the child's personality.

Freud believed that during the **phallic stage** (ages three to five) the genital area becomes the focus of sensual pleasure, even though the child's instincts are not yet directed toward reproduction. He introduced the concept of identification to explain his observations of children's anxiety about their strong but unconscious sexual attraction to the parent of the opposite sex. Freud referred to these as the **Oedipus complex** in boys and the **Electra complex** in girls, names taken from two powerful Greek tragedies. Freud believed that preschool children renounce this fantasy in exchange for positive ties with both parents. Psychologists today have a broader view of the impetus behind the processes of identification, although they recognize that children do become more like the parent of the same sex. This process involves internalizing the attitudes, values, and even the manner-isms of the parent. Thus, children learn sex roles as well as behavior that will make them feel more powerful and lovable and less anxious.

Parents almost invariably provide the models for identification, but the degree of identification varies significantly. Among the key factors involved in heightened identification are an early and strong dependency in the child, extensive parental nurturance, and demanding parental stand-ards of conduct (Sears, Rau, and Alpert 1965). Finally, both the clear presentation of models and the labeling of appropriate behavior (telling Johnny that Mommy is stepping on the match so that it will not start a forest fire) increase the child's ability to select the behaviors that he wants to imitate.

Sex-role identity

Orthodox Jewish males thank God daily that they were not born female. Most of the world's other religions also believe women to be inferior in many ways. What does being female imply? We have already described the genetic determinants of sexual identity. Some people suggest that this genetic programming is what causes dramatic differences in the psycho-logical development of men and women. Others contend that the sexes are different because they are treated differently by parents, teachers, and other cultural models.

We know that male babies are generally slightly larger than female babies and have heavier musculature (Hutt 1972). However, male children tend to lag behind females in learning to walk, in cutting teeth, and in bone development. Girls also begin to talk earlier than boys (Schachter et al. 1978). We will be noting statistical differences between the sexes at each stage of the life cycle, up to and including old age. Although sex-role identity is established early in childhood and is perhaps our most funda-mental self-concept, it is not a rigid personality trait and remains a devel-opmental issue well into adulthood.

Many sexual differences appear to be genetic; however, statistics on biological differences are often based on measurements of differences be-tween the average male and the average female. In reality, many differences that exist within the male group itself are far greater than the differences between the average male and the average female.

Equally important are the large number of developmental measures in which males and females do *not* differ. These include sociability, sug-gestibility, self-esteem, motivation to achieve, analytic ability, and response to auditory and visual stimuli (Maccoby and Jacklin 1974). The evidence suggests that cultural differences cause some of the discrepancies between males and females. However, much more research is needed in this im-portant area of human development.

Sex-role stereotypes are fixed ideas of what is appropriate behavior for males and females. These stereotypes establish distinct and mutually exclusive categories without allowance for individual variations. Most American parents expect their male children to be forceful, self-confident, realistic, assertive, and emotionally reserved. They expect their female children to be gentle, dependent, high-strung, talkative, frivolous, and impractical (Bem 1975; Williams, Bennet, and Best 1975). Children are put under strong social pressure to conform to these sex-role stereotypes, regardless of individual variations in their natural dispositions.

A study by Fagot (1978) demonstrates how parents keep their children's sex-role behavior "on track." Parents consistently react more favorably when their toddlers engage in behavior deemed appropriate to their sex and react negatively when their children engage in cross-sex behavior. For example, boys will be allowed to explore objects and learn about the physical world, but girls will be discouraged from similar activities. Girls, on the other hand, may be encouraged to ask for help or to help adults with tasks. These simple situations are precursors of more complex behavior, and it is not surprising that sex differences are fairly well set by middle childhood.

In preschool children, sex-role learning is intensified by the processes of conscious imitation and unconscious identification with the same-sex model. Children at this age play house and imitate such roles as Superman, doctor, and nurse with stereotypical gestures, language, and actions. Commercial toys also reinforce the sex roles that children are expected to imitate. For example, a Lotto game intended for three- and four-year-olds pictures over fifteen careers for boys, including truck driver, fireman, doctor, lawyer, and businessman. For girls, only three careers are pictured— nurse, secretary, and ballet dancer. Many of the toys marketed for preschool children and shown on TV commercials are even more blatantly stereotypical.

We have seen how rigid concepts of "masculine" and "feminine" behavior pervade our society. However, a recent shift in thinking has come about as more people realize that beneficial "male" and "female" traits can easily exist in the same person. Both men and women are capable of being ambitious, affectionate, self-reliant, assertive, and sensitive. This blend of personality traits goes into the makeup of what is called an **androgynous personality** (Bem, Martyna, and Watson 1976).

The studies in cultural anthropology of Margaret Mead (1939) paved the way for recent views about the cultural determinants of sex roles. She described one society in which cooperative, nonaggressive behavior was so highly valued that it was prescribed for both males and females. She also described several other cultural variations, pointing out that while every culture has in some way differentiated between the roles of men and women, they have not necessarily made these distinctions in terms of contrasting attributes of personality. She concludes that "the temperaments which we regard as native to one sex might instead be mere variations of human temperament, to which the members of either or both sexes may, with more or less success in the case of different individuals, be educated to approximate" (Mead 1939, Introduction).

The emphasis on individual differences is of paramount importance to social workers, who often see the tragic results of attempts to force a particularly unsuitable pattern of behavior on a child or adult in the mistaken belief that his or her sexual identity is dependent on acquiring a particular taste or ability. Social workers should help people to erase these stereotypes so that as many individuals as possible can live comfortably with themselves without a loss of self-esteem caused by failure to meet overly rigid stereotypes.

CASE ILLUSTRATIONS

Bilingual Child Care

Ms. Sanchez is a consultant on day care for preschool children; she works for a city-wide agency. Her job is to strengthen local day-care networks in the community and to provide them with resource material. She also serves as a legislative advocate of day care. She is particularly aware that ethnic and cultural differences influence the type of care that people want and will use, and she takes pains to work closely with parents as well as the community representatives on her local advisory committees. One of her goals is to develop local leadership.

Ms. Sanchez meets regularly with a Spanish-speaking community organization composed of small neighborhood and church groups. They want to sponsor a bilingual child-care program that will enable families and children to continue their language, cultural, and religious traditions. They also want the preschool program to teach the skills that their children will need to perform well when they enter the local public school. The community has volunteers willing to provide special programs in the arts (painting, music, and dramatics). Ms. Sanchez is providing them with material showing how these activities can be used to promote certain cognitive skills. In the past, some children have had difficulty in making the transition from home to school and suffered from a loss of self-esteem when they were suddenly evaluated as inadequate by others. Now the preschool staff will keep in touch with the children as they enter school and serve as a liaison to help their new teachers to understand them better.

The day-care program will be set up in a local church. Several neighborhood women have been hired as teachers and will work under the supervision of a bilingual director trained in preschool education. Many of the families who will use the center already know each other because they have lived in the neighborhood for many years. However, there are also some newcomers who will benefit from the supports that this network of relationships offers. One unresolved question centers on whether the program should be opened to other ethnic groups. It has been tentatively decided that other children will be welcomed if they are willing to participate in a bilingual program.

Ms. Sanchez expects to help this group become self-supporting, with the assistance of a fund-raising committee of local businesspeople, some of whom will become long-term sponsors of the program. The local priest has been active in getting the project rolling, and his support has been crucial to the success of the program.

Nicholas

Nicholas, a three-and-a-half-year-old, has been seen weekly at a child guidance clinic for the past two months. His mother is concerned about his negative, defiant behavior. One day he took a dime and walked half a mile alone in order to buy a candy that his mother had refused to get for him. His nursery school has also reported difficulty in dealing with his aggressive behavior, and the director has said that Nicholas cannot continue there unless his behavior improves. This threat of removal creates an added strain on the family, since the mother works and would have to make alternative child-care arrangements.

The clinic is part of the community mental health center. The staff is interdisciplinary. Headed by a psychiatrist, it includes psychologists who test children and conduct some therapy, as well as social workers who function as therapists. This particular center is psychoanalytically oriented.

Nicholas is a bright child whose early physical, cognitive, and language development fall within normal range. Had there been problems in these areas, he would have been referred elsewhere for special help. The social history reveals that his difficult behavior at the nursery school began immediately after his favorite teacher left to take another job. His mother is divorced and has a steady relationship with a man who appears to like Nicholas.

In therapy sessions Nicholas usually talks while he plays with the toys. His play centers around themes of "danger" and "good and bad." He insists on always being the person "in charge," and demonstrates the same problems of constantly testing authority that he shows at home and at school. He chooses toys such as guns, trucks, and sheriffs' badges that allow him to express aggressive feelings. However, he always seems anxious about leaving the therapy session and must be reassured that he can return. Several times he had difficulty leaving his mother to come to the playroom and cried about "Mommy losing me." He checked often to see if she was still in the waiting room. He is definitely not as tough and independent as he pretends to be.

At the last case conference the entire staff met to discuss Nicholas's progress. They suggested that he may act inappropriately because he is unsure about having his dependency needs adequately met; therefore, he seeks safety by trying to assert his own control over everyone and everything. It was decided that the treatment plan will include continued play therapy because Nicholas reveals his feelings through play and the therapist is able to use the situation to help him accept appropriate limits. The worker will also help his mother to encourage Nicholas to be more dependent on her, even if this means tolerating temporary regression to babyish behaviors.

Work with the mother will focus on her handling of daily routines such as eating, dressing, and sleeping. The staff notes that her handling of Nicholas is in sharp contrast to the way she relates to her daughter, who is a compliant seven-year-old. They wonder if she doesn't subtly encourage Nicholas to be overly aggressive. He is never held and comforted when he is irritable, nor is he calmed by use of humor or judicious ignoring of his provocative behavior. Since these are techniques that the mother used in raising her daughter, the therapist will probably explore with the mother some of the reasons why she responds in such a different way to her son.

SUMMARY

The physical-motor activities of preschoolers (age two to five) lay the groundwork for future cognitive and social-emotional development. The developmental sequences of such activities may be either continuous or discontinuous. Some sequences involve functional subordination.

Although there is debate about whether children should be trained in skills at this age or allowed to develop them in the natural course of exploration, self-paced learning schedules seem to be the most appropriate educational approach. The process of learning a new activity involves a state of readiness, intrinsic or extrinsic motivation, an opportunity for practice, focusing of attention on the activity, and feedback from the activity itself.

Some theorists believe that children must work out certain abstract relationships on a physical-motor level before they can deal with them intellectually. Others question this, citing the intellectual attainments of disabled children.

Four major theories have been proposed to explain the acquisition of language: imitation, reinforcement, innate language structure, and cognitive development. Most children have a basic understanding of language structure by approximately four and a half years of age. In the process of acquiring a language, they also learn cultural values and social roles. Social class and ethnic background influence language patterns; however, differences in language structure do not indicate that one or another style should be considered superior. Instead, the emphasis in social work today is on enabling minority children to be bicultural, keeping the advantages of both cultures.

While the evidence on the relationship between language and thought is equivocal, language does seem to facilitate many kinds of learning. However, the absence of certain linguistic structures does not necessarily prevent intellectual growth.

Piaget, a major cognitive theorist, has developed a framework for viewing the development of human intelligence. He sees children as able to process information from the environment by means of ready-made action patterns called *schemes*. Children build their intelligence by elaborating on and modifying these schemes through a process of adaptation. The cognitive theorists believe that humans do not simply respond to stimuli; they also give a structure and meaning to phenomena.

Preschool children are at the cognitive stage that Piaget calls *preoperational*. They develop the ability for symbolic representation and can use words and images to represent events or experiences. Preoperational children are not yet logical thinkers, and they cannot understand the principle of conservation of matter. Their cognitive processes are concrete, irreversible, and egocentric. They have difficulty with classification, time sequences, and spatial relationships. However, they can function somewhat better when given more simplified tasks than those used in Piaget's experiments.

Studies of memory tasks show that preschoolers' recognition memories are good but their recall memories are poorer than those of older children and adults. Knowledge about cognitive development can give social workers a better understanding of children's thought processes and the meaning of different levels of play. An understanding of cognitive development is also an important element in administering and evaluating educational and psychological testing.

Between the ages of two and six, children develop an elaborate set of mechanisms for expressing their positive and negative feelings in a socially acceptable way. Child-rearing practices teach children patterns of behavior through the use of rewards and punishments, modeling, and identification. Parents play a major role in helping preschoolers to achieve a balance between satisfying their own impulses and meeting demands for socialization.

In a heterogeneous society such as ours, socialization is a lifelong process and includes many influences other than those of the family. Social workers are particularly aware of the anxieties that may result from extremes in child-rearing practices, and they learn to differentiate between transitory and more deep-seated fears and anxieties. Anna Freud viewed the following defense mechanisms as strategies for reducing inner tensions: withdrawal, denial, repression, regression, reaction formation, projection, rationalization, displacement, and identification. Although these mechanisms serve a useful function, in their extreme forms they can isolate the child from reality and cause disturbances later in life.

All children have both aggressive and altruistic feelings. Aggression is believed to be related to factors other than frustration, such as the system of rewards and punishments and role modeling. Models for both prosocial and aggressive behavior are most effective when they are perceived by the child as powerful, nurturing, and with characteristics similar to the child's.

Television is another important factor in socialization. There is considerable debate about programming that portrays violence casually. Some children lack adequate real-life models to counteract the influence of television, and some suffer in other ways from an excessive amount of time spent in passive viewing.

Preschoolers must learn to express dependency needs while also exercising the degree of autonomy considered appropriate by their culture. Children who have had strong and satisfying dependency relationships often become the most self-reliant adults. Special attention should be given to the autonomy needs of disabled children.

Internalization is one of the basic processes of socialization. The individual incorporates society's standards and values and begins to develop both a sexual identity and a sense of conscience through this process of identification with the parent. Identification is heightened when there is a strong early dependency relationship, extensive parental nurturance and a clear labeling of appropriate behavior. Recently, there has been a shift in thinking about sex roles and a growing acceptance of the fact that "male" and "female" traits can easily exist in the same person.

SUGGESTED READINGS

Billingsley, A. *Black Families in White America*. Englewood Cliffs, N.J.: Prentice-Hall, 1968. A valuable presentation of the black family's strengths, with an emphasis on extended-family resources available to single-parent households.

Chukovsky, K. *From Two to Five*. Berkeley: University of California Press, 1963. In a light, anecdotal style, Chukovsky demonstrates the rather phenomenal development in thought and personality during the preschool years.

Fraiberg, S. *The Magic Years*. New York: Scribner's, 1959. A sensitive description of the evolving personality, with a blend of psychoanalytic theory and practical observation.

Ginott, H.H. *Between Parent and Child*. New York: Macmillan, 1965. Ginott presents practical suggestions and examples for increasing honest communication and understanding between parents and children.

Sinclair, C.B. *Movement of the Young Child: Ages 2 to 6*. Columbus, Ohio: Chas. E. Merrill, 1973. A description of physical-motor development, with helpful suggestions for grading activities that assist in this process.

Weikart, D.P., Rogers, L., & Adcock, C. *The Cognitively Oriented Curriculum*. Urbana: University of Illinois Press, 1970. This demonstration project translates Piaget's cognitive theories into practical suggestions for the preschool curriculum.

chapter five

MIDDLE CHILDHOOD
transition to school

outline

PHYSICAL CHALLENGES

Recreational opportunities

The school environment

COGNITIVE MATURATION

Changing abilities

Social cognition

Reality and fantasy

Moral judgments

SCHOOL EXPECTATIONS

Diversity of expectations

Goals and functions of education

Intelligence tests

Labeling and special classes

LEARNING THEORY AND BEHAVIOR MODIFICATION

Learning theory

Classical conditioning

Operant conditioning

Behavior modification

PARENTING

Dimensions of parenting

Patterns of negotiation

Current problems

PEER INFLUENCES ON PERSONALITY

Siblings

Friendship pairs

AT SIX YEARS, Esther's first bus ride to school makes her feel both proud and a little afraid. The bus seats are so high that her feet dangle and the fifth graders seem as tall as giants. She wonders about school—new rules to follow, new adults to obey, and new children to play with. And, since this is the first time she will be away from home for a major part of the day, she also wonders what her family will be doing and saying without her.

At eight years, Frank is playing marbles with his friends when his father comes home from work. The boys are intent on their game and Frank's father remembers how he used to play with his friends in the same way. He asks if he can play. As soon as he joins the game, the nature of the interaction changes. The boys lose their ease in communicating through shared verbal expressions and gestures. Frank's father feels like an intruder.

Most societies impose schooling when children are between five and seven years old. There seems to be general agreement that this is the best time for children to take on new responsibilities. In the Middle Ages, this transition was dramatically marked; after the age of six or seven, children were dressed like miniature adults and were expected to act accordingly. Modern societies take a more gradual approach, easing children into a series of age-graded tasks and responsibilities.

For most children, middle childhood is a time for settling down and building on patterns that have already been set. It is a period for learning new skills and refining old ones. Children focus on testing themselves, on meeting their own challenges as well as those imposed by the environment. Those who are successful in these tasks will probably grow to be even more capable and self-assured; those who are unsuccessful are more likely to develop a feeling of inferiority or a weaker sense of self.

Freudian theorists refer to this developmental phase as **latency,** a period of relative calm before the upheavals of adolescence. Erikson refers to middle childhood as the period of *industry.* The word captures the spirit of this period, because it is derived from the Latin word meaning "to build." In the first two sections of this chapter, we shall describe some of the ways in which children build both physical and intellectual competencies. Then we shall look at the organization of schools and the ways in which tests are used to classify children; we shall also consider some current approaches to learning disabilities. There will be an introduction to learning theory and techniques of behavior modification, with examples of their use in the schools and other institutions. Finally, we shall look at the influence of parenting styles and of peer-group relationships on personality development during this period from six through eleven years of age.

PHYSICAL CHALLENGES

Observers of school-age children are bound to be impressed by their high activity level. What function does all this activity serve? Far from being a waste of time, children's games and sports provide them with the opportunity to develop strength, coordination, and flexibility. Children can be seen testing their balance by riding bicycles through homemade obstacle courses on streets and in playgrounds. They improve their hand-to-eye coordination, strength, and speed in games of handball, stickball, and basketball. They increase their flexibility and agility by climbing trees or attempting feats of daring.

There is no rapid spurt of physical growth during middle childhood as there was in the preschool years and will be again in adolescence. Most bodily changes that occur in this period are gradual and continuous. Similarly, it is a time of gradually developing motor skills.

While many children are able to develop physical skills with little adult assistance, other children may need help because they are less resourceful, lack available playmates, or are experiencing other difficulties such as being less dexterous than their peers.

Recreational opportunities

Some of the best recreational programs resemble those that children construct on their own initiative. Groups of children have often transformed rubble-strewn empty lots into creative play areas and turned abandoned sheds into cherished club houses.

The "adventure playground" is a public area geared to the abilities and needs of the elementary school child. It may contain lumber and tools, and a carpenter may even be on hand to teach the children to build clubhouses or animal shelters. It may have piles of earth and sand that can be moved and shaped and streams of running water and gardens where children can plant their own vegetables and flowers (Stone 1970). Of course, some children still learn these things in everyday work and play tasks with their families. When parents are unable to share meaningful work experiences with children, it is important that we find substitutes that will allow for skill development and the concomitant growth of self-esteem.

The play environment affects not only children's physical-motor skills but also their personal relationships. For example, Little League games offer a competitive environment where high levels of skill are especially valued. In contrast, swimming pools offer activities at many skill levels and do not necessarily require social interaction and cooperation.

Adventure playgrounds are one example of the environmental settings that communities can provide to foster physical-motor skills and desirable social attitudes. When competent staff are provided to supervise these activities, the advantages increase. Staff can help foster cooperative activity and help children learn to mediate disputes. They can help to develop individual leadership abilities, they may set a climate of acceptance for children who are disabled in some way, and they may offer a special caring relationship to children who seek to identify with an adult other than their parent.

Social workers specializing in work with groups have traditionally played a major role in developmentally focused recreation programs in settlement houses and community centers in low-income neighborhoods, programs that were usually sponsored by private social agencies. Since the spread of public recreational programs, social group workers are involved primarily with children in special settings such as residential institutions or programs for the mentally or physically disabled.

We turn now to a description of the place where school-age children spend approximately half of their waking hours—the school itself.

The school environment

We generally think of school in terms of its effect on children's intellectual growth and interpersonal relationships. We often forget that schools must also provide for children's physical needs and skills.

The effect of the standard organization of American schools was aptly summarized by one first-grader after her first day at school. When asked how she liked her new school, she replied, "Oh, you mean sit-down school?" Her first reaction was not to the new classmates or teacher, but to the idea of being confined to a desk and chair for a whole day.

Six-year-old children are still learning with their bodies and still integrating physical and intellectual knowledge—a fact that schools can recognize and use to advantage. Children might, for example, learn math by measuring a corridor first in yards and feet, and then in terms of their own footsteps or the time it takes them to walk its length. In this way their knowledge can become both abstract and concrete. A school's design can limit or stimulate physical-motor development as well as cognitive development. There is no evidence that children learn best by sitting in straight-backed chairs for long periods of time or that lying on the floor necessarily interferes with learning.

COGNITIVE MATURATION

It is probably no historical accident that so many cultures have chosen the ages between five and seven for beginning the systematic socialization of their young. Children of this age have an increased learning potential because many of their cognitive, language, and perceptual-motor skills are maturing and becoming increasingly amenable to coordination.

Cognitive theorists find a qualitative change in thinking processes during this period. In Piagetian theory, for example, these years mark the transition from preoperational to concrete operational thought; thought becomes less intuitive and more logical. Children also begin to use language to direct thought and action, a process called **verbal mediation.**

Changing abilities

At this stage, children begin to perform the mental tasks necessary for a more realistic, logical perception of the physical world. Piaget calls these mental tasks *concrete operations* because they give children a better grasp of concepts and relationships in the physical world. This emerging ability lays the foundation for systematic reasoning.

One example of the difference between preoperational and concrete operational thought processes is that school-age children are able to make *logical inferences* (Flavell 1977). Recall Piaget's conservation of matter experiment (Chapter 4); in another example of this principle, preoperational children consistently judge that a tall, narrow glass holds more liquid than a short, wide glass, although both quantities of liquid are seen to be identical at the start. In contrast, children in the concrete operational stage know that both containers hold the same amount of liquid because they can make logical inferences. They can remember how the liquid appeared in the first container, they can think about how its shape changed as it was poured into the new glass, and they can think about the process of transformation as reversible.

Finally, children in the concrete operational stage know that differences between similar objects can be quantified, or measured. In Piaget's matchstick problem, children are shown a zigzag row of six matchsticks and a straight row of five matchsticks (see Figure 5–1). When asked which row is longer, very young children center only on the distance between the end points of the rows and thus pick the "longer" row with five match-

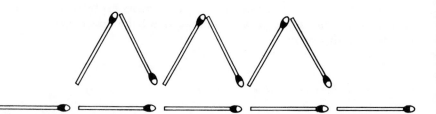

FIGURE 5–1 Piaget's Matchstick Problem   Concrete operational children realize that the six matchsticks in the zigzag top row will make a longer line than the five matchsticks in the straight bottom row. Younger children will say that the bottom row is the longest because they tend to center only on the end points of the two lines and not on what lies between them (Piaget 1970; Flavell 1977).

sticks. Concrete operational children, however, can take more factors into account and therefore choose the row with six matchsticks.

As we saw in Chapter 3, infants' cognitive development benefits from stimulation that is presented slightly ahead of their developmental level. Some researchers think that appropriate training can hasten the development of preoperational children. Piaget opposes these views, believing that cognitive development is an organic process that cannot be hurried and is resistant to outside tampering. Smedslund (1961) had some success in training preoperational children to use the principle of conservation in experiments with differently shaped beakers of water. However, the children were not able to apply this principle to other problems. His techniques were noticeably more effective with five- and six-year-olds who were nearly ready to make such discoveries for themselves. Teachers may wonder if they should spend much effort trying to accelerate children's development by a year or so instead of waiting and allowing the children to enjoy making the discoveries by themselves.

Bruner and his colleagues believe that training is most effective when children have reached a state of readiness, an **optimal period** that occurs just before they make the transition to the next stage (Bruner, Olver, and Greenfield 1966). They recommend several specific methods for promoting cognitive growth. One method is to use concrete objects in teaching five- to seven-year-olds. Children discover similarities, differences, and relationships by combining and comparing concrete objects such as blocks, rods, or seeds.

Another evidence of cognitive change is the increased stability of the IQ score. There is only a minimal correlation between a person's IQ at age two and what it will be in adulthood, but there is a highly significant correlation between an individual's test scores at age seven and as an adult (Bayley 1949). This may be related to the structure of the intelligence tests, or it may reflect real changes that make the seven-year-old's thought processes more consistent with adult intelligence.

At about six years, most children suddenly begin to use verbal mediation and to form rules and hypotheses to solve problems. Younger children approach each instance of choice separately, without forming general hypotheses for guidance. Although not all psychologists would agree, many believe that older children increasingly interpose language between thought and action, using verbal labels to direct themselves toward crucial aspects of a problem they wish to solve (Kendler 1963; Mowbray and Luria 1973).

A number of significant developments occur in the memory abilities of concrete operational children. Recall from Chapter 4 that preoperational children do well in recognition tasks but poorly in recall tasks. The ability to recall lists of items improves significantly between the ages of five and seven (Flavell 1977), when children begin to consciously memorize information. They look at the material to be remembered, begin to organize it into general categories, and then employ such strategies as rehearsal. Rehearsal consists of repeating to oneself the items to be memorized. This deliberate use of strategies makes the older child's recall more effective and efficient (Yendovitskaya 1971).

Social cognition

As we have seen, children are continually learning to deal with the complex social world both inside and outside the family. As they develop into middle childhood and adolescence, their social cognition becomes a more and more important determinant of their behavior. They must learn about concepts of friendship and justice, social rules and manners, sex-role conventions, obedience to authority, and moral laws.

One way in which they learn appropriate behaviors and attitudes is through socialization processes such as reward and punishment and the observation and imitation of a model. Another way children learn about the social world is through psychodynamic processes. Children are made to feel anxious in certain situations, and they learn to reduce this anxiety by using a number of defense mechanisms (see Chapter 4). A third way in which children learn about the social world is through processes called **social cognition**.

Just as children's understanding of the physical world changes as they mature, so does their thinking and understanding about the social world. This composite of thought processes and understandings about the social world is called social cognition. As children develop into middle childhood and adolescence, their social cognition becomes a more and more important determinant of their behavior. These social understandings have been studied by cognitive theorists who believe that all knowledge exists in organized systems. In their view, children's understanding of the social world does not consist of unrelated pieces of information but develops in a predictable sequence. Thus, the level of children's understanding of the social world will vary at different stages of their development.

As we saw in Chapter 4, egocentrism limits preschool children's understanding of the world. It is still a limiting factor for children of seven and older, even though they have reached "the age of reason" and are able to perform some logical operations. Many children seven or eight years old are still not fully aware that other persons may have points of view different from their own.

Therefore, an initial component of social knowledge is *social inference,* the act of making assumptions about what another person is feeling, thinking, and intending (Forbes 1978; Flavell 1977; Schantz 1975). By about age eight, children realize that their own thoughts may be the subject of another's thinking. And by age ten, they are able to infer what another person is thinking. A child might think, "Johnny is angry with me, and he also knows that I know that he is angry." This process of inferences continues to develop into late adolescence (Schantz 1975).

A second component of social knowledge is children's understanding of *social relationships*. They gradually accumulate information and understanding about fairness and loyalty, respect for authority, and concepts of legality and justice. A third aspect of social knowledge is *social regulations*, such as social rules and conventions. Many of these conventions are learned first by rote or imitation. Later, they become more flexible, depending on the child's ability to make correct social inferences and understand social relationships.

Psychologists find that social cognition develops in a predictable sequence and most researchers agree that children move beyond the extremes of egocentrism by age six or seven. Beyond that, they disagree as to the number of developmental stages and whether these stages are universal or dependent on the particular social system in which the child lives. The study of social cognition is still too new for very definitive conclusions.

Reality and fantasy

As we mentioned earlier, very young children cannot distinguish between behavior that is genuine and behavior that disguises true feelings. If the mother acts happy, the young child assumes that she is happy. In other words, children believe that appearances tell the whole story and that the pictures of witches, dragons, and cartoon characters represent real creatures.

Therefore, one of the complex tasks that children face is learning to tell the difference between the real and the unreal. They can only broadly differentiate between the two at the time that they enter school. As one young viewer of "Sesame Street" remarked, "I know that Big Bird isn't real. That's just a costume. There's just a plain bird inside" (Morison and Gardner 1978).

Some people believe that once children gain the ability to make this distinction, fantasy serves no useful function. However, this theory discounts the fact that Snoopy is popular because this "dumb dog" actually embodies a host of human virtues; he is wise, loyal, and independent. Bruno Bettelheim, in his book *The Uses of Enchantment* (1976) suggests that fairy tales have a special value in helping children to work out some of their existential predicaments and unconscious inner conflicts.

In the last chapter we described some of the intense emotions that children experience as they grow up: They are deeply jealous of friends and siblings, they are aware of their own good and bad feelings, they fear the dark and have terrifying nightmares, and they often have an overwhelming sense of powerlessness in a world controlled by giantlike adults.

Bettelheim suggests that hearing about fictional wicked stepmothers may help children come to terms with real mothers who sometimes act as if they were momentarily transformed from warm, loving figures to humiliating, punishing witches. Or, by identifying with the relatively powerless Jack in "Jack in the Beanstalk," children learn that powerful giants can sometimes be outwitted. This may enable them to gradually feel less powerless against adult authority and therefore less resentful against their parents.

From their experience with the emotional conflicts described in fairy tales, children may also come to a deeper understanding of the problems of good and evil. This intuitive familiarity with moral concepts may be necessary for the development of moral judgment. We shall turn now to a consideration of moral judgment, or the sense of right and wrong.

Moral judgments

Moral judgment is an area of social knowledge that involves social inferences, understanding of social relationships, and knowledge of social regulations. Mature moral judgment involves more than the rote learning of social rules and conventions; it also includes learning behavior that is kind or cruel, generous or selfish.

There is considerable debate as to how children acquire morality. Social learning theorists believe that it is the result of modeling and an appropriate system of rewards and punishments. Psychodynamic psychologists believe that it develops as a defense against anxiety over the loss of love and approval. Cognitive theorists believe that morality, like intellectual development, develops in progressive, age-related stages. We shall now take a closer look at the cognitive approach to moral development; later in this chapter we shall describe learning theory in greater detail.

Piaget defined morality as "an individual's respect for the rules of social order and his sense of justice." Justice is viewed as "a concern for reciprocity and equality among individuals" (Hoffman 1970). Piaget's stages represent the growth of a *sense of morality* rather than the existence of moral behavior as such. According to Piaget (1965), children's moral sense develops from the interaction between their developing thought structures and their gradually widening social experience. At the *moral realism* stage, children think that all rules should be obeyed because they are real and infallible. They do not consider rules to be abstract principles and judge the morality of an act by its consequences rather than by weighing the actor's intentions. For example, a young child will think that the girl who accidentally breaks twelve dishes is much guiltier than one who breaks only two dishes while trying to steal a cookie. However, when children reach the stage of *moral relativism* they realize that rules are created and agreed upon by individuals and that these rules can be changed as the need arises.

Lawrence Kohlberg (1963) has taken these two stages and extended them to six "developmental types of value-orientation" (see Table 5–1). Kohlberg discusses judgment rather than behaviors, but his model also includes examples of the kinds of behaviors that would be typical of each stage.

Baumrind (1978) has attacked Kohlberg's model on the grounds that it ignores important cultural differences in the determination of what is moral. Moral development, in Baumrind's view, may depend less upon cognitive processes than upon the values instilled during the process of socialization. Power and Reimer (1978) find other weaknesses in Kohlberg's model. They point out that there is a great difference between *thinking about* moral behavior and *acting* morally. Moral decisions are often made at times of crisis, when our behavior may not reflect our beliefs. Kohlberg reviewed his findings (1978) and acknowledged these distinctions. He decided that behavior should be studied partly in terms of people's internalized attitudes and partly in terms of the moral norms of the group to which they belong. He also concluded that his sixth stage of moral development may not apply to people in all cultures.

Table 5–1   Kohlberg's Stages of Moral Development

Stage		Illustrative Behavior
Level I. Premoral		
Stage 1.	Punishment and obedience orientation	Obeys rules in order to avoid punishment
Stage 2.	Naïve instrumental hedonism	Conforms to obtain rewards, to have favors returned
Level II. Morality of conventional role-conformity		
Stage 3.	"Good-boy" morality of maintaining good relations, approval of others	Conforms to avoid disapproval, dislike by others
Stage 4.	Authority-maintaining morality	Conforms to avoid censure by legitimate authorities, with resultant guilt
Level III. Morality of self-accepted moral principles		
Stage 5.	Morality of contract, of individual rights, and of democratically accepted law	Conforms to maintain the respect of the impartial spectator judging in terms of community welfare
Stage 6.	Morality of individual principles of conscience	Conforms to avoid self-condemnation

Source: Kohlberg, L. Adapted from "Classification of Moral Judgment into Levels and Stages of Development" in Sizer *Religion and Public Education*, p. 171. Copyright 1967 Houghton Mifflin Company.

While the cognitive approach to moral development seems to explain some of the processes that occur in middle childhood, it is well to keep in mind that social cognition is a relatively new field, and there are many important questions still to be answered.

Moral development extends into adolescence and young adulthood, and many individuals never reach the highest stages. Kohlberg emphasizes the significance of developing intellectual maturity and the capacity for reasoning. We shall consider these further in the chapter on adolescence.

SCHOOL EXPECTATIONS

This section represents a change in the pattern followed in earlier chapters, which focused almost entirely on the development of the child within the family setting. However, somewhere between the ages of five to seven most children have entered some kind of school and spend a significant part of their day interacting with a new and complex social institution.

In order to understand the school's impact on child development, it is necessary to understand some aspects of the school as a social system. First we shall discuss the diversity of school expectations regarding achievement and norms for behavior, indicating the function of the school social worker in helping to mediate the differences between child, school, family, and community. Then we shall describe some differences in educational philosophies about why and how children should be educated. Finally we shall present a summary of the controversy over the uses of testing and labeling of children in the schools, issues of particular concern to social workers.

Diversity of expectations

There are certain immediate adaptations that children must make when they enter school. If they have not been in day care or preschool, this may be the first time that they are separated from their parents or caregivers for a significant length of time. Suddenly they must learn to rely on unfamiliar adults to insure their safety and satisfy their needs. They must also start to become independent and learn to do certain things for themselves. No longer can a little boy sit down and yell, "Put on my boots!" It is time for him to put on his own boots. Even with a favorable student-teacher ratio, children must compete for adult attention and assistance. They must also learn to cooperate with others and develop a general understanding of school rules and regulations.

Formal schools usually spend a great deal of teaching time reviewing and enforcing certain codes of behavior. Children must listen when the teacher speaks, line up for recess, obtain permission to go to the bathroom, raise a hand before speaking, and so forth. It is not unusual for a teacher to spend more time and energy keeping order than teaching subject matter.

The nature of school expectations varies markedly with differences in cultural values and educational philosophy. In the "open classroom" children are encouraged to sit or lie down anywhere in the room, select their own work for the day, and interact informally with the teacher and other children. However, rules exist even in the open classroom, although they may be unspoken. Children in these classes are expected to act independently, to ask questions, and to avoid disturbing others.

Regardless of the type of school, children usually face a tremendous gap between what is acceptable at home and the new classroom demands (Kozol 1970; Holt 1964; Read 1971). This is the age at which children have just begun to internalize the rights and wrongs of family life, and suddenly they are expected to adapt to a whole new set of procedures. Children's success in school is related to the width of the gap in expectations and how great an effort school personnel make to help children with the transition. Successful adaptation also depends on other factors of individual development, such as how well the child has previously coped with dependency, autonomy, relationship to authority, the need to control aggression, and the promptings of conscience.

Children must face another change when they enter school. They now must spend a major part of their day with a fixed number of agemates, many of whom will be unfamiliar to them. We shall discuss the impact of peer relationships on personality development in the last section of this chapter. However, at this point it is important to note that most schools expect children to be able to function as a member of a rather large group for a significant part of the day. Children also are expected to interact successfully with peers during the rather loosely supervised recess and lunch periods. Children are sometimes referred to school social workers because they are unable to manage these unstructured recreational periods without getting into fights, even though their classroom behavior may be acceptable. Sometimes the school environment offers other options for such children, and sometimes they are expected to either adapt or be limited to a minimal school day.

Many children also experience difficulties when their level of skill development varies significantly from the normative, age-graded structure of most schools. In fact, very few five- to seven-year-olds are able to meet the teacher's expectations in every respect. A child's reactions to the demands of schooling result from the complex interplay of all personal resources: intellectual, perceptual, physical, social, and emotional. For example, reading readiness in the first grade requires sufficient perceptual maturity to identify letters and follow a left-to-right sequence, enough fine motor coordination to write letters, and the ability to discriminate among phonetic sounds. If children learn to read in a large classroom, they must be able to sit attentively for long periods of time, follow directions, and inhibit irrelevant impulses. Those who are immature or unfamiliar with these expectations may not learn to read.

We have already learned that there is no such thing as an "average" child and that individual children often have uneven levels of skill development. A very bright six-year-old may read at the third-grade level but be unable to participate in a reading group because of emotional immaturity and disruptive behavior. Or, as frequently happens, a teacher may have a poor view of a pupil's general ability when the problem is merely underdeveloped motor coordination and poor writing ability. It is hard for teachers to make demands that are appropriate to each child's maturational level, particularly in schools where all lessons are taught in fixed-age groups.

Teachers must take also into account the extent to which the child is familiar with the English language. Some children who speak another language learn English rapidly, but others experience a repeated sense of frustration and failure that may result in general school failure. Some schools have tried to correct this situation by offering bilingual classes as needed, enabling children to have successful experiences in a familiar language while they are learning a new one. When there is no program of bilingual education, social workers may help to locate or develop community resources to assist teachers and children with the transition to a new language and culture.

The social worker often serves as the liaison between school and parent. In such cases the worker must become as familiar as possible with the requirements of the home culture and points of similarity and difference from the school culture. For example, an Indian child's withdrawal and noninvolvement in classroom discussions may elicit negative adult responses. The teacher may not understand the meaning of behavior such as refusal to make eye contact or failure to respond to well-intentioned inquiries. The social worker, in such cases, should be in a position to explain about tribal traditions of avoiding activities at which failure is likely or that might be done better by others. Indian children generally deal with unpleasant situations by withdrawal rather than action and confrontation, and they may consider "normal" teacher-pupil interactions to be overly intrusive rather than helpful (Blanchard 1979).

Goals and functions of education

Americans today do not agree about the purposes of education. We shall examine a few prominent educational philosophies and show how they lead to the setting of different goals and expectations for students. However, it is important to remember that students may be more deeply affected by the qualities of the teaching staff than by the educational philosophy of the school. Adults can often recall the impact of a sympathetic teacher who bolstered their self-esteem or an enthusiastic teacher who motivated a lifelong interest in a particular subject. School social workers are particularly aware of the crucial effect of a proper fit between student and teacher, and part of their function is to offer assistance in instances of a poor fit.

Both educators and parents hold diverse views about the purposes of education. Schools vary widely within a single district, and views about teaching may vary considerably even within a single school. Recently parents have demanded more power to determine educational policies, some seeking more alternative-style education and others more emphasis on "basics."

Some "back to basics" proponents merely want to insure that their children will obtain a certain degree of proficiency in reading, writing, and arithmetic by the time they graduate. Others are traditionalists, believing that the primary task of the school is to transmit the accumulated knowledge, skills, and values of past generations. They value a formal educational approach that uses carefully structured lessons to inculcate a particular set of skills.

Other theorists disagree with this approach because it focuses too heavily on teaching facts and principles by rote memorization and ignores the student's ability to apply new learning, analyze concepts, synthesize ideas, and evaluate the merit of information (Bloom and Krathwohl 1956). They emphasize the need to teach children *how* to think rather than *what* to think, because we live in a world where "facts" may change every day.

The educational literature of the late 1960s was replete with biting criticism of our schools. The reformers believe that students become frustrated and unhappy because they are taught subjects in which they have no interest and which are unrelated to their needs (Holt 1964; Kohl 1968; Kozol 1970). The solutions they proposed have been incorporated in a number of experimental *alternative schools* in both the public and private sectors. While proponents of innovative, informal teaching methods claim that they are also successful in teaching basic skills, most voluntary alternative schools have attracted mostly white, middle-class families, and few minorities.

Still other educators have drawn upon the work of such diverse theorists as Piaget, John Dewey (1916), and Susan Isaacs (1930) to develop the concept of *open education*. This approach encourages children's natural developmental progress by presenting them with skills and concepts at the point of natural readiness. Children are given learning materials appropriate to each stage of growth so that all areas of the mind are stimulated, and learning is regarded as an active rather than a passive process.

The emphasis on individualized planning for the needs of the whole child leads open-classroom advocates to resist external demands for all children to attain a fixed degree of skill within a strictly limited time frame.

Instead, they favor heterogeneous grouping and individual learning contracts based on the child's particular interests, cognitive level, learning style, life experience, and physical and emotional maturity. The teacher aims at maximizing the child's strengths rather than focusing on tests that determine areas of deficit.

This educational reform movement, based on humanistic values and psychological theories about readiness for learning, continues to attract both teachers and social workers. However, it has been countered in recent years by renewed pressures for greater accountability in measuring the acquisition of specific skills. The latter view is particularly popular among those who believe that a good education is the key element in achieving a higher income and occupational status later in life.

The debate as to how best to attain greater equality in student achievement has intensified in recent years, partly as a result of the Supreme Court's 1954 decision declaring that state laws requiring or permitting racially segregated schools violated the equal protection clause of the Fourteenth Amendment of the United States Constitution (Clark 1963). Current research indicates that school behavior and achievement levels are affected by social class as well as racial segregation (Wilson 1963). Working-class students are more likely than middle-class students to reflect peer values rather than adult expectations for achievement. The evidence thus far is that while black students' scores on standardized tests rise somewhat if they attend desegregated elementary schools, these benefits are dependent on the new schools' having a greater proportion of middle-class students (Wilson 1967).

Christopher Jencks (1972) and his associates have made significant new contributions to the research in this area. They conclude that individual differences in achievement test scores are largely dependent upon a combination of genetic and environmental factors. They also estimate that the elimination of racial and socioeconomic segregation in the schools will reduce the gap in test scores between black and white children and rich and poor children by about 10 to 20 percent. However, their most controversial finding is that the widespread individual inequality of income distribution in America cannot be explained by either cognitive ability, family background, or achievement test scores. They believe that greater economic equality must come from direct intervention in the workings of the economy and not from changes in the school system. Following this logic, we should expect schools to provide a more satisfying learning environment and a desegregated setting because of their intrinsic values and not because of any future "pay-off" they may provide.

There is continued debate over the role of the schools in lessening the achievement gap among individuals and groups, and professionals differ as to the best course of action. Meanwhile, social workers will continue to focus on individuals whose needs are not adequately met by the present system, helping them to make better use of the schools and helping the schools to be more responsive to individual differences.

We have already considered many of the factors that contribute to effective learning ability: adequate motivation, the presence of meaningful role models, rewards for good performance, and adequate physical, cognitive, and emotional development. We have also discussed how different educational philosophies lead to different expectations of children. We turn now to a brief review of the debate over testing, labeling, and the use of separate classes for children with special needs.

Intelligence tests

During the 1940s and 1950s, there was a great increase in the testing of American schoolchildren; they were given IQ tests, achievement tests, psychological tests, and career-aptitude tests. School files were filled with scores of varying degrees of accuracy and significance. The rationale for testing is that schools must assess student abilities in order to plan efficient educational programs. However, teachers and administrators have been criticized for using test scores to deny some children access to educational opportunities. It has also been charged that only rarely is constructive use made of the information provided by tests. It is not unusual for a child to enter the first grade with reading-test scores at the third-grade level only to be assigned to a class in reading readiness for six months because he or she "has not had that subject yet."

In the 1960s, many parents and educators reacted against what they considered to be the abuse of diagnostic tests. Today these tests are still used, but teachers have become more aware of the dangers of misinterpreting the results. School social workers often interpret tests results to parents, and therefore need to obtain an understanding of the specific tests used in their school districts; this text will provide only a general introduction to some of the issues posed by testing procedures.

Probably no issue is more controversial in the field of developmental psychology than that of intelligence testing. The academic debate has become public, largely because the test scores have been used to provide or deny educational and social opportunities. IQ scores can affect the extent and quality of children's education, limit the kinds of jobs they obtain as adults, and leave a lasting imprint on their self-images. Intelligence tests have been administered more widely and taken more seriously in the United States than in any other country.

Why do we hold "intelligence" in such high regard? What are we actually trying to measure? In this section we shall explore the concept of intelligence, beginning with some early attempts to measure and define it.

The first comprehensive intelligence test was designed for the French government in the late nineteenth century by Alfred Binet, a psychologist.

He was commissioned to devise a method of identifying those children who would not profit from a public education. His theoretical definition of intelligence includes such complex intellectual processes as judgment, reasoning, memory, and comprehension; he measured these capabilities with test items for problem solving, word definition, and analysis. Since he believed that intelligence grows and changes throughout life, questions had to be carefully arranged to reflect this growth. A good test item differentiated between older and younger children. If more than half of the five-year-olds were able to define the word *ball* and fewer than half of the four-year-olds were able to do so, then the definition of *ball* was included on the test for five-year-olds (Binet and Simon 1905; 1916). This empirical basis for selecting and ordering items was a landmark in the testing field. The resulting test score was called a *mental age*.

In 1916 an American version of this test was introduced by Terman at Stanford University. The American test was the first to present the concept of an **intelligence quotient,** or IQ—a ratio between an individual's mental and chronological age. It was computed by dividing the mental age (MA) by the chronological age (CA) and multiplying the result by 100.

The quality that is actually measured on the Stanford-Binet or other intelligence test constitutes the operational definition of intelligence. These tests generally measure a number of abilities: the Wechsler Intelligence Scale for Children (WISC) provides separate scores for subtests on information, comprehension, mathematics, vocabulary, digit span, picture arrangement, and other abilities. Subtest scores are helpful because the same individual may have a good memory and be adept at perceiving similarities, for example, but do poorly on tasks involving spatial relationships.

Arthur Jensen (1969) is a controversial researcher who believes that genetic inheritance accounts for 80 percent of the abilities measured on IQ tests, and experience accounts for only 20 percent of the score. His theories have been strongly criticized for underrating the impact of training and environment (Kagan 1969; Williams 1974). One of the most important studies of the relationship between race and IQ (Klineberg 1935) shows a clear relationship between IQ and length of residence in a northern city as compared to a southern rural background. This relationship existed for both blacks and whites at a time when northern cities provided a relatively enriched environment for the education of children.

However, the most telling argument against the indiscriminate use of standardized intelligence tests is the uncertainty about the meaning of the measurements. It would be fairest to say that the tests measure some combination of innate ability, acquired learning, motivation at the time of the test, and environmental factors (Lyman 1971). We also know that many test questions refer to subjects that are less familiar to children from low-income families than to others. In order to measure intelligence, as opposed to learning, one must assume equal familiarity with the content of the

MIDDLE CHILDHOOD 159

questions. Children's life experiences vary greatly, and considerable evidence attests to cultural bias that strongly favors middle-class whites (Kagan 1973).

In spite of these problems, tests and informal assessments can be useful aids in diagnostic-prescriptive teaching. Such teaching assumes that educators will be better able to prescribe appropriate learning tasks if they know precisely what an individual child is able to do. Instead of labeling a child as "mildly retarded" or a "slow learner," teachers measure a child's specific knowledge, skills, and abilities at a given moment. Sometimes a diagnosis is based on classroom observation or a diagnostic lesson; sometimes it is based on criterion-referenced tests (Glaser 1963). **Criterion-referenced tests** focus on the skills a child must acquire, in contrast to the more familiar **norm-referenced tests** that compare one person with others in the same age group.

Social workers often work with children who have been labeled mentally retarded, developmentally disabled, emotionally disturbed, or hyperactive. The passage of the *Education for All Handicapped Children Act* in 1975 gave a legislative mandate to extend public education to all children and to provide it in the least restrictive setting possible. This law required a yearly individual educational plan for each handicapped child, to be drawn up in consultation with the parent or guardian. In addition to the necessary special education, which can be offered in a range of settings from a regular classroom to a hospital, handicapped children must also receive whatever related services are needed, including such support services as speech therapy and social work. Unfortunately, as with much other social legislation, implementation has been hampered by lack of fiscal appropriations for expanded services.

Labeling and special classes

Along with increased emphasis on the rights of the handicapped has come increased opposition to the use of standardized tests for placing children in special classes. The antilabeling movement holds that classifying children as "deficient" is injurious to their self-esteem and that special classes are ineffective and limit the development of individual potential. While recognizing that specialized small-group instruction may offer some benefits, opponents of labeling feel that the losses often offset the gains (Cromwell et al. 1975).

Critics of labeling claim that a label often becomes a self-fulfilling prophecy and that even children who are erroneously placed in a class for slow learners will in fact suffer from retardation as a result of the placement. The Rosenthal and Jacobson study (1968), often cited as evidence of the prejudicial effects of labeling on teachers' expectations about individual potential, has been criticized for its faulty methodology (Fleming and Anttonen 1971), and at present we have no clear experimental proof of the extent to which teachers' expectations are dependent on the labels given to children. However, we do know that labels affect children's perceptions of themselves, whether they are "class clown," "underachiever," or "bright."

A more theoretical criticism of labeling is that it makes a pretense of diagnosis when it is merely an identification of symptoms. For example, one can usually predict that a child who does poorly on an IQ test is likely to have problems succeeding in school without special help. However, the tester often cannot explain the cause of the problem or the extent to which cognitive, emotional, or physical difficulties are responsible for the observed symptoms (Mercer 1975).

Although social workers generally try to consider as many factors as possible in making a diagnosis as to probable causes of learning difficulties, the options for special education are apt to be limited. Funds for individualized or small-group instruction are usually only available for children who have been tested and placed in an eligible category. Social workers must examine the possible options in each case, and a major consideration will be the quality of the available teachers. A skilled teacher in a class for the retarded may bolster a child's self-image more than a punitive teacher in the regular classroom. Other considerations are the teacher's ability to handle a wide range of abilities within a single classroom and the climate of the peer group within the classroom. There is some evidence that special classes provide a more supportive setting for children's social adjustment in spite of the negative effects of labeling (Blanton 1975). This issue has become highly politicized, especially since a disproportionate number of minority children have been placed in special classes.

Similar problems in the use of testing arise in the diagnosis of children who have learning disabilities. The term **learning disability** refers to the difficulties encountered by a broad category of children who often share few characteristics other than the label itself. In today's school system, children are usually described as learning disabled when they are of normal intelligence and have no obvious physical or sensory defect (such as poor vision, deafness, cerebral palsy) that can account for the learning difficulties that they experience in the classroom. Although experts may differ, symptoms often include an unexplained discrepancy between the child's general ability and his specific performance in tasks such as reading. Educators then look for causal factors such as deficits in visual and auditory perception, sensory integration, and memory. They may also look for problems in selective attention, such as overattention to irrelevant details or an inability to concentrate.

Cruickshank (1977) considers the central factors to be neurologically based deficits in perceptual processing, such as an inability to recognize and integrate written and spoken forms of words and attach the proper meaning to them. Ross (1977), however, focuses on selective attention, which he believes to be a learned response amenable to corrective training. A third point of view has a medical bias; Wender (1971) describes a set of organically based learning disabilities that arise from minor brain damage. He lists the following as difficulties attributable to **minimal brain dysfunction:** impaired motor coordination, problems with cognitive functions, and disturbed interpersonal relationships.

These symptoms may be caused by a variety of factors, and professionals cannot accurately separate symptoms caused by minimal brain damage, prenatal or birth difficulties, poor nutrition, anxiety resulting from family problems, and inadequate early cognitive stimulation. Because there are so many unanswered questions about learning disabilities, professionals should approach these problems with a healthy amount of skepticism and carefully evaluate each case.

One behavioral syndrome frequently discussed in the literature on learning disabilities is **hyperactivity.** The term is often used to characterize children who have a high activity level, impaired coordination, and difficulties in learning because of a short attention span. The issue of hyperactivity has generated considerable controversy, with no agreement so far about its definition, causes, or treatment.

There are presently three major approaches to the treatment of learning disabilities: *drug treatment, educational management,* and *psychotherapy.*

The history of *drug treatment* for hyperactivity provides an interesting example of the accidental ways in which we sometimes learn about the causes of certain behavior patterns. In the 1970s, it was discovered that some children with symptoms of hyperactivity responded to a drug called Ritalin, a stimulant in the amphetamine family. These children, who had been unaffected by tranquilizers or depressants, actually calmed down in response to a drug that ordinarily speeds up activity. This unusual response gave rise to the hypothesis that hyperactive children actually require more than the average amount of environmental stimulation in order to function effectively and that their high activity level represents their attempt to seek this stimulation. Ritalin thus calmed them by lessening their need to seek external stimulation. Although this drug has seemed effective with some children, the precise mechanisms by which it operates remain open to further research. Meanwhile, its widespread overuse has raised serious questions about the ethics of recommending drugs for children on the basis of a sketchy diagnosis and inadequate information about possible side effects. Aside from any long-term physiological effects, there are psychological consequences when children believe that a pill causes them to "be good."

The second kind of treatment is *educational management,* both at home and at school. In most cases, this involves an attempt to restructure a child's environment by simplifying it, reducing distractions, making expectations more explicit, and generally reducing confusion. The specific educational plan depends on the theoretical position of the therapist or educator. Although no single educational plan seems to work with all children, most programs have some record of success.

Although schools recommend *psychotherapy* less often than various types of symptom management, social workers believe that the symptoms of hyperactivity are often attributable to emotional problems and look to possible therapeutic intervention in the family system. However, they must first rule out the possibility of an organically based disability and so will usually recommend a complete medical examination, including a neurological evaluation. For example, a child's reading difficulty might prove to be caused by an undetected auditory or visual deficit.

Coles (1978) suggests that the battery of tests designed to diagnose learning disabilities represents an attempt to find a biological explanation for problems that may actually have social and emotional causes. Sapir and Wilson (1978) are less skeptical about the usefulness of tests but stress the importance of skillful interpretation to insure that social and emotional difficulties are not mistaken for neurological problems.

On another level, one might even question whether some of the symptoms we have described really do represent disabilities. They may instead represent minor variations in the normal pattern or a simple developmental lag. For example, many four-year-olds would appear hyperactive if placed in a first-grade classroom, and many boys appear hyperactive only because the school setting does not allow them enough physical activity. Boys are classified as learning disabled four times as often as girls and as hyperactive nine times as often. Schools also are often unresponsive to the special needs of the creative child who does not conform readily to the rules and restrictions of the classroom. Perhaps we should revise our concept of "normal" to include a wider range of variations in behavior.

There are still many unanswered and controversial questions in the area of learning disabilities. Further research may also help us to gain a better understanding of the processes of normal child development. Meanwhile, both educators and social workers have shown increasing interest in techniques of behavior management that offer the possibility of controlling and changing behavioral symptoms without needing to specify the underlying causes. In this next section we shall briefly outline some learning theories and techniques of behavior modification.

LEARNING THEORY AND BEHAVIOR MODIFICATION

All theories of human development must consider the nature of the changes that occur over a life span. Does development occur in sharp distinct stages? Is the infant qualitatively different in some significant ways from the adolescent? Or is development continuous, with many more similarities than differences in the nature of the individual?

The learning theorist sees development as a gradual accumulation of knowledge, skills, memories, and competencies. Learning is not confined to formal and informal education; it also includes the acquisition of moral views, mannerisms such as gestures or stuttering, and characteristic forms of emotional response. There are no sharp stages, and the learning process is the same for all age groups. This learning theory model of continuous, cumulative development contrasts sharply with the cognitive theories that we have examined in Chapter 4.

Learning theory

Psychologists in the learning theory tradition are interested in developing a science of human behavior. Their thinking has been stimulated by the work of John B. Watson, the originator of the behaviorist school of psychology. They build their assumptions from an empirical base, collecting their facts by observing what actually happens in nature or in the laboratory, much as biologists or physicists do. Researchers carefully define and control the stimuli present in the experimental setting and then observe and record their subjects' behavioral responses to these stimuli. They attempt to use objective methods, generally through an inductive approach. This means that researchers do not start from a "grand design" as some theorists do, but rather construct their theory bit by bit, moving from simple laboratory experiments to more complex applications to human behavior. Many learning theorists have concentrated on descriptions of the **stimulus–response** connection, which they believe to be the basic unit of human behavior. This approach has led to an amazing amount of research and resulted in some very interesting discoveries.

Followers of this theoretical perspective assume that human nature is neither bad nor good. People simply react and respond to environmental influences and are shaped by the rather automatic process of associating stimulus (behavior) and response (consequences). Some psychologists say that this explanation is too simplistic and that it views people as machines stimulated by an input and responding with an output. Learning theorists have given little attention to internal mental processes because these cannot be observed and objectively described. They also believe that people are unable to give accurate reports of their subjective thoughts and feelings.

The learning theory model has also been described as *deterministic.* Everything in the individual's behavior, including values, attitudes, and emotional responses, is believed to be determined by either the past or present environment. Therefore, such concepts as blame, respect, and dignity are considered irrelevant. People are products of their past learning history and deserve neither credit nor blame for their actions (Skinner 1971).

Classical conditioning

In their search for the "basic laws of learning," researchers have divided human behavior into two general categories. People either act in *automatic* response to a stimulus (the pupils of our eyes contract in bright light; a newborn infant sucks the finger placed in his mouth), or they act *voluntarily* (a child kicks a ball; a woman paints a picture). The terms **respondent** and **operant** are used to describe these two types of behavior. Sometimes the same behavior may be both respondent and operant. Putting a finger into a newborn's mouth elicits a sucking reaction, but slightly older infants have some voluntary control over their sucking behavior. They can start and stop it, slow it down, or speed it up. Similarly, a knee jerk can be both respondent and operant. The patient's leg will respond with an automatic kicking reflex to the doctor's knee tap, but the patient can also decide to kick the leg voluntarily at any other time.

The process of conditioning varies according to whether it is applied to respondent or operant behavior. **Classical conditioning** takes a respondent behavior and brings it under the control of a previously neutral stimulus. The experiments of Ivan Pavlov (1928) are among the most famous examples. Pavlov, noting that dogs salivate when offered food, began to strike a tuning fork each time that he offered food to a dog. He repeatedly paired the neutral stimulus (the fork) with the food; soon the sound of the fork alone was enough to make the dog salivate, even when no food was within sight or smell. The fork had become a conditioned stimulus, eliciting the same response from the dog as the food had produced.

A famous experiment on the classical conditioning of an emotional reaction was performed by Watson and Raynor (1920). An eleven-month-old infant named Albert showed no fear when first confronted by a white rat. Then the experimenters made unpleasant clanging noises every time they showed the rat to Albert, causing him to cry and crawl away. It did not take many associations of the unpleasant noise with the previously neutral stimulus of the rat for Albert to respond with anxiety and fear to the rat alone. Reportedly, Albert was soon frightened by other white furry objects, even a Santa Claus beard. This spread of response to related stimuli is called *stimulus generalization.*

We can see clear parallels to this dramatic example of conditioning in children's everyday lives. Doctors' white uniforms may arouse fear in children because they are associated with unpleasant experiences such as painful injections. Positive emotional reactions can also be conditioned by associating pleasurable reactions with previously neutral stimuli. For example, an old song may bring back memories of an enjoyable high school dance.

Common phobias such as fear of flying or of snakes have been treated by the use of counterconditioning techniques such as relaxation training, or **desensitization.** These techniques teach clients a new relaxation response to replace the old anxiety response. Rather than focusing on analyzing the reasons for the anxiety, clients are conditioned to learn a new competing response, while the old response is extinguished by withdrawing reinforcement.

Operant conditioning

The foregoing examples of classical conditioning and respondent behavior do not apply to operant behavior. In operant conditioning, behavior cannot be elicited automatically; however, once the behavior occurs, it can be strengthened by rewards or reinforcements. For example, suppose that a child is learning to put on socks. At first the parent puts one sock nearly all the way on, then praises or rewards the child for completing the task. The next day the parent does less of the work, and before long the child can complete the entire task. Skinner used this concept to develop teaching machines that structure learning tasks in small incremental steps (Skinner 1968). The desired behavior or answer is reinforced at each step by positive feedback from the machine and by the appearance of a new problem to solve. Eventually, the student succeeds in mastering a fairly complex problem.

These concepts are most useful when dealing with specific behaviors rather than large areas of human development. Recent investigations indicate that some more complex mental structures and processes may be innate (Horton and Turnage 1976). Specifically, conditioning and modeling do not totally account for the processes of language acquisition, which seem to depend largely on innate mechanisms for processing information (Spiker 1977).

Cognitive theorists such as Bruner and Piaget (see Chapter 4) find that the learning theorists' emphasis on repeated practice and positive reinforcement ignores many of the complexities of human thought and understanding. They believe that people are *motivated* to solve problems and that one cannot reduce beliefs, attitudes, and values to a simple stimulus–response behavior (Bruner 1971). These psychologists believe that cognitive theories about language and thought pick up where learning theories end.

Other students of human behavior believe that learning theories do not adequately recognize positive emotions and behaviors such as love, joy, and creativity. Indeed, purists such as Watson advised psychologists to ignore such mental concepts because they cannot be scientifically observed. However, *social learning theorists* are currently attempting to explain more complex social patterns. They do not limit themselves to seemingly automatic conditioning, and they give conscious thought a larger role in guiding behavior. For example, Albert Bandura (1977), a leading social learning theorist, points out that people usually notice the consequences of their own actions and those of others. They also notice which actions succeed or fail and adjust their thoughts and behavior accordingly.

Behavior modification

Programs of **behavior modification** use principles of operant conditioning to shape human behaviors for therapeutic goals. Such programs may use praise, attention, tokens, or other positive reinforcers to achieve the desired behavior. For example, a counselor working in a residence for disturbed children may decide to pay attention only to those requests that are made in a reasonable manner and to ignore demands that are accompanied by temper outbursts. Or children in the residence may have to earn certain privileges by accumulating poker chips or tokens that are given as rewards for desired and agreed upon behavioral objectives. The behaviors that earn chips can be expanded and changed, as can the prizes or privileges that the chips will "buy." Undesired behavior is generally ignored, lest the child feel rewarded for behaving badly by receiving adult attention.

A host of techniques have been developed for increasing the effective use of both positive and negative reinforcers to influence behavior (Gardner 1974). Some techniques have gained more widespread support among social workers than others, but their impact has been widely felt in schools and in residential institutions for children and adults with special behavioral problems. Part of the attraction of these techniques is that they can be used to modify behavior, and the degree of change can be measured without the worker having to diagnose the underlying causes of the problem. However, some social workers believe that this approach has only limited usefulness unless it is balanced by providing stable, nurturing relationships with caring adults. There has also been a concern with possible abuses of this technology in settings where clients have little opportunity to control their own lives.

There may be need for a broader perspective, even when behavioral techniques focus on a limited objective. For example, a social worker may be able to change a specific behavior only by removing all rewards and satisfactions until the desired behavior is achieved. In such a case, we must carefully question whether the results are worth the cost to the client. We may eliminate hair-pulling behavior by pulling the child's own hair each time the child does it to another child, but we must look also at whether or not the child has become a social isolate in order to avoid the unpleasant consequences of previous patterns of interaction (Gardner 1974).

In summary, behavior therapy, like other interventive techniques, requires a worker who has humanistic values, empathy for others, and the skill to diagnose the individual's total situation before selecting appropriate objectives and appropriate methods for achieving them.

PARENTING

Neither cognitive nor learning theories adequately cover all the factors that influence the social and emotional development of children. Therefore, we shall return to some of the concepts of socialization and relationships introduced in Chapters 3 and 4. Social workers, educators, and other professionals seeking to influence the behavior of school-age children recognize the influence of parents and peers in the lives of children. In these next two sections we shall examine some ways in which these systems of relationships operate and some of the problems of parenting in our society.

Dimensions of parenting

One way to examine parenting is to observe the particular behaviors and attitudes of parents and the resulting behavior of their children. Parents' behaviors affect children's behavior in at least three ways. First, parents serve as models. Second, most parents have specific expectations about the way they want their children to behave. Finally, parents control the rewards and the punishments that their children receive. We have already discussed the ways in which child-rearing practices affect socialization and personality development. Now we shall examine broad patterns of parenting styles in order to see their differential effects.

Becker (1964) has developed an excellent model for examining parenting. In his view, every parent's attitudes and actions can be placed along continua involving three key dimensions: restrictiveness–permissiveness; warmth–hostility; and anxious emotional involvement–calm detachment. By describing dimensions of parental behavior instead of specific acts, Becker's model encompasses not only examples of extreme behavior but also the actions of the great majority of parents whose behavior is not excessive.

Becker's model demonstrates the ways in which these three dimensions interact. For example, if we were to look only at their specific acts and attitudes, we might assume that two highly permissive mothers were raising their children in the same manner. This assumption might be far from the truth when the other two dimensions are considered. Both mothers may be highly permissive and both may deal calmly with their children, but one could be a warm person and the other coldly hostile—a critical difference in parenting styles. Becker describes the calm, permissive, warm parent as *democratic* and the calm, permissive, but hostile parent as *neglectful*.

Several research studies have given us important insights into the effects of restrictiveness and permissiveness. The principal finding has been that restrictive parents tend to have dependent, submissive, and compliant children. And in at least a few studies, permissiveness (defined as a noncontrolling, undemanding atmosphere) was related to active, outgoing, creative, and constructively aggressive behavior in children (Baldwin 1949; Watson 1957). However, permissiveness does not necessarily produce independent children; the way in which permissiveness interacts with the other parenting dimensions is of crucial importance. When permissiveness is accompanied by high hostility (the neglectful parent), it is more likely to result in noncompliance and aggressiveness. Many studies of young delinquents show that their home environments have had exactly this combination of permissiveness and hostility (Bandura and Walters 1959; Healy and Bronner 1926; McCord, McCord, and Zola 1959).

Some extensive research done by Baumrind (1972) examines parenting styles in a different way. She describes three distinct patterns of parental authority and emphasizes the differences between the authoritative parent and the authoritarian parent. *Authoritative parents,* who combine high controls with warmth, receptivity, and encouragement of independence, produced the most self-reliant, self-controlled, and self-satisfied children. *Authoritarian parents,* who are warm but more detached and controlling, had more withdrawn and distrustful children who were less assertive and independent. *Permissive parents,* who combine high warmth with few controls or demands, had the least self-reliant, explorative, and self-controlled children.

These models are useful to the social worker, pointing out the importance of examining many dimensions of parenting when assessing the strengths and weaknesses of a particular family constellation. It is also important to remember the findings in Chapter 3 about reciprocity and mutuality, and to consider the particular fit between the needs of each child and the parenting styles of the caregiving adults. Social workers involved in family counseling and in placing children in foster homes and adoptive families must continually make assessments about the appropriateness of a particular combination of parenting styles in any given situation.

Patterns of negotiation

Maccoby (1979) has expanded Becker's model of parenting styles to include not only the effects of parental behavior on children but the effects of children's behavior on parents. Although parents are better able than children to exercise control, it is the interaction between parent and child that affects the climate of family life. Maccoby has studied how controls are exercised in the course of these interactions. In some families parents are highly controlling; in families at the other extreme the children are in control. Ideally, neither side dominates all the time, a situation that is true of both Becker's democratic family and Baumrind's authoritative family. Maccoby indicates that this balance comes about when parents and children engage in a long-term dialogue that results in an agreement on *shared goals.* When decisions are reached without much struggle for control, there is a harmonious atmosphere. Families that enjoy this balance have a fairly high degree of intimacy, and their interaction is stable and mutually rewarding.

Families that are unable to achieve shared goals must negotiate every-thing—from what to have for supper to where to go on vacation. This can be an adaptive style, in spite of the necessity for constant communication among family members. However, if either the parents or the children dominate the situation to an extent that makes negotiation impossible, the family atmosphere will be unstable. Preadolescent children may learn to avoid excessive domination by staying away from home as much as possible. And when aggressive children can control overly permissive parents, the parents may also seek to avoid the situation by, for example, coming home late from work. Either of these two extremes weakens the socialization process during middle childhood and adolescence and makes the transition from family life to independence more difficult for children.

Current problems

Many recent articles and books have described the American family as in a state of transition, decline, or liberation, depending on the biases of the author. We shall point out just a few recent changes affecting parent-child relationships and note some ways in which social workers are helping people deal with the resultant stresses.

Urie Bronfenbrenner (1970) characterizes modern America as a so-ciety that is increasingly segregated by age, with children spending greater amounts of time apart from their parents. He cites evidence that children fill this gap with increased peer contact, although this is not altogether satisfying to them. Christopher Lasch (1977) thinks that this leads to a lessened capacity of parents to transmit adult values and the growing dom-inance of the values of the peer culture.

The erosion of parental authority is related to many factors, among them the family's loss of many of its traditional functions. The family is no longer the unit of economic production, and it is unlikely to include one parent who works and another exclusively involved in child rearing. This situation, in which child rearing is delegated to outside institutions, is less evident among some traditional ethnic communities in the United States. However, even in these communities, traditional ties are being weakened by the processes of assimilation and acculturation. Parental controls are further undermined when children learn to speak English while language barriers limit their parents' ability to deal with the outside world. Social workers in such communities should take care that they do not institute programs that hasten the breaking of traditional authority before there is an alternative to take its place. School values may also undercut family standards that are considered old-fashioned and authoritarian from the American perspective.

The rising incidence of divorce is also causing strain in parenting. An intensive five-year study of the children of divorce (Wallerstein and Kelly 1980) documents divorced parents' increased difficulty enforcing limits with their children. In part, this is caused by their fear of increasing their children's anger toward them, fear of being rejected in favor of the other parent, guilt, and lowered self-esteem. Children suffer as a result of this parental vulnerability, but they also take advantage of it.

Even intact marriages do not always result in consistent parenting, and family counseling sessions often deal with battles over how to "discipline" the children. Sometimes parents make contradictory demands; they may themselves be aggressive but at the same time punish their children's aggression. Or they may want their children to be emotionally strong and self-confident but are unaware that they really are encouraging excessively dependent behavior. Needless to say, the children receiving these conflicting messages cannot possibly please their parents, and this causes both parties considerable distress.

There has been an increased effort by professionals to work with groups of parents to teach more effective parenting skills. Some programs use volunteers and members of the community under professional supervision. Some programs are aimed at the community at large, and some serve special groups, such as single mothers, abusive parents, foster parents, and parents of the handicapped. The methods used vary and often include role playing, supportive counseling, peer counseling, role modeling, and setting tasks to modify specific behavior. Almost all attempt to involve parents in solving of their own problems (Gordon 1979; Ryan 1979).

Social workers also help parents through counseling based on psychoanalytic theories. This counseling is usually offered during a period of crisis, and the worker's purpose is to help parents understand what is happening and to help the entire family cope more adaptively with the effects of the crisis (Parad 1977).

PEER INFLUENCES ON PERSONALITY

It may seem a bit dramatic to say that children have their own culture, but in many ways it is true. The world of the preadolescent child at play often has its own customs, language, rules, games, and even its distinctive beliefs and values. What is this "culture of childhood" and what role do **peer groups** play in a child's development? Although childhood rituals may mirror adult social conventions, in some ways they are even more strict and demanding. Rhymes must be repeated in an exact fashion, and rigid rules dictate the one right way to play each game. Peer relationships may also be ritualized, and children make lifelong pledges to each other in private clubs. These prescribed games and customs of childhood are often adopted without adult direction, and some of them have been transmitted from older to younger children for countless generations in almost every culture (Opie and Opie 1959).

How and why do elements of this culture remain so constant? Children seem to derive a sense of competence and mastery from learning how to do things correctly. The rituals and rules of middle childhood provide a period of practice in learning the detailed behavior expected of adults. Remember Erikson's formulation of this period as one of industry versus inferiority? A sense of security is gained from being able to master the familiar framework of rules that govern the play situation.

These rules and standards may help children to contain intense emotions and to defuse intense peer relationships by playing make-believe roles of victim and conqueror. They may also teach complex social concepts such as justice, power, or chivalry.

Siblings

Brothers and sisters offer the first and probably the closest peer relationships. Sibling relationships differ from parent-child interactions and siblings are strongly influenced by experiences of living with other children who are unequally competent and powerful.

What influence do brothers and sisters have on each other? And how does birth order affect each child's personality? It is difficult to generalize about sibling status without knowing whether the siblings are male or female, how many there are, and the age differences between them. Many variables must be considered before any conclusions can be reached. In general, the first child tends to be more achievement-oriented than any other siblings and the most likely to achieve eminence in academic and scientific areas and in business (Sutton-Smith 1958). The same is true for the only child, whose status is similar to that of the firstborn. Second and third children seem to have greater social skills and are better able to get along outside the family. A possible explanation for this finding is that firstborns are only children for several months or years, during which their parents give them exclusive attention and provide sophisticated behavior models. Parents also tend to be more anxious about the firstborn's achievements. As a result of this attention they are more likely to speak at an early age (Koch 1956), and are also apt to be adult-oriented and anxious about achievement (McArthur 1956).

However, these effects are greatly modified by factors other than birth order, including the number of children in the family, the sex of the siblings, their closeness in years, and their individual personalities (Sutton-Smith and Rosenberg 1970).

Friendship pairs

Sibling relationships may be the most intense peer influences affecting a child, but they are not the only important ones. Middle childhood is a time of movement away from the family, and friendships outside the home are increasingly important in modeling children's attitudes and behavior.

Friendship patterns shift during childhood from the egocentric pattern typical of the preschool years (Piaget 1965) to the close relationships with a best friend typical of early middle childhood. These friendship ties are very strong, but they also tend to be erratic and short-lived. It is not until late childhood and adolescence that stable friendships are formed.

We have already discussed social cognition and the ability to understand social relationships. Now let us consider some of the functions of friendship in middle childhood. First, friendship pairs satisfy certain needs in each child. One friend may be dominant and the other submissive, or the relationship may be egalitarian. Generally, stable and satisfying friendships allow some flexibility in roles so that each child may fulfill a broad range of needs.

A friendship pair may also act as a vehicle of self-expression. Children often choose friends whose personalities are quite different from their own. An outgoing, expressive child may choose a reserved or conscientious close friend. Such a relationship allows a maximum amount of self-expression to each member of the pair with a minimum amount of competition between them (Hartup 1970a; 1970b). Of course, long-lasting friendship pairs usually share many values, attitudes, and expectations about themselves and others.

The friendship pair serves other functions; it intensifies exclusivity, and it provides a practice ground for competition both within the group and beyond it (Hartup 1970a). These functions are also served by larger peer groups; there is an extensive research literature on the formation of children's peer groups and their structures and functions.

Peer groups

Social work has a long tradition in settings serving children in groups; these include residential institutions, camps, community centers, and youth-serving agencies such as the YMCA. Professional practice in these settings has drawn heavily upon the large body of sociological research on small groups and group processes (Hartford 1971).

Our concern here is not with aggregations of children who happen to be in the same place, such as the audience at a puppet show. Social workers are more interested in the **primary group** that is relatively stable over a period of time and has common norms governing behavior. The interaction within such groups leads to some degree of status differentiation, and there is at least a temporary division into leaders and followers.

Charles Horton Cooley (1909) was the first to conceptualize and define the primary group as a small, informal group in which the members interact closely with each other and which provides a sense of solidarity and mutual identification. He recognized that such groups provide socialization experiences and are major factors in the development of the child's values and standards of behavior. Along with the family, friendship groups and play groups frequently function as primary groups.

Although many forms of peer groups are important throughout middle childhood, the forms of group organization and their importance to the child shift during this six-year span. Peer groups in early middle childhood are relatively informal. They are usually formed spontaneously, and they have a rapid turnover in membership and few operating rules.

The group takes on a more intense meaning for its members when they reach age ten or twelve. Group structure solidifies, and conformity becomes extremely important. Children may show an almost compulsive reverence for rules and norms in all areas of social interaction, and peer pressures assume a coercive influence on the child. Formal groups may have special membership requirements, meetings, and initiation rites. Some groups, such as the Scouts, are organized by adults around specific interests; other groups may be formed by adults whose major goals are improved socialization. Formal and informal groups of children of this age are often composed of one sex, as interests and activities reflect sex-role differences. There have been recent legal challenges to the institutionalized exclusion of either sex from formal single-sex athletic activities such as Little League baseball teams. However, psychologists disagree as to the boundaries between normal developmental processes and culturally imposed role distinctions regarding appropriate activities for boys and girls.

Group processes

Groups are constantly being formed as children gather together in school, in camps, in recreation agencies, and in neighborhoods. Some will remain simply interest groups, with minimal interaction among members, but many will develop role differentiation, common values, and standards. We shall look at just a few of the studies of small group formation and how groups affect individual thought and behavior.

Muzafer Sherif set out to test three hypotheses about groups. He theorized, first, that a hierarchy of roles will form when a group of children share both physical closeness and a common goal; second, that the individual members of the group will discover shared values and attitudes; and third, that if two groups are brought together in competitive circumstances, intergroup hostility will develop (Sherif and Sherif 1953; Sherif et al. 1961).

Sherif's first experiment, the "Red Rover" study, took place in three phases (Sherif and Sherif 1953). In phase one, ten-year-old boys with similar backgrounds were sent to summer camp. They lived in two separate groups for a few days, and budding friendships were observed. Then the experimenters divided the groups along new lines, splitting up the friends. Stage two of the study lasted for five days, and during this period new in-group friendships formed. A clear hierarchy of leadership also emerged very quickly. Group names were chosen and group rules and norms were developed.

In stage three, the two groups took part in competitive games that were rigged so that one group was almost never allowed to win. At first, the competition resulted in animosity and even open hostility between the groups, with powerful feelings of in-group exclusivity. Later, the frustrated group's structure fell apart, their leadership disintegrated, and intragroup disharmony developed.

A second study (Sherif et al. 1961) duplicated this first experiment with one important change. The competition between the groups was now equalized, and this revealed some interesting findings about group structure. The feelings of in-group solidarity were intensified in both groups, reinforcing their norms and expectations. Feelings of exclusivity and out-group hostility were also intensified, as the experimenters had hypothesized. The hierarchical structures of both groups also changed, with leadership shifting to those who did best in the current competition. In other words, group roles were shown to be strongly related to group goals. When the goals changed, so did the leaders.

In both of these studies the experimenters had created a situation of open hostility, and in each case they tried to "undo the damage" before the boys were sent home from camp. The hostility was never completely erased in the highly frustrating "Red Rover" study, but in the second case the experimenters were able to break down the hostility by bringing both groups together to work toward a common goal—both groups saw the necessity of cooperating on a camp project to fix the food truck so that all campers could eat.

These studies are worth describing because they were conducted in natural settings common to almost every child's experience, and therefore they tell us a lot about groups. The findings about the development of shared norms and the development of exclusivity and hostility under predominantly competitive situations add to our understanding of how groups form and compete in classrooms, athletic events, and neighborhood ethnic rivalries.

Other studies have documented some of the factors leading to popularity in the peer group. We can easily observe the process of selection that takes place even among children who are not involved in close group interactions. During school recess, some children are surrounded by others seeking their attention, and other children are off in a corner or ignored.

Several factors seem to contribute to this status differentiation. Peer acceptance is often related to an individual's overall adjustment, to the degree of enthusiastic participation in activities, cooperation with group routines, and sensitivity to social overtures. This kind of attunement, or lack of it, tends to reinforce itself (Glidewell et al. 1966). Well-liked children's good adjustment is bolstered by their popularity, and awkward children become even more ill-at-ease when they are ignored or rejected by the group.

Intelligence is a second factor influencing popularity or leadership. Popular children generally have fairly high IQs (Roff and Sells 1965). Slow learners are often ridiculed or ignored by their classmates. Athletic ability is a third factor contributing to group status, particularly in settings where the entire group is involved in sports.

Less popular children usually have "undesirable" traits, such as high anxiety, excessive dependence on adults, rebelliousness, or a physical problem such as obesity—all traits that reduce children's level of conformity to group standards. During middle childhood there are opposing needs for autonomy and mastery of the environment and for the security of being accepted by others. For children between six and twelve, the peer group often offers a solution that satisfies both needs.

Peer-group conformity is a normal and often desirable behavior, if it is not followed to excess. However, some children tend to be more dependent on outside approval than others. Social workers who deal with groups of children at this stage may set goals of helping those in leadership roles to allow a higher degree of nonconformity and to develop a more democratic process of decision making. The worker will often simultaneously help individual members to respond more appropriately to group demands in order to gain greater acceptance by peers. Adult leaders may choose to influence group standards and values if they feel the group is too intolerant of individual differences or if the staff wishes to reduce the amount of tension and feelings of social distance between racial and social-class groups.

As children move away from their families during middle childhood, they often must strain to reconcile their own self-images with the new and often unpleasant prejudices and stereotypes they encounter. As a result, they often become anxious and self-denigrating (Boyd 1952; Deutsch 1960; Palermo 1959). *Prejudice* may be defined as "the negative attitudes directed toward members of social groups who are perceived by themselves and others in terms of racial, religious, national, or cultural-linguistic attributes" (Proshansky 1966, p. 311). We tend to think of prejudice as an adult attitude, but racial awareness begins to develop by four years of age. Studies of both Jewish (Radke, Trager, and Davis 1949) and black children (Goodman 1952) show that ethnic awareness often appears earlier in the minority group child than in the general population. Minority children, especially black children, often direct these learned prejudices against members of their own group. Studies done in the late 1940s and the 1950s show that black nursery schoolchildren preferred white dolls to black dolls (Clark and Clark 1947; Goodman 1952). This preference for white persons was found to decrease with age, but these studies also show that white children's tendency to reject blacks and Jews increased as they got older, and their early prejudices were reinforced by the peer group. Although group attitudes have changed a great deal since the 1950s and ethnic pride has increased, the majority group prejudices and stereotypes still have a great influence on the development of the minority child.

One of the best-known analyses of the personality traits of prejudiced persons (Frenkel-Brunswick 1948) found an association between prejudice and authoritarian traits. The authoritarian child has rigid concepts of good and bad, either looks up to or down on others, and has little tolerance for ambiguity or nonconformity. These children are often difficult for social workers to reach. Although their personality characteristics often create great problems for them later in life, such children may defend their attitudes and beliefs very rigidly.

Racial awareness is an important issue for children in middle childhood because it is the time when a child signs an implicit contract with society (Comer and Poussaint 1975). In return for "swearing allegiance" to the standards of society, minority children must gain a sense of acceptance by the larger, more powerful group. If the majority group does not value them equally and offer equal rewards, then they will experience conflict about accepting the norms of the larger society.

The minority child's ethnic awareness is often increased by membership in a homogeneous neighborhood peer group. This makes adjustment easier during middle childhood, as it tends both to improve self-esteem and to increase in-group solidarity and out-group hostility. However, sometimes the norms of the neighborhood peer group conflict with the norms of the larger community (Rainwater 1966). We shall return to some of these issues in the next chapter on adolescence.

CASE ILLUSTRATIONS

Central School

David Prince is a school social worker assigned to two schools. Central School uses a team approach effectively, and therefore he frequently hears from teachers who are concerned about a particular child's emotional development. Most teachers seek advice on better management techniques, although some want a child removed from the classroom immediately.

The social worker tries to look at all aspects of the child's functioning and then make recommendations based on an evaluation of the child's strengths and weaknesses and an assessment of the child's interaction within the family and the school. David has just started looking at Larry's situation. Larry is a ten-year-old boy whose teacher finds him intelligent but hyperactive and unable to concentrate on school tasks. He is very disruptive in class and often speaks out of turn in a bid for attention. He is easily provoked into fighting with other children. David asks the school psychologist to test Larry and is told that Larry's IQ is 105, but that he might score higher if he was not so impatient in frustrating situations and prone to give up rather than risk failure. A breakdown of his test scores reveals that his verbal and analytic abilities are much higher than the norm for his age.

The social worker has involved Larry's mother in the evaluation process as soon as he received the teacher's referral. She has had problems with Larry since her divorce six years ago and is relieved that others now realize how difficult he is. For the past two years she has been unable to ignore demanding behavior that she could tolerate when he was only five or six years old. She is also relieved that the social worker does not blame her for Larry's problems but rather offers to strengthen her own efforts to help her son to function more adequately. She has a vague sense that she may have "spoiled" him in the past by being overindulgent to make up for her husband's violent behavior in the home. However, after several conferences, David concludes that she is probably not aware that she has also demanded too much of Larry by expecting him to be "the man of the house."

As part of the evaluation process, Larry's doctor conducts a complete physical examination and finds no evidence of neurological problems. The social worker finally decides to refer the mother to a family counseling agency. David chooses an analytically oriented agency in this case because the mother is verbal and highly motivated to understand more about her present and past relationship with her son. He thinks that an improvement in the parent-child relationship will help reduce Larry's anxiety and improve his school performance.

The second phase of David's task is to offer immediate help with the school environment. Here he decides, in consultation with the teacher and principal, to put Larry in a highly structured classroom with a warm teacher who uses behavior modification techniques successfully. The teacher gives Larry small tasks that he can easily succeed at and gradually increases her expectations. He is given clear instructions and sees equally clear and consistent consequences for his success or failure to reach the agreed-upon goals. His disruptions and manipulative behaviors are largely ignored, although sometimes he is given "time out" away from the other children until he can return to the task at hand. For the most part, he is given attention and other rewards when he displays appropriate behavior. One reason that this system is successful is that Larry knows the teacher likes him, and he wants her approval very much.

Oakwood School

The staff at David's second school are overwhelmed by problems. A very large number of their children, particularly the boys, are two or more years behind grade level in reading by the time they reach the sixth grade. Some of the children have been in Head Start and did not fall behind until they reached the third or fourth grade. The principal knows that these children display more than adequate intelligence in other areas of problem solving; they easily learn the intracacies of car mechanics or other knowledge that interests them.

Morale at Oakwood School is low. Some staff believe that it is too late to compensate for the lack of cognitive and social skills that should have been acquired earlier. Others believe that students living in overcrowded homes and experiencing frequent family crises cannot be expected to settle down to hours of formal instruction and pay attention to rules and regulations. There is a wide divergence between the culture of the school and that of the community.

A large part of David's time is spent filling out forms certifying children as eligible for learning-disability status. This enables the school to receive additional funding to provide separate remedial instruction in reading and math, mainstreaming the children in these programs for the remainder of the school day. This is not always successful, as the lack of reading skills affects children's status and self-esteem in classes such as science and history unless the teacher does a great deal of individualized curriculum planning.

David's most exciting project at Oakwood School has been the formation of an after-school group of fifteen boys. He selected them from a list of fifty names submitted by various teachers. The boys all presented behavior as well as academic problems in the classroom. However, David was careful not to select only aggressive boys, but to balance the group with children showing other developmental and socialization problems.

David's goals were to use group processes to help members learn more acceptable ways of handling aggressive feelings, to help increase their tolerance for frustration, and to help build their self-esteem as students at the school. While not directly aimed at reading ability, these achievements were expected to help group members respond more positively to classroom remedial efforts. This did in fact happen.

The members' goals varied: Some valued the opportunity to use the school gym after hours; others joined because their friends knew and liked David; still others wanted to join because some of the members already had a reputation in the neighborhood for being "tough." David was careful to talk over his program suggestions with the unofficial clique of four boys who had the most power in the group and to establish himself as an advisor rather than as a rival for leadership.

At first the activities centered around athletics, which should have provided the boys with easy successes. However, the members could not benefit from their high level of physical skill until they were better able to follow the rules. At first many simply left the game, cursing when they disliked the umpire's decision. The group eventually took on a project of cleaning up an empty neighborhood lot to make a playing field, working closely with a group of adults who made them feel that they were doing "men's work." They received special recognition for this project at a school assembly; this was the first time many of the members had received so much praise from the school staff.

The group was then ready to tackle more complex projects that required them to plan ahead, such as organizing fund-raising activities and saving enough money for club jackets. Such projects would add to their cognitive skills as well as their emotional development.

SUMMARY

Most societies consider children between five and seven years old as entering a new period of reason and responsibility. Increased cultural demands seem to parallel a period of gradual growth in children's thought, use of language, and perceptual-motor skills. Middle childhood is the time when children settle down and develop more fully the patterns that are already set. It is also a time when they develop new skills and are increasingly motivated to gain the approval of parents and peers. School and recreational environments should be responsive to the physical-motor, cognitive, psychological, and social needs of children.

By age seven or eight, children come to perceive the physical world more logically and realistically. They move from intuitive thought to the stage of concrete operations. They begin to make logical inferences and become capable of reversal in their thinking. The seven-year-old's IQ score correlates more closely with his or her mature adult IQ than did earlier scores. Children of this age use verbal rules and hypotheses to solve problems and become more deliberate in their use of memory strategies. Attempts to speed cognitive growth have had mixed results.

Children acquire important elements of social knowledge in middle childhood, and they develop more refined concepts of friendship and morality. The three broad areas of social knowledge are social inference, social relationships, and social regulations. They also learn to distinguish between fantasy and reality. Bettleheim believes that fairy tales help children's emotional growth and convey important meanings about life.

Moral judgment is believed to arise from social learning, as a defense against anxiety, or as a result of developing cognitive processes. Cognitive theorists, such as Piaget and Kohlberg, believe that the child's moral sense develops in stages. Kohlberg's stages of moral development range from simple obedience to a high level of morality in which an individual's behavior is internally motivated.

When they enter school, children must cope with a new set of demands from teachers and peers. The greater the gap between expectations at home and at school, the more difficult it will be for the child to adjust to the classroom. Peers begin to have an increasingly strong impact on children's behavior, as models to be copied and as reinforcers of personal behavior.

There is a great deal of controversy about the purposes of education. Traditionalists believe its purpose is transmitting knowledge; others stress goals of self-actualization and spontaneous growth. Some educators believe that school activities should be geared to each child's stage of development and favor the "open classroom" in which the teacher plans carefully enough to allow individual growth in a heterogeneous setting. Professionals still differ as to the role of the schools in lessening the achievement gap among individuals and groups.

Although psychologists agree that intelligence is modified by experience, they strongly disagree about the definitions of intelligence implicit in standardized tests. The Stanford-Binet and the Wechsler tests measure deviation IQ, which is based on a comparison between the scores of an individual and those of others of the same age. All diagnostic and achievement tests should be interpreted with caution, taking account of individual differences, including cultural and emotional factors.

Further research is needed to define learning disabilities and to determine how they can best be treated. At present there are different approaches to the diagnosis and treatment of children who have reading and language problems or who show a range of symptoms labeled as *hyperactivity*. Although drug treatment and educational management are the most common forms of intervention, social workers are concerned that emotional as well as biological factors be considered. Meanwhile, there is considerable opposition to the practice of labeling children on the basis of such limited understanding of the problem.

Learning theories have greatly influenced the management of children's behavior in schools and residential treatment centers. Learning theories are based on a deterministic view of human nature, and learning theorists attempt to use objective, experimental methods of gathering data. Behavior is perceived to be an automatic response to stimuli, and is considered to be neither good nor bad.

In classical conditioning a respondent's behavior is brought under the control of a previously neutral stimulus. In operant conditioning new learning is shaped or strengthened by a series of reinforcements. Some psychologists believe that learning theories are inadequate to explain complex mental structures and processes and certain positive emotions. Behavior modification programs use principles of operant conditioning to shape human behaviors for therapeutic goals. These programs have had numerous successes, but there is also concern about the possible abuse of some of the techniques.

Because parents strongly influence children's personality and social development, the multiple dimensions of parenting behavior have attracted the attention of researchers. Becker examined the areas of restrictiveness–permissiveness, warmth–hostility, and anxious involvement–calm detachment. Baumrind described the dimensions of warm–detached, and authoritative–authoritarian behavior. Maccoby looked at the degree to which families have shared goals and a balance of control between parents and children.

Children's behavior is also strongly affected by sibling relationships, friendship pairs, and primary groups. Primary groups have shared values and standards, are relatively stable, and interaction among members leads to status differentiation. As children move toward adolescence, peer groups become more formal and demand a greater degree of conformity. Conformity to group standards is very important during middle childhood because it satisfies needs for intimacy and acceptance. Just as important, however, are children's needs for autonomy—their need to understand and control their environment.

Children from minority groups must often cope with prejudice from members of majority groups. Prejudice causes problems for both the aggressor and the victim. Group experiences can reinforce a positive or a negative self-image in a circular process that is dependent on parental influences, previous group experiences, and the degree of social knowledge that children have achieved.

SUGGESTED READINGS

Coles, R. *Children of Crisis. Vol. 1: A Study of Courage and Fear.* Boston: Little, Brown, 1967. The author explores the impact of racial integration in the schools of New Orleans through interviews with children, families, and others.

Gardner, W. *Children with Learning and Behavior Problems: A Behavior Management Approach.* Boston: Allyn & Bacon, 1974. An excellent practical guide to the theory and techniques of behavior modification. The concepts are clearly presented and illustrated.

Jencks, C. *Inequality: A Reassessment of the Effect of Family and Schooling in America.* New York: Basic Books, 1972. A controversial and stimulating review of recent research dealing with the impact of family background, schooling, and IQ scores on adult success.

Keniston, K., & the Carnegie Council on Children. *All Our Children: The American Family Under Pressure.* New York: Harcourt Brace Jovanovich, 1977. The problems of parenting and sibling relationships are discussed in the context of broad contemporary social conditions in the United States.

Kohl, H. *36 Children.* New York: W.W. Norton & Co., 1968. A personal account of efforts at developing an alternative style of education and a description of classroom dynamics in a multiethnic setting.

McCarthy, J.J., & McCarthy, J.F. *Learning Disabilities.* Boston: Allyn & Bacon, 1969. A review of the major categories of learning disabilities, assessment procedures, and educational strategies.

Redl, F., & Wineman, D. *Controls From Within: Techniques for the Treatment of the Aggressive Child.* New York: Free Press, 1957. A small group of delinquent children are described both before treatment and as they progress in a residential treatment program designed to develop "controls from within."

chapter six

Marc Anderson

ADOLESCENCE
the search for identity

outline

PHYSICAL CHANGES

> *Growth and body size*
>
> *Sexual maturation*
>
> *Adjustment to body image*

COGNITIVE DEVELOPMENT

> *Formal operational thought*
>
> *Reasoning and morality*
>
> *Values and ideology*

THE SEARCH FOR IDENTITY

> *Ego identity*
>
> *Disengagement from family*
>
> *Adolescent sexuality*
>
> *Social roles and group membership*

YOUTH UNEMPLOYMENT: A SOCIAL PROBLEM

JUVENILE DELINQUENCY

> *Causal factors*
>
> *Drug use*
>
> *Status offenders*
>
> *Diversionary programs*

CASE ILLUSTRATIONS

SUMMARY

SUGGESTED READINGS

IN INDUSTRIALIZED COUNTRIES such as ours the transition from childhood to adult status is a prolonged process. Long years of education are required, while technical skills are learned, and large numbers of relatively unskilled youth are kept in school and out of the labor force. As a result, the age at which youth achieve full adult status has been delayed beyond the age of physical maturity. In contrast, the transition from childhood to adulthood in hunting and agrarian societies is fairly abrupt and adult status is often marked by a symbolic ceremony at the time of physical maturity, followed by a year or two of apprenticeship before assuming the full rights and responsibilities of adulthood at age fifteen or sixteen.

Today we generally accept adolescence as a rather lengthy transitional period between childhood and adulthood. How do we define *adolescence*? It is not synonymous with *puberty*, which refers to the point at which an individual is capable of procreation. Nor does it coincide with the *genital period* that Freudians describe as the final stage of psychosexual development, in which the individual turns to satisfying heterosexual relationships.

Adolescence generally refers to the lengthy period in which full sexual maturation takes place. Adolescence also refers to the period in which the individual makes the transition from school to the world of work and from childhood dependency to adult self-sufficiency and responsibility. In the United States, this transition usually extends to age eighteen, twenty, or even twenty-two (Rogers 1977).

Adolescence may be considered to have early, middle, and late periods (Konopka 1973). *Early adolescence* is the period when most individuals are in junior high school or the first year of high school. They are undergoing the bodily changes of pubescence and some of the mental changes of cognitive maturity. *Middle adolescence* is a period of seeking an independent identity and of beginning to date. It is also a time when increased importance is placed on peer relationships. During *late adolescence,* or youth (Keniston 1975), decisions are made about careers, further schooling, and the selection of paths toward adult life. Thought processes have matured, and youth lack only the experiences of adulthood.

This chapter describes physical and cognitive development during adolescence, then outlines how adolescents attempt to integrate these changes in order to achieve a satisfactory sense of identity apart from their former identity as dependent child in the family. For some young people, this is a period when cognitive skills are used in developing new values and ideologies.

While adolescents experience these developmental changes, they are also influenced by situational factors that shape their current behavior and future course of development. In this context, we shall discuss youth un-employment as an environmental factor that has a critical impact on ad-olescent development. The chapter ends with a discussion of delinquency as another example of how individual and social factors interact to deter-mine the course of adolescent behavior. Delinquency prevention and treat-ment are areas in which social workers have traditionally been involved.

Edgar Friedenberg, in considering the social context in which today's adolescents develop, characterizes our society as "untrustworthy," in the sense that people cannot rely on large impersonal organizations in the same way that they had trusted the structures of more stable societies in the past. He characterizes the effects of this change as follows:

> ... the social climate itself is inimical to personal clarity and commitment, which are the chief developmental tasks of adolescence . . . Personal isolation and a sense of abandonment are among the costs of constructing an open, technically advanced social system whose chief boast is the opportunity it gives its members to alter the circumstances of their lives. And they are costs that bear disproportionately on adolescents (Friedenberg 1966, pp. 74–75).

PHYSICAL CHANGES

The rapid rate of physiological change during adolescence is similar to that of the fetal period and the first two years of life. Adolescence is marked by an increase in the rate of growth, rapid development of the reproductive organs, and the appearance of secondary sex characteristics. These changes are precipitated by *hormones*, the chemical products of the endocrine glands. Some of these changes occur universally, but most are sex-specific.

During adolescence, there may be an increased production of hor-mones that were previously present only in trace amounts, or a new hor-mone may be produced (Tanner 1971). Each hormone is designed to in-fluence a specific set of targets, or receptors, although these receptors are not necessarily located in the same organ or type of tissue. For example, the sex hormone testosterone affects areas as diverse as facial skin, sections of the brain, cells in the genitals, and cartilage in the shoulder joints (Tanner 1971). The target tissues have the ability to respond selectively to hormones circulating in the bloodstream; the uterus, for example, selectively responds to two sex hormones, estrogen and progesterone (Garrison 1973).

Normal growth and functioning is dependent upon the extremely delicate balance of endocrine gland secretions. The **pituitary gland,** located on the underside of the brain, is sometimes known as the master gland. It produces several varieties of hormones; among the most important is the growth hormone, somatotrophin (Garrison 1973). The pituitary also pro-duces secondary hormones that stimulate and regulate the functioning of a number of other glands, including the sex glands. The sex glands (the testes and the ovaries) have two functions: to produce gametes (sperm or eggs), and to secrete the hormones vital to the development of the reproductive organs. The secretions of the pituitary and the sex glands have an emotional as well as a physiological impact upon the developing young person; hormonal changes may be an important source of stress.

Males and females develop at different rates, with females rather uniformly experiencing extensive bodily changes about two years before males (Tanner 1971). Moreover, the rate of development among members of the same sex varies widely. Some boys have completed the physiological changes of adolescence at an age when other boys have not begun to change. However, once the sequence of sexual maturation has begun, it progresses in fairly predictable order. (During the last century, these biological changes have begun at an earlier chronological age in each generation.) Keeping in mind the differences from one individual to the next, let us look at the general pattern of physical change that characterizes adolescence.

Growth and body size

The high *rate* of growth, equaled only by the two-year-old, reaches its peak in girls at age twelve and in boys at age fourteen (Tanner 1971). Both bones and muscles are developing, triggered by the same set of hormones. However, different parts of the body develop at different rates, often following a sequence that appears comical to the observer. Because the extremities—hands, feet, and head—reach adult size before the torso, and because the legs lengthen rapidly in advance of other parts of the body, the adolescent is often caricatured as gangly and ill-proportioned.

During this period, there is a loss of fat that is more marked in boys than in girls. Fat accumulation resumes at the end of the growth spurt. Boys also develop more red cells and hemoglobin in their blood than girls at this time. Both sexes show superior athletic ability at this stage, as evidenced by the performance of adolescents in national and international athletic competitions.

Sexual maturation

The second major biological change during adolescence is the development of the reproductive system. The term *puberty* refers to the maturation of the reproductive organs. However, *sexual maturation* also involves the much longer process of social and psychological adjustments related to the physical onset of puberty. We shall deal with the nonphysiological aspects of sexual maturation later in the chapter when we discuss sexual identity.

In males, the first indication of puberty is often the accelerated growth of the testes and scrotum. Approximately one year later there are spurts in both height and penis growth, with concurrent development of the seminal vesicles and the prostate gland. Boys are usually sterile at the time of the first seminal emission. Pubic hair begins to appear in the interim between testicular and penile development, but it attains full growth only after the completion of genital development. During this period there is also an increase in the sebacious (oil-producing) glands and sweat glands, resulting in new concerns about acne and body odors (Tanner 1971).

In girls, the "breast buds" are usually, but not always, the first sign that puberty has begun. There is simultaneous development of the uterus and vagina, with enlargement of the labia and clitoris. **Menarche** (first menstruation), although perhaps the most dramatic and symbolic indication of a girl's changing status, occurs later in the period of accelerated growth. The current age range for menarche is generally from ten to fifteen years. These early menstrual cycles are often irregular and vary from one girl to another. For most girls, menstruation begins before the ovaries can produce mature ova and before the uterus is ready to support a pregnancy.

The psychological acceptance of the menarche appears greater when girls receive information and emotional support from their mothers and other significant females. The traditional psychoanalytic view focuses on the potential for emotional distress resulting from menstruation while paying scant attention to girls who readily accept this symbolic entry into a feminine sexual role (Melges and Hamburg 1976).

In discussing the biological bases of sexual differentiation, it is important to recall the presentation in Chapter 2 of the differential development of the male and female fetus. In addition to the chromosomal determinants of sexual identity, sexual response biases are built into the prenatal nervous system and sexual predispositions are created by the hormonal system (Diamond 1976). Nonetheless, the majority of these biologically based sex differences represent quantitative distinctions rather than discrete categories (Beach 1976), and the major part of gender identity occurs after birth, as other factors intervene from earliest childhood through adolescence and into young adulthood (Kagan 1976).

Adjustment to body image

We turn now to a consideration of how adolescents perceive the rapid and dramatic physical changes associated with puberty. Adolescents have the pain and pleasure of being able to observe the change process, watching themselves with alternating feelings of fascination and horror. Embarrassed and uncertain, they continually revise their self-images based on a comparison with others. Both sexes anxiously monitor their development, or lack of it, with knowledge and misconceptions, pride and fear. They constantly compare the perceived reality with the prevailing ideal, and the ability to reconcile differences between the two is crucial for maintaining self-esteem during this transitional period.

Adolescents are neither children nor adults. Their insecure status increases their need for conformity, and they can be extremely intolerant of deviations in body types such as obesity. The mass media support this conformist tendency by presenting stereotyped images of attractive youths who glide through adolescence without pimples, braces, or unattractive proportions.

Children are aware of their own body types, skills, and proportions long before adolescence. But their self-image receives renewed scrutiny at this time (Dwyer and Mayer 1968–69). Some teen-agers in our society subject themselves to intense dieting, either to counteract overweight or to achieve idealized body proportions. Others embark upon rigorous regimens of physical fitness and strength training—weight lifting, athletics, and exercise. There are interesting differences in the types of changes sought by the two sexes (Frazier and Lisonbee 1950). Girls want very specific changes: "I would make my ears lie back" or "I would make my forehead lower." Boys do not articulate their dissatisfactions as precisely. A typical boy's response is: "I would make myself look handsome and not skinny." In general, girls worry about being heavy, and boys are concerned about being too thin in the upper arms and chest. Girls think of themselves as too tall; boys worry about being too short.

The impact of timing in maturation has engrossed researchers almost as much as it has adolescents themselves (Mussen and Jones 1957; Clausen 1975). Investigators have found that the social stigma of ill-timed maturation falls more heavily upon late-maturing boys (Hamachek 1973). Because girls generally mature two years earlier than boys, the late-maturing boy is the last to come of age. He may be at a disadvantage in athletics if he is smaller and somewhat weaker, and he is generally treated as a younger, more immature individual. Late-blooming boys have a far more difficult adjustment than early maturers, who tend to gain much more social and athletic prestige among their peers.

In contrast, the early-maturing girl may be at a slight disadvantage in comparison with her peers. Her greater height makes her stand out awkwardly in the elementary grades. She has fewer chances to exchange confidences about her body changes with peers, and there is no particular prestige value attached to her precocious development (Hamachek 1973). However, the effect of developmental variations is generally less traumatic for girls than for boys.

Social workers find that adolescents vary greatly in their ability to handle these social responses, depending on the amount of positive self-esteem they have developed earlier in childhood. Indeed, those with low self-esteem sometimes exaggerate the differences associated with rejection by others, as with the plump girl whose sloppy clothing calls attention to her heaviness. The ability to cope is also related to the *amount* of stress the individual must deal with. A vulnerable person may become upset by the slightest hint of rejection, but even relatively strong individuals may be upset by peer groups that consistently reject them on the basis of their physical characteristics. Social workers must objectively assess the total situation, including the degree to which the adolescent may have unrealistic expectations of others. The problem may be to help adolescents find a satisfying "fit" with a more appropriate peer group. Encouraging a child with poor athletic skills to "make the team" is not helpful unless there is the possibility of developing more skill with increased practice. It may be more useful to help the child understand why such a goal is so important. Other interventions include providing a variety of athletic opportunities that can include less skilled and even disabled individuals.

Social workers can sometimes be effective as advisors to teen-age groups, using their skill to influence the mutual process of individual and group acceptance. For example, if a group broadens its program to include activities other than athletics, it is also more apt to accept some members with other than athletic skills. Or, the social worker may encourage the local community center to offer group activities such as ceramics classes, which base their membership on shared interests rather than intimate social acceptance. In this way more individuals have an opportunity to increase their social skills as well as their self-esteem.

COGNITIVE DEVELOPMENT

Along with sexual maturation, adolescents develop broadened cognitive capacities such as greater awareness, imagination, and judgment. These abilities facilitate the rapid accumulation of knowledge about a broad range of issues and problems that can both complicate and enrich adolescents' lives.

Formal operational thought

In Piaget's developmental theory, formal operational thought is the hallmark of adolescent cognitive change. It involves being able to critically examine one's thoughts, conjecture about the effect of one variable on another, and differentiate between the possible and the probable (Gallagher 1973).

Adolescents typically make frequent use of their newly developed ability to analyze their own thought processes, gaining insight into themselves and others. However, because of their preoccupation with their own metamorphoses, adolescents frequently assume that others are as fascinated by them and their behavior as they are themselves. They also tend to anticipate the reactions of those around them and to assume that their own self-assessment is matched by the approval or criticism of others. These assumptions about other people's opinions make up the adolescents' *imaginary audience* (Elkind 1975), which they use to anticipate the reactions of others as they mentally "try on" new attitudes and behaviors.

At the same time that they fail to differentiate the feelings of others, adolescents may overdifferentiate their own feelings, believing that their emotions are unique, that no one has ever known or ever will know such personal agony or rapture. This kind of egocentrism begins to recede by the age of fifteen or sixteen, as adolescents replace their imaginary audiences with real ones. In the formal operational period, as described by Piaget, adolescents become more accurate at seeing themselves from another's point of view and begin to incorporate a variety of outside judgments into their self-concept (Elkind 1975).

Not all psychologists agree with Piaget's formulation of this final cognitive stage. They point out that not all adolescents or even adults are able to think in formal operational terms. A certain level of intelligence seems to be necessary; cultural and socioeconomic factors, particularly educational level, also play a role (Neimark 1975). Furthermore, even those who attain this level do not always maintain it consistently. For example, many people facing unfamiliar problems are apt to fall back on a much more concrete type of reasoning. These facts have led some psychologists to suggest that formal operational thought be considered an extension of concrete operations rather than a stage in its own right. Piaget himself (1972) recognizes that this may be the case, but he emphasizes that elements of this last cognitive stage are essential for the study of advanced science and mathematics.

Another limitation in Piaget's formulation of higher-level cognitive skills—those that enable an adolescent to speculate, analyze his own thoughts, and form a self-concept—is that it does not completely explain creative ability. Some creative adolescents exhibit capacities for unusual ways of thinking that are different from the cognitive modes typically employed by adolescents with high IQ scores. The latter group typically uses conventional thinking in searching for the "right" or "customary" solution. Educational institutions and society in general tend to reward this conventional model rather than the highly creative and divergent person. This results in an unfortunate loss of a great deal of creative potential (Getzels and Jackson 1959).

Reasoning and morality

As the adolescent's thinking and reasoning mature, increased attention is given to the selection of ideals and moral values. This is part of a long developmental process that begins when the toddler is taught not to pull hair, lie, or steal. An external morality is taught by processes such as modeling, identification, and rewards and punishment. The child later internalizes this morality. However, many psychologists believe that in order to become mature adults, individuals must eventually reassess these principles and build their own coherent set of values. We turn now to a discussion of this process.

Cognitive theorists believe that preadolescent children probably cannot construct an independent value system because they lack the mental capacity to consider all the possible alternatives, to generalize from the specific, and to logically examine cause and effect. These new intellectual abilities are the major reason why the adolescent years are so full of changing ideals, values, and attitudes. Jane Loevinger (1976) and Lawrence Kohlberg (1966) are researchers who have described the process of developing this personal moral system.

In the last chapter, we introduced Kohlberg's theory of the development of moral reasoning. He believes that most children in our culture have outgrown the first stages of moral development by the time they reach their teens, when they are at the level of conventional role conformity. They are motivated to avoid punishment, are obedience-oriented, and are ready to abide by conventional moral stereotypes. They may stay at this "Law-and-Order" level for the rest of their lives, especially if they receive no stimulation to think beyond this level. The final two stages of moral development—morality by social contract and morality as derived from ethical principles—require that adolescents develop more sophisticated thought processes.

What is the process by which these changes in thinking occur? Can one teach more advanced forms of moral thought? Kohlberg thinks that "moral education" is possible, and that people learn through experience in making moral judgments. He has set up experimental classes in which children from all types of social backgrounds discuss hypothetical moral dilemmas. The child is presented with an ethical problem and asked to give a solution. If the answer is argued at level 4 (conformity to avoid censure by authorities), then the discussion leader suggests a level 5 rationale as an alternative (conformity based on awareness of moral principles). The student almost always finds that this slightly more advanced reasoning is more attractive and, over time, begins to form judgments at level 5 (Kohlberg 1966). It would seem that the consideration of moral paradoxes and conflicts forces the child to question older patterns of analysis and to begin making increasingly mature judgments about social situations. However, it is not clear that superior moral judgments necessarily lead to superior behavior, and there is very little research on the relationship between the two.

Values and ideology

The development of new cognitive abilities in adolescence is of central importance in the ability to integrate new ideas and ideals and to satisfactorily formulate a sense of individual identity. We shall address the first of these issues in this section, before discussing the adolescent's "search for identity."

It is often tempting to dismiss adolescent ideals by explaining that they represent "rebellion against authority," rooted in the developmental need to separate from dependence on one's parents. There are always some individuals who personify the psychoanalytic perspective in which conflict between adolescents and their parents leads to the excessive repudiation of parental ideals in order to shore up youths' shaky sense of individual autonomy. There are also some individuals for whom the emotional satisfactions of belonging to or leading a movement outweigh the intellectual commitment. Some youth movement leaders turn from one ideology to a completely different one within the space of a few years.

However, one must also remember that youths acquire new intellectual abilities that may be put to excellent use in thoughtfully questioning established traditions. This is especially true in a period of rapid technological change, accompanied by a correspondingly rapid change in traditional social institutions. Adolescents are in a transitional period in which they often try out new views about the world and about themselves. Edgar Friedenberg (1966) calls those who make a commitment to idealistic causes and ideas "pro-social youth." He concedes that only a small percentage of American youths' behavior is influenced by a strong value commitment, but points out that a high proportion of those who do show such a commitment are young.

The specific content of the youth culture depends very much on the social and historical period. Perhaps this relationship is even more evident with adolescents than with adults because of their greater involvement with peers and the youth culture. Among the causes attracting youthful idealism in the past fifty years have been fascism, socialism, communism, utopian communalism, pacifism, environmentalism, and religious fundamentalism. There is obviously an enormous difference in the values represented by these movements and the types of youth attracted to each of them. However, they all appeal in some way to youthful idealism in stating that the present values and traditions are no longer relevant or adequate and that a new morality is called for.

Like any other culture, the youth culture consists of a set of shared attitudes, values, and expectations about behavior. The term *counterculture* was applied to the youthful rebellion of the 1960s against traditional values perceived as irrelevant. This included a denunciation of the ethics of individual achievement, the discipline of delayed gratification ("doing without today so we can be better off tomorrow"), and the self-denying Puritan morality (Getzels 1972). The counterculture emphasized social responsibility, authenticity, and sharing, rather than independence. While some of these shifts in values were already underway, the counterculture was nourished by the strong opposition to the war in Vietnam, particularly on college campuses.

In a rapidly changing society such as ours, many of the counterculture values of one decade are absorbed by the dominant culture in the next decade; other values and beliefs are discarded. For example, many of the recent environmental-impact studies required for government and business are an outgrowth of the counterculture's concern with ecology. In the next chapter, we shall discuss new family styles and the increased tolerance of varied expressions of sexuality that were championed by youths before gaining wider acceptability.

The counterculture's interest in self-awareness and spiritual values has also continued into the 1980s (Glock 1976). The disillusionment with rational scientific thinking is expressed in a variety of counterculture religious groups appealing primarily to youths, along with quasi-religious movements emphasizing personal growth. Adherents of these groups also tend to show higher than average tolerance for alternative life styles and radical political activity (Wuthnow 1976).

THE SEARCH FOR IDENTITY

In the last two sections we have outlined several developmental tasks of adolescence: acceptance of a changed and sexually developed body, mastery of new intellectual challenges, and the integration of a set of moral values. In this section, we shall consider the impact of the psychological need to form what Erikson calls an **ego identity.** In part, this identity formation consists of achieving emotional separation from earlier patterns of dependency on parents, learning satisfying sex roles, making friendships, and achieving a sense of group identity.

Children move into adolescence with varying abilities to cope with these challenges, and they receive varying degrees of support from the family, school, and larger community. When the adolescent experiences a strong sense of failure, loss of self-esteem, and feelings of isolation from loved ones, there may be danger of severe depression and attempts at suicide. However, most adolescents are successful in adapting to these new demands and opportunities.

Ego identity

Erikson (1959) describes adolescence as a "normative crisis," involving a number of elements that converge to form a consistent ego identity. This requires an integration of constitutional predispositions, prior identifications, and characteristic roles and defenses. Erikson shuns the view of adolescence as an affliction and focuses on the potential that it offers for increased growth in many areas. Subsequent researchers (Offer and Offer 1975) cite evidence to support the view that the developmental tasks of adolescence can be accomplished over a rather long period of time without the major emotional crises that we have been led to expect.

According to Erikson (1956, 1968) adolescence can be conceived of as a moratorium, a period of freedom to explore various roles and alternatives. Individuals living in a consistent and homogeneous society find it relatively easy to achieve a *normative identity*, that is, an identity conforming to the values and expectations of the surrounding culture. In contrast, our society offers many choices of occupation, sexual role, and life style. However, even in a heterogeneous society it is possible for an individual to select a *deviant identity*—that is, one considered to be at odds with the expectations of the majority culture or of significant reference groups. For example, an adolescent in an athletically oriented family may experience stress if he decides to join a chess group rather than a basketball team. Or, an Asian youth may choose to identify with a non-Asian peer group, in opposition to family tradition. Adolescents who deviate from expected group norms may do so in order to avoid closing off directions and relationships that offer the potential of enriching their lives.

Finally, an adolescent may choose a *negative identity* in order to avoid feeling channeled into an unwanted life pattern. Adolescents who need to assert a measure of control over their destiny may do the opposite of what is expected of them. They may deliberately choose what seems to be a dangerous or undesirable role out of anger at a parent or in preference to having no separate identity at all. Classic examples of this are the general's son who becomes a pacifist or the minister's daughter who becomes sexually promiscuous. Sociocultural barriers also affect the search for identity; low-income and minority children may feel that there are insufficient social and economic rewards for conforming to majority-held values.

Erikson emphasizes that adolescence, as a dynamic and open-ended period in our lives, is subject to two particular dangers. One is the danger of *premature identity formation*, whereby individuals close off potentials for a more mature identity by choosing their future roles in life too early. The other is a prolonged period of *identity confusion*, a lack of closure that leads to the continuance of unattached and uncommitted selves. Although this leaves adolescents free to choose among many possibilities by trial and error, it is inconsistent with the need for a unified sense of identity. This situation may result from too many simultaneous demands—social, occupational, and sexual—for commitment before the individual is ready to deal with them.

Disengagement from family

According to psychoanalytic theory, adolescence is a period of great inner turmoil, characterized by the need to master increasingly strong sexual impulses and the revival of unresolved oedipal conflicts. The adolescent tries to deal with these frightening impulses by disengaging from the family but experiences inner conflict because of the simultaneous desire for continued parental love and support. The resulting ambivalence accounts for a great deal of the stormy character of family life when children become teen-agers. Anna Freud (1969) calls adolescence a "developmental disturbance" that is necessary in order for the individual to form a new identity apart from the earlier role as a dependent child in the family. This theory also explains how increased identification with the peer culture offers adolescents a substitute for dependency on their parents.

Anna Freud (Lidz 1969) mentions the need for parents of adolescents to be tolerant of inconsistent behavior and to exhibit confidence that their teen-agers can eventually work things out satisfactorily. While recognizing that conflict with parents is normal at this stage, she also points out that the extent of conflict is dependent on parental abilities to tolerate the child's new competencies and to set appropriate limits on behavior. The amount of conflict is also dependent on situational factors, such as whether parents are undergoing a divorce.

Offer and Offer (1975) cite some recent research attesting to a smoother course of adolescent development than has just been described. They point out that much of the analytic literature reflects therapeutic work with disturbed adolescents rather than longitudinal studies of average subjects. Their own research points to the existence of smooth and continuous growth toward adulthood and to growth in "spurts" as well as the more frequently documented tumultuous growth pattern. The pattern of growth is dependent on the course of earlier childhood development as well as on the ability of parents to allow their children increased independence and freedom of action.

It is important that we also remember to look at cultural influences on behavior. For example, a study comparing a group of middle-class Chinese adolescents in Hawaii with a similar group of white Americans in Chicago noted significant differences between the two groups in personality and social adjustment (Hsu et al. 1961). The Chinese teen-agers were markedly less rebellious than the Chicago subjects. The researchers' explanation is that Chinese parents generally expect their children to conform to adult standards at a very young age; their children learn gradually to participate in the adult world. In contrast, American children are raised in an artificially ideal children's world; they are shocked and disillusioned when they encounter adult inconsistencies and injustices and therefore tend to rebel against their parents.

Adolescent sexuality

Catherine Chilman (1979a) published a review of research findings on adolescent sexual behavior, from the pioneer work of Kinsey in 1948 to the present. Her review suggests an increasing trend toward sexual liberalization that is reflected in the lives of adolescents. However, adults must remember that adolescence is a period of beginning sexuality and that because of their lack of experience much of young people's sexual behavior is of an experimental nature. Adults may misinterpret this behavior by superimposing their own perspective.

Early adolescents may be involved in sexual experimentation, but full sexual intimacy usually is not achieved until late adolescence. Young adolescents need to be liked and to think well of themselves, and this causes them to feel strong pressures for peer group conformity. The pre-sixteen-year-old may still prefer meeting the opposite sex in groups to the closer relationships of a dating system (Douvan and Adelson 1966). "Hanging out" (sitting around and chatting at a pizza parlor, park, or other public place) is a popular pastime. This type of interaction becomes increasingly coeducational as adolescence progresses, and it is the first step in learning to relate to the opposite sex.

Early adolescence is often an awkward stage of imagining and testing what it is like to function in coeducational groups and pairs. During this trial period young people can form basic attitudes about sex roles and sexual behavior without feeling pressured to become too deeply involved.

The custom of dating as we know it is a mixed blessing. Although we usually think of the dating system as helpful in preparing youths for deeper relationships, the personal qualities that are rewarded by popularity in the dating system are often not the qualities that make a good marriage partner or parent (Douvan and Adelson 1966). The popular date is one who can "keep the ball rolling" on a superficial level, a skill of little importance in a sustained adult relationship. In addition, the competition for dates and the desire for popularity can make the identity search of the adolescent years more painful and difficult than is necessary.

As sexual drives are integrated with other aspects of the personality, there are noticeable differences in male and female behavior. Early male sexual impulses are most often expressed through masturbation. This is less true of adolescent females. Although masturbation is gratifying, it may lead to a pattern of emotionally detached sexual activity (Simon and Gagnon 1969). Until recently, class differences were also an important factor in sexual behavior—more so for males than females. For example, the ability to develop a rich fantasy life during masturbation was reportedly related to high socioeconomic status and greater experience in the manipulation of symbols. Guilt over the "unmanliness" of masturbation was of greater concern to working class males. Recent studies, however, report a lessening of social class differences in this area of behavior (Dryer 1975).

Males of all classes receive little training in linking up sexual feelings with emotional relationships: This remains an area of female concern. Adolescent females do not have the same level of hormonal sensitization to sexual arousal as males, but this is not a sufficient explanation of the behavioral differences between the sexes. Girls in our society are not encouraged to be sexual, and their extended period of sexual inactivity may be related to social forces urging repression of the sexual drive and a failure to learn how to be sexual (Simon and Gagnon 1969). However, girls do receive more social training than boys in evaluating themselves and others as desirable mates; this definition of attractiveness usually has a strong sexual component. Girls also develop a greater interest in intense relationships that have a romantic quality.

The data on sexuality does suggest that an increased amount of premarital sexual intercourse is occurring at a younger age. There is also a lessening of the "double standard" that previously allowed more sexual experimentation among the upper and lower classes than among the middle class and among males than females. The widespread availability of birth control measures has supported this trend, although there still seems to be a negative attitude toward casual sex that is unrelated to a caring relationship (Sorensen 1973; Konopka 1976). However, other studies (Offer and Offer 1975) indicate that sexual attitudes are changing more than the actual behavior, and that the nonexperienced teen-ager may be mistakenly convinced by the media that he or she is more deviant in behavior than is actually the case. Statistical data gathered in the seventies (Chilman 1979a) shows that about 25 percent of both males and females were nonvirgins by the ages of fifteen or sixteen, and that the percentage was higher among poor children and minorities living in urban ghettos. Findings from these studies indicate that about half of today's youth are sexually active by age eighteen, and about 75 percent by age twenty-one (Zelnick and Kantner 1977; Chilman 1978).

Several factors influence adolescent sexual behavior. Chilman (1979a) cites the role of *education, psychological makeup, family relationships,* and *biological maturation.* Let us consider these four factors in more detail. *Educational achievement* is associated with middle- and upper-middle-class status and a correspondingly more conservative attitude toward premarital sex. This is especially true for females who place high value on intellectual pursuits and career goals. Academic failure in high school, on the other hand, may cause adolescents to turn to sexual relationships in order to feel successful. This is more prevalent among females because nonacademic males have traditionally achieved success through athletic prowess.

The *psychological factors* associated with early sexual experience differ in males as opposed to females. High self-esteem is characteristic of sexually experienced male high school students, but the reverse is more likely to be true for females. In both sexes, sexual intimacy may occur before the development of the capacity for true mutuality in a relationship (Erikson 1968). In some cases, "falling in love" may serve mainly to bolster a low sense of self-esteem.

In the area of *family relationships,* a number of studies indicate that parent-child interactions are related to adolescent sexual behavior. The children of mothers with nontraditional attitudes who fail to combine affection with firm, mild discipline are more likely to become sexually active. Sexually active adolescents are more likely to see themselves as having poor communication with their parents. However, good parent-youth communications will not necessarily prevent young people from experimenting with sexual relationships.

According to Chilman (1979a), more research is needed on the *biological factors* influencing early sexual relationships—a subject that is frequently overlooked. She believes that adolescents in general may be sexually active at an earlier age because the mean age of puberty is declining. This hypothesis is supported by other research showing that both males and females who mature early are more likely to become sexually active at a young age. Individual differences in temperament also cause some individuals to be more sexually active than others and to begin at an earlier age.

The rising incidence of very young mothers and unmarried mothers has been of special concern to both researchers of adolescent sexuality and social workers attempting to provide services for this group. From 1971 to 1974, unwed parenthood for girls under fifteen years old increased by 35 percent (Schwartz 1977). Illegitimate births in the United States for females ages fifteen through nineteen have tripled from 1940 to 1975 (Chilman 1979b). During 1976 about 25 percent of the babies of white adolescent girls and 80 percent of those of black adolescents were born out of wedlock (National Center for Health Statistics 1978). Many professionals are concerned about the ability of these young and single mothers to adequately care for their children.

Why do these births occur when contraceptive measures and abortions are widely available? A national survey of women between fifteen and nineteen (Zelnik and Kantner 1977) reported that while 30 percent of sexually active women said that they always used contraception, 25 percent said that they never used it. Teen-age girls are often sexually active for a year or more before seeking contraceptive advice (Lindeman 1974; Zabin, Kantner, and Zelnik 1979), sometimes because they want to postpone facing the reality of their changed sexual behavior.

Research also shows substantially higher rates of illegitimate births among blacks than whites. This is related to blacks' higher rates of early premarital sex, more inconsistent use of contraceptives, and preference to have members of the extended family rear the illegitimate child rather than to seek an abortion (Chilman 1979b). These statistical differences between blacks and whites seem to be related to the higher number of blacks who have moved to the city from southern rural areas and who encounter poverty, discrimination, and lack of opportunity for educational and occupational mobility, rather than to the single factor of race (Billingsley 1970; Stack 1974; Chilman 1978).

Another factor affecting the rate of illegitimacy is that many young mothers wish to have and to keep their children because of their own needs to be loved. In such cases, the teen-age mother has often been deprived of affection as a child. Misinterpreting reality, she now expects to be cared for by her infant. Fosburgh (1977) records an adolescent mother's feelings toward her parents and her baby: "It was mine, all mine, NOT theirs or my brother's, just mine. And if they didn't ever really pay attention to me, my baby would. He would love me and hold me . . . ."

Today fewer than 10 percent of unmarried pregnant women relinquish their babies for adoption, although the unmarried father is unlikely to offer a permanent relationship (Schwartz 1977). After an extensive review of the literature, Chilman (1979b) concludes that being a teen-age parent only adds to the difficulties of adolescents who are already likely to be burdened by childhood experiences of racism, poverty, troubled family relationships, and low levels of school achievement.

Social roles and group membership

Before leaving the subject of the adolescent search for identity, let us examine the group memberships and alternative roles available to adolescents. **Roles** are norms or standards of behavior that apply to certain categories of persons. For example, there are male and females roles, occupational roles such as plumber and lawyer, roles of student, parent, and son and daughter. Each of these roles has certain requirements and rules for judging appropriate behavior.

During middle childhood, an individual learns from peers and family what it means to fill roles such as student, devout Catholic, and team member. By adolescence these roles must be integrated into a personal identity, and the conflicting roles must either be reconciled or discarded. This process is more difficult when roles conflict. For example, a female Hispanic teen-ager may be expected by her parents to follow the traditional role of wife and mother; as a good daughter she wants to meet this expectation. However, her teacher may expect that she use her exceptional talents in pursuing a professional career; as a good student, the teen-ager would like to meet this expectation, although it conflicts with her role as good daughter. At the same time, her childhood peer group may define "desirable behavior" in yet a third way.

Adolescents may find that some of the groups that had the most influence on them during childhood, such as the family, the neighborhood gang, or the church youth group, are now no longer attractive. As they turn to new affiliations they may experience conflict between old and new loyalties.

There are times when the adolescent is drawn to the values and attitudes of a single individual rather than those of an entire group. This person might be a close friend, an admired teacher, an older sibling, or a music or sports hero whose opinions are highly valued. Although significant others may exist for individuals at all stages of life, they often have their greatest impact during adolescence, when the teen-ager is actively seeking role models.

As individuals become increasingly independent of their families during early adolescence, they come to depend more on friendships in working out a personal identity. Between the ages of twelve and sixteen, children—especially girls—increasingly demand greater loyalty, conformity, and intimacy from their friends (Douvan and Adelson 1966). Boys sometimes continue the loose childhood pattern of activity-based or sports-based friendships. At this age, adolescents also tend to select friends who are from a similar social class and who have similar interests, social maturity, and moral values. They become increasingly aware of peer groups and are concerned about whether their group is "in" or "out." Adolescents usually know how the groups they belong to will affect their status and reputation. Once an adolescent has become established in a clique or group, he or she may find it difficult to join another, perhaps more desirable, group (Douvan and Gold 1966). Socioeconomic and ethnic patterns often contribute to this rigidity.

Since the United States is culturally heterogeneous, the youth culture has a number of ethnic subgroups. Racial, ethnic, and religious identity is more important for some groups and individuals than for others. For some adolescents, it becomes important to decide whether they wish to identify with a minority group and how significant a part of their lives they wish this group membership to play. For others, their physical characteristics leave them no choice as to racial identity, but they still must decide how to integrate this identity with others they wish to assume.

We have already noted how some children, from early childhood, suffer from low self-esteem because of prejudice and discrimination. This will adversely affect their attempts to achieve success in other roles later in life. The Hispanic-American family, traditionally patriarchal, expects the father to be the primary wage-earner, respected and obeyed by his family. If the father is unable to continue in this role because of low social and economic status in the American community, then the self-esteem of all family members is apt to suffer (Thornberg and Grinder 1975).

Ralph Ellison (1947) gives a moving account of his experience as an "invisible man" to others who never saw aspects of his identity other than his color. A young Chinese-American writer (Kingston 1977) describes with eloquence another aspect of ethnic identity as she writes of her struggle to escape from the narrow role prescribed for her by family tradition while still drawing on those aspects of her rich heritage that are useful in her personal struggle for identity. These two examples are based on the experience of creative individuals who were able to forge a unique self-image. Many adolescents lack the strength to deal with these complexities. They are more apt to look for peer group memberships that will bolster their sense of self-esteem by providing a clear definition of who they are.

YOUTH UNEMPLOYMENT: A SOCIAL PROBLEM

Most adolescents are successfully moving toward a new identity as an adult. However, social workers are most likely to see those adolescents experiencing serious difficulties in making this transition and who are defined by the community as a "school problem" or a "behavior problem." Because professionals see a select population, there is a tendency to discuss delinquency and behavior disorders as if they were problems of adolescent development rather than individual and group problems that are affected by the social environment. One major social problem affecting teen-agers' transition to adulthood is society's inability to provide sufficient employment for youth who are no longer in school or are alienated from the educational system.

By late adolescence, the problem of entering the world of work assumes a primary importance. For those leaving school at age sixteen or eighteen, the immediate problem is to find full-time employment. Other adolescents need part-time work while attending school. Failure in these early efforts to enter the labor market can have disastrous effects on the self-esteem of adolescents and damage their prospects for successful employment as adults. The consequences of this problem are extremely serious, both for the development of individual potential and for the society as a whole.

Recent statistics (Ginzberg 1980) show that from 1955 to 1978 the rate of unemployment among teen-agers (sixteen through nineteen years old) increased from three times the rate for adults (twenty-five years and older) to four times that rate. During this period of population increase, the total number of jobs in the economy increased, and a larger percentage of the total population sixteen years and older were employed. However, while a higher proportion of white teen-agers were employed than formerly, the proportion of employed black teen-agers declined. While blacks were remaining in school longer than before, their ability to find part-time and full-time employment had not increased; the figures for young adults show a similar trend.

Young whites suffer proportionally less from unemployment than blacks, but since they represent a greater percentage of the total population, they constitute a greater proportion of the total unemployed population. Hispanics fall midway between whites and blacks in terms of rates of unemployment (Ginzberg 1980).

A number of hypotheses have been offered to explain these statistics: The minimum wage discourages employment of unskilled youths; adolescents are unwilling to work at the wages presently offered them; unemployment is high because of the great population increase in the past thirty-five years (the "baby boom" after World War II); as jobs shift from manufacturing and agriculture to the service sector, higher levels of skill are required by employers; racial discrimination in employment still exists;

and factories are moving away from the cities where minority youths are most heavily concentrated.

Some of the problems adolescents encounter in obtaining employment are related to the poor match between their skills and the skills demanded by employers. We noted in the last chapter that many children in middle childhood are labeled as school failures; these children will probably encounter increased problems in school as they move into adolescence. Some become truants, others fail to graduate, and still others remain in school physically but become disengaged from the educational process.

Jenck's research (1972) points to the possibility that success in the world of work depends on variables other than competence in the cognitive tasks measured at school. In addition to competence at school-based skills, adolescents benefit from having positive adult role models, a high degree of motivation, a pleasing personality, and family who can introduce them to potential employers (Jencks 1972). If we follow this line of reasoning, on-the-job training may be one way to ensure that a greater number of potential employees gain necessary job skills, rather than relying so heavily on school credentials as evidence of ability.

At present, there are still no satisfactory solutions to this major social problem. Our economy, for a variety of reasons, simply does not employ all youths, and many unplaced adolescents remain unemployed or underemployed throughout their lives (Ginzberg 1980). Social workers are involved in programs such as the Summer Youth Employment Program, the Job Corps, and other programs of subsidized job training that attempt to provide remedial education as well as job skills. The programs are offered too late in the developmental sequence for some youths; interventive programs are needed when problems in the child's development are first noticed.

Social workers obviously cannot provide all the answers to these problems. Nonetheless, it is important that professionals who work with adolescents in schools, neighborhoods, and the juvenile justice system address themselves to the need for improved employment programs for youths. There can be no healthy psychological and social development if adolescents have reason to believe that they are unlikely to ever attain regular employment and an adequate income.

JUVENILE DELINQUENCY

Social workers have traditionally been involved in programs seeking to treat or rehabilitate adolescents labeled as juvenile delinquents. They offer counseling through family or youth agencies, they work with groups involved in "anti-social activities," they function as placement workers and caseworkers with residential institutions, and they are employed by the juvenile justice system as social workers and probation officers. We shall present a number of perspectives on the causes of delinquency and its prevention and treatment, because in our present state of knowledge we cannot say that any particular theory is correct.

Adolescents are labeled *delinquent* for different reasons. Some violate the criminal law by actions such as theft, rape, assault, and even homicide. Others come under the jurisdiction of the juvenile justice system for **status offenses.** Status offenses are actions that are illegal for minors but not for adults, such as truancy, promiscuity, or refusing to accept parental supervision.

The question of which adolescents should be labeled as delinquent is further complicated by the fact that statistics are commonly compiled by looking at arrest records to see who has broken the law. However, arrest practices for teen-age lawbreakers vary widely; some communities are prone to let minor offenders off with a warning, while others are inclined to "book" the offender. Members of a fraternity are less likely to be labeled as delinquent for causing property damage than are low-income and minority youths who commit similar offenses. Many adolescents have at some time in their lives engaged in illegal behaviors such as shoplifting, drinking, and drug use. Whether they are considered juvenile delinquents depends in part on whether they are caught, where and by whom they are apprehended, and what their race and socioeconomic status is.

Thus far, we have emphasized delinquent acts of a relatively minor nature. However, there is a grimmer aspect to the problem of adolescent crime. United States Department of Justice statistics for 1977 show that 41.2 percent of all persons arrested for serious crimes were under the age of eighteen. A closer examination of this percentage reveals that youths under eighteen years were arrested for 9.7 percent of all homicides, 11.1 percent of negligent manslaughters, 16.5 percent of forcible rapes, 32.0 percent of robberies, 16.3 percent of assaults, 51.5 percent of burglaries, 42.9 percent of larcenies, and 53.0 percent of motor vehicle thefts (U.S. Federal Bureau of Investigation 1977).

The available evidence strongly suggests that crime rates tend to be much higher during middle and late adolescence than at any other period of life (Wheeler 1967). There also tend to be higher rates of crime against property in inner-city slums than in suburban areas. These and other observations have led sociologists to theorize that certain characteristics of our society are responsible for the pattern of delinquent behavior.

Causal factors

Sociologists have been greatly influenced by the work of both Emile Durkheim and Robert Merton, whose theories provide a way of looking at the breakdown of social bonds and shared norms in our society. In a time of rapid social change and social mobility, deviant subcultures are more likely to develop, with values that differ from those prevailing in the community. Our social structure offers both legitimate and illegitimate means of achieving income and material goals. According to some theorists, delinquents share the value traditionally placed on success but deviate from middle-class means of achieving it. Thrasher (1927), Cohen (1955), Miller (1958), and Cloward and Ohlin (1961) are among the researchers whose theories identify social class as a determinant of delinquency. Some theories emphasize the fact that delinquent behavior is learned as part of lower-class culture, and others see delinquency as a substitute means of achievement for groups whose legitimate opportunities for advancement are blocked.

Sykes and Matza (1957) present an interesting alternative theory—that delinquent values do not greatly differ from those of the middle class and that much of delinquent behavior is situational. In other words, one is more apt to steal if it is relatively easy to do so without being caught and if the benefits are relatively rewarding compared to other activities. This theory accounts for the fact that the crime rate decreases as lower-class adolescents grow into less impulsive adults with jobs and families that make their former high-risk activities less worthwhile.

A number of the "War on Poverty" programs of the 1960s were based on Cloward and Ohlin's opportunity theory and attempted to decrease delinquency among low-income youths by increasing the range of legitimate opportunities available to them through job training and improved education. Other programs sought to counter social disorganization by helping to develop new sources of community leadership and to increase the ability of the poor to deal with powerful institutions through welfare rights and legal aid organizations (Rector 1977). Although a number of these innovations have continued, it is still unclear what their impact on preventing delinquency has been.

As instructive as sociological theories about the structural causes of delinquency may be, they lack the ability to explain why some individuals in the same environment are delinquent while others are not. Therefore, we shall summarize a number of theories that deal with individual *psychological variables* associated with delinquent behavior.

Psychoanalytic theorists tend to see adolescent delinquency as symptomatic of personality disturbances originating in earlier stages of the life cycle. These disturbances include unsocialized patterns of aggression, inadequate development of defenses against anxiety, and either a lack of guilt feelings or an unconscious need to be punished for guilt feelings.

Other researchers focus more on immature cognitive development and poor integration of moral values. They point to immature thought processes in which delinquents see themselves as the center of the universe and are unable to understand why others respond to them so unfavorably. In contrast, behavioral theorists focus on delinquency as learned behavior that is environmentally reinforced for some individuals more than for others. Finally, some researchers focus on possible physiological and constitutionally based temperamental similarities among those who become delinquent (Rector 1977).

Unfortunately, professionals working with delinquents and in programs seeking to prevent delinquency still do not have a consistent, proven theoretical framework on which to base their efforts. However, systematic evaluations of program efforts should enable researchers and practitioners to build a satisfactory knowledge base for the future (Rector 1977). Such a base will undoubtedly have to take account of both individual and social factors.

Drug use

Drug use is included under the heading of juvenile delinquency because of the large numbers of adolescents who break the laws against its use. However, drug abuse is obviously a much more complex and widespread problem. If all the users of prescribed and unprescribed psychoactive compounds were counted, one would have to conclude that "the American who has never 'used' drugs is a statistical freak" (Keniston 1968, 1969).

Gisela Konopka's study of adolescent girls (1976) reveals a widespread acceptance of drug and alcohol use among teen-agers, even among those who are not themselves users. She found that drug use often starts in early adolescence, and that a knowledge of drugs and their effects is apparently not a deterrent. The users interviewed indicated that drugs provide an escape from problems and an opportunity to be part of the peer culture. The nonusers indicated that these pressures were offset by a strong motivation in regard to other life goals such as health, school success, and a desire to please a boyfriend or girlfriend. These responses indicate the importance of adolescent peer relationships as a determinant of behavior.

Every drug has the potential of being abused, even drugs that may be beneficial in moderate doses, such as a judicious use of opiates to kill pain. Alcohol and nicotine, two drugs that are more powerful and addictive than marijuana, are legally consumed by millions of Americans (National Institute on Drug Abuse 1977). In fact, the conspicuous use of alcohol and tobacco may be seen as a hallmark of adulthood to a great many adolescents. Teen-agers are taught by their parents' example and the media that drinking is a sophisticated activity.

Alcohol acts as a depressant; its effects are similar to those of sleeping pills. In small amounts, the psychological effects include lowered inhibitions and heightened feelings of well-being. Many drinkers use alcohol to ease tension and to facilitate social interaction. The physical effects may include distorted vision, impaired motor coordination, slurred speech, and loss of consciousness when taken in large doses. Both mental and physical effects vary with individual tolerance and the amounts taken. Long-term habitual use of alcohol results in damage to liver and brain cells.

Tobacco use is another habit that the adult world encourages by example. Although cigarette advertising has been banned from television and the overall incidence of smoking has declined, cigarette smoking continues to appeal to teen-agers. One study has shown that one-third of all high school students smoke (Consumers Union 1972), and that the practice is on the rise, particularly among adolescent girls.

Smoking has long been known to present a serious health hazard. It increases the heart rate, causes shortness of breath, constricts the blood vessels, irritates the throat, and damages lung tissues. Years of smoking lead to an increased incidence of premature heart attacks, lung and throat cancer, emphysema, and other diseases. Yet most adult smokers started in their teens in response to peer pressure and continue to smoke because the addictive qualities of nicotine make it difficult for them to stop.

Along with alcohol and cigarettes, marijuana use is widespread among today's youth. A survey taken by the National Institute on Drug Abuse (1977) shows that 47 percent of sixteen- and seventeen-year-olds and almost 60 percent of the eighteen- to twenty-year-olds had smoked marijuana at least once in their lives. However, only about 30 percent of these age groups reported using it the past month. This shows that a large number of adolescents have broken the law and would be juvenile offenders if caught, even though they may be only occasional users. During the past fifty years, law-enforcement agencies have spent a large amount of time and money prosecuting violations, and many states retain harsh penalties for offenders.

While marijuana is not as dangerous as the legal restrictions imply, neither is it a benign drug. In fact, its widespread use among teen-agers creates some real dangers. For example, a survey of research on the topic (Schmeck 1979) shows that smoking marijuana alters perception, impedes motor coordination, and interferes with problem-solving abilities. The physical effects are just as potentially cancer-causing as cigarettes; smoking damages the lungs of the user.

For adolescents, there are a number of offenses that are considered illegal only because of the offender's youthful status. We turn now to a discussion of status offenders.

Status offenders

We have mentioned that adolescence is generally a time in which the boundaries of established authority are tested and new life styles are tried. At various times, our society has been more or less tolerant of specific forms of deviant behavior. When youthful behavior is not considered tolerable, it may be defined as a juvenile offense, subject to criminal penalties. For example, adolescents who are habitually truant or runaways are status offenders because social norms dictate that fifteen-year-olds must attend school, live with their families, and obey their parents. In fact, the laws on this score are frequently ignored if no one makes a complaint. However, in 1974 approximately one-third of those under eighteen years old in correctional facilities were status offenders (Sarri 1978).

In recent years there has been a growing awareness that legal controls over minors may be more harmful than helpful. Incarceration in a correctional institution may harm an adolescent more than doing nothing about the situation. There is also increased reluctance to labeling youths as delinquent when they may be running away from intolerable family situations, as is often the case. The appropriateness of legislating different standards of morality for adolescents than for adults and of treating runaways as offenders is also being questioned.

On the other side of the debate about status offenses, many people point to the sexual exploitation of minors who run away from home and need society's protection, whether they seek it voluntarily or not. Some of the children whose behavior is at issue are early adolescents, fifteen years old and younger. Freedom may be a meaningless benefit if prostitution is the only means of employment immediately available to adolescents who do not have parental care and supervision.

The Juvenile Justice and Delinquency Prevention Act of 1974 dealt with one aspect of this longstanding problem by prohibiting the use of federal funds for facilities that mix status offenders with those who have committed more serious crimes. The intent of this legislation was to force communities to create alternative programs and services for adolescents outside of the juvenile justice system (Sarri 1978). We shall turn now to a discussion of some of these programs.

Diversionary programs

The concern with keeping minors who have not committed serious offenses out of the criminal justice system has led to a search for suitable noninstitutional alternatives. Unfortunately, there is a lack of suitable foster home and group home placements for this population of adolescents. While they are not "criminals," they have often suffered early neglect or abuse, have low self-esteem, and need to be supervised by adults mature enough to handle constant testing of limits. Foster home parents or group home counselors may not be able to deal with problems of sexuality, drug use, truancy, and defiance.

A major goal of diversionary programs is to avoid long-term placements by offering family counseling and other services designed to allow the adolescents to return to their own families. Some families are able to respond to crisis intervention. Other family problems, however, are far too serious to respond to such "band-aid" remedies. Great skill is required to assess adolescent offenders and their families and recommend the most suitable program. Often the family will need a multiservice approach that offers remedial education, job placement, housing assistance, and coordinated medical care, as well as counseling services.

By looking at the total family situation rather than merely punishing the adolescent who exhibits deviant behavior, we realize that intervention is often needed at many levels if our goal is to restore the adolescent to a family that is functioning at a minimally adequate level. As we pointed out earlier, a crucial variable is the degree of the "fit" between parent and child. Some families can tolerate and successfully help a teen-ager who gets into all sorts of trouble; others lack the resources to handle the situation. On the other hand, some teen-agers have the inner strength or enough support from significant others to enable them to successfully deal with neglectful or abusive parents or a neighborhood with a high delinquency rate.

In summary, we need a range of services for troubled youths and their families. Some families will improve as a result of expanded community-based programs to divert youths from the juvenile justice system, but others will not. For the latter, a range of alternative placements are needed—from foster homes to locked facilities for those who are dangerous to themselves or others. At present, alternatives are limited, and reformers are dismayed to find that even when alternative dispositions are available, the rates of commitment to correctional institutions have not appreciably diminished. Instead, programs have expanded and the number of persons served has increased, causing concern that many of the youths now being referred to community-based programs would formerly have been released because their offenses were minor (Pabon 1978).

CASE ILLUSTRATIONS

Fred Collins is a social worker for a community agency that operates a group home for adolescents. The following are descriptions of some of the children with whom he works.

Jonathan

Jonathan is a sixteen-year-old who has been in several other diversionary programs in the past few years. He has been dismissed from each program because of continued stealing. He is underweight and very self-conscious about his severe acne. He feels very angry toward his parents because of their divorce and his father's subsequent abandonment of the family but is unable to express this anger directly toward them. Instead, he bullies his peers and is antagonistic toward other adults. He has excellent scholastic skills but constantly "messes up" by cutting school. He has been stealing since he was eight years old, and when caught he confesses readily. He has little expectation that he will do well in life in spite of his considerable ability but indulges in grandiose fantasies about becoming a millionaire.

His present placement offers a fairly strict regime where he can earn rewards for appropriate behavior. Although Jonathan continues to earn privileges, he always falls back to "step one" because of stealing. He is very manipulative and demanding of others.

Mr. Collins is counseling Jonathan and his mother, trying to help his mother set more appropriate and consistent expectations for her son's behavior during family visits. Although the social worker's goals are based on his diagnosis of Jonathan's particular problems he also applies his general knowledge of adolescent development. He secures medical treatment for Jonathan's acne and tries to involve him in satisfying recreational activities that may help him to improve his relationships with peers. Mr. Collins will also help Jonathan find a part-time job to increase his self-esteem and provide him with spending money. The agency and the public school are working cooperatively in this case, but it is not certain that they will succeed in eliminating Jonathan's stealing.

Darryl

Darryl is thirteen and has run away from home several times. His mother feels that she has no control over his behavior; the school is having similar problems controlling him. His teacher has made a referral to the group home because she thinks that Darryl's behavior will not improve if he continues to live with his family.

Mr. Collins has met several times with Darryl, his mother, and his teacher. He finds that the mother is afraid of Darryl and expects him to become violent like his father, a man she has not seen in twelve years. His mother also worries about his hanging around with and imitating some older boys in the neighborhood who are members of a gang. He is large for his age, and people therefore expect him to act more maturely.

The school records indicate that Darryl has serious learning problems. He is reading at a third-grade level, and his speech patterns show that he is not able to deal with complex thoughts and has difficulty in conceptualizing time sequences.

Mr. Collins thinks that Darryl should remain at home and attend the agency's day treatment program as an alternative to residential placement. He thinks that the mother will benefit from supportive counseling for her own social and medical problems and that learning more effective parenting methods will help her in dealing with all her children. He fears that out-of-home placement will weaken the parent-child bonds before Darryl is ready. Funding for placement is contingent on a judgment that he is out of control of his parents and is therefore a dependent or neglected child in need of court supervision. Mr. Collins feels that this process will only add to the damaged self-esteem of mother and son.

Fortunately, the agency services include an alternative day-school for troubled adolescents. Darryl's strengths and weaknesses in the cognitive area will be carefully assessed, and necessary remedial instruction will be available. Darryl will also be able to study the guitar, which interests him greatly. The treatment plan will emphasize helping him to identify with at least one of the male teachers at the school so that he starts to see himself in a more positive way. In addition, it is hoped that gains in cognitive development will enable him to make better judgments and be less likely to thoughtlessly follow his peers.

Fred Collins knows the neighborhood Darryl has lived in throughout his life and sees no reason to sever the ties he has with individuals and groups in the community. While the neighborhood adolescent gangs look and talk "tough," delinquency seems confined to individual rather than group actions. The usual pattern is for the youths to settle down to marriage and employment in the local factory when they are in their twenties. Fred hopes that as Darryl matures in his cognitive and emotional development he will be able to deal successfully with neighborhood peer groups. Learning to play the guitar well enough to perform with a group will give him some of the status he needs.

Joan

Joan is a fourteen-year-old girl who lives in a group home because, after working with her family for two years, the county Child Protective Services Unit recommended that she be removed from her own home. Her father had abused her sexually numerous times while her mother protected the father by denying knowledge of the situation. After Joan reported the situation to the school nurse, the family was supervised by a protective services worker. However, the situation became unstable because both parents blamed their daughter for breaking up their marriage. Joan is expected to remain in the group home until she is eighteen years old because relatively few foster home placements are available for adolescents.

The treatment plan includes the objective of allowing Joan to become dependent on an adult so that she can experience appropriate parenting. Luckily she is small for her age, and people respond to her as to a younger child. It was decided to place her in junior high school for another year instead of enrolling her in high school. Her cognitive skills are excellent, but she daydreams a lot and has little motivation to do homework or to hand in written assignments.

Until now, Joan has not had much of a social life with children of her own age. She has had "best friends," but she always becomes disappointed in them and loses interest in the relationship after an initial period of enthusiasm. She usually expects too much of her friends. Because of a lack of friends and interests of her own, Joan often feels bored and lonely. Therefore, the treatment plan includes helping her to develop interests and skills that will lead to participation in activities with children of her own age. She appears to like roller skating and making jewelry, and the staff will encourage her to participate in these activities.

The staff's prognosis for Joan is optimistic. This is partly because she looks attractive and staff find her appealing. As the youngest girl in the group home she looks to staff as role models. They are somewhat apprehensive about the future, when the novelty of being babied wears off and Joan follows the pattern of the other girls who are all sexually active. Although the girls eventually go to Planned Parenthood for birth control pills, most delay this move for some time after they become sexually active. Even afterward, they are prone to forget about taking the pill. They seldom take precautionary measures against the possibility of a future occurrence, tending to deal with events as they happen.

As the home's social worker, Fred Collins offers individual counseling to help the adolescents to build a more positive self-image based on real accomplishments and successful moves toward independence from their families. He also seeks to find the most favorable combination of environmental factors that will foster skill development and improved peer relationships for each child. Emphasis is also placed on helping staff to understand the special developmental needs of adolescents and to respond appropriately to behavior that is often provocative and inconsistent.

SUMMARY

Adolescence in industrial society is rather lengthy, involving an extended period of education and dependence. Although *puberty* refers to the onset of reproductive ability, *adolescence* includes the period between childhood and the attainment of adult self-sufficiency.

The biological changes of adolescence proceed at a rapid pace. The body growth and hormonal changes begin at an earlier age for some than for others. Sexual maturation has psychological as well as physiological effects, since adolescents place a high value on conformity in looks. Professionals must often deal with problems of damaged self-esteem among adolescents.

Formal operational thought, which involves the capacity to critically analyze one's own thought processes and to see oneself from the point of view of others, develops at this time. Not all people achieve this ability or use it consistently, but it does represent the most complex stage of cognitive ability and is necessary for the construction of an independent and logical system of values. Kohlberg has developed a system for increasing this ability by "moral education."

A significant proportion of those who are concerned with idealistic causes and value commitments are older adolescents. The youthful counterculture of the sixties was followed by an increased general acceptance of varied forms of sexual expression, use of drugs, and emphasis on self-awareness.

Erikson characterizes adolescence as a time when a number of elements converge to form a consistent ego identity. The search for identity may be a time of growth rather than stress, depending on a number of internal and external factors. Sometimes options are closed off too quickly, and at other times there is continued lack of attachment and commitment.

The evidence points to increased liberalization of sexual behavior and experimentation by adolescents. However, young adolescents still socialize in single-sex groups. The age at which adolescents become sexually active is related to factors such as education, psychological makeup, family relationships, and biological maturation.

The rising incidence of unmarried and very young mothers is of particular concern to social workers. There are substantial differences in the illegitimacy rate of whites and blacks, differences that appear to be related to social factors such as immigration from the rural South and the incidence of poverty.

Adolescence may be a time of increased role conflict; reference groups differ in their behavioral expectations, and teen-agers who make new group affiliations may experience conflict between old and new loyalties. These problems may be greater for ethnic and racial minorities.

Unemployment is a major social problem with a special impact on youths. Although a higher percentage of white teen-agers are employed than formerly, the reverse is true for blacks. Many adolescents who are unplaced in their teens will remain unemployed or underemployed throughout their lives—with drastic psychological as well as economic effects.

Juvenile delinquency is another social problem affecting adolescents; the crime rate is higher during middle and late adolescence than at any other period of life. There are numerous psychological and sociological theories about the causes of delinquency. Adolescents currently come under the jurisdiction of the juvenile court not only for criminal activities but also for offenses such as truancy and incorrigibility, illegal only because of the offender's minor status. Drug offenses also account for a number of juvenile arrests, although the use of alcohol and drugs is widespread in adult society.

There have been recent moves to divert adolescent offenders from the criminal justice system into community-based alternative programs. Social workers are often involved in helping to establish alternative foster and group home programs. Some offenders can return to their families after a period of counseling; others need long-term placement.

SUGGESTED READINGS

Cohen, A. *Delinquent Boys: The Culture of the Gang.* Glencoe, Ill.: Free Press, 1955. A clear presentation of one perspective on delinquency—the "delinquent subculture" of the lower-class adolescent gang.

Erikson, E.H. *Identity: Youth and Crisis.* New York: W. W. Norton & Co., 1968. A discusson of adolescent identity formation, with many examples from case studies.

Glock, C.Y., and Bellah, R.N., (Eds.). *The New Religious Consciousness.* Berkeley: University of California Press, 1976. A sociological analysis and empirical study of the religious aftermath of the counterculture of the 1960s.

Josselyn, I.M. *Adolescence.* New York: Harper & Row, 1971. While emphasizing psychosocial problems as seen by an analytically oriented therapist, this book also discusses adolescence in a physical, cognitive, and cultural context.

Kingston, M.H. *The Woman Warrier: Memoirs of a Girlhood Among Ghosts.* New York: Knopf, 1977. A forceful presentation of a young woman's attempts to forge her own identity, selecting some parts of her Chinese tradition and rejecting other parts.

Konopka, G. *Young Girls: A Portrait of Adolescence.* Englewood Cliffs, N.J.: Prentice-Hall, 1976. An overview of the issues that concern adolescent girls today, their interpersonal relationships, and their connections with the adult world.

Offer, D., and Offer, J.B. *From Teenage to Young Manhood: A Psychological Study.* New York: Basic Books, 1975. Based on an innovative study of the normal male adolescent, this book challenges some traditional views about this stage.

chapter seven

Christa Armstrong, Photo Researchers

YOUNG ADULTHOOD

establishing
a new household

outline

PERSONALITY DEVELOPMENT

Developmental tasks

The Grant study

Levinson: The novice phase

Gould: Outgrowing illusions

THE WORLD OF WORK

Characteristics of the labor force

Occupational choices

Work and leisure

SEXUALITY AND INTIMACY

Cultural differences

Dimensions of human sexuality

Sexual orientation

Sexual therapy

MARRIAGE AND OTHER ALTERNATIVES

Married and unmarried couples

Divorce

Singleness

Communal families

PARENTHOOD

Tasks of parenting

Decisions about parenthood

The single mother

CASE ILLUSTRATIONS

SUMMARY

SUGGESTED READINGS

WHEN DOES ADOLESCENCE end and adulthood begin? Legal definitions of maturity vary. A person is mature enough to vote at age eighteen, but a candidate for the U.S. Senate must be at least thirty years old, and the presidency is open only to those age thirty-five and over. There are informal social definitions of maturity: someone who is regularly employed, financially independent, or who is a parent. There are also psychological characteristics associated with maturity, such as autonomy, reliability, and integrity. Psychologists may emphasize one set of characteristics or another (Bischof 1969), and cultures vary in their expectations of adults. Freud defined psychological maturity quite simply as the ability to work and to love.

Whatever combination of characteristics is included in a psychological or social definition of maturity, it has no clear age demarcation. Nonetheless, studies of human behavior suggest that each of us has an internalized clock by which we judge whether activities are age-appropriate (Neugarten 1968a). Most often these built-in expectations for various stages in life represent learned responses. For example, we would probably have dramatically different reactions to a fifty-year-old couple seen dancing enthusiastically at a disco club than to a twenty-five-year-old couple. This is because we frequently interpret people's motivations in accordance with their age.

Neugarten and Moore (1968) define three stages of adulthood: young adulthood (twenties and early thirties), middle age (forties and fifties), and senescence (sixty-five and over). But within these broad categories many other factors affect judgments of behavior. Socioeconomic status, ethnic background, rural or urban setting, historical period, and other life events also influence definitions and expectations of adulthood. The higher a person's social class, for example, the more likely he or she will be able to afford the luxury of delaying movement from one stage to another (Neugarten and Moore 1968). Persons who are dependent on physical labor for their livelihood may feel that they have reached their prime at age thirty, while professionals may be viewed as still gaining maturity, experience, and recognition as they approach forty. An important aspect of an individual's self-concept is whether or not that person considers himself or herself to be in the prime of life.

Although men and women are emotionally still somewhat immature in their early adult years, they enjoy a peak of vitality, strength, and health. Physical strength is at a maximum between the ages of twenty-five and thirty, after which it declines slowly but significantly. However, most physical skills and capacities will remain functional if used regularly. Generally young adults enjoy better health than children, they have few acute illnesses, and they have not yet begun to experience the troubles of middle age (Timiris 1972).

Theorists used to believe that intellectual capacities peaked in the late teens—a view that stemmed from an undifferentiated, simplistic concept of intelligence and intelligence testing. Developmental psychologists now chart the differential growth of specific cognitive functions such as memory, reaction time, reasoning, and creativity. We now know that some skills do peak in the late teens—for example, rote memory and speed-related performance. These early-peaking proficiencies may have a physiological basis, or they may simply reflect the fact that many of those tested are full-time students who constantly practice and rely on these skills. Other cognitive abilities such as judgment, reasoning, and creativity continue to develop throughout life, as is apparent in the artistic and scientific achievements of many mature and elderly people. Creative processes that depend on originality and innovation, however, seem to peak earlier than those requiring maturity and accumulated experience.

In the first part of this chapter we shall examine some basic theories of adult development and describe a few recent studies. We shall then discuss the importance of adults' entry into the job market. Social workers must be aware of the characteristics of the labor market as well as the psychological and vocational prerequisites for job success.

Finally, we shall examine the social and cultural milestones generally reached in early adulthood and the patterns of adaptation associated with career, marriage, and the establishment of a new family unit. The timing of these events varies from individual to individual and among ethnic and socioeconomic groups. Choice of career or the birth of a first child may take place at age fifteen or forty. Marriage may occur in adolescence, early adulthood, old age, or not at all. As we have seen in earlier chapters, expectations about marital roles and parenting vary markedly among individuals and groups.

PERSONALITY DEVELOPMENT

Development, or at least the potential for development, continues throughout life. Although some theorists believe that there are developmental stages in adulthood, others believe that the developmental process in maturity is somewhat different from that of childhood and adolescence (Havighurst 1953). The latter point out that changes after adolescence are primarily due to social and cultural forces rather than to new body functions or intellectual operations. The social milestones and cultural demands of young adulthood may disrupt behavioral patterns laid down in the teenage years and require that new patterns be developed. However, these crises and conflicts need not be considered as undesirable, as the ability to respond to change and to adapt successfully to new conditions is a hallmark of maturity (Datan and Ginsberg 1975). Although less has been written about personality development during the adult years, the journey through adult life does follow certain general patterns. We shall describe three theories of adult personality development in the following section.

Developmental tasks

Erikson (1963) sees the establishment of intimate relationships as the major developmental task in adulthood. *Intimacy* requires self-awareness, self-acceptance, independence, and trust. Trust is necessary if the young adult is to allow expressions of vulnerability and inadequacy without fear of rejection by the intimate partner. By the same token, the other partner's inadequacies can then be acknowledged without a diminished sense of worth or desirability. Intimacy is destroyed if one partner's needs consistently dominate a relationship.

Erikson's theory is that the adult process of establishing intimacy draws on the skills and resources developed in earlier stages. Recall that Erikson identifies these as: trust (birth through age two); autonomy (two to four years); initiative (four to six years); industry (six to twelve years); and identity (twelve to eighteen years). To be capable of intimacy, young adults must be convinced that those who love them will act in their best interests (trust). They must be prepared to do without the help of others (autonomy), and must take the first steps toward obtaining their own support and affection (initiative and industry). All this frequently takes place in the context of sexual attraction. Healthy young adults accept and enjoy the sexual desires they feel for and evoke in others (identity). Intimate friendship without a sexual component also requires a satisfactory resolution of the identity task of adolescence, so that tenderness, openness, and vulnerability are seen as appropriate qualities in mature men and women. Ideally, intimacy replaces parental love, and equal partnership supplants domination and obedience.

Bühler offers a different framework for viewing the developmental tasks of this period (Bühler and Massarik 1968). He considers the period from ages twenty-one to thirty as a stage of experimentation, parallel in some respects to the period of growth and exploration from eight months to four years. Children in this earlier stage master many bodily functions and test the boundaries of dependence on their parents. Young children mark a major social achievement when they are able to let their mothers leave them, trusting in her eventual return. Similarly, young adults seek to establish loving, trusting bonds with an intimate partner while guaranteeing independence for both. Young adults require a period of experimentation as they set out on the uncharted waters of adult love and work. Many tend to make impulsive choices at this time, lacking the wisdom and experience to reach satisfying solutions. However, once they have gone through the experimentation stage, adults proceed to a stage that Bühler terms *consolidation*. This represents the final establishment of occupational, financial, and emotional security. Consolidation occupies the approximate age span from thirty-five to fifty.

The third theory we shall present emphasizes the role of the ego in adult growth. *Loevinger* (1976) sees the ego as an overseer that exerts conscious control of the personality. From infancy through adolescence, the child's ego is primarily involved with the reactions of others, their blame or approval. However, the young adult gradually turns inward for standards of right and wrong. In the *conscientious stage*, the individual measures ideals, achievements, and traits by inner standards. These inner standards may differ from those of peers and authority figures and may vary from one context to another. What is morally correct in one situation may be wrong in another, and the individual is now capable of self-criticism in thinking about these problems. Loevinger's next adult stage is the *autonomous period*, in which young adults can understand and tolerate paradoxical relationships without having to condemn or approve of them. They become more aware and tolerant of inner conflicts between needs and personal ideals. It also becomes increasingly easy for them to accept differences between themselves and others. Autonomous people let others make their own decisions about work, love, family, and friends. Loevinger's final development is the *integrated stage*, in which an adult not only permits differences between self and others but values and enjoys them. Loevinger estimates that only about 1 percent of all adults achieve this final stage.

The Grant study

Adult development cannot be studied in a controlled laboratory setting. Cultural and historical factors influence each generation of adults in unique ways. We shall examine three major studies of adult development that have been completed in the last few years. In each an attempt is made to view individual personality traits over a period of time. We should keep in mind the tentative nature of the concepts developed by these theorists; they are not supported by empirical research as are Piaget's stages of cognitive development.

The Grant Study (Vaillant 1977) was a developmental project that began in 1938. The researchers wanted to learn how and why some men succeed in life while others fail. A group of almost three hundred Harvard students were tested, interviewed, and followed over a period of years. The students had been recommended by their classmates as outstanding in health, self-reliance, achievement, and stability. Interestingly, one of the group, described as a statesman who was "pointlessly murdered" before his prime and "destined to play a role in every child's history book," was undoubtedly John F. Kennedy, Harvard '40. JFK and others in the cohort went through twenty hours of tests and interviews while in college. Researchers compiled detailed family histories for each subject, and each was rated for twenty-five personality traits. The subjects continued to complete detailed questionnaires at regular intervals after graduation.

"Blind" evaluators, who never personally encountered the young men, divided the group into "best" and "worst" outcomes. These were determined by the criteria of material wealth, professional prestige, mental stability, and satisfying family life. Both the criteria and the scales were defined in rather elitist terms, reflecting the power and prestige of a Harvard degree. For example, occupational success was measured in part by being listed in *Who's Who in America* and *American Men of Science*.

Researchers combed the records of the "best" and the "worst" for childhood clues to later success. They found that classic childhood traumas such as strict toilet training, bans on nail biting and thumb sucking, and emotionally distant mothers did not necessarily result in emotional illness in adulthood.

Adult success of the JFK generation was then compared with adolescent profiles. The researchers expected to document a relationship between the lively, outgoing, altruistic teen-ager and the prosperous, well-adjusted man. This hypothesis, however, was not supported by the data. Gregarious, idealistic students were no more likely to succeed than shy, self-contained youths. The Grant Study analysts concluded that easy amiability is a hallmark of adolescence that does not necessarily appear in the mature personality. The traits in teen-agers that most clearly predicted later success were practicality, organization, and personality integration—traits not usually associated with late adolescence.

The researchers also looked at defense mechanisms in order to determine their adaptive function. Interestingly, they even identified *repression* and *projection* as among the successful adult coping styles (although they usually are labeled as pathological processes). According to Vaillant, these defense mechanisms perform five important functions in adult life: (1) containing emotions within acceptable limits during times of extreme emotional stress, such as the loss of a loved one; (2) maintaining stability by channeling biological drives; (3) permitting adjustments in self-image following important changes such as a job promotion or major surgery; (4) resolving conflicts within one's intimate circles; and (5) rationalizing major conflicts involving the dictates of conscience, such as killing in wartime.

It was found that to some degree even repression and projection help the individual's ego to survive. However, the most successful mode of adaptation was *sublimation*. According to Freudian theory, sublimation involves channeling anxiety and unacceptable impulses toward acceptable goals.

Which factors are related to the development of mature defenses? Successful maturation (as defined by this study of a select population of Harvard students) was found to be surprisingly independent of the effects of sheer intelligence, happy childhood, and affluent background. Vaillant suggests that variations in adult brain development may account for some of the successes and failures. However, environmental influences also affect the capacity to build intimate relationships, and the most successful subjects were those who acquired mentors and role models in early adulthood and later became protectors and advisors to others.

Levinson: The novice phase

Another intensive study of male adult development was conducted by Levinson (1978). Unlike the Grant Study, which interviewed adult subjects at fixed intervals for over a decade, this study conducted several intensive interviews during a period of a few months. Levinson was primarily interested in learning about middle age, so his subjects consisted of forty men, aged thirty-five to forty-five, drawn from different racial, ethnic, and professional groups. His data is based on his subjects' memories and introspection and therefore is more subjective than the tests, scales, and "blind" evaluations used by Vaillant. Along with the reconstructed biographies of these forty men, Levinson and his assistants also studied the biographies of great figures such as Dante and Ghandi for clues to patterns of adult growth.

The study identifies three major "eras" in the male cycle, each approximately twenty-five years long. While Levinson was primarily interested in the decade from thirty-five to forty-five, he found that maturation and adjustment at this stage was highly dependent on the individual's growth in the *novice phase, from seventeen to thirty-three years of age.* This period is the time when young American men resolve adolescent conflicts, create a place for themselves in adult society, and commit themselves to stable, predictable patterns.

According to Levinson, the young man must master four main developmental tasks in order to complete entry into adulthood: (1) *defining a "Dream"*; (2) *finding a mentor*; (3) *developing a career*; and (4) *establishing intimacy.*

Levinson considers the **Dream** as a vision, "an imagined possibility that generates excitement and vitality" (Levinson 1978, p. 30). At the beginning of the novice phase, the Dream is not clearly linked to reality. It may consist of modest aspirations, or it may involve a grandiose goal such as becoming a movie producer, business tycoon, or famous poet. It serves the important function of inspiring a young man so that he begins to structure his life in realistic, optimistic ways that help realize the Dream.

However, fantasies and utterly unattainable goals do not encourage such growth. It is important to note that the Dream may undergo change over time. The young man hoping to become a basketball All-Star may later find satisfaction as a coach, thus incorporating some of the elements of the youthful Dream.

Even when the Dream is realistic, it may remain unfulfilled because of lack of opportunity, excessive parental pressure, or individual traits such as guilt or passivity. Thus, a young man may enter and master an occupation that holds no magic for him. When this happens, there may be continuous career conflicts in adulthood and a limited self-investment in work. Levinson believes that those who struggle to fulfill some version of the Dream are more likely than others to achieve a sense of fulfillment.

A **mentor** can be of enormous assistance to the achievement of a young person's Dream. The mentor can instill self-confidence by sharing and approving of the goal and by imparting skill and wisdom. As a sponsor, the mentor may use influence to advance the career of the protégé. However, the major function of the mentor is to provide a transition from the parent-child relationship to the adult relationship with peers. The mentor must be sufficiently parental to represent a high level of achievement, yet sufficiently sympathetic to overcome the generation gap and establish a peer bond. Gradually, the apprentice may acquire a sense of autonomy and competence and may even overtake the mentor. Given the intense nature of the relationship, this growth may lead to bitterness, conflict, and distance. The mentor may find the youth rebellious and ungrateful; the youth may see the mentor as critical and oppressive. They frequently break off their relationship and drift apart.

Besides forming the Dream and acquiring a mentor, youths also face a complex, sociopsychological process of *career formation* that goes well beyond the mere selection of an occupation. Levinson views this developmental task as spanning the entire novice phase. We shall examine this process in more detail in the next section of this chapter.

Similarly, the formation of *intimate family relationships* does not coincide with the time of marriage or the birth of the first child. The young man is constantly learning about himself and the ways in which he relates to women. He must ascertain what he likes about women and what they like about him, and must define his inner strengths and vulnerabilities in sexual intimacy. While some self-discovery takes place in adolescence, it is not until his early thirties that the young man develops the capacity for a serious, democratic partnership. Furthermore, relating to the feminine aspects in his own personality and that of others remains a lifelong developmental task.

A primary relationship with a "special woman" (Levinson's term) may fill a need similar to that of the mentor-pupil bond. The special woman may facilitate realization of the Dream by believing in her partner. She aids his entry into the adult world by encouraging adult hopes and tolerating his shortcomings. According to Levinson, the male's need for the special woman decreases by the time of mid-life transition, when most men achieve a high degree of autonomy and competence.

Levinson's study, although covering a broader cross-section of men than the Grant Study, still does not answer any questions about the growth patterns of women. There is a need to replicate these studies with women in order to see how female subjects establish a Dream, mentor, career, and patterns of intimacy. Such questions are of particular interest because of the increased number of women who are now planning careers in professions and trades that were formerly all male.

Gould: Outgrowing illusions

Gould's studies (1978) include both men and women, although his subjects are by no means representative. Gould and his colleagues examined extensive life histories of a large group of psychiatric outpatients, age sixteen to sixty, and compared them with a similar sample of nonpatients. From these profiles, they extracted world views characteristic of different adult stages. Gould views growth as the process of casting off childish illusions and false assumptions in favor of self-reliance and self-acceptance.

According to this view, sixteen- to twenty-two-year-olds must challenge the false assumption that "I'll always belong to my parents and believe in their world." In order to discard this illusion, young adults must start building an adult identity that their parents cannot control or dominate. However, the sense of self is still fragile at this stage, and self-doubt makes young adults highly sensitive to criticism. Gradually, they are able to see their parents as imperfect and fallible people rather than the all-powerful controlling forces they once were.

From ages twenty-two to twenty-eight, young adults make another false assumption that reflects their continuing doubts about themselves: "Perseverance in doing things my parents' way will eventually bring results. But if I become too frustrated or am unable to cope, they will step in and make things all right." To combat this notion, the young adult must accept full responsibility for his or her life, surrendering the expectation of continuous parental assistance. This involves far more than freeing oneself from parental domination. It requires the active construction of an adult life, as energies are rechanneled toward adult work instead of ancient grievances. Conquering the world on one's own also diverts energy from constant introspection and self-centeredness. Gould found that young adults progress during this period from flashes of insight to a cognitive style characterized by perseverance, discipline, controlled experimentation, and goal orientation.

Gould says that another significant shift occurs during the period from twenty-eight to thirty-four years of age. The major false assumption during this period is that "Life is simple and controllable. There are no significant contradictory forces within me." Growth during this time is dependent on developing competence based on effort and on acknowledging a sense of limitations. Adult consciousness allows one to accept inner turmoil without feeling that one's integrity has been seriously threatened.

At this stage there may also be a reemergence of talents and desires that were suppressed because they did not fit the earlier blueprint for adulthood. Gould cites examples of the ambitious young partner in a prestigious law firm who begins to consider entering public service, or the carefree bachelor who suddenly recognizes that his many relationships with women are not satisfying because of some of his own inadequacies. (This developmental process closely resembles Levinson's prediction that those who ignore and suppress the Dream in early adulthood may be haunted later by the unresolved conflict.) Even those who have fulfilled youthful ambitions may experience some doubt and depression during this period. They may begin to question the very values that helped them to gain independence from their parents.

The period from thirty-five to forty-five years of age brings definitive involvement in the adult world. As adults move into middle age, they become the final authority to those both younger and older than themselves. Their parents no longer have control over them, and their children have not yet effectively challenged them. At the same time, they experience a sudden time pressure and fear that they will not accomplish all their goals. The beginning physical changes of middle age frighten and dismay them. The drive for stability and security that was paramount in the thirties is replaced by the need for immediate action and results. There can be no more procrastination as the awareness of their own mortality brings them face to face with the unfairness and pain of life. Gould believes that a full, autonomous adult consciousness is achieved when people become free to examine and finally discard the deep sense of their own worthlessness and wickedness that was left over from childhood.

These presentations of personality development in the adult years are of particular relevance to social workers who offer counseling services in settings such as colleges, family agencies, mental health centers, and special settings such as correctional institutions or agencies serving the handicapped. Some young adults seek support in order to cope with tasks that seem temporarily overwhelming; others have become seriously immobilized by the challenges of adult life.

Although limited in their range of subjects, these studies do provide an intensive view of how some young adults utilize cognitive and emotional patterns developed earlier in order to cope with new challenges. They show the young adult years as a time of gradual rather than sudden transition from dependence on parents to autonomy. Counselors, therefore, should be alert to the possibility that establishing independence from parents may continue to be a central issue throughout the young adult years.

Social workers must understand individuals' hopes and aspirations as well as their capabilities if they are to help them formulate realistic yet exciting goals for themselves. Some people accomplish the transition from illusion to acceptance of one's limits more easily than others. The Grant Study illustrates how success in adult life may be related to personality traits that differ from those leading to popularity and success during adolescence. Counselors should be sensitive to this factor in helping individuals make the transition from the adolescent peer culture to the demands of the world of work.

Social workers in institutional settings can make a special contribution by pointing out that issues of developing autonomy and intimacy are usually not resolved during adolescence but continue to be salient throughout the young adult years. Individuals with disabilities need opportunities for emotional growth, but many institutional settings cast them into roles of greater dependency than necessary.

We turn now to some of the adjustments involved in entering the labor market.

THE WORLD OF WORK

The ability to provide a livelihood for oneself and one's dependents is considered to be an important indication of maturity for men and increasingly for women as well. It is a major task for young adults and usually involves the expenditure of considerable time and energy. Individual attitudes toward work vary considerably with social class, age, sex, and personality differences. For most persons, work is necessary to survive; some also view it as an opportunity to be productive, to gain self-esteem, or to be creative. For still others, work may be something they are driven to do in order to feel adequate. A person may achieve a sense of pleasure and fulfillment from work or feel burdened, frustrated, and dehumanized by it (Keniston 1963).

Most males are socialized to feel that their work is a central part of their identity (Moore 1969). Women, on the other hand, have a rather mixed socialization toward work. Some are clearly socialized to aspire to careers and achievement; others see work as an unsatisfying alternative to marriage and motherhood. Some women take jobs out of economic necessity but still identify themselves primarily as wives and mothers.

In this section, we shall consider both psychological and socioeconomic factors associated with young adults' choice of occupation and successful entry into the labor market. Because unemployment, underemployment, and low wages result in both individual and social crises, we shall turn first to a consideration of some characteristics of today's labor force.

Characteristics of the labor force

One of the most striking changes in the character of today's labor force is the increase in the employment of women, particularly married women. The labor force participation rate of single women has remained fairly constant at close to 50 percent from 1900 to 1974; however, the participation rate for married women of all ages (with husbands present) rose from 6 percent to 43 percent in that same period (Cain 1977). The labor force participation rate of all women twenty to twenty-four years of age rose from 57 percent in 1969 to 64.3 percent in 1975 (Heath and Somers 1977). By 1978, over 60 percent of American women, ages twenty to fifty, were employed outside the home (U.S. Bureau of the Census 1978b). This situation reflects both increased employment opportunities for women and changes in the socialization of females to allow variations from the traditional sex-role orientation.

Of course, the male labor force participation rate remains much higher than the rate for women. Many adult women either do not enter the work force or else they leave it during the childbearing years of twenty-five to thirty-four.

Women with little formal education are less likely to be in the work force than other women because less educated women earn less, they are likely to have less interesting jobs, and they are more apt to think of homemaking and motherhood as women's primary functions. In addition, less educated men are more likely to disapprove of their wives working. The more male-dominant the culture, the greater the likelihood of conflict over wives working (Scanzoni and Scanzoni 1976).

Women who interrupt their careers when they have children suffer a relative disadvantage compared to men who have never left the work force. However, it may not be economically advantageous for a woman earning low wages to purchase child care, and therefore those women who earn higher salaries are more likely to continue working while their children are young (Cain 1977). Policy decisions about day-care subsidies and taxation rates on second incomes will continue to influence women's decisions about uninterrupted working during the childbearing years.

Black married women have higher rates of employment than white married women. One cause of this is the relatively lower earning rates of black men as compared to whites. Also, there are proportionally more black female heads of households who must work to support minor children. Currently, the differential between black and white female incomes is less than the comparable differential among males (Cain 1977).

Social workers are most likely to be involved with young adults seeking services because they have been unsuccessful in entering the *primary labor market.* The primary market includes jobs that offer stable employment and good salaries and benefits; examples are unionized industrial and clerical jobs, public service employment, and the professions. Young adults who fail to enter this mainstream of the work force because they are competitively disadvantaged must seek employment in the *secondary labor market,* where employment is less stable and wages are low (Heath and Somers 1977). Minorities, women, the unskilled, and the handicapped are over-represented in this secondary market. The critical issues for individuals in this group are their limited access to employment and the relatively low wages they receive. This situation has a psychological as well as an economic impact, affecting individuals' aspirations and their perceptions of what is possible for them to achieve.

As we mentioned in the chapter on adolescence, current social policies do not adequately assist workers in the secondary market. Suggested solutions include increasing the number of private-sector jobs, providing greater opportunities in public employment, and a guaranteed minimum income for all workers. It has been estimated that 1.5 million new jobs a year must be created in the 1980s if we are to keep unemployment at a 4 percent level (Heath and Somers 1977). Social workers and others have also suggested a family-income policy to correct the present situation in which unskilled male heads of household may earn less than their families would receive in welfare payments if they were without a male wage earner. However, there is also concern that by offering welfare supplements to heads of households earning low wages, the government is helping to maintain them as a semipermanent class of cheap labor (Wattenberg and Reinhardt 1979).

Occupational choices

Occupational decisions are influenced by socioeconomic conditions such as the rate of general unemployment, the state of the economy, the degree of discrimination in hiring practices, and the skills most in demand by employers. However, a host of other factors that people may not even be aware of also influence their decisions. These include social class, sex, race and ethnicity, intelligence, education, and parental occupation. The social and psychological bases of conscious career choices are often rooted in childhood. Long before we consciously choose a formal program of instruction, we begin absorbing informal norms and values and learning sex-role differences. Our tutors are numerous: parents, teachers, workers in a particular occupation, actors in movies and on television, and characters in books. This informal socialization may be a key determinant in choosing a career (Moore 1969).

Individual personality styles also play an important part in career choice. Some people experience so much stress from fear of making an unsatisfactory decision that their judgment is impaired. Janis and Wheeler (1978) have identified four modes of coping with career choice. The first is *complacency,* or passively letting matters take their own course. Second is *defensive avoidance,* or using techniques such as procrastination and rationalization to avoid assuming control and responsibility. Third is *hypervigilance,* or making impulsive decisions because of feelings of panic, rather than taking the time to weigh the alternatives. *Vigilance* is the fourth and most mature style. Vigilant persons take the time to make an effective search, they construct alternate possibilities, and they try to anticipate possible outcomes. In this way, they can avoid the most obvious errors and develop flexible and effective strategies for making decisions.

Having made either definite or tentative career choices, young adults become ready to enter the work force. Entrance into an occupation is only the first of several critical stages in the work cycle (Moore 1969). There will be other changes, such as dramatic promotions, reassignments, and changes in occupational choice. There may be a career plateau, a holding period, which begins earlier and lasts longer than is desired. Some people encounter frequent or protracted periods of unemployment, often resulting in financial and psychological stress.

Workers enter the marketplace seeking to strike a contract of wages for services that is as advantageous as possible. Their success will depend in part on how well they have been prepared and socialized for a particular job and how well they can cope with difficult new challenges. The Gould Study cited in the previous section describes a number of useful skills, as young adults shift in intellectual style from reliance on intuitive insights to patterns of systematic effort, goal orientation, and perseverance. The studies by Levinson and Valliant emphasize young adults' increased ability to associate personal aspirations with occupational realities.

In making the transition from student or unemployed person to member of the labor force, people must acquire a number of new skills, values, and attitudes, through both formal and informal instruction. Formal career preparation includes structured learning in high school, college, vocational training programs, and on-the-job instruction. Informal career development takes more subtle forms but is equally important. It is the process of absorbing the attitudes, norms, and role expectations appropriate to a particular job. These are the unwritten rules of the game.

College is often considered a critical phase of career preparation, but for many students it does not provide training in readily marketable skills. Liberal arts curricula seek to develop basic language and analytic skills and to broaden students' awareness of the physical and social world. These relate to developing intellectual maturity more than to employability. Programs such as engineering and other professional schools do provide substantive knowledge and practical skills, but they usually attract motivated students who have already defined their goals.

A massive survey of hundreds of thousands of college students (Astin 1977) found that for most students the emotional and attitudinal changes occurring during college are far more significant than any specific career preparation. Beliefs and self-concepts undergo major revisions, and students learn to rate and assess themselves in increasingly complex and realistic ways. The musician accepts her shortcomings in history with greater equanimity; the writer acknowledges his lack of mathematical aptitude without downgrading his other achievements.

For both college and noncollege young adults, information about jobs and the labor market is often hard to obtain. Initial job decisions may be made on the basis of very limited information, thus partly accounting for the high turnover among younger employees. Too often, the emphasis has been on the prompt location of employment rather than on whether there is a good match between the job and the employee (Heath and Somers 1977). This is particularly important to high school dropouts and those with other characteristics associated with a high rate of unemployment.

Since the 1960s, manpower programs have addressed themselves to problems of young persons who are relatively disadvantaged in the competitive labor market. These are individuals who have limited education or job experience, lack knowledge about job openings, and have been burdened from birth with the disadvantages associated with poverty and discrimination. Initially, manpower programs were aimed at increasing employability through skills training. Gradually, the program emphasis has turned to preparing job applicants for the discipline and structure of the world of work (Heath and Somers 1977). The concept of job readiness now includes teaching basic educational skills and providing auxiliary social services as needed. Such services might include health care, legal assistance, and counseling on work-related problems.

At the end of the 1960s, public subsidies were offered to private employers willing to hire disadvantaged unemployed persons. An increasingly tight job market led to renewed, although limited, programs to assist localities in creating new employment opportunities for disadvantaged populations (CETA [Comprehensive Employment and Training Act]). Many of these new jobs have been in social service areas, enabling agencies to temporarily expand the range of services they can offer. However, it remains to be seen how many of these experiences have led to permanent employment once subsidies are terminated.

Work and leisure

While the problem of finding a job is paramount for many young adults, for others the predominant issue is whether their expectations about personal fulfillment will be met through the occupation they select. Some may be torn between the desire for material success and the desire to do something worthwhile. Others wonder about the impact of their occupational choices on their life style and whether they will live in the city or the country, the East or the South. Until recently, occupational roles tended to define individual identities and priorities. Workers sacrificed and suppressed conflicting values for the sake of job stability, and few expected to be psychologically fulfilled by their jobs. Today, the importance many young people assign to work as opposed to other parts of daily life has changed, and they are less willing to compromise other goals for the sake of a job.

This change in priorities has occurred only in the last decade. Until 1970 a coherent value system dominated the attitudes of most twentieth-century American workers (Yankelovich 1978). This value system had several distinct components: Women were expected to stay at home if their husbands could afford it; men tolerated unsatisfying jobs for the sake of economic security; and the main motivations for workers were money and economic security.

Today workers enter the labor force later and retire earlier than in the past. They live longer after retirement, and they enjoy paid vacations and holidays that were virtually nonexistent for many workers years ago (Cain 1977). Partly in response to these economic shifts, and partly in response to the counterculture's emphasis on individual creativity, many young adults view their jobs in a different way. They try to establish greater control over their work schedules and to avoid an excessively depersonalized work environment. A survey of young, well-educated professionals indicates that over half contemplated changing occupations in the next five years (Renwick and Lawler 1978). Heading their list of demands was a desire for greater opportunities for growth, learning, and self-actualization. Executives, professionals, and others with a high degree of autonomy and responsibility expressed job satisfaction more often than clerical and unskilled workers. They were also less likely to feel trapped in their jobs than the lower-paid, less-educated workers.

Young adults may also face problems in using their leisure time. Those who are unmarried may find young adulthood an especially lonely period unless they are able to maintain old friendships or establish new ones. Married people also may experience a sense of loss if their close group of peers from adolescence is no longer available for leisure-time activities. Some communities offer more opportunities than others for unmarried young adults to meet each other through participation in activities. Dances, bars, sports programs, educational activities and campaigns for political and social causes offer young adults some opportunities for leisure-time socialization.

SEXUALITY AND INTIMACY

Whether single, married, widowed, divorced, or cohabiting, adults are to some extent involved with the issue of sexual intimacy, even though it may remain unresolved. Adolescent sexual experiences are often tentative, confusing, overwhelming, and embarrassing. Adults gradually abandon these explorations of newly acquired powers and feelings and attempt to integrate sexuality as part of an enduring and satisfying emotional bond. They may also have intimate relationships that do not include an explicit sexual component.

One researcher (Calderone 1972) suggests that the development of intimacy involves several distinct components: choice, mutuality, reciprocity, and delight. Two people choose each other because of a mutual attraction. They exchange reciprocal confidences and develop a sense of trust by accepting each other's vulnerabilities in a sharing, predictable way. These factors lead to the achievement of intimacy—mutual acceptance in an atmosphere of safety and delight (Calderone 1972; McCary 1978).

An enduring intimate bond helps a couple deal with other problems that may arise. Intimacy may be blocked by denial of feelings such as anger, or denial of one's emotional needs because of a fear of rejection. Even traditional courtship and dating patterns may discourage intimacy if they emphasize ritual behavior rather than an honest exchange of feelings (McCary 1978).

Cultural differences

Perhaps we can better understand sexuality in our culture by first introducing two extremely different patterns of sexual behavior, one from Polynesia and the other from an island off the coast of Northern Europe (Gagnon 1977). The Polynesian peoples of Mangaia are vigorously sexual in a direct and casual way. Intercourse may occur after the slightest display of interest by the male or the female, without prior courtship. Sexual education occurs spontaneously; children frequently go nude, masturbation is done openly, and young children are free to watch teen-age boys slip into the family hut for intercourse with one of the daughters. After a male puberty rite, young Mangaian men receive instruction in various sexual techniques and are told of the importance of the female orgasm.

In contrast the farmers and fishermen who live on the island of Inis Beag in the North Atlantic receive very little sexual education. Women do not learn of menstruation until it occurs; men are fearful that ejaculation will rob them of their energy and power. Nudity is not tolerated, and intercourse is performed quickly without removing one's nightclothes. There is little or no sex education or premarital sexual experience, and neither marital partner expects to derive much satisfaction from sexual activity. Historically, men in this culture could marry only after inheriting property, usually in their late thirties or forties.

Imagine a Mangaian finding a mate in Inis Beag! This couple would probably be doomed to failure in the task of establishing a close, enduring bond. Expectations for sexual behavior are often resistant to change, and attitudes such as those concerning the appropriate level of nudity or sensuality are often reinforced by religious beliefs. It is therefore not surprising that couples in our culturally pluralistic society often have difficulty in finding patterns of sexual behavior that are mutually acceptable.

Individuals in every culture learn sexual roles and are taught behaviors considered appropriate to that role. In many cultures, males and females are expected to acquire distinctly different behavior patterns. In our own country, we seem to be moving toward a lessened reliance on sex differences as a determinant of behavior and a tolerance for a wider range of sexual activity within each gender.

In earlier chapters, we described the process of forming a sexual identity, starting with the biological predispositions of the prenatal period and continuing through the socialization and social learning processes that occur during childhood. By young adulthood, almost all individuals have formed a clear sense of gender identity. However, there is evidence that the sex roles learned in childhood do not reliably predict specific adult sexual behaviors (Simon and Gagnon 1974). Although sexual identity is formed in childhood, adolescent sexual development may represent the beginning of newly learned adult sexual behavior. In the following discussion we shall see that human sexuality is a much broader concept than the mere awareness of gender identity and gender-appropriate behavior.

Dimensions of human sexuality

Harvey Gochros (1977) identifies five dimensions of human sexuality: sensuality, intimacy, reproduction, interpersonal influence, and sexual identity.

Sensuality describes the psychological and physiological enjoyment associated with release of sexual tension. In our society, sexual satisfaction is most often associated with a love relationship, but sexual pleasure and orgasm are also achieved through self-stimulation (Masters and Johnson 1966).

Intimacy describes the pleasure of closeness and interdependence with another person. Because of their early socialization, many Americans experience psychological intimacy only with a spouse or other person with whom they have an intimate sexual relationship, but other physical expressions of intimacy are possible, such as hugging and kissing close friends.

Reproduction is only part of human sexuality, but the historical connection between the two remains strong, even though contraception is widely used today. The battle about whether public funds should be used to pay for abortions revolves in part around the continuing issue of people's being responsible for bearing any children that may accidentally result from sexual intercourse.

Interpersonal Influence refers to the use of sexual activities for nonsexual purposes such as dominating, punishing, pleasing, or bargaining with a partner. Young adults may engage in sexual activities in order to prove their adequacy and rapists may use sexual attacks to express aggression or assert dominance.

Sexual Identity is an extremely complex concept. It involves our biological gender and our self-image as well as our sexual preferences or choice of love objects. Occasionally there is physiological or psychological ambiguity about gender: Hermaphrodites are persons whose physical characteristics are not entirely male or female; transsexuals are persons whose anatomical features are clearly of one sex but who subjectively perceive themselves as belonging to the opposite sex. However, social workers are much more likely to see young adults whose *gender identity* is clear, but who may be confused about their *sexual identity* because of their choice of love objects. Individuals may wonder whether they fit the classifications of "straight" (heterosexual), "gay" (homosexual), or "bisexual." These terms refer to sexual orientation or preference in selection of a love object.

Sexual orientation

The term *homosexual* refers to persons who are sexually attracted to others of the same sex. Homosexuality has existed in all societies. In ancient Greece the philosophers idealized the bond between a male teacher and his young male disciple. The evidence from studies of other societies suggests that although heterosexuality is generally the preferred pattern, homosexuals and bisexuals are not necessarily stigmatized (Davenport 1976). Homosexual behavior may also be considered as acceptable for heterosexuals when women are unavailable for sexual relations, such as at childbirth and when men are in prison or in the army. While recognizing the increased public acceptance of homosexuality, Judeo-Christian ideology still generally labels it as an unnatural relationship.

There is no general agreement as to the causes of homosexual or heterosexual preferences, but the trend in professional thinking has been away from the orthodox psychoanalytic view that homosexuality results from flawed family relationships. There is evidence that homosexuals are not inherently less well-adjusted than the rest of the population and that psychiatrists have tended to generalize about an entire group based on their experience with the most troubled segment of the particular population (Hoffman 1976). Although seductive mothers and passive fathers may be a causal factor of homosexuality in some cases, other children grow up in similar families and choose heterosexual love objects (Hoffman 1976). Today, there is less interest in questions of causation and "cure," and greater emphasis on accepting the variety of sexual preferences that individuals learn throughout their lives (Gochros 1977).

Although homosexuality often involves an exclusive attraction to people of one's own sex, many people have both homosexual and heterosexual feelings. As we have pointed out, some societies are more accepting of bisexuality than others; in our own society, sexual behavior is generally governed by the predominant tendency. The incidence of homosexuality is difficult to measure because many people are reluctant to acknowledge their actual behavior for fear of social sanctions. In Kinsey's 1948 study it was estimated that one-third of American men and one-eighth of American women had homosexual experiences to the point of orgasm at least once in their lives (McCary 1978). Kinsey also reports that 25 percent of the male population had more than incidental homosexual experiences for at least a three-year period of time (Hoffman 1976).

In a study of homosexual men in the San Francisco area, Bell and Weinberg (1978) found that those who were interviewed showed a significant mixture of homosexual and heterosexual behavior. Although the San Francisco area is notably more tolerant of homosexuality than many other parts of the United States, most respondents concealed their homosexuality from large numbers of friends and acquaintances. The researchers' main conclusion is that gays exhibit as much diversity of attitudes and behavior as the rest of the population. They have career patterns similar to those of straight men and must cope with some of the same conflicts between career demands and domestic obligations.

While many male and female homosexual couples do achieve longterm, stable relationships, they also encounter special problems such as whether to reveal their homosexuality to friends, family, and colleagues and how to integrate children from previous marriages. Because they are often discriminated against socially and in employment, we cannot know the extent to which the current marketplace character of many sexual relationships in the gay world is due to discrimination and low self-esteem. We do know that gay men currently tend to be more sexually active than gay women (McCary 1978).

Sexual therapy

Social workers, along with other professionals, are gradually changing their views about sexual preferences from trying to "cure" deviants to helping individuals achieve greater sexual satisfaction. William Masters

(1970) estimated that about 75 percent of all sexual problems were treated by professionals other than doctors. Social workers are among this group, and professional organizations now offer continuing education in human sexuality in order to help clinical social workers better understand sexual functioning.

Most problems brought to sexual counselors involve heterosexual adults—married couples and single individuals concerned about either their own or their partner's sexual adequacy. One very common problem reported in studies of sexual behavior is that women generally achieve less physical gratification than men do (Hunt 1974; McCary 1978; Hite 1976). Female dissatisfaction may be related to differences in the physiological and psychological patterns of men and women, with men climaxing before their partners have had sufficient stimulation to reach orgasm (Gebherd 1966). There is a growing awareness of the importance of the clitoral rather than vaginal orgasm in women and correspondingly less emphasis on simultaneous male and female orgasm (Gordon and Shankweiler 1971).

Psychologically, it is important for many women to express tender emotions along with sexual intimacy, whereas men are more likely to have been taught to suppress their emotions. Because of these substantial differences in male and female needs, couples who can improve their communication can usually adapt more successfully to each other's needs.

After publication of the Masters and Johnson study, *Human Sexual Inadequacy* (1970), there was a surge of optimism about short-term behavioral techniques that were claimed to be effective in achieving erections, delaying ejaculations, and facilitating orgasms (Fischer and Gochros 1975). However, several psychologists specializing in sexual counseling now report that the Masters and Johnson research is too methodologically flawed to provide a sound theoretical basis for sex therapists and that its claims of curing sexual dysfunction are highly inflated (Zilbergeld and Evans 1980). Their criticism centers on the fact that Masters and Johnson do not set behavioral criteria for defining successful treatment outcomes; they simply speak of having only a 20 percent failure rate. The extent of change achieved by the 80 percent the therapist does not regard as failures remains unclear.

Zilbergeld and Evans (1980) also question how one measures success in treating a man's premature ejaculation when the criterion for success is the partner's subjective sense of satisfaction. What if the partner's dissatisfaction stems from other than physiological causes, such as interpersonal conflict and struggles for power? Perhaps what is needed is an integration of the newer techniques of behavioral management with the insights into relationships provided by psychodynamic theories. In this way, symptoms may be relieved by short-term methods when the client lacks proper information and instruction. In other cases, however, the therapist may have to deal with the client's total pattern of relationships to be helpful.

MARRIAGE AND OTHER ALTERNATIVES

Young adults generally seek a source of emotional intimacy that will replace their family of origin. (Recall that Erikson ranked intimacy versus isolation as the central task of early-adult development.) Many cultures permit such intimacy only within the confines of marriage. In our own society, alternative life styles have generally been considered deficient as compared to the nuclear family (Keller 1971). However, critics of this view point out that the nuclear family (husband, wife, and children) has never been a universal family form (Skolnick and Skolnick 1974) and that the family pattern in which the wife stays home to rear the children while the husband goes off to work is of relatively recent origin.

Prior to the industrial revolution, all members of the family were likely to work as part of an agricultural production unit. But by the end of the nineteenth century, men increasingly worked away from the home and the socialization of children became the primary function of the family. Today, the family no longer is the primary provider of education, religious training, and recreation for its members. Instead, it functions primarily to meet its members' affective needs for love and understanding. Family members today are increasingly asserting their rights to challenge the authority of the family if it does not meet their emotional needs (Duberman 1977). The current emphasis on achieving sexual satisfaction is probably related to the fact that marriages are no longer evaluated in terms of their functioning as economic partnerships.

Much has been written in the past decade about the changing nature of the American family. Indeed, the 1980 White House Conferences on Families were scenes of heated debate between traditionalists and those suggesting that the family be redefined to include such relationships as homosexual couples and unmarried persons living together. Whether we call them families or not, the fact remains that there is increased acceptance for varied types of independent households today. Single persons are establishing households with greater frequency, more divorced and single women are raising children in separate households, more homosexual couples live together openly, and some people are choosing to form communal families. Social workers have had to make a number of adaptations in order to respond to these changing needs. We shall discuss a few of the alternative life styles in this section.

Married and unmarried couples

Rates of marriage in the United States have fluctuated over the years. The massive economic depression brought a sharp dip in the marriage rate in the 1930s. By the late 1940s and the end of World War II, the rate had doubled (National Center for Health Statistics 1973a). Since 1945, the rate of first marriages of single women ages fourteen to forty-four has been steadily declining (Glick and Norton 1973). The rate of remarriages had been rising during most of this period, but since 1972 even this rate has declined (Glick and Norton 1977). Later in this chapter we shall discuss the significance of these figures for those living as singles and for the single-parent family.

We know relatively little about how individuals go about selecting a marriage partner. Some theories consider the search to be for an ideal type similar to one's own parent, some look to the common traits among couples, and others focus on the functional nature of attraction among opposites. Thus far, there is little substantive evidence to support these psychological theories. On the other hand, we do know that there is still a very high probability that individuals will marry within their own racial group and a more than average chance that they will marry within their religious and social-class group (Eckland 1968).

Middle-class young couples today may live together before marriage; there is increased acceptance of this pattern. Sometimes this is seen as "trial marriage," but at other times it is simply an extension of the pattern of dating behavior (Macklin 1972). Some of these relationships are highly structured; others are not bound by any explicit expectations about financial and other responsibilities.

A Census Bureau study indicates a large increase in the number of young adults acknowledging **cohabitation.** The reported increase among those under twenty-five years old was from 29,000 couples in 1970 to 236,000 couples in 1978 (Reinhold 1979).

Even when couples are living together in an informal arrangement, they face many of the same problems as newlyweds. Not only must they make major decisions about jobs and housing that will be suitable to both partners, they must also make many minor decisions about daily routines. Curley and Skerrett (1978) offer the following as typical of the major interpersonal adjustments all new couples must make. First, the partners' togetherness makes them more acutely aware of flaws and habits that formerly went unnoticed, and a partner's excessive neatness or casual housekeeping may suddenly become irritating. The couple also works to define their relationship by sorting out the small but important differences in their needs for dependence and independence. Each gives up some activities for the sake of the other, and each must also cultivate individuality to relieve the pressures of intimacy. Couples must agree on how to divide household chores, which may be divided according to traditional role assignments, on the basis of equality, or according to individual preferences. The couple must also find an effective way to cope with anger and conflict. Typically, they make several unsatisfactory attempts at resolving newly identified issues before arriving at a predictably satisfying style of solving problems. Finally, they must establish a satisfying sexual relationship, and they must reevaluate intimate bonds with family members and friends and resolve competing loyalties.

The above briefly describes the lengthy adjustment period faced by any new couple. Those who are living together without being married must cope with these issues and with others based on the ambiguous nature of the relationship. For example, they face the initial problem of how to describe their relationship to others. There is no really suitable label for their mate, and a variety of terms are used, such as "friend," "roommate," and "lover." According to one study (Almo 1978), unmarried couples find it difficult to deal explicitly with their concerns about fidelity and commitment, even though both partners have strong feelings about each other. Some couples have an implicit agreement that "outside relationships" are unacceptable. Others explicitly agree that they will not demand sexual exclusivity, but this may be stressed by one partner and merely accepted by the other. As with other adjustments, nothing can be resolved without timely and unambiguous communication. Clear communication may be both more important and more difficult for those who have vague boundaries regulating their life together. Family counselors should make efforts to reach new couples experiencing adjustment difficulties, whether or not they are married.

Divorce

Sociologists tend to view the increasing rate of divorce as inevitable in urban industrial societies (Scanzoni 1976). In our own country the divorce rate in 1973 was 18.2 for every thousand married women (National Center for Health Statistics 1975). The rate is even higher among women who married very young, had little schooling, and have low family income. Census figures from 1970 indicate that divorce is more common among blacks than among whites—figures that reflect blacks' overrepresentation among those with low incomes and less education. Overall, it is predicted that almost a third of current marriages among young couples will end in divorce (Wattenberg and Reinhardt 1979). Half of all divorces take place within the first seven years of marriage (National Center for Health Statistics 1973b).

Divorce seriously disrupts a couple's lives and the lives of any children they may have, and results in temporary feelings of loss and anger. In addition, legal and socioeconomic settlements must be arranged, new social roles must be learned, and a new sense of identity as a single person must be developed. Divorce may be a response to stresses other than marital incompatibility, and in such cases divorce may not provide relief from the problem. For example, a parent may suddenly seek a divorce in reaction to the depression brought on by the death or injury of a loved one (Wall-erstein and Kelly 1980). In other cases, divorce may bring welcome relief from an intolerable marriage.

Among the factors underlying the current high divorce rate are the increased numbers of women in the labor force and the increased accept-ance of the view that unhappy marriages ought to be terminated. Recent income maintenance experiments indicate that an improved economic sit-uation apparently leads to an increase in the rate of divorce among the very poor (Hannan et al. 1977). Presumably, the increased income gave these couples the option of separating.

Approximately two-thirds of divorced women remarry, and the av-erage time for remarriage is about six years after their divorce (Glick and Norton 1977). However, demographers predict that 44 percent of these second marriages will also end in divorce. Nonwhites and welfare recipients have lower rates of remarriage (Wattenberg and Reinhardt 1979). These demographic patterns of high rates of divorce and remarriage suggest a growing acceptance of "serial monogamy" as a style of family life.

Singleness

Census figures show a recent increase in the percentage of single young adults (U.S. Bureau of Census 1974). The proportion of women aged twenty-five to twenty-nine who remained single rose from 28 percent to 48 percent from 1960 to 1976 (Glick and Norton 1977). This trend toward remaining single and delaying a first marriage is most prominent among white women with relatively high levels of education and occupa-tional achievement. They are the least likely to choose both work and marriage (Scanzoni and Scanzoni 1976). However, the 1970 census indi-cates that those least likely to ever marry are the functionally illiterate with the least educational and occupational skills.

It is too early to tell whether this increase in the percentage of young adults remaining unmarried will continue, accelerate, or reverse itself. Meanwhile, more research is needed on the subject of singleness and es-pecially on the single man; studies of the "unmarried" usually refer to the unmarried woman. One study (Stein 1976) of single young adults finds that their greatest perceived need is for networks that will provide sup-portive relationships, intimacy, and continuity. Close and sharing friend-ships are of great importance as a supplement to continued family ties and work-related acquaintances.

The women's movement has brought to light many of the inequities in the treatment of single women that make life relatively more difficult for them—for example, the discrimination they face when they travel and apply for bank loans or credit cards. Not only are women gaining legal rights to equality, but a gradual change is also occurring in the public's perception of the single woman. This may be partly in response to the swelling of the ranks of the singles by large numbers of newly divorced persons.

At this point, the social services must differentiate among this large group of singles in terms of life patterns and needs for services. We cannot categorize all singles as people who have never had the opportunity to marry. Women as well as men may prefer the freedom to pursue a career without the responsibilities of marriage. Others may wish to combine a career with marriage if they can work out the accommodations for a two-career family. Some single men and women already have very satisfying supportive social relationships, yet others are at a loss in finding opportunities to form new and close relationships. Some communities include many single working people, and others have few unmarried young adults and few recreational facilities geared to their social needs. Agency workers should be attuned to the social needs of singles who will never marry as well as those who are interested in courtship and dating. Finally, social workers should be alert to the needs of the least socially adequate group of singles, those with minimal levels of intellectual, occupational, and social skills and who need assistance in meeting their needs for friendship and intimacy. Part of this handicapped adult population live in group homes or halfway houses, but others live in isolation from their peers. For both groups, opportunities for socialization may be limited by a lack of appropriate recreational programs and staff assistance.

Single persons today have greater freedom than formerly to live away from their family of origin. They are more apt to form a separate household, share a household with someone of the same or opposite sex, or live in a communal family. Singles who are the heads of households are usually females with children; their special problems and needs will be considered in the final section of this chapter. We turn now to a description of communal families.

Communal families

Communal families are an alternative to nuclear and extended families. They provide a context for intimacy, and for the development of a shared life style. In a study of contemporary communes, Berger and his associates (1974) found that they may be characterized as creedal or noncreedal, with the former having a firm system of beliefs that guide relationships and expected behavior. However, Berger notes that even noncreedal communes tend to have an ideology based on countercultural values such as open expression of feelings and affirmation of natural and mystical rather than scientific values. Although urban communes are easier to start, rural communes call for a more serious commitment from members and therefore have a more stable membership. Rural communes are more likely to involve a shared economic enterprise, whereas urban groups vary in their economic arrangements from those where members contribute all of their earnings to the group, as in religious communes, to those where members merely share household expenses. At present, welfare payments to individuals and to unmarried mothers with babies are a significant source of income for many communes, which indicates that communes may be a valuable resource for persons who would otherwise have financial difficulty in living on their own. Communes also offer emotional supports to individuals who might otherwise be living alone. Nevertheless, the indications are that the heterosexual couple is still the backbone of most communes (Berger et al. 1974). Group solidarity and continuity appear most often in communes that are organized around a clear-cut purpose and that include some system of rules and responsibilities as well as shared ideas (Cross and Pruyn 1973). A few communes have been successful, but many more have been unable to develop an enduring alternative life style.

PARENTHOOD

Families go through cycles that usually begin when an individual leaves his or her original family (the family of orientation) to establish an independent household. This is usually followed by marriage, involving a relationship with a new individual and probably a new family network. The most common third stage in the family cycle is the birth of the first child and the beginning of parenthood (the family of procreation). There are still other milestones, such as the birth of the last child, the departure of the last child from the family, and the death of a spouse. In an extended family several of these events will overlap, providing rehearsal and repetition that makes each individual member's adjustment somewhat easier.

During the last fifty to one hundred years, family cycles have changed in timing as well as in nature. Not only are people living longer than ever before, but their ages at various points in the family cycle have also changed. The average time span between marriage and the first child has increased, along with an increased span between the time the last child leaves home and the parents' retirement or death. There has also been a recent increase in the number of women deciding to have their first child after thirty-five years of age.

Tasks of parenting

The initial adjustment to parenthood may be difficult, particularly if the new parents have not anticipated the infant's demands on their time and energy. Previous routines are disrupted, and both parents usually find their freedom curtailed. In addition, this new and demanding family member often strains the existing relationship between husband and wife (Komarovsky 1964). Along with these major changes in life style, the couple must make many relatively minor adjustments, such as learning the details of child care, buying baby clothes, and choosing a name for the child.

Rossi (1968) has divided parenthood into four stages: the anticipatory stage, the honeymoon stage, the plateau stage, and the disengagement or termination stage. The *anticipatory stage* refers to pregnancy and the new roles and perceptions that it requires. Couples face both domestic and external social adjustments as they become a family.

The *honeymoon stage* of parenthood is when the parent-child attachment is formed. Although parents must make difficult adjustments during this time (lessened intimacy, less freedom, greater fatigue), they also derive excitement and pleasure from the new infant and their role as parents.

During the *plateau stage,* parents assume the roles of father and mother and learn to deal with family and community problems. Parenting includes socialization of the child, but it may also include future family planning, involvement in schools and religious training, and participation in community groups. The final stage, *termination,* is usually reached when the last child leaves home permanently. (However, it may be prematurely and painfully terminated by divorce and loss of child custody.)

Parenthood confers new social status on young adults; it also makes demands that vary considerably with the age of the child. An infant demands almost total and constant nurturance. Some parents find it comparatively easy to satisfy this need but others are overwhelmed by such intense dependency requirements. Some parents cannot bear to hear an infant cry; it triggers their own feelings of helplessness, dependence, and anger. When the child's urgent needs stimulate similar needs in parents, they may need help in coming to terms with their own needs and feelings. Crisis intervention is often appropriate, through hot-line numbers, drop-in centers, and parent-support groups.

Benedek (1970) believes that each critical period in the child's development produces or reactivates a critical period in the parents' lives. Some parents are able to resolve their own conflicts at a new and more advanced level of integration. Others cannot cope with newly aroused feelings and develop pathological problems that often result in family crises.

Parents who are unable to deal effectively with children at one stage of development may be quite competent at another stage. Parents who have difficulty with an infant may cope quite well with a preschool child or an adolescent, or vice versa. In such cases it may be helpful to have more than one or two persons involved in child rearing so that adults may complement each other's areas of strengths. Responsibilities may be shared through extended families, supportive networks of friends, and nursery and play groups.

Decisions about parenthood

Young adults face difficult decisions about whether to have children, when to have them and with whom, and how many to have. When a couple disagree about these issues, anger and bitterness often result. Not only are these decisions difficult, but they are irreversible once the child is born. The child continues to need care, even if the parents separate or decide that parenthood was a mistake. The women's liberation movement has led to increased communication about and awareness of the liabilities of parenting from the woman's perspective.

Wife and mother, husband and father, marriage and family, home and children—these coupled words are based on cultural assumptions. Although research indicates that only about 8 percent of all married couples voluntarily remain childless (Veevers 1973), a number of recent articles have presented the argument for rejecting parenthood. Some speak to the problems of overpopulation and shrinking natural resources; others focus on women's need to liberate themselves from traditional roles. Motherhood is depicted as a barrier to fulfillment and an essentially burdensome chore (Millet 1969; Rollin 1970; Jones 1970). The position taken is that our society has oversold the idea of childbearing as the biological and psychological high point in women's lives, thereby arousing expectations that are far beyond reality (McBride 1973). Emphasis is placed on the burdens of pregnancy and the physical and emotional strains experienced by parents. Finally, it is pointed out that a demanding baby often has a detrimental effect on the close relationship between husband and wife.

Lott (1974), in reviewing these arguments, points out that motherhood is being rejected because of its association with women's inferior status, and that once childbearing is shared equally by men it will no longer seem demeaning. Others who share Lott's opinion recommend changes in the organization of employment, such as flexible hours, half-time employment, and paternity leaves that will enable men to share more fully in child rearing. Lott concludes that without these and other accommodations by husbands, women who desire autonomy and a career will not wish to accept the burdens involved in rearing children. Nonetheless, a recent study of Ivy League college men (Komarovsky 1973) shows that males often have positive attitudes about female equality, but they are not willing to significantly modify their own career patterns to assume equal child-rearing responsibilities.

We turn now to the reasons why most married women continue to want children. Lowenthal and her colleagues (1975) found that the middle- and lower-middle-class women they studied as newlyweds had markedly traditional views about female roles and expected to find happiness through nurturing rather than achieving. In contrast, the newlywed men in the study focused on their sense of mastery and independence. In spite of the fact that 84 percent of newlywed women in the study were employed, they were motivated more by the desire for two incomes in order to further family goals than by the desire for a dual-career marriage.

In addition to those women whose jobs do not offer them as much personal satisfaction as their parental roles, there are career women who have personal needs to parent a child. As a single woman applying to adopt a child stated, "I had love that needed to be given and I need to be needed. I wanted some purpose to my life other than my work and my cat" (Dougherty 1978, p. 312).

The birth rate is highest among those with lower socioeconomic status and those who marry youngest (Scanzoni and Scanzoni 1976). One explanation for this correlation is that large families are a source of pride to couples who have few alternative sources of authority and status. Rainwater (1960) found that children provide emotional satisfactions to blue-collar wives who do not obtain self-esteem from their relationships with their husbands. Children are especially valued when motherhood is seen as the major role in a woman's life—when it provides a sense of personal achievement as well as an opportunity for vicarious achievement through the activities of her children. Other reasons noted for having children are concern with increasing the population of minority groups and a sense of religious obligation (Scanzoni and Scanzoni 1976).

We cannot predict what proportion of future marriages will be equal partnerships in which both parents are responsible for rearing the children. Duberman (1977) and others anticipate the need for major shifts to provide alternatives to full-time motherhood. They suggest equal parenting responsibility by men, professional surrogate parents, and publicly subsidized child care, including the possibility of twenty-four-hour care. However, while we cannot predict the extent to which families will choose these alternatives, we do know that many women are already working and in need of some form of child care. In 1972, 50 percent of married women who were living with their husbands and had children between the ages of six to seventeen were in the labor force and 30 percent of married women with children under six were in the labor force (Department of Labor 1973).

The single mother

The 1970 Census indicates that approximately 13 percent of all American families are headed by single, separated, widowed, or divorced women (U.S. Bureau of the Census 1978b). Some writers indicate that the increase in single-parent families over the past twenty years is due to the rising divorce rate and the increased rate of illegitimacy among white women, many of whom are teen-agers (Ross and Sawhill 1975). Others point out that these statistics may merely reflect the fact that unmarried women today are more apt to form separate households than they once were (Wattenberg and Reinhardt 1979).

A salient fact for social workers is that more than half of all families headed by a woman rely on welfare payments as at least a temporary source of income. Such families are heavily overrepresented among those living below the poverty level (U.S. Bureau of the Census 1976). The incidence of female-headed households is three times higher among nonwhites than whites (Ross and Sawhill 1975), and is reflected in the high proportion of black families among the very poor. Because social workers tend to see only groups with serious problems, we often forget that two-thirds of urban black households are headed by a man and wife living together (Scanzoni 1971).

Many female heads of households do not receive alimony or child support, and even women in the middle- and upper-income brackets are usually deeply concerned about the loss of income following a divorce (Wallerstein and Kelly 1980). Reductions in income often necessitate a change in residence and life style at a time when parent and children are already under great strain.

In 1975 one-quarter of the parents under twenty-five years old consisted of a single head-of-household (Wattenberg and Reinhardt 1979). Almost all these single parents are women who face great difficulty in locating other than marginal employment; they often are the sole source of both financial and emotional support for their children. Nonetheless, there is still no general consensus about the need to provide financial supports above the poverty level for the single parent. Nor is there agreement about whether governmental support payments (AFDC [Aid to Families with Dependent Children]), should be used to subsidize women to stay home with young children or whether payments should be conditional on their accepting employment at any level available. Further evaluation is also needed to determine the effectiveness of job training programs and to understand the needs of single parents for supportive social services as well as income supports.

It is not within the scope of this text to provide answers to these complex issues of public welfare policy. However, the student will realize that in developing appropriate policies the developmental needs of both parents and children must be considered, along with an awareness of individual and group differences within the single-parent category. For example, single fathers have different needs than single mothers, just as single parents living far from relatives have different needs from those living close to supportive family members. Some single parents are in a transitional stage before remarriage; others are not. A recent five-year study of divorce points out that children, because of continuing emotional ties to both parents, generally do not receive the same emotional relief as their parents when an unhappy marriage is terminated. The authors suggest that more counseling be made available when divorce is first contemplated (Wallerstein and Kelly 1980).

We should recognize that not all single parents are living in poverty or having difficulty in coping with their situation. A study of highly educated, mature, single adoptive mothers indicates that these women have adequate coping skills (Dougherty 1978). Although they expressed interest in participating in a group for single parents, they appeared to have adequate financial and emotional resources.

Single parents have varied needs and possess internal and external resources to varying degrees, but their most serious problem remains that of obtaining an adequate income. The single mother living in poverty is often handicapped in her ability to offer her children the resources they need to realize their own developmental potential.

CASE ILLUSTRATIONS

Mr. Chase

Mr. Chase, a social worker for a welfare department, is helping to develop a list of resources for young adults. The list will be part of the county's new information and referral system, a telephone service that he hopes will assist adults from all income groups to make use of community resources. Among the areas included in the file are employment services, including special training programs for the long-term unemployed, the unskilled, minorities, and women; information on applying for subsidized housing; legal resources relating to discrimination, divorce, and child custody; resources for financial subsidy, medical benefits, and food stamps; counseling agencies; and mental health clinics.

Mr. Chase often asks which services provide child care for clients. However, he refers those seeking regular child-care programs to a switchboard operated by a voluntary agency listing specific facilities. In a number of other areas he also decides to use existing information and referral services that have developed to meet special needs, such as those of the physically or mentally disabled.

The number of privately operated switchboards serving special groups in Mr. Chase's community has grown in the past few years. Some receive public funds because they reach a population not adequately served by the traditional community agencies. One recent example is the switchboard referring callers to health, counseling, legal, and other services operated by gay and lesbian organizations. Members of the city government disagree about whether to continue funding this privately operated switchboard or whether to require that it be integrated into the county-wide referral system. Mr. Chase thinks that there is value in maintaining these private services because they are better able than the large, impersonal public agency to offer emotional support and individualized services. Although he does not believe that only gay counselors can help gay men, he recognizes the need for transitional services until a mutual accommodation is worked out between traditional agencies and groups that have just recently asserted their needs and rights.

Betty Carr

Ms. Carr works for an adoption agency that handles hard-to-place children. When she first became an adoption worker, only young married couples were considered as suitable candidates for parenthood. However, with the recent emphasis on trying to place older children and those with special problems, the agency is now accepting single persons as adoptive parents. The definition of a family has been broadened to include the single-parent family and, in some cases, the gay couple.

Cynthia Hughes is a thirty-five-year-old black professional woman who has never married. She comes from a loving family and has satisfying relationships with family and friends. She doubts that she will marry and would like to participate in the emotional intimacy of parenting a child. She will also satisfy her idealism by adopting a child who would otherwise have to remain in foster care. Since Ms. Hughes has helped raise several younger siblings, she is well aware of the emotional burdens and responsibilities of raising children. Ms. Carr is pleased to be able to place an older child in her home for adoption.

Norma Masters

Norma has come to a family agency for marriage counseling. She is depressed and fearful of what will become of her if she is unable to "save" her marriage. She and her husband, Ron, were scheduled to participate in family counseling, but Ron refused to come to the agency and two weeks later he disappeared.

The social worker and Norma decide that the first priority is to help Norma apply for financial assistance, including eligibility for free medical care for herself and her three children. The social worker acts as a resource and supportive person, being careful not to "take over" and make Norma feel even more helpless than she already does.

Norma spends some time discussing her marriage, trying to gain a sense of "what went wrong." She had married as a teen-ager because she wanted to escape from an unhappy situation at home. She had no clear goals for her life other than wanting a new family to replace the one she was leaving. Ron was a handsome football hero when they met in high school, and she was flattered by his attentions. However, Ron had been unable to hold a steady job after graduation; he always felt disappointed by what life had offered him after his hopes of entering professional football were dashed. After a while he started drinking heavily and began seeking out old friends while increasingly avoiding his family responsibilities.

In discussions with the social worker, it soon becomes clear that Norma has inner strengths that can help her to move past this crisis. She has been competently managing her own household and raising three children during her six-year marriage. She is more mature now at twenty-four than she was at eighteen, but is only beginning to recognize her own abilities.

The social worker helps Norma to handle her children's anxieties and to reassure them that she will not also disappear from their lives. Eventually Norma chooses to enter a two-year community college training program for vocational nursing; the school has a day-care program she can use for her youngest child. In preparation for this big step, the social worker helps Norma learn to set limited goals and as Norma accomplishes each task, she finds it easier to take the next step. Aside from the job training she receives, the other students provide Norma with a supportive social group, and her teacher, a divorced woman, becomes an important role model for her. The future looks hopeful for Norma, although she now feels that she has a lot of growing up to do before she considers remarriage.

SUMMARY

Human development takes on a new character in adulthood, no longer stemming primarily from physical growth and the rapid acquisition of cognitive skills. Adult growth is defined largely in terms of social and cultural milestones, as young people begin to terminate dependence on parents and assume responsibility for themselves and for others. Maturity is culturally defined and is also dependent on individual "age clocks."

Three recent studies offer perspectives on adult growth. The Grant Study of Harvard graduates concludes that success is most related to the development of effective patterns of coping with the challenges of adult life rather than to factors such as childhood trauma or adolescent success. A crucial aspect of maturity in the men studied was the development of intimate relationships with both older and younger generations. The Levinson study emphasizes the mythical "Dream," a vision of future accomplishments that effectively inspires adult growth. The Gould study describes adult growth as repeated moves toward a more complex and realistic view of one's own relationships to others, leading to eventual autonomy and discipline.

The ability to work is an important measure of maturity. Most males feel that work is a central part of their identity. Some women view their careers in the same way as men, and others define themselves primarily by their familial roles. The proportion of married women who are employed has greatly increased, especially among the well educated. However, many women in the labor market continue to hold marginal jobs with low wages.

Preparation for work includes both formal and informal training. Early socialization and cognitive and emotional development throughout childhood set the stage for later career choices. Career choice is a crucial decision for young adults, and they may need assistance in developing effective strategies for making choices. College often does not result in crystallized vocational choices; however, higher education does influence social and emotional growth.

Success in work depends on prior socialization, the ability to adapt to new challenges, and the relationship between the individual's skills and the demands of the labor market. Many young adults fail to locate other than marginal employment offering minimal income. Others are more concerned that their work offer personal fulfillment. Today's workers generally have more leisure time than those of earlier generations and place more value on leisure activities.

Another central task of adult life is the development of intimacy, which usually includes sexual intimacy. Sexual relationships are affected by both internal and external factors. Adults' sexuality includes more than simple gender identity. It includes sensuality, intimacy, reproductive behavior, interpersonal influence, and a sexual identity with an orientation toward a particular sex as love object. Many problems faced by homosexuals today are related to social disapproval and discrimination against them.

Social workers are beginning to learn more about sexuality in order to meet the demand for sexual counseling. There is some question about early claims of high success rates with short-term treatment of sexual dysfunction.

Much has been written about the changing nature of the American family. More people are remaining single, and more singles are establishing separate households. The number of unmarried couples living together is also increasing and communal families are drawing interest as an alternative style of life. New couples face many adjustments, whether or not they are in a traditional marriage. The divorce rate is also climbing, requiring many adults and children to make difficult readjustments. People who remain single and those who become single later need to develop supportive networks of family and friends that will provide intimacy and continuity.

Family cycles are often marked by events such as marriage and parenthood. Parenthood confers new social status on young adults, and it also makes some demands they may be unprepared to meet. The women's movement has challenged the view that every woman will feel fulfilled by motherhood, pointing out the negative aspects of that role. An increased number of women are calling for greater equality in child-rearing responsibilities among men and women. It is too early to predict the influence these views will have on working-class families that hold more traditional views about the family. It is this group that has the most children and who find work relatively less satisfying.

There are more single parents today, and they are usually women. The rise in single-parent households is partly due to the high rate of illegitimacy and the high divorce rate. A distressingly large number of single parents live on the edge of poverty and need adequate financial and social supports if they are to cope with their own problems and those of their children.

SUGGESTED READINGS

Duberman, L. *Marriage and Other Alternatives.* New York: Holt, Rinehart & Winston, 1977. A discussion of changes in patterns of courtship, marriage, and parenting, with speculations about future trends.

Reisman, D., Glazer, N., and Denney, R. *The Lonely Crowd: A Study of the Changing American Character.* Garden City, N.Y.: Doubleday, 1956. An outstanding analysis of the effects of our changing social structure on adult personality development. Reisman characterizes our society as "other-directed" rather than "inner-directed."

Scanzoni, L., and Scanzoni, J. *Men, Women and Change: A Sociology of Marriage and Family.* New York: McGraw-Hill, 1976. This text covers recent trends in sexual relations, marriage, and parenthood, pointing out the differences among racial and socioeconomic groups.

Skolnick, A., and Skolnick, J.H. *Intimacy, Family, and Society.* Boston: Little, Brown, 1974. A contemporary reader that emphasizes interpersonal relations. Numerous articles discuss alternative life styles.

Wallerstein, J.S., and Kelly, J.B. *Surviving the Breakup: How Children and Parents Cope with Divorce.* New York: Basic Books, 1980. A report of a ground-breaking study of the impact of divorce, this book will be of interest to those counseling adults as well as children.

chapter eight

VISTA, Pennsylvania, Conklin

MIDDLE AGE

continuity and change

outline

IN EARLIER CHAPTERS we looked at childhood, adolescence, and young adulthood. We described the developmental steps by which a child becomes an individual with a relatively stable outlook and personality, and we noted the social milestones that mark the adolescent's entrance into the world of the adult.

After this, what next? Is adulthood merely one long living out of the decisions made earlier in life, possibly with a few corrections here and there? How much continuity do we find during the adult years? If John Smith is not the same person at fifty-five that he was at twenty-five, how much of the change is attributable to biological decline, to increased life experience, and to the expectations that others have of him? Does his wife respond differently to these same factors?

This chapter will focus on continuity and change in the years between forty and sixty-five—the middle years. We shall consider the viewpoints of psychologists, sociologists, and economists in discussing the following areas: middle age as a stage in the lifelong process of growth and development, biological changes that accompany aging, and social role changes in middle age. We shall conclude with a discussion of the theories of humanistic psychology. This is the last of the theories of human development presented in the text and is discussed at this point because it often provides the framework for social workers' therapeutic efforts with adults experiencing mid-life crises.

MIDDLE AGE AS A DEVELOPMENTAL STAGE

Chronologically, middle age lasts from age forty to age sixty or sixty-five, but the period may be longer or shorter for different people. Although many cues inform people that they are no longer young, individuals are not equally aware of these changes. Some cues are biological. A woman suddenly realizes that her son is taller than she is, or a man finds his jogging hampered by arthritis. Other cues are social and positional (Neugarten 1968b). People in mid-life are aware of being separate from both young adults and the elderly. In fact, one of their major responsibilities may be to simultaneously develop new ways of responding to grown children and aging parents.

There are also social and psychological cues to middle age, centering on issues of continuity and change. People realize that they have made certain basic decisions about career and family, and that the future no longer holds limitless possibilities. Some people meet this challenge confidently; others experience a sense of crisis. Women have tended to clock middle age according to the family cycle—either their children have left home or they realize that they will no longer have any children. Women who have primarily been homemakers ask themselves, "What shall I do with the rest of my life?" In the future more women may be evaluating the success they have achieved in careers, as men do today. They may feel satisfied with their status or keenly aware that they have little time left in which to achieve their original goals. If they have been successful, they may suddenly ask if it was worth the struggle (Levinson 1978). For many people, this is a time of reassessing old goals and setting new ones. However, neither researchers nor the middle-aged themselves agree on whether this is the "prime of life," a time of new fulfillment, stability, and potential leadership, or the dreaded "mid-life crisis," a period of dissatisfaction and inner turmoil. We shall consider the reasons for these differences in outlook in the later section on role changes and interpersonal adjustments. First, we shall examine the responsibilities that help to define middle age as a developmental stage.

Tasks of middle age

Havighurst and Erikson both define the "developmental tasks" that people must accomplish to feel satisfied with their lives. Havighurst (1953) described these tasks of middle age in a pragmatic way: to achieve adult civic and social responsibility; to establish and maintain an adequate standard of living; to help teen-age children become responsible, fulfilled adults; to develop suitable leisure-time activities; to relate to one's spouse as a person; to accept and adjust to the physiological changes of middle age; and to adjust to one's aging parents. According to Erikson, the basic issue facing people at this time is *generativity* versus *self-absorption*. By generativity, Erikson means that people must go beyond the few intimate relationships established in young adulthood—with spouses or close friends—and become concerned with the next generation and humanity in a broad sense (Elkind 1970).

In both of these models, the challenge of middle age is to develop a command of one's inner impulses as well as a competence in dealing with the responsibilities of the outer world. Another way of phrasing this is to say that the middle-aged must assume the power of the older generation and ensure the future for the younger generation.

Issues of adult life

Peck (1968) has expanded on Erikson's formulation by adding a number of key conflicts present in adult development. Peck believes that Erikson's formulation of eight stages of life places too much emphasis on the first twenty-five years. Six of Erikson's eight developmental issues—trust versus mistrust, autonomy versus doubt, initiative versus guilt, industry versus inferiority, identity versus role confusion, and intimacy versus isolation—pose conflicts that individuals must resolve in their early years. But what of the last forty to fifty years of life? Peck agrees with Erikson's descriptions of the two developmental stages reached in adult life—generativity versus self-absorption and integrity versus despair—but thinks them inadequate to sum up all the issues that arise during these years.

Occasionally, earlier issues that had been temporarily resolved reappear during these later years. A sudden physical impairment, such as a heart attack, may reawaken struggles with autonomy and dependence in a forty-five-year-old. The death of a husband may renew strong intimacy needs in a woman. Social workers often see individuals and families when some life crisis has stirred up old issues and offered the opportunity for reevaluating old solutions to problems. For example, the death of a spouse may make a woman aware of strengths and capacities for independent action that she was formerly unable to express.

Peck proposes seven issues or conflicts of adult development, four of which are particularly important in middle age. The first of these adjustments Peck calls *valuing wisdom* versus *valuing physical powers*. Decreasing physical stamina and increasing health problems may cause people to shift a good part of their energies into mental rather than physical activities. The second developmental task is to find a new balance between *socializing* versus *sexualizing* in human relationships. Physical changes, as well as social constraints imposed by divorce or widowhood, may force people to redefine their relationships and emphasize companionship rather than sexual intimacy or competitiveness.

In dealing with these first two issues, social workers should probably not make judgments about the way in which individuals choose to resolve the issues they face. A temporarily satisfying state of equilibrium may be attained in many ways. Some people will make great efforts to prevent a decline in their physical stamina, and others will surrender easily to the notion of being "over the hill" athletically. Similarly, some widowed or divorced people will want to reenter the competition for a new partner, and others (particularly women) will substitute friendships that are largely single-sex. It is important that we provide activities that meet the differing needs of people who choose these differing forms of adaptation. For example, the needs of the many single middle-aged women can best be met by providing some programs that help them meet men, and others that focus primarily on sharing enjoyable activities.

Peck's remaining tasks of middle age involve *emotional and mental flexibility* versus *rigidity*. These refer to the adjustments that people must make in middle age as families and friends move away and as new situations call for new mental attitudes. In these cases, social workers do make judgments, by considering flexibility as more desirable than rigidity. People often seek help during a crisis when the old ways of coping are no longer adequate, and the social worker can help free them from the inflexible domination of past experiences and judgments. An example is the couple who must learn to modify their rigid disapproval of how their grandchildren are being raised if they are to benefit from a continued relationship with their children.

Although Peck's final three dimensions are particularly relevant to the older years described in Chapter 9, individuals do begin to deal with these issues during middle age. The first is *ego differentiation* versus *work-role preoccupation.* If people define themselves solely in terms of the work they do in their jobs or families, then they become disoriented when they lose those roles because of retirement, unemployment, or children leaving home. The second conflict, *body transcendence* versus *body preoccupation,* centers around the individual's ability to avoid preoccupation with the increasing aches and pains that accompany age. A third dimension, particularly important in old age, is *ego transcendence* versus *ego preoccupation.* This requires that people not become mired in thoughts of death. People who age successfully transcend the prospect of their own extinction by becoming involved with the younger generation—the legacy that will outlive them.

Like Erikson's stages, none of Peck's dimensions are confined solely to middle age or old age. The decisions made in early life act as building blocks for the solutions of the adult years, and the middle-aged begin to resolve the issues of old age. In fact, research suggests that the period from fifty to sixty is often when people make critical adjustments that determine how they will live out the rest of their years (Peck and Berkowitz 1964).

BIOLOGICAL CHANGES

"Age is like love; it cannot be hid," wrote a seventeenth-century dramatist. For many middle-aged people, there is a "moment of truth," when the mirror reveals new wrinkles, a thicker waistline, and a receding hairline. These reminders that their bodies are aging are more disturbing to some people than to others, depending on their attitudes toward aging and their sense of self-esteem. Some people have already noted that their physical abilities have peaked during adolescence or early adulthood. Others will follow the teaching of health experts who believe that middle-aged people can continue to function with youthful vitality by following a program of regular exercise, lessened stress, and good diet. Peck refers to this adjustment to physical changes as the first issue of middle age.

Physical capacities

Some physical decline or slowing down will occur during middle age (Birren 1959). Visual acuity may begin to decline in the forties or early fifties. Near-sighted people, however, often see better in middle age than they did as young adults. On the average, hearing declines gradually after the age of twenty, causing particular difficulty in hearing high-frequency sounds. Sensitivity to taste, smell, and pain also decrease at different points in middle age, although these changes may be more gradual and less noticeable than visual or auditory problems (Ebersole 1979).

Other biological functions, such as reaction time and sensorimotor skills, are also likely to slow down. Motor skills may decline, but usually the actual performance remains constant, probably as a result of long practice and experience (Ebersole 1979). Someone who chops firewood or plays tennis every day will probably not experience any change in performance. But it does become a bit more difficult to learn new skills.

Internal changes occur, such as a slowing of the nervous system and a stiffening of the skeleton. Skin and muscles begin to lose elasticity, and the body shows a tendency to accumulate subcutaneous fat, especially around the midriff. The heart pumps less blood to the body, and the opening of the coronary arteries is nearly one-third less in middle age than in young adulthood. Lung capacity decreases as well, thus lowering the capacity for enduring hard labor (Brody 1979).

By adjusting one's life to a slower pace, reserving energy for special occasions, and exercising regularly, people can conserve and maximize strength in middle age (Timiras 1972). Numerous studies have shown that exercise before and during middle age can increase physical capacities and endurance. Certain kinds of exercise—especially aerobic exercises—are designed to increase heart and lung capacity by supplying the body with more oxygen. Exercise can also slow the deterioration of muscle tissue, reduce body fat, help prevent deterioration of the joints, and combat some kinds of arthritis (Brody 1979).

We shall discuss the causes and symptoms of biological aging at greater length in Chapter 9. Meanwhile, it should be noted that people age at very different rates, both in the middle years and in later life. By paying attention to some of the factors influencing the aging process, people can often alleviate some of the unpleasant aspects of growing older.

Intellectual functions

We have looked at continuity and change in the biological aspects of middle age. What about intelligence? Intelligence testing in childhood is a well-established (although controversial) process, but it is more difficult to test the accumulated knowledge and experience of adults. Until recently, studies of adult intelligence ignored substantial complexities. However, in the last few decades significant advances in methodology have clarified some of the issues.

Traditional investigations of adult intelligence relied on simple **cross-sectional studies,** without taking into account differences between age cohorts (Schaie 1970). Age cohorts are those groups born at the same historical time. Such a cross-sectional study might compare the IQ scores of a group of twenty-year-olds with a group of forty-year-olds and a group of sixty-year-olds. The differences in performance among the three groups would then be considered the result of the aging process. But this design ignores the historical period in which each group has lived and the wide differences in their educational and socioeconomic backgrounds. Since the older groups contain more individuals with little education, with low socioeconomic level, and in poor health, it is not surprising that the older groups score lower on the IQ tests. Aging is only one of the factors that may account for the differences in the test scores of a sixty-year-old farmer who dropped out of school during the Depression years to earn a living and the scores of a twenty-year-old New Yorker, who grew up in the city during the 1960s and is now in college.

If cross-sectional studies have tended to maximize a decline in intelligence with age, **longitudinal studies** have tended to minimize such a decline. These studies measure the same person's IQ at age twenty and again late in life. This method provides more dependable information about individual intellectual growth and decline than the cross-sectional method, but it too has its limitations. For example, the people who show up for retesting at age seventy-five are likely to be the healthiest and most able of the test group. Their IQ scores tend to be higher than those of study participants whose health prevents them from retaking the tests (Botwinick 1977).

A third method of measuring changes in adult intelligence was developed in 1965 by Schaie (Schaie and Param 1977) and was designed to reconcile discrepancies between the cross-sectional and the longitudinal methods. Schaie's method is called **cohort-sequential analysis.** Groups of twenty-year-olds, thirty-year-olds, and forty-year-olds are tested and then retested ten, twenty, and thirty years later. At the time of the second testing, another group of twenty-year-olds is added. This procedure is repeated so that all the groups may then be compared both with each other and with their own performance at a different time.

Cohort-sequential and longitudinal studies have indicated that although aging is associated with some decline in cognitive functioning, the decline is much more gradual than researchers assumed even ten years ago, and it is more evident in the older years, which are discussed in the next chapter. In fact, some facets of intelligence appear to increase during middle age.

To better understand these changes in intelligence, we should examine the two kinds of intellectual abilities that people use as they age. The first broad area of intellectual functioning is called **fluid intelligence** and is based mainly on the speed and effectiveness of neurological and physiological factors. It includes such abilities as motor speed, induction, and memory. The term *fluid* refers to the fact that this kind of intelligence can "flow into" various intellectual activities, including perception, recognition, and dealing cognitively with new information (Horn 1970; Neugarten 1976). Fluid intelligence seems to increase until late adolescence and then decline gradually (Knox 1977; Neugarten 1976). However, by the end of middle age it has only declined to the point that it occupied during the middle of adolescence—still quite high.

Crystallized intelligence reflects the ability to process and record the kind of information that people acquire through both formal and informal education. It includes verbal reasoning, vocabulary, comprehension, and aspects of spatial perception. Unlike fluid intelligence, crystallized intelligence increases over the life span, including the middle years (Neugarten 1976).

This increase in crystallized intelligence helps people in their forties and fifties to compensate for any decline in fluid intelligence and to maintain their earlier overall level of intelligence. The exception is in skills requiring speed, as various psychomotor processes do slow down in the later years (Botwinick 1977). The declines in intellectual performance due to memory problems are more noticeable after middle age, and we shall discuss them in Chapter 9.

Is there a cognitive style or characteristic pattern of thinking that remains constant as people grow older? Does a fifty-year-old woman approach a problem in the same way she did when she was 20? Knox (1977) and others use the term *cognitive style* to refer to a person's characteristic pattern of information processing. For example, we find that some people are characteristically reflective and deliberate, and others are impulsive; some see the world in a simple black-and-white framework, and others look for shades of gray; some are tolerant of ambiguity, and others intolerant.

Research seems to indicate that most of these cognitive patterns are developed in childhood and continue to become individualized in adulthood. They seem to be primarily related to personality types, early training, and cultural life styles. For some, there appears to be a shift toward analytic thinking somewhere between childhood and adolescence, with the shift becoming stable in early adulthood. After that, many aspects of cognitive style become more rigid between middle age and old age (Knox 1977).

The issue of cognitive style is particularly important in casework services, work-training programs, and formal and informal education for the middle-aged. It is important to recognize that some middle-aged people may have difficulty in learning concepts not because they lack intellectual ability, but because of their inflexible cognitive style. Recognizing differences in cognitive styles may enable educators to help older students improve their intellectual performance (Knox 1977). If educators understand a person's thought processes, they are better able to present information in a way that is easily understood. This understanding is also of value in helping caseworkers to assess the cognitive style of their clients.

Sexual changes

The term **climacteric** refers to a broad complex of physical and emotional effects that accompany hormonal changes in middle age. In women, this change is usually called **menopause,** in reference to the end of menstruation and the ability to conceive children. Many professionals believe that in middle age men also undergo sexual changes that are accompanied by emotional readjustments. However, these effects are more gradual and less dramatic than the female menopause. Sometime during the middle years most men experience delayed erection time and reduced pressure for ejaculation; women have a shortened orgasmic experience and a lessening of vaginal lubricaton (Masters and Johnson 1974).

Menopause in women generally occurs around the age of forty-seven, although the time of onset and length of the transitional period will vary from individual to individual. Although many glands secrete hormones that are involved with the climacteric, the major changes result from the decreased production of estrogen by the ovaries. This creates a temporary hormonal imbalance, which some doctors correct by estrogen replacement therapy. Although the artificial supplementation of the female sex hormone reduces the unpleasant physical symptoms some women experience, potentially damaging side effects have been identified, such as an increase in the likelihood of uterine cancer.

Some women experience headaches, dizziness, palpitations, and "hot flashes" during menopause. Some may also feel depressed over the loss of the reproductive function and regretful if they have never had children. However, Neugarten and her colleagues (1968) found that about 75 percent of the women in their study did not feel that menopause affected them in any important way. As with other changes, reactions to the climacteric depend on the extent of hormonal imbalance, individual personality makeup, cultural expectations, and the degree of situational stress. Some women may become temporarily depressed and therefore enjoy sex less than they did before; others may enjoy sex more once they no longer have to worry about becoming pregnant.

Less is known about the male climacteric. We do know that middle-aged men experience a gradual decrease in the level of androgen, a male hormone, and a decrease in fertility and potency (Fried 1967). But unlike estrogen, androgen declines over a longer period of time. Even so, many men have reported physical symptoms such as impotence and frequent urination. Some even experience the symptoms common to female menopause (Ruebsaat and Hull 1975). Others may experience a loss of self-confidence or become irritable, fatigued, and depressed. These can result, in turn, in diminished sexual ability. Whereas some symptoms are caused by changes in hormonal levels, some are due to psychological stresses such as job pressure, boredom with a sex partner, family responsibilities, ill health, and the fear of ill health.

Although most individuals are healthy and can enjoy full sex lives for many more years, the overall level of sexual activity tends to decline in the middle years. Usually, people can handle these changes without outside assistance. However, some people may need help in coping with increased inner stresses, which have been compared to the hormonally based stresses of adolescence (Fried 1967). Although sexual dysfunction is more openly discussed today, people may have difficulty obtaining competent sexual counseling. Medical schools have only recently begun to offer courses in human sexuality (Masters and Johnson 1974). The same is true of training for social workers, although most sexual problems are treated by nonmedical professionals such as social workers (Gochros 1977). There are still individuals and couples with sexual problems who turn to people making false claims of competence as sex therapists.

Health and disease

As the body ages, it becomes increasingly vulnerable to disease. Middle-aged people often become aware of the effects of aging and their own mortality as they or their friends become ill. For Americans under the age of thirty-four, accidents are the single highest cause of death; after this age, death is increasingly the result of disease (U.S. Bureau of the Census 1978a). Certain diseases are major problems in middle age, and some diseases affect one sex more than the other. Men are more apt to work in dangerous occupations, they are less apt to show concern about their health because they have been taught that it is "manly" to ignore weakness, and they may have a higher genetic predisposition to disease than women. There is also a growing awareness of the extent to which nonwhites suffer poorer health because of their relatively higher concentration in hazardous occupations.

Cardiovascular diseases—heart disease, arteriosclerosis and hypertension—are the leading cause of death among the middle-aged. Heart disease accounts for nearly 40 percent of all deaths in the United States (U.S.

Bureau of the Census 1978a). Throughout middle age, this disease is a much greater threat to men than to women, although heart attacks increasingly become a problem to women after menopause. One third of all deaths for men between the ages of forty-five and fifty-four are due to coronary arterial problems (Ebersole 1979).

Cancer is the second highest cause of death in the United States, and it too claims more men than women. Middle-aged men are particularly prone to lung cancer and women to breast cancer. Men are also more prone to respiratory diseases in middle age. Diabetes occurs in increasing rates and severity in middle age, but it claims more women than men (U.S. Bureau of the Census 1978). Some diseases of middle age are less life-threatening than cancer or diabetes, but nevertheless interfere with activity and cause considerable discomfort. Arthritis, for example, troubles many middle-aged people of both sexes.

Many of these diseases seem to reflect a complex interrelationship between stress, personality, and genetic factors. Since men are more often the victims of heart disease than women, most of the studies on stress and coronary disease have involved men. However, some recent changes in the pattern of sex-related diseases among the middle-aged should be noted. For example, although the rate of death from breast cancer in women has declined dramatically, the rate of death from respiratory cancer has been rapidly increasing among middle-aged women for the past fifty years (U.S. Bureau of the Census 1978a). Presumably, this rise is due to the increase in women smokers during this period. We may also expect a similar rise in the rate of heart attacks in middle-aged women as more women are employed in stressful executive positions.

In one study (Rosenman 1974) 3,400 men from thirty-nine to fifty-nine years of age were examined and then reexamined at the end of two and one-half, four and one-half, and eight and one-half years to determine how behavior patterns might affect the incidence of heart disease. The men were typed according to their personality styles. At one extreme is what the researchers called the **Type A** personality, people who are highly competitive, aggressive, impatient, and achievement-oriented. Their facial muscles are often tense, and they are plagued by a constant sense of urgency. At the opposite extreme are **Type B** persons, who are patient, easygoing, and relaxed. About 10 percent of Rosenman's subjects had clearly defined Type A or Type B personalities; the rest were somewhere in bewhere in between.

At the beginning of the study, none of the men had experienced any coronary heart disease. Follow-up studies found that twice as many Type A men had developed coronary heart disease as Type B men, and that twice as many Type A men had suffered fatal heart attacks. The researchers found that the biochemistry of Type A personalities was similar to that of people who had a history of heart disease. They were found to have higher serum cholesterol levels and accelerated blood coagulation than Type B men. They also had more stress hormones in their blood during working hours. The Type B subjects rarely developed any coronary disease before the age of seventy, regardless of how much fatty food they ate, how many cigarettes they smoked, or how little they exercised (Rosenman 1974; Eisendorfer and Wilkie 1977).

Dramatic as these findings are, it is important to remember that 90 percent of the men in the study were somewhere between these two behavioral extremes, and some of these men also developed coronary problems. Like the men who were studied, most middle-aged people do not fit neatly into either of these extreme categories. For the vast majority of middle-aged people the interrelationships between disease, stress, personality style, diet, and exercise are still unclear.

Social workers are aware of the drastic effects that the health breakdown of a middle-aged wage earner can have on the entire family. The hospital social worker may be involved in locating resources to assist the family of the disabled wage earner. The worker in a family or children's agency sees the effects of family stress on the child's relationships with others and on his or her school performance.

A less familiar role for social workers involves working directly with industry or with public and private insurance plans to help prevent disabilities and to rehabilitate those who might otherwise remain disabled. Compulsory worker's compensation laws in the United States provide income maintenance and medical and rehabilitative services for job-related disabilities. When temporary disabilities are unconnected with work, the employee must rely on benefits from private disability plans, which usually do not cover the costs of extensive rehabilitative services. When long-term health services are needed, most people must turn to federally funded programs for financial assistance to the permanently disabled.

All these options may present problems for the middle-aged wage earner who must adjust to a restricted life style and a significant reduction of income. Few resources offer retraining of middle-aged workers for new types of employment. Because these disabilities are costly to both employers and the government, who must pay benefits to the worker who is no longer on the payroll, both groups have an interest in the prevention of work-related disabilities. Social workers may be employed by the government or private employers as members of interdisciplinary teams that participate in preventive education, diagnosis, referral for job training, and counseling families of disabled workers (Spencer, Mitchell, and Salhoot 1977).

We have discussed some of the physical adjustments required in middle age. In the next section, we shall examine some of the social adjustments peculiar to middle age—changes that are sometimes lumped together under the single term of *middle-age crisis*. However, we shall see that although some people consider these adjustments as a crisis, others see them as an opportunity for growth.

CHANGING ROLES IN MIDDLE AGE

Crisis or opportunity?

In our introduction to this chapter, we presented middle age as a period of both continuity and change. After presenting some of the biological changes of this period, we now come to the changing social roles of the middle-aged person, changes that further characterize this as a period of transition. Women may experience greater role changes than men if they have centered their earlier adult lives around their families. We shall see how individuals deal with these changes in a manner consistent with their previous behavior patterns; however, we shall also present evidence that adults are still capable of developing new and more satisfying patterns of coping with life.

Marjorie Fiske (Fiske 1979; Lowenthal 1975) has categorized the different reactions people have to the stresses of middle age. Some experience little stress but feel defeated by life nonetheless, and others happily ascribe their nonstressful life to good luck. Some experience many stresses, such as poor health, job loss, and widowhood. Of these, some people become preoccupied and overwhelmed by the situation, while others may experience the same stresses as a challenge. The latter group feels that they are in the prime of life, able to make decisions with an ease and self-confidence previously beyond their grasp.

The women in Lowenthal's study (1975) were more likely to be overwhelmed by stress than the men. Although half the women were employed outside the home, they continued to assume major responsibility for the household chores and the burdens of caring for other family members. Lowenthal also found that women who coped less successfully with stress in middle age usually had suffered the loss of a parent early in life. This finding is in accord with theories about the long-term effects of early emotional deprivation. However, loss of a parent early in life did not seem to affect the middle-aged men in the study who, presumably, were able to utilize positive work experiences in adult life to strengthen their ability to cope with stress. Their personal characteristics were not as fixed in early childhood as has been assumed by the theorists (Fiske 1979).

We turn now to the stresses resulting from the position of the middle-aged between two generations. We shall also describe the adjustments caused by divorce or death of a spouse and the changing work roles of men and women.

Between two generations

The middle-aged must often function as both parents and children, meeting the simultaneous demands of both an older and a younger generation. The degree of change in their relationships with aging parents depends on a number of factors: whether both parents are alive, the state of their health, the extent of their financial independence, and whether they maintain a separate household, to name but a few. Social workers must examine both *cultural factors* and *family histories* to understand these relationships. Sometimes the elderly expect power to be transferred to their middle-aged children, in at least a partial reversal of childhood roles. Sometimes everyone expects the older generation to continue to dominate family life. Conflicts may develop unless both generations can reach substantial agreement on such issues (Gould 1978; Neugarten 1976).

In many families, it is the middle-aged woman who takes care of dependent parents (Fiske 1979). Wives are often expected to assume responsibility for aging in-laws as well. However, as more women work outside the home, they are less available for this caretaking function.

While they are developing new relationships with their parents, the middle-aged must also build new relationships with the younger generation. Middle-aged women have sometimes been considered prone to depression when the last child leaves home—the so-called "empty nest" syndrome. However, in many families women do not react in this way (Deutscher 1972). Middle-class families are particularly able to deal successfully with this transition by anticipating the child's eventual departure during the college years and by using their new-found freedom to enjoy a more flexible and possibly more affluent life style. Women who have not made their children the sole focus of their lives also make the transition more easily and are likely to experience a sense of relief as well as sadness when the responsibilities of child rearing have ended.

Individuals or couples with children must often adjust to the fact that the younger generation may have a very different life style from their parents. In addition, when their children marry, parents are suddenly confronted with the need to work out still another set of relationships. Divorced children may return home, bringing grandchildren with them at a time when financial resources are already strained to the limit. Families may seek counseling on how to deal with these changing and potentially troubling relationships. As we shall see in the next chapter, many older adults rely on their children for support in times of crisis. Even if they live at a great distance, there is strong evidence of the continued strength of family ties. Unlike the later years, however, the middle-aged may still be called on for financial help by both their parents and their grown children.

The middle-aged have contact with the younger generation, whether or not they have children of their own. They may relate to members of the extended family such as nieces or nephews, or they may work with young people in their jobs and in the community. In doing so, the middle-aged play different roles at different times, such as supportive mentor, aging competitor, boss, and partner. If middle-aged people withdraw from the world in which young people live, they are likely to become stagnant, self-absorbed, and unhappily isolated from the continuum of life.

We have discussed the shifts in the relationships of the middle-aged with the older and younger generations. Equally important, and presenting somewhat more difficult adjustments, are changes in marital status that may be caused by separation, divorce, and widowhood.

Separation, divorce, widowhood

In 1977 nearly 2.8 million American women between the ages of forty-five and sixty-four lived alone. The number of men in that age group living alone was about 1.4 million (U.S. Bureau of the Census 1978). In other words, twice as many middle-aged women as men live alone in the United States. The two major reasons for these disproportionate statistics are the soaring rate of separation and divorce and the high death rate among middle-aged men.

The rate of separation and divorce has increased dramatically in recent years and shows no signs of leveling off. In 1974 there were 424 divorces for every 1,000 marriages, or nearly one divorce for every two marriages and these figures do not include informal or legal separations (Goode 1976).

Divorced women are most likely to remarry if they are divorced before the age of thirty. In 1975 the U.S. Bureau of the Census found that 75 percent of the women who had remarried were divorced from their first husbands before the age of thirty. Only 32 percent of women who were divorced in their forties remarried, and of women whose marriages ended between the ages of fifty and seventy-five, only 12 percent married again. Divorced men over thirty years tend to remarry more often than divorced women of that age group; by the age of about forty-five, nearly twice as many divorced men as women have married again (Troll 1975).

We can see that a large number of middle-aged people are affected by divorce. They are likely to experience substantial and difficult readjustments, even when the breakup comes as a welcome relief. These are problems common to all ages, but they present particular difficulties for the middle-aged, who are more likely to have maintained long-term interdependent relationships. Therefore, they find it more difficult than young adults to adjust to the emotional, social, and economic disruptions caused by death, separation, and divorce. This disruption is particularly evident in women who have defined themselves primarily as wives and mothers rather than by their occupational role. These women also suffer the most serious income problems when they lose a spouse. Women's groups have recently intensified efforts to achieve reform in the distribution of social security and other pension benefits. At issue is the plight of women who have contributed to the well-being of the family unit as a full-time mother and homemaker but who are entitled to no pension benefits such as their husbands receive after years of work outside the home. At present a woman must be at least fifty-five years old or still have dependent children living at home in order to be eligible for social security survivor's benefits.

Social workers should also be aware that while divorced young adults and middle-aged men are very likely to remarry, most middle-aged women will need to find substitute relationships other than marriage. This is important to remember when designing group activities for adults. Another difference is that middle-aged women who have never married have probably adjusted to social life as a single person, but the recently widowed and divorced are experiencing the stresses of making a sudden transition in life style. As a result, the social and emotional needs of these groups may differ.

Friendships are particularly important for the newly single and those who have never married. Intimacy will often be expressed through friendships rather than marriage and through relationships with family other than a spouse. Social workers should increasingly look at the roles of a variety of "significant others" in assessing the supportive network that an individual may draw on in time of crisis.

Lowenthal and her associates (1975) interviewed people at four different life stages about their friendships. In general, the most complex friendships occurred among the late middle-aged group. In early middle age, people were more involved with families and establishing job security. They had less time to devote to friends, and their friendships were less involved. More complex and multidimensional relationships began to form by late middle age, perhaps as a result of certain personality shifts. Jung (1961) described the period from forty to sixty years as a time of inner awareness, when people turn away from the activities of the conscious mind and confront the unconscious. Lowenthal and her colleagues suggest that as people become aware of the subtleties of their own natures, they may also come to appreciate complexity in others more than they did in earlier life.

Social workers sometimes work with groups of individuals who share similar problems, as with the recently widowed and divorced. Some such groups meet under agency auspices; others are led by clinical social workers in private practice. Very often these groups utilize the sharing of feelings and the support of peer relationships to help individuals make a successful transition to their new roles.

As mentioned earlier, the death rate for middle-aged men is much greater than for women. Overall, nearly twice as many men as women die in middle age. Over half of all widows in the country are under sixty (Troll 1975). In fact, the average age at which women are widowed is fifty-six (Burnside 1979). These statistics reflect the fact that women tend to marry men older than themselves as well as the higher mortality rate for men (Troll 1975).

Nearly twice as many men as women remarry within five years of the death of their spouse (Goode 1976). Older men feel free to choose new partners from a relatively large population of younger women while many widows still feel socially constrained to choose partners from the comparatively small group of older men. We shall discuss the problems associated with widowhood at greater length in the next chapter.

We have already noted many of the reasons why divorce and widowhood are most stressful for middle-aged women. Compared to men, their social and financial status often radically deteriorates. They also face special problems in reentering the labor market or seeking a job for the first time. Women often enter the job market with the disadvantages of being both "older" and "untrained," or considered ineligible because of lack of recent work experience. It is often difficult for them to find work even when they are highly motivated and capable.

Divorced and widowed women often need a job to support themselves. They may also seek work to reestablish contact with the world outside the family. The experience of being rejected as unsuited for employment can have a devastating impact on the self-esteem of women who are already feeling vulnerable. Some states have introduced "displaced homemakers" programs to assist middle-aged women without recent employment experience. These programs provide counseling and peer support to build self-confidence as well as advice on assessing marketable skills developed during the homemaking years and using available retraining opportunities.

Career adjustments

Past studies of mid-life career adjustments focused only on men who were reassessing their life achievements. Since then the number of young women in the labor market has increased strikingly and some of these women are about to enter the ranks of the middle-aged. We do not yet have evidence as to what their timetable will be for mid-career evaluations. We do have evidence about yet another group, women who have been homemakers during most of their adult years and then seek employment in middle age. We shall discuss the first and the last of these groups as they face the prospects of mid-life career adjustments.

As middle-aged men reassess their work lives, they may experience regret about the career they have chosen (Sarason 1977). Our rapidly shifting technology also makes some jobs redundant, leaving employees in need of assistance and retraining for new types of employment. Both of these groups require opportunities to update their skills and make career changes. However, social agencies are more likely to see the latter group because of the additional stress placed on the family system when the wage earner becomes involuntarily unemployed.

Health problems are still another cause of involuntary unemployment in middle age. The rate of participation in the labor force for white males between the ages of forty-five and fifty-nine who have health problems has decreased 16 percent between 1966 and 1969, partly because of the greater availability of disability pensions (Kreps and Clark 1975).

As we noted in the last chapter, the norm for educated young women today favors uninterrupted participation in the labor force. However, women who have always worked are just beginning to reach middle age, and married women who reached young adulthood during or before World War II by and large have never worked or temporarily withdrew from the labor market during their child-rearing years. By 1974, the rate of participation in the labor force of married women between the ages of thirty-five and forty-four, with husbands still alive, was triple what it had been in 1940 (Kreps 1975). The rate of participation in the labor market for nonwhite married women has always been higher than for whites because on the average their husbands earn less than white men.

Despite the great increase in the employment of women, there remains a residual problem of unemployed women who do not appear in the Labor Department statistics because they are too discouraged to register as actively seeking employment. Men also find it difficult to find new jobs after the age of fifty-five. Better educated men tend to remain in the labor force, but the participation rate of men aged fifty-five to sixty with only a grade school education drops to about 70 percent (Kreps 1975). In a competitive job market younger workers with higher educational levels are usually chosen over less educated older workers.

HUMANISTIC PSYCHOLOGY: THEORIES OF THE SELF

Personality theorists disagree as to how the personality develops during adulthood. Does it simply reintegrate itself and repair earlier damage, or does it continue to grow and change? Some theorists believe that the major task of adult personality development is to work out the problems caused by faulty development earlier in life. They assume that many people have been "bent out of shape" by their early socialization. According to this view, the task of adult development is to straighten out the old conflicts of dependence and autonomy, correct dysfunctional patterns of coping, and overcome conditioned anxieties.

In contrast, some theorists have begun to see the potential for continued growth and development in adults. This view of lifelong development owes much to the humanistic psychology of *Abraham Maslow*. He saw the individual as constantly "becoming" and never arriving at a point where he or she can say "this is me," with finality. O'Connell and O'Connell (1974) suggest four key dimensions to this process of becoming. First, we never stop learning who we are and what our world is all about. Second, we never stop growing in awareness of our emotional needs and the needs of others. Third, we never stop trying to be ourselves and to direct our own destinies. And fourth, we never stop trying to find a meaningful and comfortable fit between ourselves and our world.

Humanistic psychology has been called the *third force* in psychology (Maslow 1968) because it rejects both the environmental determinism of learning theory and Freudian instinctual determinism. Humanistic psychology and related "self" theories center on the individual's self-concept, the perception of personal identity. These theories provide a conception of human nature that is close to experience and view people as more than the sum of stimulus–response patterns or animal drives.

Proponents of these theories point out that experiments with lower animals often do not tell us much about humans, who are set apart from other animals by their superior ability to use symbols and think in abstract terms. Although some of the higher primates are able to learn to use symbols, their abilities in no way approximate the richness and flexibility of human language and abstract thought.

Humanistic psychologists also emphasize consciousness as a basic human process and reject the sharp division between subject and object in psychological research. People experience themselves and others as spontaneously self-determining and creative persons striving consciously toward goals (Severin 1974). This approach provides a holistic theory of personality and is closely tied to existential philosophy in maintaining that people can make choices about their lives and feel responsible for their actions in everyday life (Severin 1974). Because it focuses on people's potential to be self-determining and creative, it presents a more hopeful philosophy than alternative theories of human development that have been presented elsewhere in the text.

Abraham Maslow's theory of self, proposed in 1954, stresses each person's innate need for self-actualization. According to Maslow, this striving for fulfillment of one's potential can be expressed only after "lower" needs, such as the needs for food and shelter, have been met. For example, children who are hungry most of the time will not properly attend to reading or other school tasks.

Maslow arranges human needs in a pyramid with the most basic physiological survival needs of all animals—food, warmth, and rest—at the bottom. At the next level is the need for safety; people must be free from constant fear. The next most pressing needs are for love and a sense of belonging. Beyond this, people must have a sense of self-esteem, and they need positive responses from others. The satisfaction of these needs contributes to the basic sense of well-being that enables people to reach toward their full potential (Maslow 1954). Maslow believes that the need for *self-actualization* is basic to human nature. "What a man *can* be, he *must* be." In a sense, this need can never be entirely satisfied, because it involves "no less than a search for truth and understanding, the attempt to secure equality and justice, and the creation and love of beauty" (Shaffer 1978).

In Maslow's studies, self-actualized people tended to be older—most over sixty. They had satisfied their lower-level needs and were now motivated by a higher scale of values. They tended also to be more spontaneous, creative, self-sufficient, and freer of cultural stereotypes and limitations than the rest of the population. Most had formed close relationships with a few friends but frequently needed privacy and solitude (Maslow 1968; Shaffer 1978). Maslow found that many self-actualized people have "peak experiences." These are times when people experience joy from a sense of fulfillment and feelings of oneness with the universe.

Carl Rogers is a humanistic psychologist who has had great influence among educators and psychotherapists. Unlike the Freudians, who believe that human nature is controlled by inner drives, some of them destructive in nature, Rogers (1961) holds that the core of human nature consists of positive, healthy, and constructive impulses that exist from birth. Unlike Maslow, Rogers derived his theory from extensive clinical observations. He found that the greatest personal growth occurred when he was genuinely and totally involved with his clients, and when his clients knew that they could express their true feelings in the assurance of his full acceptance. He called this accepting attitude **positive regard** (Rogers and Stevens 1967). He felt that positive regard from the therapist would foster more self-accepting attitudes in the client and lead to a greater tolerance and acceptance of others (Shaffer 1978).

Rogerian techniques are used in social work with both individuals and groups. Sometimes the worker encourages group members to express their feelings and then reflects these back in a nonjudgmental manner. However, sometimes groups wish to focus on achieving specific action goals and will then want a worker who is more task-focused and less client-centered.

Humanistic psychology, although a comparatively recent approach to human development, has begun to influence adults' counseling and has contributed to the "humanizing" of interpersonal relationships within schools. However, it has had comparatively little impact on theories of child development and has yet to mature as a developmental psychology. Although Maslow's hierarchy of needs suggests developmental stages, little is known about the self-actualizing person. Some writers criticize humanistic theory because concepts such as *self-fulfillment* are difficult to define and nearly impossible to test. This is in sharp contrast to behavioral theory, which deals only with researchable problems and clearly defined units of behavior.

Social workers have sometimes turned to humanistic theories to guide their work with adults as individuals, in families, and in peer groups. This move parallels the shifting of social workers toward private practice and short-term treatment of voluntary clients. Social workers today often serve clients whose major stresses come from problems in interpersonal relationships rather than from adverse environmental conditions. Humanistic theories seem ideally suited for clients whose major complaints are that their lives are less fulfilling then they would like (Child 1973). However, social workers are also involved in developing better institutional means for satisfying those human needs lower on Maslow's hierarchy, such as the need for basic subsistence and the need for self-esteem.

The theoretical emphasis in humanistic psychology on the "here and now" rather than on the reconstruction of past crises or developmental problems is particularly suited to short-term treatment. However, the notion of accepting clients' feelings, and the use of techniques for clarifying clients' current thoughts, feelings, and actions have long been a part of casework practice. What is unique to this type of therapeutic intervention is the assumption that emotional clarification on a conscious level can lead to positive behavioral change (Gilbert, Miller, and Specht 1980).

This approach also places a high value on individual freedom and self-expression but otherwise makes few value judgments. In applying self-actualization theory, we assume that positive actions will result from a lightening of the heavy hand of outer-determined obligations (Hale 1978). While it may be helpful to view divorce as a transition in life style rather than as a failed relationship (Chiancola 1978), there are great difficulties in extending this approach to the parent-child relationship. Christopher Lasch (1977) refers to this extension of humanistic psychology as "the ideology of non-binding commitments."

Social work practices change as the family changes in structure and function. Today, for example, we see an increased awareness of the need for services to the single-parent family. We are also aware that today's middle-aged, whether living alone or as couples, retain few of the historical functions of the family member. However, family ties are still highly rated as a personal value and as a source of emotional satisfaction for most people (Rice 1977). The current consensus among social work practitioners seems to be that we should continue to support family relationships while recognizing a variety of family styles and structures.

CASE ILLUSTRATIONS

John Wong is a social worker at a community mental health center in a predominantly middle-class community. His agency has decided to develop a few groups for adults facing situational crises, on the assumption that serious breakdowns in functioning can be minimized if early crisis intervention is available.

Women in Transition

The first group is for recently widowed women. John's goals are to help members to maintain their self-esteem against the depressing effects of a serious personal loss, to increase their ability to draw upon existing inner strengths, and to help them develop new ways of coping with present difficulties. He limits the membership to one sex in order to maintain the focus on learning new coping skills. He thinks that a mixed-sex group would attract some members who have a primary interest in seeking a new partner. While this is a worthwhile interest, it is not within his agency's function to sponsor groups whose primary function is socializing.

In the initial meetings the wide age range of the participants created no problems, and discussion centered on shared experiences. All the participants seemed to benefit from an increased awareness that their painful experiences were not unique, and all seemed to appreciate the group leader's acceptance of their feelings of depression. Some were relieved to be able to air feelings of guilt and anger toward the dead spouse for the first time.

However, as the meetings continued, it became clear that most of the younger widows were employed full-time and the job satisfactions and positive relationships with coworkers supported a fairly rapid return to their normal patterns of problem solving. They generally dropped out of the group after three or four sessions, leaving only the middle-aged women for whom the group relationships had become a significant source of support.

John realized what was happening, and he offered the middle-aged women an opportunity to continue meeting for another six months. The members were enthusiastic about continuing and decided to call their group "Women in Transition." They were fast developing the characteristics of a social group, visiting each other's homes and sharing holiday meals. The social worker had to continually reestablish the focus of the meetings, which was to help the women make connections with other parts of the community as well as with each other.

As some members became better able to assess their financial situation, they realized that they would need to seek employment to make ends meet. This led to a group decision to spend a number of sessions learning about opportunities for paid and volunteer jobs. They also decided to focus on ways of improving their relationships with other family members who had come to assume greater significance in their lives.

Mid-life Career Changes

John also meets weekly with a group of ten men to discuss "mid-life career changes." As he had anticipated, discussion has focused on the desire for a career change, with little attention given to other existing problems such as shaky marital relationships, anxieties about health, and doubts about competency. John is aware of these other problems but knows that the group is not ready to deal with them. He waits until the members themselves begin to question each other about why they "keep complaining about the job but never do anything about it." At this point, the participants who were clear about their desire to pursue a different vocation decided that they no longer needed support and left the group. The remaining participants decided to look more closely at the reasons why they felt so dissatisfied with their lives at this particular time. Two of the men accepted a referral, along with their wives, to a caseworker experienced in sexual counseling. Both men were in their fifties, involved in highly competitive jobs, and depressed about the possibility that they might never "make it to the top." These pressures, along with the unrealistic expectation that they would continue to function sexually as they had when they were younger, were causing feelings of depression and occasional impotency.

The Rogersons

Most of the time John works with individuals or couples. He has been seeing the Rogersons, a couple in their mid-fifties, for the past three months. They were referred to the mental health center by their pastor, who recognized that Mr. Rogerson seemed continually angry and obsessed by thoughts of his daughter's ruination. Mr. Rogerson has had several heart attacks and has been advised by his doctor to avoid stress.

The Rogersons are extremely worried about their daughter, a young woman who is now living in a commune. She is their only child and is still unmarried. Because her life style conflicts with her parents' values, and because family relationships had been very close until this year, the situation was causing the Rogersons great stress.

John's assessment of the situation is that the Rogersons probably have always been inflexible in their ways of thinking about people and that they had little experience in weighing complex issues. They have always considered their daughter to be well behaved, and they now face the risk of losing all contact with her unless they are able to modify their attitudes about her life style.

John is successful in helping the Rogersons to see some of the ways in which their daughter's behavior reflects some of their own values. Although they still disapprove of many things about their daughter's life, the Rogersons are able to change their perceptions enough to enable them to continue to accept her as a member of the family.

SUMMARY

The middle years extend roughly from forty years to sixty-five years, but individuals vary in their response to the biological, social, and psychological cues of mid-life. Middle age is a time of reassessment, which can lead to a sense of fulfillment and leadership or a period of turmoil and dissatisfaction. The middle-aged have a general sense that the future no longer holds limitless possibilities. Their life tasks center on taking over the responsibilities of the older generation and being concerned about the future of the younger generation. These tasks require mastery of earlier conflicts and an acceptance of growing older. Peck has expanded on Erikson's conceptualization by adding four issues that are particularly relevant to adult development.

The recent development of cohort-sequential analysis has given us a better understanding of how intelligence changes over time. Intelligence may be divided into two broad areas: fluid intelligence, which declines gradually after adolescence; and crystallized intelligence, which continues to increase with age. Cognitive styles tend to become more rigid with age.

Both sexes undergo physical and emotional changes that are related to hormonal shifts. These changes occur gradually in men. The menopause often brings radical physical changes in women, but this is not necessarily the cause of great stress.

Biological, intellectual, and social functioning are affected by internal changes and external factors such as divorce, widowhood, and unemploy-ment. Physical abilities level off in middle age and serious diseases become more common. The death rate for men during this period is much higher than for women, although the pattern of sex-related diseases may be shift-ing. Further research is needed to determine the exact relationship between stress, diet, exercise, and disease.

The middle-aged are between two generations that often make si-multaneous demands on them. Some women look forward to the release from child-rearing responsibilities, but others become upset by the loss of a familiar function. Stresses may lead to feeling overwhelmed or feeling confident of one's coping capacities. Some of the stresses common to middle age are separation, divorce, and widowhood.

A high percentage of widowed and divorced middle-aged women are unlikely to remarry and face serious financial and emotional strains. They often have no pensions, and they experience difficulty in obtaining em-ployment. Men may also experience special problems if they become un-employed due to poor health or employer preferences for younger workers. Social workers should be aware of the varied needs of the middle-aged for services, including the availability of job retraining.

Some researchers feel that adult personality development is primarily a process of repairing earlier developmental problems and resolving old conflicts. A more optimistic approach is taken by humanistic psychologists, who deny the determinism of both the learning theorists and the Freudians. They feel that life can be a continuous process of maximizing potential. Maslow believes that basic needs must be met before higher personality integration can be achieved. Rogers developed clinical techniques for help-ing clients achieve greater self-acceptance. Humanistic psychology has had a great impact on clinical social work practice with adults, particularly on techniques of short-term therapy.

SUGGESTED READINGS

Davitz, J., and Davitz, L. *Making it from Forty to Fifty*. New York: Random House, 1976. A popular account of the thoughts, feelings, and actions characteristic of mid-life adjustments.

Fiske, M. *Middle Age: The Prime of Life?* London, San Francisco: Harper & Row, 1979. An excellent summary of our knowledge about middle age, written for the general public by a prominent researcher.

Hale, B. J. Gestalt Techniques in Marriage Counseling. *Social Casework*, July 1978, 59:7, 428–433. An example of casework techniques that focus on dealing with crisis in a way that maximizes individual freedom.

Rogers, C. *On Becoming a Person*. Boston: Houghton Mifflin, 1961. A prominent therapist talks about continued personal growth and creativity during adulthood, using theories of humanistic psychology.

Rubin, L. B. *Women of a Certain Age: The Midlife Search for Self*. New York: Harper & Row, 1979. An anecdotal report of a study of women today and how they are affected by the feminist movement.

chapter nine

Grete Mannheim, Photo Researchers, In

THE OLDER YEARS

strategies for coping

outline

THE ELDERLY IN SOCIETY

Population statistics

Retirement from the workplace

Family relationships

PHYSICAL AGING AND DISEASE

Physical changes

Chronic illness

Mental illness

Physiological theories of aging

COGNITIVE CHANGES

Intelligence

Memory and new learning

PERSONALITY AND AGING

Disengagement theory versus activity theory

A developmental perspective

Retirement

Liberation from role stereotypes

Coping with loss

Reflections on the past

DEATH AND DYING

Stages of adjustment

The right to die

CASE ILLUSTRATIONS

SUMMARY

SUGGESTED READINGS

THIS LAST STAGE OF LIFE includes many more years than any previous stage. Even though all stages encompass a process of growing older, or "aging," this is the only time when people are labeled as such. It is the time when individuals must come to terms with declining capacities and eventual death, although the age at which this occurs varies widely.

The Social Security Act of 1935 established age sixty five as the rather arbitrary definition of "old," as political and economic factors determined that job retirement was to begin at that age. Since then, developmental psychologists have identified several categories of older adults. Three groups may be distinguished: the *"young" old* (sixty to sixty four years), the *"middle" old* (sixty five to seventy four years), and the *"old" old* (over seventy four years) (Brody 1977). The sixty- to seventy-year-olds are similar in many ways, but those younger than sixty five differ significantly in that most are employed. Those older than seventy four are characterized by lowered incomes, more severe health problems, and a greatly increased need for community services.

The chapter begins with a discussion of the elderly in society. We shall examine some of the major shifts in American society that have affected the relationships of the elderly with their families and communities. This description of the social context in which aging takes place should prepare the student to understand the later discussion of physical and cognitive functioning and theories about interpersonal relationships. Special emphasis is given to problems of institutionalization and community care for the severely impaired. The chapter closes with a brief overview of social programs that have been developed to help individuals cope more successfully with these later-life changes.

THE ELDERLY IN SOCIETY

Butler (1974) seeks to counter the mistaken view that all the elderly are dependent, in poor health, or in need of institutional care. He chides us for not placing more emphasis on normal development, as 95 percent of the elderly live in the community rather than in institutions. However, social workers must be particularly aware of the special problems of the 5 percent who do need institutional care as well as those in the community who live in poverty and substandard housing or suffer from poor health. These groups, whose basic needs are still unmet, constitute the traditional concerns of social workers.

Cowgill (1972; 1974) theorizes that the status of older people declines as their proportion of the population increases. Moreover, he claims that industrial changes have created a high degree of competition for technical jobs, which puts a premium on youth and leads to early obsolescence of job skills. It certainly is striking to note that the median age in the American colonial period was only sixteen, and that only 2 percent of the population reached age sixty five. Today the median age is thirty and 10 percent of all Americans reach sixty five (Fischer 1978).

However, we should not paint an overly romantic picture of the high status the elderly attained in the past, in contrast to their present position in society. A reading of Western literature suggests that it has always been considered undesirable for the elderly to be in poor health or without financial resources. Often parents were held in high esteem only so long as they maintained control over the estate that younger family members hoped to inherit. And in our own times, it is the poor rather than the rich or powerful who lose status with advanced age, as evidenced by the ages of members of the United States Senate and Supreme Court and the list of millionaires in America. Neugarten (1976) claims that present studies show that the aged have not lost status as a result of urban industrialization.

The Harris Poll (Harris et al. 1978) points out that while elderly individuals tend to think they are doing pretty well, they also believe that they and their friends are the exceptions to the rule that "life was really tough for most people over 65." Harris finds that the rest of the population holds an even more pessimistic view of the condition of the aged than do the aged themselves. Similarly, the myth persists that families no longer care about the elderly today, despite persistent evidence to the contrary (Brody 1977).

Population statistics

Although attitudes toward aging have changed less than is popularly believed, demographic studies (statistical information about the population) indicate that great shifts have occurred in the characteristics of the elderly population. The U.S. Census is an excellent source of information about the needs for services of different population groups.

Let us now examine four sets of statistics on the percentages of aged in the population and on differences in life expectancy. Then we shall consider what these figures tell about the changing role of the elderly in our society.

1. In 1900, approximately 3 million people, or 4 percent of the population, were over sixty five years old; by 1975 approximately 22.4 million people, or 10.3 percent of the population, was in this age group. It has been predicted that by the year 2000 there will be 30.6 million people sixty five years or older (Brody 1977).

2. In 1900, 29 percent of those sixty five or over were age seventy five or older; by 1975, 38 percent of the elderly were seventy five or older (National Council on Aging 1978). It has been predicted that by the year 2000, 44 percent of the elderly will be seventy five years or older (Brody 1977).
3. Life expectancy in the United States has increased from about forty seven years in 1900 to about seventy two years in 1974. This is almost entirely due to many fewer people dying in infancy and early childhood. Life expectancy for those reaching age sixty five has not changed significantly, despite many scientific advances in disease control (Brody 1977).
4. The life expectancy for women is about eight years longer than for men, with the gap widening with increasing age. Life expectancy is approximately six years shorter for nonwhites as compared to whites (National Center for Health Statistics 1975).

What do the above figures suggest about needs of the aged? First, it is evident that an increasing percentage of the population will be not only elderly but also located in those upper age ranges that suffer the most from poor health, limited mobility, and loss of income. This suggests an increasing need for economic and social programs, which will be financed by a smaller proportion of younger workers than are presently in the population. The figures also indicate a disproportionately high number of widows among the elderly, and this group suffers from loss of companionship as well as income loss.

An examination of the statistics on women working outside the home reveals other factors affecting care of the elderly. As increased numbers of younger and middle-age women enter the labor market, fewer women are available to care for the frail elderly at home. This leads to an increased need for supportive social services in the community if the family is to continue its traditional role of caring for its elderly members.

We conclude with a brief look at population statistics that show median income in 1974 for single elderly who are living alone. Table 9–1 relates income to three other variables: sex, race, and age. These data indicate that problems of poverty are more prevalent among aged women, blacks, and those over seventy three years of age. Aged black women who live alone are in the greatest jeopardy due to lack of income sufficient to provide adequate housing, nutrition, health care, and other necessary services.

Overall, about one-sixth of the elderly live in households with incomes below the official poverty threshold for that kind of household (Brody 1977). Compare the life style possible for the frail elderly person who is able to afford a live-in housekeeper to that possible for a comparably handicapped person who is only provided four hours a week of subsidized household help. As we shall see later, some countries subsidize home helper services for a much larger proportion of the needy population than we do in the United States.

Although these statistics may be useful in predicting future behavior,

Table 9–1 Annual Income of Single Elderly Living Alone, by Sex, Race, and Age

		Age 65–72	Age 73 or Over
W H I T E	Male	$3882	$3037
	Female	$3024	$2516
B L A C K	Male	$2029	$1890
	Female	$2127	$1775

Source: *U.S. Bureau of Census 1975:* 114–115

one must exercise caution in making assumptions. For example, the present cohort of aged people (those born at the same historical time) are characterized not only by their age, sex, and income. The life experiences of people born at the turn of this century have been very different from the experiences that today's college students will have in their lifetimes. Today's elderly frequently immigrated from another country, and they generally received little education compared to young people today. In 1974 only 7 percent of the elderly were college graduates (Brody 1977). Many had worked for years in blue-collar jobs that were not unionized and that paid very low wages. Their lives were often characterized by a struggle to provide for a well-deserved retirement. Their parents rarely lived to enjoy retirement, and their last child often did not leave home until they were already old. Students can see how different their own generational life style is and can imagine the ways in which their lives will be different when they are elderly.

Retirement from the workplace

Retirement from paid employment changes one's way of life substantially. When we discuss theories of personality later in this chapter, we shall consider the emotional implications of retirement and why some people regard it as a blessing and others as a curse. First, however, we will look at some of the social factors related to retirement policy.

The social security retirement system was established in the 1930s partly in response to the fact that the elderly were not needed or wanted in the work force. Pincus and Wood sum up the situation as follows:

> The continuing argument over the merits of compulsory versus voluntary retirement is to a large extent an argument over the adequacy of the legal

definition of old age. Many of these arguments are academic in that retirement policy seems to depend primarily on the state of the economy rather than on the attitudes of particular employers or the competence of individual employees. In fact it has been argued that retirement practice (compulsory versus flexible) could come to be viewed as one of the measures by which the balance between total labor requirements and total labor supply is maintained (1977, p. 1219).

Social workers need to know not only the economic determinants of social policy but also people's beliefs about these policies. The social security retirement system embodies the prevalent view that a worker is entitled to a pension. Furthermore, this is held to be a right that is earned after years of labor. Many elderly today keenly feel the distinction between social security as an earned right, and SSI (Supplemental Security Income) as a welfare payment. Although SSI is administered by the Social Security Administration, it requires proof of financial need and therefore is still closely associated in the public mind with the assistance programs administered by county welfare departments. In fact, recipients of both social security and SSI may have been wage earners and taxpayers for many years. Many recipients of SSI are also receiving social security retirement benefits but their retirement income is so low that they qualify for an income supplement.

In 1900, 63.1 percent of men sixty five or older were in the labor force. The corresponding figure in 1972 was 24.4 percent, and by 1985 it is expected to drop to about 20 percent. However, due to the recent increase of women in the labor force, the proportion of workers supporting non-workers is still as large as previously (Pincus and Wood 1977).

It remains to be seen how much the relative economic costs of supporting a large retired population will increase in the future. Monk (1979) points out that the government will have to alter the financing of social security either by increasing the taxes of future wage earners or by increasing the age at which people retire. Federal legislation in 1978 has already raised the mandatory retirement age to seventy years for most employees and abolished it for federal employees.

We still do not know what effect this new legislation will have on retirement patterns because most workers retire voluntarily. Experience thus far has shown that where adequate income is provided, blue-collar workers prefer to retire by the age of sixty five. At present those who prefer to remain on the job tend to be better educated workers with more interesting occupations (Pincus and Wood 1977). The retirement preferences of women who have just recently entered the labor market and of the cohort of older workers who made career changes in middle age are still undiscernible.

There is another form of involuntary retirement that can have an even more devastating effect on the individual. This occurs when an individual is unemployed and unable to secure new employment. It is particularly tragic when subtler forms of age discrimination force a competent worker into early retirement with a concomitant reduction in pension benefits.

Another form of involuntary retirement occurs when an individual wishes to work, needs the income desperately, but has health problems that prevent employment or has job skills that have become obsolete. Thus far, rehabilitation and retraining programs have focused on the younger worker. We will return to the plight of the older worker when we discuss personality adjustments among the elderly.

Family relationships

Over 80 percent of elderly people are heads of households, either living alone, with a spouse, or with a nonrelative. As a result of the lower mortality rate of females, three-quarters of older men and only one-third of older women live with a spouse (Brody 1977). Of American women over sixty five, more than one-half are widowed and more than one-third live alone. Of American men over sixty five, only one-seventh are widowed and about the same number live alone (Murphy and Florio 1978).

On the average, older widows tend to survive about 50 percent longer than widowers following the spouse's death (Burnside 1979). These statistics spell loneliness for a good many older people, but aged women are eight times less likely than aged men to remarry following the death of a spouse (Burnside 1979). This is partly due to our society's favoring the pairings of older men and younger women (one of the reasons for the disproportionate number of widows in the first place) and partly because fewer men are available for remarriage. Thus we can see that the preoccupation with widowhood among middle-aged and older women is firmly rooted in reality.

Despite the number of elderly who live alone, there is considerable evidence that the norm continues to be family contact with the elderly (Atchley 1977). Adult parents continue to maintain relationships with their adult children. Although these relationships are generally most successful when both parties have the physical and financial resources to remain independent, children often do live close enough to their parents to visit them regularly and can respond to crises even when they live at a distance (Shanas et al. 1968; Shanas et al. 1979).

The elderly may rely on other kinship relationships if they have no spouse or child. Siblings are chosen more frequently than other relatives for assistance in a crisis (Atchley 1977), and many old people have some contact with grandchildren and great-grandchildren. However, as Monk (1979) points out in his review of family supports for the elderly, the three- or four-generation extended family serves mainly as emergency assistance in acute illness or disaster. Even closer relationships, as between parents and children, may not be capable of providing long-term support to the elderly.

A recent study by Kulys and Tubin (1980) looked at the relationship between a group of elderly over seventy years old who still lived in the community and the persons whom they designated as "responsible others" in the event of crisis. About 18 percent of the elderly respondents were having difficulty in caring for themselves. The results confirmed earlier findings that the elderly rely most often on family even though they have friends to whom they feel personally closer. Spouse, children, siblings, and other family members were chosen in decreasing order of importance. A number of the respondents had no living spouse and frequently the relative who was chosen in lieu of the spouse was unaware of being designated as the emergency resource. Other respondents had no back-up person who might serve as an alternate resource. It was evident that a sizable minority of those studied had a rather fragile support system. Blacks in this study were found to have a wider range of kinship-type relationships they could count on for assistance than did the whites. Later in the chapter, when we look more closely at the institutionalized population, we shall see that it includes a much higher proportion of widowed and never-married persons than exists in the population of elderly still living in the community (Shanas et al. 1979).

It has been estimated that only about 5 percent of the elderly have no close kinship relations (Atchley 1977). However, social workers tend to see a disproportionate number of those without close family ties or for whom these ties have been broken. Social workers also tend to become involved when families are no longer able to cope with the severe health problems of an elderly member and are considering an institutional placement.

The institutionalized elderly constitute about 5 percent of the total aged population, but for those eighty five and over the figure is close to 20 percent (Brody 1977). The needs of the institutionalized occupy much of our attention, both because good care is very costly and because those most likely to have severe physical and mental problems are also the most likely to have outlived their family and friends. There are special difficulties when an older child is also over sixty five years and possibly in poor health or when a middle-aged married daughter has reentered the labor market and has less time available to tend to the needs of an ailing parent. We shall return to this discussion of family relationships when we discuss health care and alternatives to institutionalization.

Some elderly couples choose to retire to Sunbelt states such as Florida, California, and Arizona. This arrangement may become problematic if the spouse dies, leaving the partner with no other close supportive relationships in the new community. Another option is to move to a housing development serving only the elderly. This type of age segregation suits some people but is quite unsatisfactory for others. Some affluent elderly choose to live in retirement communities that provide lifetime care, thus ensuring that their needs will be met if they become unable to live independently. A down payment and monthly fees are usually required for lifetime care. In return, the retiree is assured of a full range of services as needed, including nursing care. Students working with the elderly will want to be knowledgeable about these varied arrangements and how they affect the care of the elderly.

PHYSICAL AGING AND DISEASE

Physical changes

What happens in fifty five years to change a twenty-five-year-old quarterback into a sedentary, fragile old man? Which elements of the aging process are predictable and which are not? We cannot say that the predictable biological course of nature is the only explanation of physical aging. Genetic inheritance is modified by the physical environment as well as by the social and psychological environment of a lifetime. For example, the physical changes we shall discuss are influenced by whether the lungs have been exposed to the dust of a coal mine or the skin to excessive radiation by the sun. Physical aging is dependent on whether nutrition has been adequate or poor and whether income has been sufficient to provide for proper dental care. Research cannot tell us exactly how much influence each of these factors has nor the extent to which a particular individual is showing signs of aging or the symptoms of a particular health problem that may be remediable. One further caution: We should avoid associating all physiological changes with a comparable rate of either psychological aging or cognitive decline. An individual may be confined to a wheelchair or be totally blind, yet still be more mentally alert than another individual who may look years younger.

With these cautions in mind, let us consider the changes the elderly observe as they look in the mirror. To see oneself growing older can be something of a shock, particularly if one has been avoiding such an awareness during the middle years. Our society encourages such avoidance, advertising hair dyes and face lifts as ways of dealing with the physical signs of aging. Nonetheless, the elderly will find their skin becoming less elastic, drier, and more wrinkled. Warts on the trunk, face, and scalp may increase, and small blood vessels may break, producing tiny black-and-blue marks. Brown areas of pigmentation, popularly called "liver spots," may appear.

Years of poor posture may be accentuated by shrinking muscles, a decrease in elasticity, calcification of ligaments, or loss of space between the vertebral disks. These skeletal and ligament changes in old people are responsible for their becoming shorter or showing a slump in posture (Tonna 1977). As muscle weight decreases with age, the structure and composition of the muscle cells themselves are altered as they accumulate more fat. Muscles also function less efficiently if the cardiovascular system becomes impaired. Or, they may be adversely affected by weak bones, which are more likely to fracture and slower to mend in the very old. We still lack adequate longitudinal studies to provide definitive conclusions about what causes these changes and whether they can be forestalled by regular exercise and improved nutrition.

The heart, although a highly specialized muscle, nevertheless suffers from some of the same problems as other muscles. In addition, the heart depends on the efficiency of the entire cardiovascular system, which itself develops a variety of problems as it ages. Lungs also may suffer from reduced capacity.

Hearing becomes less efficient as people age, with deficits occurring most often in the high frequency tones. Severe hearing loss results in communication problems that increase the social isolation of the elderly. The rate of blindness also increases sharply after the age of sixty.

Many of these disabilities reduce the mobility of the elderly—a significant disadvantage in our society with its suburban sprawl and dispersal of family and friends over great distances. Even seemingly minor sensory or motor impairments can make life extremely difficult. Reduced mobility constricts the elderly person's range of activities and social contacts, and for some it may mean confinement to their homes, or even to their beds. Reduced mobility also has symbolic meaning. In adolescence, getting a driver's license is an important rite of passage that not only increases mobility but signifies independence. The teen-aged driver gains control over his or her comings and goings, and can get away from the family to visit with friends. Loss of the ability to drive in old age may be seen as symbolizing a loss of independence.

Until recently, the elderly generally were ignored in serious discussions of *sexual functioning*. When institutionalized, couples were often assigned to single-sex living arrangements. Sex was considered normal for middle-aged men, but when these same men continued to show interest in women years later, they were called "dirty old men."

Masters and Johnson (1966) helped dispel some of these myths by including the elderly in their study of human sexual response. They found that older women engaged in less sexual activity, largely because hormonal changes resulted in discomfort during sexual intercourse. Both men and women who remained sexually active were better able to maintain their capacities than were less sexually active people. However, it was more difficult for women to remain sexually active because of the relatively small proportion of elderly men in the population.

Masters and Johnson found that men's sexual responsiveness declined after age sixty. They attributed this mainly to increased physical and mental infirmities or to psychosocial factors such as fear of failure rather than to aging per se. We may speculate that the fear of failure among the aged has been heightened by our cultural emphasis on intercourse as the only proper form of sexual expression. In fact, the elderly can continue to express sexual intimacy in other ways.

To some extent, the increased health problems among the elderly reflect the body's decreased ability to cope with stress, including the stress of disease. A disease that may have easily been shaken off by a younger person—such as a respiratory infection—may linger on and perhaps cause permanent damage, thus increasing the likelihood of recurrence.

Socioeconomic factors, race, and sex all play a part in the occurrence of illness in old age. The large majority (80 percent) of deaths in those over sixty five fall into three categories: cardiovascular disease, cancer, and accidents. In all categories the rates are higher for men than for women. The rate of cardiovascular disease among blacks is twice as high as among whites (Kimmel 1974).

The poor health of old age may also be related to poor diet. Because of the lessened physical activity of old age and slowdowns in body metabolism, the elderly require less food than younger adults. However, the eating habits of a lifetime cause many elderly people to become overweight at the same time that they may be anemic or malnourished because they do not eat sufficient quantities of nutritious food. Inadequate income, depression or loneliness, and problems in obtaining transportation to shopping areas are among the reasons for poor eating habits. The Federal Government has subsidized a program of noontime meals for the elderly that provides both a nutritious hot meal once a day and a setting that encourages socializing. Many of these meal programs are in churches or senior centers.

What impact do these physical changes have on an individual's self-image? As older people become aware of their stiff joints, shortness of breath, or longer reaction time, they begin to revise their ideas about who they are and what they can do in the world. They may have to give up driving a car, for example, because their reaction time has slowed and their eyesight is failing. They may become cautious about going down a staircase or feel vulnerable while crossing an intersection. They may cut down on their after-dinner walks because they feel too tired or fear being mugged.

Sometimes physical changes force the elderly to make major psychological adjustments, especially when aging seems to occur suddenly. After a prolonged illness or a serious fall, for example, an individual may feel that he has turned into an old man overnight, before he is ready. He may not be able to regain his usual energy level, muscle tone, and quickness of thought or action. The suddenness of this drastic change may cause considerable confusion, stress, and frustration.

Social workers in senior centers or mixed-age leisure settings must appreciate that most elderly people are not as capable of strenuous physical exercise as they once were, nor are they ready for the rocking chair. Physical activities can often be modified so as to afford safe and enjoyable participation by many people. This same approach should be taken in nursing homes and other settings serving the more seriously impaired. Here too, creative social workers are finding ways to modify exercises so that those in wheelchairs may maintain their mobility. Social workers in these settings often work with other specialists as part of a rehabilitative treatment team.

Chronic illness

Hippocrates, in the fourth century B.C. wrote, "Old people have fewer diseases than the young, but their diseases never leave them." Chronic conditions still account for much of the health care required by the elderly. The *Fact Book on Aging* of the National Council of Aging (1978) reports that about 85 percent of the population over sixty five has at least one chronic condition. The most prevalent are arthritis and rheumatism (38 percent) and hearing impairments (29 percent), followed by vision impairments, hypertension, and heart disease. However, studies indicate that not all chronically ill people are functionally impaired and that about 32 percent of those with chronic conditions are not at all limited in their activities (Brody 1977). For the remaining group, the degree of impairment ranges from slight to severe, with 15 percent suffering major limitations in their activities.

The elderly need careful individual evaluation of their capacities; even among nursing home residents with similar diagnoses, some will struggle to compensate for their impairment and succeed in functioning at a much higher level than others. Social workers have traditionally advocated comprehensive diagnoses that enable more appropriate treatment plans to be made for residents of institutions.

Although only a small percentage of the elderly suffer severe restrictions due to chronic conditions, the elderly do account for nearly one-third of the nation's health expenditures. They are more frequently hospitalized, have longer and more costly hospital stays, and are the major users of long-term care facilities. They also consume one-fourth of all drugs purchased (Butler 1975).

Long-term care becomes necessary when the elderly can no longer perform the daily services necessary to maintain themselves. This is usually caused by irreversible, chronic health problems (Kaufman 1980). Some people can receive this care in their own homes; others cannot. Some people now in institutions might be better served in their own homes, if money now earmarked for medical services could also be used for home help and housekeeping services. The reimbursement rate is highest for institutions whose residents are the most disabled, need the most medical services, and are the least able to function on their own. This does not provide institutions with incentives to rehabilitate their residents.

On the other hand, some of the chronically ill now living at home might receive better care if good institutions were available to them. Shanas and her associates (1979) estimate that about 10 percent of those over sixty five and living at home are disabled to the point of being totally house-bound, with about one-third of them unable to leave their beds without assistance.

The major criticisms of institutional care are the high cost of the service and inadequacy of the care, as well as the fact that many elderly people prefer having the option of remaining in their own homes. If we are going to develop increased alternatives to institutionalization, then we must develop policies and programs to encourage existing family support systems and supplement them as necessary.

Sweden provides a good example of the range of services needed to ensure good community care (Little 1978). Swedish state-subsidized services include meal distribution, transportation, day centers, and home helpers. Home-help services include assistance with shopping, cooking, housekeeping, hairdressing, bathing, and snow removal. Local social service departments coordinate the delivery of these services. Older people who are unable to manage independent living, even with these supports, have the option of alternative housing, such as residential hotels or service flats where meals, recreation, housekeeping services, and easily available medical care are provided.

Although communities in the United States may provide some of these services, they are not available to all who need them. Compare, for example, the statistics on home helpers: In 1976 Sweden had 923 home helpers per 100,000 total population, Great Britain had 265 per 100,000, and the United States had 28.7 per 100,000 (Little 1978).

Until such time as we expand alternative housing and home-help programs to include a much larger proportion of those in need, we will continue to require institutional facilities. These facilities must be adequately funded and supervised to ensure that standards of professional care are met. Programs must be developed that show concern for residents' needs for autonomy and privacy. There must be individualized treatment plans, and the staff who care for the elderly must be caring people. We could go on with this list, but there is no lack of information about what is needed to improve our existing facilities. What is lacking is a public commitment to provide the full range of services needed by the elderly in our society.

Mental illness

Some mental problems of the elderly, called **organic disorders,** are related to the physical aspects of aging. They involve temporary or permanent damage to the brain tissue, causing symptoms such as impaired memory, poor judgment, intellectual decline and disorientation. The degree of impairment may vary from slight to serious enough to require hospitalization (Manney 1975). Again, individuals with the best coping skills before they became disabled will be the most successful in dealing with organic impairment.

Old people with serious physical illnesses are more likely than others to suffer from organic brain damage. Because of the incidence of organic disorders, it is estimated that the rate of psychosis for those over sixty five is about three times that of the thirty-five- to sixty-four-year group (Brody 1977). Sometimes these mental symptoms are caused by strokes, heart failure, or alcoholism and can be reversed. **Chronic brain syndrome,** however, refers to the gradual, irreversible deterioration of the brain cells, or to cerebral arteriosclerosis, which impairs the flow of blood to the brain.

These facts are particularly important to social workers in community mental health programs. The public policy on care of the mentally ill has shifted, since the 1960s, away from care in state hospitals and toward the use of community facilities. Many of the elderly, however, had been hospitalized for many years, and when discharged, they no longer had any family able to care for them. This situation resulted in the rapid growth of small, privately owned residences and nursing homes, which stepped in to care for this population. Operators of nonmedical facilities are paid a minimal amount through the SSI program, to provide care and supervision for the financially needy part of this population, while payments to those in nursing homes are made through the Medicaid program. The amount of payment in both these programs varies from state to state. Social workers are concerned about the difficulty of enforcing minimum standards of care in these facilities, most of which are ill-equipped for handling mental disorders.

There has also been a recent expansion in the number of *community mental health centers.* Although the centers provide outpatient psychiatric services to the entire population, they do not see many of the elderly. It is estimated that 10 percent of the elderly population are likely to experience severe mental problems, but only 2 percent of this population are seen in outpatient hospital clinics and 4 percent at community mental health clinics (Kramer, Taube, and Redick 1973). One reason for this underutilization of services is the tendency of professionals to mistakenly regard all symptoms shown by the elderly as irreversible. Programs dealing with the elderly should use a multidisciplinary assessment of problems to determine which are organically based and which can be expected to change in response to improved treatment and rehabilitative services. For example, overuse of drugs and improper monitoring of medication are common problems of the elderly, and even the excessive use of tranquilizers may result in greatly reduced physical and mental activity.

Physiological theories of aging

How does aging actually happen? Does the genetic clock simply run down, or must cells and organs be damaged by chemicals or radiation? Here are a few of the more popular theories.

The *homeostatic theory of aging* views the body as increasingly inefficient at maintaining stable levels of the various chemical elements. Since these processes are delicately interrelated, deterioration in one area can have a great cumulative impact on the body as a whole. Some of the mechanisms involved are the acid–alkaline balance and sugar levels in the blood, internal regulation of body temperatures, and filtration and excretion of toxins by the kidneys. Interestingly, when the body is at rest, these self-regulating processes in older people operate at a level similar to those observed in younger people. The crucial difference is found in older people's decreased ability to return to homeostasis, or a normal balance, after physical or emotional stress such as exercise, anger, high sugar intake, and great changes in temperature. Thus, the emotional stresses that normally accompany old age, such as loss of spouse, retirement, and environmental change, may have severe consequences for physical health (Timiras 1978).

The *cellular aging theory* is actually a set of theories that focuses on various aspects of cellular change in aging bodies. Body cells divide and reproduce a finite number of times and some researchers believe that cells may begin to reproduce imperfectly (by inserting the wrong amino acid into a strand of DNA). Other researchers believe that cells deteriorate in response to an accumulation of insults and injuries (Timiras 1978). They compare the human body to a machine that simply wears out as a result of constant use, with the added accumulation of insults and injuries (Kimmel 1974; Timiras 1978). Schock (1977) criticizes this model because it fails to account for the fact that many body systems are in fact self-repairing. For example, skin and red blood cells constantly replace themselves; and while nerve and muscle cells do not redivide in adults, they are capable of self-repair.

The *auto-immunity theory of aging* is the last that we shall mention, although there are many others. This approach is based on the fact that human beings, as they age, show an increasing tendency to reject their own tissues. Among the diseases linked to auto-immunity are rheumatoid arthritis, cancer, diabetes, vascular diseases, and hypertension. This theory has been criticized on the ground that it may refer to symptoms of deeper processes rather than to the cause of aging itself.

Elderly individuals often differ in their beliefs about "what keeps people young." Currently, many people believe that certain diets will delay the aging process. Social workers should avoid proselytizing for any particular theory or type of medical treatment; at the same time, they should recognize that a strongly held belief may in fact prove beneficial for the particular individual believer.

COGNITIVE CHANGES

The common belief in an inevitable and substantial mental decline in old age is not supported by research. Older people vary widely in their level of cognitive functioning.

Intelligence

Recall from Chapter 8 the developmental differences between fluid and crystallized intelligence. As long as the older person is alert and capable of taking in new information, crystallized intelligence can compensate in some ways for losses in fluid intelligence. The losses in speed and memory that begin in late middle age are frequently offset by gains in reasoning and understanding.

Reliable data on the IQ of older subjects are hard to obtain, since many external factors such as test format, motivation, and social isolation can substantially affect performance (Hooper and Sheehan 1977). It is difficult to make accurate estimates of intellectual functioning in old age, and while there does appear to be some decline, it is not as great as was previously thought (Botwinick 1977). Neugarten (1976) states that age is generally not a reliable index of cognitive performance. However, she does note major changes in the speed with which older adults perform both mental and physical activities. Thus, older subjects consistently scored lower than younger ones on speed-related tests.

One reason for the difficulty in generalizing from the studies on intelligence is that such studies are usually based on a cross-sectional sample of the population. In other words, the same test is given to all ages of the population and the results compared. But, as has been pointed out, respondents differ not only in age but also in life experiences that affect their scores. For example, do older persons score low on abstract thinking because of their age or because their earlier education did not emphasize abstract thinking? If rigidity of thinking is being tested, how do we determine whether the older people being tested were always more rigid in their thinking than the younger people with whom they are being compared? Neugarten (1976) points out that much of our **gerontological** research is based on cohorts born in the late nineteenth century. They include a high proportion of the foreign-born, the uneducated, the unskilled, and the poor. Cohorts that will enter old age in the 1990s will be quite different, having lived through periods of greater affluence, mobility, and accessibility of higher education.

A few longitudinal studies have followed the same people throughout their entire life span to determine which of their characteristics change over time. Although those who perform the least well in tests of ability tend to drop out of the study group, the evidence from longitudinal research is that those with relatively high levels of ability early in life tend to stay relatively high (Botwinick 1977). To cite an extreme example, Albert Einstein would score higher than most of the population, even were he to suffer some loss of capacity due to aging.

There is increasing awareness that optimal intellectual functioning in the later years is related to the maintenance of good health, regular physical activity, and intellectual interests throughout life. Reduced physical and mental activity may be caused by emotional crises, such as grief or depression, or it may be brought on by pessimistic expectations of deterioration. Social workers are sometimes involved in programs to maintain cognitive functioning in residents of institutions. Meditation, exercise, and guided imagery have been successfully used to reawaken thoughts and communications made dormant through neglect and isolation.

The single most reliable indicator in predicting intellectual functioning in old age, according to Neugarten (1976), is a person's educational level. Increased education may stimulate a desire to stay mentally active; it may also impart skills that help the elderly adjust to old age. Educated people continue to enjoy reading, analyzing, criticizing, and discussing throughout their lives.

Many communities now have library outreach programs that bring books and cassettes to the homebound. In addition to offering intellectual stimulation, the staff assigned to the program may perform the social service functions of friendly visiting, assessing unmet needs, and making referrals to other agencies when needed.

In sum, Neugarten (1976) concludes that the most influential factors in cognitive decline in old age are not intrinsic to the aging process itself, but rather are attributable to failing health, social isolation, minimal formal education, poverty, and low motivation. Although there is some inevitable drop in cognitive abilities, there is also much that can be done to improve socioeconomic conditions and prevent unnecessary decline.

Memory and new learning

In Chapter 4 we discuss an information-processing model of memory: Information is fleetingly retained by sensory processing mechanisms, sent to short-term memory for organization and encoding, then stored in long-term memory. Gerontologists differ about the changes in these mechanisms that occur in old age. A number of the existing studies lack sound methodology, and further research is needed. In some studies the sample tested does not accurately represent the general population of elderly persons; in others the results could well have been affected more by poor health than by aging per se. A host of other factors can call into question the "evidence" presented for or against a particular theory.

After evaluating a number of memory studies Craik (1977) summarized the major findings. He found that memory loss is not an all-or-nothing occurrence, and some individuals compensate for deficits better than others. Moreover, the elderly do not have significantly greater problems than the rest of the population in immediate recall, but they are slower when memory retrieval is involved. The elderly also have particular problems when their attention is divided—for example, when information is coming from two sources at once. Recall appears to be improved if the elderly are given more time for a task, with careful instructions on how to organize the material to be learned. He also found that performance is improved by past education and experience with the organization and recall of learned material.

None of the above should lead us to conclude that people past sixty five cannot learn and utilize completely new material. They may not be as efficient as younger students, but their past experience and knowledge may more than compensate for this. Adult education is growing in both traditional and nontraditional settings, and continuing education is helping to facilitate the difficult adjustment faced by retirees in our work-oriented society (Timiras 1978). Because the new cohort of retirees is better educated, the number of college programs geared to the elderly is increasing.

Adult education is growing in both traditional and nontraditional settings, and continuing education is helping to facilitate the difficult adjustment faced by retirees in our work-oriented society (Timiras 1978). Because the new cohort of retirees is better educated, the number of college programs geared to the elderly is increasing.

PERSONALITY AND AGING

One of the most important psychological factors of the aging process is a person's subjective perception of his or her position in the life span. Recall from Chapter 8 that middle-aged adults stop thinking in terms of "time from birth" and begin to think in terms of "time left to live" (Neugarten 1977). This perception becomes intensified for those entering old age. People in their late fifties and early sixties begin to be concerned about how much longer they have to live, whether they will be seriously ill or hand-icapped, what kind of life style they can maintain on a fixed pension, what they will do with their time after retirement, and how they will cope with the death of their spouse.

We have already discussed some ways in which elderly individuals adjust to diminished physical or mental capacities. For most, it is merely a question of not seeing or hearing as well, not moving as quickly, or noticing that "my body just doesn't work as well as it used to." However, some elderly must make adjustments to severe mental or physical impair-ments. Older people who cannot expect to recover lost functions may suffer severe restrictions on their autonomy, making them much more dependent on others. People who formerly took care of their own needs may now need to ask others for help, even with such simple tasks as getting dressed.

Some adjust to these changes better than others. Peck's term *body preoccupation* (Peck 1968) and Shanas's term *health pessimism* (Shanas et al. 1968) describe the tendency of some old people to become overwhelmed by the limitations of their bodies. *Body transcendence* describes the ability to find life satisfying despite changes in health. Research indicates that the physical self-evaluation of the aged is a good measure of their psychological well-being (Shanas et al. 1968). Many elderly people have serious ailments that they consider as "little aches and pains," and others in relatively good health magnify their minor problems. The sicker that people think they are, the more lonely and alienated they are likely to be.

Disengagement theory versus activity theory

Disengagement theory presents the aging process as a mutual with-drawal of the individual from society and of society from the individual (Cumming and Henry 1961). According to this theory, the withdrawal is natural and even beneficial, because the aging individual's diminished life span matches his decreased physical and psychic energy. Thus, the indi-vidual maintains a feeling of life-satisfaction as social involvements and activities are curtailed because he or she has less desire for them.

The **activity theory** presents a different picture of old age. According to this theory, the pattern of withdrawal that characterizes many elderly people is the result of society's withdrawing from those individuals, usually against their wishes. Therefore, older people will stay more satisfied with life if they remain active and involved, resisting the isolating effects of social attitudes toward the aged. According to the activity theory, older people will make the best adjustment to retirement loss by finding substitutes for work, and individuals who lose a spouse will benefit from finding new friends to fill the emotional gap.

A developmental perspective

Social workers will probably find a developmental perspective the most functional way to view the transitions and adjustments that the elderly must make. This perspective emphasizes the *continuity of personality structures* throughout life and recognizes that there are as many different personality types in old age as in youth.

Williams and Wirth (1965), in a major study of styles of successful aging, found successful adaptations within life patterns that differed significantly from each other. For example, some people attach primary meaning to the work they do, and others focus more on family relationships. Some rely heavily on the couple bond; others have adapted successfully to living alone. Within each of these groups some individuals make more successful adaptations than others.

Social workers see some individuals who can accept dependency more easily than others and who can accept help without loss of self-esteem. An awareness of these differences enables workers to offer services, wherever possible, in the manner most suited to the personality, or life style, of the client. An example comes to mind from a recent newspaper story about an elderly couple who had once been quite wealthy but now were living in very reduced circumstances because inflation had wiped out the value of their savings. Although they supplemented their social security checks by selling furnishings from their house and had restricted their life style by foregoing all recreation and entertainment, they were unwilling to sell their expensive house and add the profits from the sale to their monthly income. The reason they gave was their very strong desire not to renege on a promise to leave the house to their daughter. This is an excellent example of a couple who held rigidly to a strongly felt value in the face of "good reasons" for selling their house. The house probably also represented the last tie to a way of life they had cherished throughout their adult years. In such a case, it is well for the worker to recognize and accept this framework, possibly helping them to accept some modifications within the basic pattern. Clearly, other couples might have no such strong desire either to maintain a large house or to provide for the future of a grown child at the expense of their own standard of living. Part of the skill in helping people plan for retirement is the ability to recognize that people have very different values, needs, and goals for themselves. They also vary considerably in the capacity to be flexible and make changes in their customary pattern of adjustment.

Retirement

Retirement marks a major change in status for the individual in our society. It is a time when the person works out choices, negotiations, and coping patterns consistent with his or her own set of meanings. As Pincus and Wood state: "Viewing the retirement process from the perspective of developmental psychology enhances the possibility of eventually understanding the interplay of physiological, psychological, and social factors that influence this transitional process" (1977, p. 1220).

Obviously, the ideal approach to retirement would be for society to provide the elderly with the maximum number of options. One person may want to continue working and another may be eager to retire. One may start a new career, and another may prefer to withdraw from former social obligations. Still others may prefer to disengage but cannot afford the resultant loss of income.

More research has been done on retired men than on retired women. The studies that have examined factors determining the quality of life during retirement, find that *health* is a significant factor. Many older men leave the work force, either willingly or unwillingly, because of ill health. Levy (1978) studied a large group of men who were about to retire, comparing their state of health and their willingness to retire. As one might expect, healthy men who wanted to retire fared the best. Healthy men who were initially opposed to retirement gradually took on more favorable attitudes after an initial period of adjustment. Those in ill health fared the worst, regardless of their willingness to retire.

Contrary to some popular beliefs, there is no evidence that health deteriorates as the result of retirement (Pincus and Wood 1977). This belief stems from drawing the wrong conclusions from a piece of evidence. True, the evidence shows a higher death rate for newly retired workers than for those who have not yet retired. One possible explanation is that retirement causes premature death among the elderly. However, before coming to such a conclusion, we must ask whether there are any other possible explanations for this relationship. More careful studies suggest that those who retire have poorer health than those the same age who continue working (Pincus and Wood 1977). In other words, the retiree's state of health accounts for the different death rates noted. Researchers are often able to control for intervening variables affecting the results of a study. For example, we might compare retirees and nonretirees who are equally healthy and have the same incomes, then see if their degree of life satisfaction and rate of death varies significantly.

Economic status also affects the retiree's adjustment to a new way of life. A few individuals have accumulated no savings and have no pensions. To them, retirement means permanent impoverishment. Most retired people, while not impoverished, must learn to live on less than their former income. If this retrenchment cuts deeply into people's favorite pastimes or lifelong retirement dreams, they may feel sharply restricted in their last years of life.

Friends and colleagues also affect the quality of life after retirement

(Cox and Bhak 1979). If an individual's significant others—friends and associates in clubs and organizations—hold positive attitudes toward retirement, the individual will tend to look forward to retirement and make a successful adjustment.

As mentioned earlier, an individual's lifelong *attitude toward work* also affects feelings about retirement. Many people have spent so much time at their jobs that their sense of worth and self-esteem is embedded in their work. For them, retirement means stepping out of the important, productive stream of life. Disengagement is especially hard for those who have never found other satisfactions, such as hobbies, reading, continued education, or involvement in organizations. The problem tends to be worse for the less educated, the financially strained, and those with few social or political involvements, but the professional individual or the business executive may also have difficulty organizing leisure time.

Social and economic circumstances have an important impact on an individual's adjustment to retirement. But even under the same external conditions, people react differently. Many studies have suggested that *personality type* determines a person's reaction to retirement. One study (Reichard, Livson, and Petersen 1968) tentatively identified five different personality types. Among the well-adjusted, the largest group were the "mature"—those who had no regrets about their past lives and who accepted their present circumstances realistically. They made the best of old age by finding genuine satisfaction in their activities and friendships. A second group, the "rocking-chair men," welcomed old age as a time when they were free to sit back, relax, and do nothing. They, too, seemed to find genuine satisfaction—but in passivity, instead of activity. The third group, the "armored," used activity as a way of fending off old age. They developed a highly satisfying life style in the years after retirement, but this system served as a defense against anxieties about feeling old. Other individuals found little satisfaction in retirement. Some poor adjusters, the "angry men," bitterly blamed others for their own failures in life. Others, the "self-haters," blamed themselves.

Whether an individual reacts well or poorly to retirement is the result of many different factors: health, economic status, need for a sense of fulfillment, flexibility, personal history, and the reactions of significant others. Retirement is not merely a break with the past; it is also a continuation of what has gone before. Coping styles and patterns of adaptation are well established by this time of life, and social workers need to understand these patterns if they are to be successful in helping elderly individuals.

Liberation from role stereotypes

Researchers have tried to determine whether any distinct pattern of personality change can be observed as people grow old. Gutmann (1964) found, in a longitudinal study of middle-aged and aged in Kansas City, that middle-aged men tended to view the environment as within their control. They saw themselves as possessing the energy to take risks and meet the challenges presented by the outside world. In contrast, older men saw the world as more complex and dangerous, no longer within their power to change according to will. They saw themselves as conforming and accommodating to their environment. Gutmann called this change in perspective a shift from active to passive mastery.

Gutmann (1975) later hypothesized that men and women respond differently to this aspect of aging. As men adapt to the shift from an active to a more passive style, they are freed from the necessity of being the masterful decision maker and seem better able to express the neglected, or feminine, sides of their personalities. Gutmann found that women, on the other hand, tend to become more aggressive, instrumental, and domineering as they age. He hypothesized that both sexes are responding to liberation from the "parental imperative," the social pressure for women to conform to nurturing roles and for men to be financially responsible and to suppress any conflicting traits.

It will be interesting to see whether further research substantiates this theory. Meanwhile, social workers should be aware of the possibility that the elderly truck driver in the senior group might be looking forward to becoming a really good cook. It is also important to be aware of the possibility for increased family conflict, should the roles of one partner not mesh with the roles of his or her spouse. A family diagnosis is one way of looking at the roles of each family member and seeing how they differ from previous roles and previous patterns of adaptation.

Coping with loss

The **role-exit theory** (Blau 1973) describes old age as a time when many old roles are terminated and new roles must be found as substitutes. This theory is similar to the activity theory described earlier, but it examines old age from a sociological perspective. A *role exit* is the cessation of a stable pattern of social interaction; old age is characterized by many such exits. Friends may die, children and grandchildren may move far away, physical ailments may curtail activities, and a reduced income may force the individual to move to a smaller home in a new neighborhood. Most of these role exits signal the end of lifetime attachments. When one exit follows another in rapid succession, as they often do in old age, the cumulative effect can be devastating.

We have already discussed loss of physical and mental capacities and loss of the work role. Another major loss often experienced by the elderly is loss of spouse or friends through death. We have shown how the meaning of these events differs with the individual. Although retirement is generally thought of as signaling the end of an individual's usefulness in the work force, it may mean something quite different to someone who has hated his or her job for the past thirty years. Similarly, widowhood may mean sudden release from the toil of caring for a chronically ill spouse and the freedom to structure one's own time.

As we saw in Chapter 8, many married women become widows in middle age; by age sixty five and beyond, widowhood is the common pattern. For some, this is the last significant status passage before their own deaths and may indeed hasten their own deaths. For others, it may provide a long-awaited opportunity to assume control of their own lives.

Widowhood poses some of the same problems as impending retirement; foremost among them is the threat of financial insecurity. By the time they have reached old age, most women have several friends who are widows, and anticipation of their own possible bereavement becomes almost unavoidable. For many, the anticipation of loss may create anxiety, excessive worry over a spouse's health, and strained personal relationships. Older women use a number of coping strategies to work through these problems. The anticipation of loss is very similar to the separation anxiety that many infants experience, with its stages of protest, despair, and detachment (see Chapter 3). Just as in infancy, adults in later life need to work through their emotional reactions to come to terms with an inevitable separation. Surely, no one can have survived to old age without having experienced several separations and losses, which provide a rehearsal for more intense later losses. The anticipation of loss may lessen the ultimate pain and shock of a critical loss if it leads to an acceptance of the inevitability of the loss. Also, an older woman's friends and acquaintances may serve as role models in helping her adapt to widowhood.

Despite all the preparation and rehearsal, most individuals will have to make a difficult emotional adjustment after the death of a spouse. At this point, social customs may be of assistance. A funeral, memorial service, or other rite can impart a sense of order, comfort, and continuity, and it can help to reaffirm the bereaved person's ties to the broader social group. Sometimes ties that have been only loosely held in the past now acquire a new meaning for the individual.

Grief takes a considerable amount of time to work through. It often involves mulling over the circumstances of the spouse's death. Although repetitive accounts of the terminal illness may seem morbid to the outsider, they may provide needed opportunities for the bereaved to express his or her feelings or simply to cry. The bereaved person needs time to lose the recurring expectation that the spouse will really return. Psychosomatic complaints also may be part of the grieving process, although physical symptoms seem to be more common among those bereaved earlier in life than among the aged (Burnside 1979b).

The clergy have traditionally been "grief counselors," and for many individuals they still offer the most solace. Some clergy have training in psychology in addition to their traditional preparation. However, some · elderly individuals do not identify with a religious group or no longer live in the same neighborhood as the minister with whom they have had a lifelong relationship.

Social workers have also become more aware of the grieving process. Sometimes they use group discussions as a vehicle for allowing individuals to express their feelings. At times the peer group can offer the most meaningful help in accepting the often ambivalent feelings people have about the death of a spouse or another significant person. Social workers in residential settings should be particularly aware of the importance of rituals to appropriately mark the death of an older person. Staff sometimes mistakenly think that elderly residents will be spared grief if no mention is made of the deaths that continually occur in an institution. Yet how much more frightening it is to think that one's death will be unnoticed or unmarked by others.

Some elderly people will find it comforting to turn to activities at a senior center, church, or volunteer program. Activities are one means of creating new relationships and repairing the damaged self-esteem that sometimes accompanies the death of a loved one. Irrational as it seems, the person left behind sometimes feels betrayed, as if he or she would not have been left behind, alone and unprotected, if he or she were really loved by the dead person. Sometimes individual counseling will be better suited to a person in temporary need of a one-to-one relationship.

One of the new realities that widows and widowers must often face is living alone. For the first time in many years they must now run errands, maintain social contacts, and make financial decisions on their own. Some may welcome the opportunity for personal growth and the development of new competencies. Others may have difficulty living alone because their spouse has always taken care of practical matters for them, particularly finances. Unfortunately, this new freedom may come at a time of reduced mobility, limited finances, and a constricted social environment, all of which make independence more of a burden than a joy.

Living alone need not mean loneliness. *Loneliness* is the perceived lack of *any* intimate relationship with another. The mere reduction in the amount of social interaction is not in itself associated with poor emotional adjustment (Lowenthal et al. 1967). Conversely, an older person can live in a family and essentially remain an isolate, or even be physically and emotionally abused by other family members.

Widows may find it easier than widowers to maintain a social life since wives traditionally keep lines of communication open with family members and initiate social activities with friends (Lopata 1975). Widowers, therefore, are more apt to become isolated from the couple's previous social contacts. Widowers are also generally less active in social organizations than widows. Men may face sexual problems when they attempt to reinitiate sexual activity following a long period of bereavement or sexual inactivity due to a wife's prolonged illness. Sometimes a feeling of guilt toward the dead spouse intensifies these problems.

Suicide is not an uncommon response to the problems the elderly face. Although the most publicized suicides are those of young adults and children, by far the greatest number of suicides occur among people over forty five years of age. Those over sixty five years account for 25 percent of all suicides in the United States (Butler 1974). Four times as many men commit suicide as do women, and their suicide rate rises steadily with age, reaching a peak among those over eighty years (Riley and Waring 1978; Miller 1979). These statistics do not take into account the more passive forms of suicide, such as letting oneself die, or the indirect forms of dying through excessive drinking, smoking, or drug abuse (Miller 1979).

Suicide among the elderly is almost always a result of major accumulated losses. Both widows and widowers, therefore, are at a greater risk of committing suicide. The risk falls off sharply after the first year of bereavement but still remains higher than average for several years (Miller 1979). Old people who always feel lonely or who have a history of emotional instability are also highly prone to suicide.

Social service programs for the elderly sometimes include a component that attempts to reach out to the isolated elderly, through home visits by volunteers, through church programs, or through outreach services of public or private agencies. However, it is always a difficult task, because the isolated elderly rarely come to the attention of any agency, and many live out their last years in run-down hotel rooms. Even their death may go unnoticed for days.

Reflections on the past

The reminiscences and ruminations of old age lead to an overall evaluation of the way a lifetime has been spent and of the legacy one will leave behind. Older people wonder whether their lives have fulfilled their earlier expectations and have conformed to deeper belief and values. Erikson calls this final crisis of ego development *integrity versus despair*. Those who can look back and feel satisfied that their lives have had meaning will have a sense of integrity. Those who see nothing but a succession of wrong turns and missed opportunities will feel despair. Most people will experience each of these feelings to some degree. Shakespeare's Macbeth, commenting on his evil deeds, anticipates the effect which this will have on his later years: "I have lived long enough, my way of life is fall'n . . . and that which should accompany old age, as honour, love, obedience, troops of friends, I must not look to have; but in their stead, curses . . ." However, it is only by coping with the reality of approaching death that one can ultimately decide what is really important and who one really is (Kübler-Ross 1975).

Butler (1974) points out that successful aging involves both a life-review process and also the shifting of focus from consideration of the future to enjoying the quality of life in the present. Indeed, the process of life review leads to decisions as to how best to live in the present. He recommends that psychotherapy, or counseling for the elderly, make use of this review process to help the individual relieve old guilts and resolve old conflicts.

Social workers in residential settings have also noted the improved sense of self-esteem that often results from programs such as taping oral histories, preparing individual scrapbooks, and other evidences to mark the person's existence. In many institutional settings a sense of anonymity and isolation is created among residents, hindering the process of life review and reconciliation with the past.

DEATH AND DYING

Although the inevitability of death increasingly crosses the older person's mind, few people can fully grasp the idea of their own extinction, especially by natural causes (Kübler-Ross 1969). In their unconscious minds, they think of their own death only as something done to them by an outside force—either an accident or someone's deliberate act. It is almost impossible for them to imagine growing old and dying quietly in bed.

For a long time, the psychological realities of facing death received little professional attention. In recent years, however, a profusion of research, books, and articles have appeared on the subject. The helping professions are now beginning to help the critically ill and dying to discuss their feelings, and to work with doctors and relatives of the patient so that they can also recognize the emotional needs of the dying person. Doctors are apt to feel disappointed when their skills do not cure the patient, and therefore may sometimes prefer to withdraw from further interaction. Relatives may not know whether to mention the imminence of death or to pretend that all will be well. The proper approach to these matters, of course, will depend on the individuals' previous patterns of coping with crisis as well as their present preferences.

Stages of adjustment

Elisabeth Kübler-Ross (1969) was one of the first to make a detailed study of dying. She focused on the relatively short-term situation when a person first recognizes death as an immediate possibility—for example, when a fatal illness is discovered. She identified five stages in the process of adjusting to the idea of death: *denial, anger, bargaining, depression,* and ultimately *acceptance.* Let us consider how these stages apply to a man who has been diagnosed as having a fatal illness and told that he has only a short time to live.

Once the initial shock wears off, he will *deny* the possibility of death. He will simply refuse to believe that it can happen to him. He may suspect there has been some mistake and "shop around" for other diagnoses and reassuring opinions. The denial stage is often characterized by an intense feeling of isolation, as the person attempts to cope with this tremendous problem that has suddenly fallen on him and him alone. Even as the initial stage of anxious denial subsides and the person begins to consider the possibility of death more realistically, partial denial may persist for some time longer.

Disbelief gradually gives way to an awareness that there was no mistake, and that he is indeed going to die. The next question becomes "Why?" Denial is now replaced by "anger, rage, envy, and resentment" (Kübler-Ross 1969). The *anger* is born of frustration. After a whole lifetime of planning, preparing, dreaming, and striving, suddenly it's all for nought. Projects remain unfinished, dreams unfulfilled. Since the anger usually has no particular object, it will probably be indiscriminate and unfocused, directed at any object or individual within reach, at God, at medical professionals, and at family members.

Once the person calms down to the point where he begins to accept his fate more stoically, he looks around for ways to *bargain* for more time. If the inevitable cannot be avoided altogether, perhaps it can at least be postponed. And if not, then perhaps the suffering patient can at least be spared a day or two of pain and discomfort. Again, the dying person, not knowing where to turn, will turn in all directions. Promises are offered in exchange for relief.

As this bargain ultimately fails—or time runs out—hopelessness and depression take hold. The *depression* may be either of two types: *reactive depression,* which is a response to the losses incurred so far—physical deterioration, depletion of financial resources, and the crumbling of one's hopes and dreams; or *preparatory depression,* which anticipates impending death and separation from one's family and friends. Just as many elderly married persons suffer anticipatory grief at the prospect of the spouse's death, the person facing death may grieve for himself. It is difficult to talk the dying person out of his grief and probably unwise to attempt it. His expressions of sorrow probably ease the transition to final acceptance.

Finally, given sufficient time and support, the dying person will leave fear, anger, and depression behind and simply await and accept his fate quietly. *Acceptance* does not necessarily mean happiness, but it may mean rest, peace, and probably relief. In fact, there is a notable absence of any strong feelings, which is often reflected in the dying person's silence. He withdraws into himself and becomes uncommunicative. In one sense, this stage represents a return to the passivity and egocentrism of early infancy: "we are going back to the stage that we started out with and the circle of life is closed" (Kübler-Ross 1969, p. 120).

Not every person will in fact progress through to the final stage, and social workers may be called on to work with those who maintain denial or anger until the time of their death. The form of the final stage of acceptance will also vary with the individual's religious or personal philosophy of life. The patient may choose this time to return to a previously held religious belief, particularly if this brings about a desired family reconciliation.

Butler (1974) observes that Western society, with its emphasis on man's ability to control the environment, is particularly unsuited for teaching people to accept death as an integral part of life. Indeed, one need only look at popular magazines or newspapers to see accounts of individuals "conquering" death by one means or another. The hero is usually the person who "battles" death without ever relinquishing hope, rather than the person who quietly accepts the fact that further battle is useless. There is, however, a growing recognition that some people do prefer to do without "heroic measures," or actions that use the very vocabulary of the battlefield.

The right to die

A growing number of professionals and lay persons feel that dying patients should have more control over the manner of their death. Specifically the "right to die" movement aims to counteract a situation in which doctors may prolong the life of a terminally ill person regardless of the patient's own wishes about continued medical intervention. The pros and cons of artificially maintaining life-support systems beyond the point at which the patient is ever able to regain consciousness are widely debated. Professionals may wonder whether they prolong the life of others because of their own fear of death, even when the patient is ready to die. Social workers, of course, must not allow their own preferences to prevent them from accurately perceiving and accepting the patient's preferences. Some patients may prefer to "fight to the last" because they have always "tackled" a crisis aggressively.

We are remarkably good at providing medical care to dying patients, but often we offer no human support system to supplement the technical support system. Patients are often isolated from their loved ones in a sterile environment, and decisions are made for them without regard to their own wishes.

Euthanasia, or mercy killing, is an idea that goes back to ancient times. It refers to letting nature take its course, or even lending a helping hand to hasten the end in a painful terminal illness. An interesting case example of one person's handling of a painful, inoperable, and incurable cancer is Sigmund Freud, the father of psychoanalytic thought. Ernest Jones's biography of Freud (1957) gives a moving account of his final months. After suffering from cancer of the jaw for sixteen years, the ninety-three-year-old Freud had exhausted the possibilities for treatment then available. He had undergone both surgery and radium treatment, using this extension of time to continue his analytic work. He continued to show an interest in world conditions and accepted his personal fate with complete resignation. He avoided drugs as long as possible, commenting that "I prefer to think in torment than not to be able to think clearly" (Jones 1957, p. 245). Then, in September 1939, the last year of his life, he sank into a state of complete pain and exhaustion. Two days before his death, he reminded his doctor: ". . . you remember our first talk. You promised me then you would help me when I could no longer carry on. It is only torture now and it has no longer any sense" (p. 247). The doctor responded by providing sufficient morphia for Freud to sink into a peaceful sleep until his death the next day. His biographer, Jones, said of Freud at the funeral,

> It was hard to wish that he would live a day longer when his life was reduced to a pin point of personal agony. Nor did he in any way dread death . . . what in others expresses itself in religious feeling did so in him as a transcendent belief in the value of life and in the value of love. . . . He had lived a full life, had experienced its heights as well as its depths . . . and life had nothing left to offer (p. 241).

The **Living Will,** prepared by the Euthanasia Educational Council, is a recent effort to assure a greater measure of individual autonomy for the dying patient. This document informs the signer's family, or others who may be concerned, of the signer's wish to avoid the use of "heroic measures" to maintain life in the event of irreversible illness. Although it is not legally binding, it does protect those who observe its terms from legal liability (Shapiro 1978).

In 1977 California passed the first American legislation that affirmed the right of the patient to offer written instructions to the physician about terminating life-sustaining procedures at a certain point. Patients already had the legal right to verbally refuse further treatment, but the purpose of this new legislation was to protect those who become unable to communicate with their physician at the time they wish to terminate treatment. The directive was to be *legally* binding on the physician only if signed at least fourteen days *after* a person was medically certified as having a terminal condition. A number of safeguards were also built into the legislation to protect misuse of such a document, and it did not sanction hastening the moment of death by any positive action. The example of active euthanasia, cited in Freud's case, remained illegal.

Hospice programs are another recent development in the United States. They are based on the idea that hospitals are for patients undergoing medical treatment to "get well," and that dying patients, who have different needs, should be treated in a different place. The first hospice for the dying was started in England in 1967 as a place where the terminally ill could have their needs attended to when medical intervention could no longer prevent imminent death. The English hospice views death as a difficult task that, like childbirth, can be made easier by appropriate assistance and comfort from others. The first aim of the hospice is to manage pain of all sorts: physical pain, mental pain, social pain, and spiritual pain (Garrett 1978). In addition, the hospice helps the family to understand the dying person's experience and needs and helps keep communication with the family open so that the dying person will feel less isolated. The hospice remains in touch with the family throughout the period of bereavement. Of particular benefit to those in extreme pain, such as cancer patients, is the willingness of the hospice to administer painkillers to make the patient more comfortable in the last weeks of a terminal illness, without the usual medical concerns that the patient might become addicted to the drugs used.

The hospice idea spread to America in 1974, and four years later there were some two hundred programs in various planning stages (Abbott 1978). Most of the first American programs were limited to outpatient services that provide the care and support needed to enable the patient to remain at home for as long as possible (Garrett 1978).

Some of these innovative ideas could beneficially become an integral part of the procedures in all institutions caring for the terminally ill. The vast majority of the elderly continue to die in hospitals and nursing facilities, and social workers can play a significant role in helping these facilities deal more adequately with the multifaceted needs of the dying patient.

CASE ILLUSTRATIONS

Mary Longwood is a social worker from the local family service agency. She is assigned to a senior recreation center two days a week. Approximately 250 elderly people use the center daily, primarily for the hot noontime meal. This nutrition service is subsidized by the federal government under the Older Americans Act.

One condition of government funding is that additional supportive services be offered along with the meals program. Many centers offer an information and referral service, using volunteers to provide information on a wide range of available resources. However, this center has decided that their members require more comprehensive services and wants to offer brief counseling and assistance in locating resources, with professional expertise in coordinating the available services. Our examples will illustrate how Mary uses the concepts of human development presented in this chapter. For each example, we shall also indicate how public policies set the framework within which the social worker operates and suggest ways in which these policies might be altered to improve the availability of needed services. The case illustrations in this chapter go beyond the specific focus of this text in order to offer students a glimpse of the breadth of concerns and the variety of methods of intervention in the field of social work.

Income assistance

One of Mary's first tasks has been to acquaint herself with the provisions of the SSI program. We have already mentioned this supplemental income program but should further note that those on SSI are also presumed financially eligible for a number of other subsidized benefits, such as Medicaid or special transportation assistance. Mary's intent is to encourage those who might be eligible for benefits to apply for SSI. To further this goal, she has invited a representative from the social security office to the center to answer questions about the program.

It is soon evident that a number of senior center members are reluctant to discuss their finances with a stranger, although a full financial statement must be made to apply for SSI. Mary is careful to arrange a private space for interviews so that the conversations will not be overheard.

She also notices that some applicants for SSI misinterpret or misunderstand what is explained to them at the social security office. She tries to remedy this situation by making a brief presentation on the special problems of the elderly at one of the regular social security staff training sessions. She discusses the need to be aware of potential hearing problems and suggests that some information be put in writing so that applicants can think about it and return later to ask questions. This leads to a discussion of the general procedures for making an application, and Mary points out how difficult it is for the elderly to wait so long to see a worker, only to be told to return with documentation.

Mary's concerns, which are shared by social workers concerned with the mentally ill as well as the elderly, eventually result in the development of a program whereby volunteers accompany those who need assistance in applying for SSI. The staff at the senior center also decides to distribute written material about the program and to discuss it frequently at group meetings so that people will be familiar with the requirements before making an application.

Mr. Seely is a neat but shabbily dressed widower who attends the meals program but rarely socializes with anyone. Today, Mary notices that he has initiated a brief contact with the social security representative. She asks him whether he received the information he needed. Mr. Seely firmly replies that he could never get involved with any scheme that required him to surrender his small savings account of five thousand dollars. He had just learned that his monthly income was low enough to entitle him to financial aid, but first he would have to "spend down" his savings to the maximum amount allowed by law, which is currently $1,600. Logically, it would be sensible for him to do this, since the benefits would far exceed the amount of the lost savings. But to Mr. Seely the savings account represents a degree of independence that he is not willing to surrender and an achievement of which he is proud.

After listening carefully, Mary realizes that Mr. Seely feels very strongly about this matter. She also knows that inflation is fast making many government income restrictions unrealistic and that it would be beneficial to allow the elderly to keep a larger amount of personal savings.

In order to find some way of helping Mr. Seely improve his standard of living, Mary suggests that he get on the waiting list for the subsidized housing program. He is eligible for the federal program that allows him to choose from among the public and private units provided by the local housing authority. He is then required to pay only 25 percent of his income toward the rent, with the remainder being subsidized by the government.

Housing help

Edna Brown, an eighty-year-old woman who is quite sociable, has been growing noticeably frailer over the past six months. She finds it more difficult to move around and tells Mary that she fears she will not be able to continue shopping, cooking, and cleaning for herself. She is on SSI and eligible for publicly subsidized household help of four hours a week. However, she cannot find someone to work for the minimum wage that she is allowed to spend.

Edna is widowed, with one son, fifty years old, who has recently moved to Hawaii. He writes to his mother but rarely sees her. He has recently remarried, and his new wife is considerably younger, with three children to support. Since his re-marriage, he has discontinued the small monthly checks he used to send his mother. Mary is able to find Edna a place in a nonprofit housing development designed for the elderly. In six months she will have a studio apartment, for which she will pay 25 percent of her income. In the meantime, the local volunteer agency is able to provide some temporary assistance with shopping chores. Edna's new apartment will provide cafeteria meals for all residents, and assistance with cleaning and maintenance of the apartment.

Mary checks around to see if the community offers any housing that includes multiple levels of care, such as units for the nonambulatory or even those requiring nursing care. With such arrangements the disruptions caused by poor health are not compounded by those of having to leave one's friends and neighbors. However, this community does not have such a housing program, and Edna must live with the possibility that illness may force her out of yet another home. Even a temporary stay in a nursing home might force her to give up her apartment, since she cannot receive Medicaid and rent subsidies at the same time.

The social worker could not continue doing her job if she had to find perfect answers to the problems faced by the elderly. In this case, Mary is reasonably convinced that Edna will enjoy the studio apartment, which is in the same neighborhood in which she presently lives. She expects that Edna will be able to remain there at least five years, barring an unexpected physical crisis. She has contacted

Edna's doctor, and he makes a referral for a physical therapist to visit Edna once a week to help her maintain her present degree of mobility. Unfortunately, such assistance is costly and only available to a limited extent. It is easier to obtain funds for nursing home care than to obtain the same amount for the care needed to maintain people in their own homes.

Mary feels certain, having observed Edna's enjoyment of the activities at the senior center, that she will like being in housing occupied entirely by the elderly. Frances, on the other hand, makes it quite clear that she comes to the center only for the inexpensive meal and that she does not wish to identify in any way with "these old people." She is sixty six years old, looks young, and is quite active in political activities that involve people of all ages. She continues to pursue her many other interests actively; for her, having to live in age-segregated housing would be a disaster. Frances is also looking ahead to the time when she might no longer be able to get along entirely unassisted, and since she is divorced, she has decided to rent one of her rooms to a college student who will help out with the chores in exchange for a room.

Mary has noticed that several of the elderly black women who come to the center are still providing child care for their sons or daughters. The possibilities for successfully multi-generational family life styles are increased when there is a continued exchange of services within the family, but Mary is not sure whether this pattern will continue among younger black families. She also wonders whether the Hispanic and Asian families in the city will continue their strong cultural emphasis on taking care of the elderly within the family. She knows that younger members of the new immigrant communities have begun to help their parents or grandparents use various community resources. The older generation is often unfamiliar with these resources, which did not exist in their native countries.

We often see many separate ethnic groups among the elderly, particularly when there are language barriers as well as marked cultural differences. Mary does not have contact with all the ethnic groups, although organizational efforts have been made to coordinate church programs serving the immigrant communities. These efforts have been resisted by group members who have strong feelings about maintaining food programs that serve the foods they have eaten since childhood. For them, there would be a great sense of loss at having to abandon their traditional diet at the point when they could no longer cook for themselves.

Health care

Verena Thomas, who is seventy five years old, has recently suffered a stroke. After initial treatment in an acute-care hospital, she was sent to a nursing home— or convalescent hospital. After a brief period of nursing care and rehabilitative treatment, she had to leave because her Medicare health insurance had run out and the fee for the facility was higher than Medicaid (medical payment plan for the financially needy) would allow. In order to find a facility that would accept the Medicaid rate, Ms. Thomas would have to go far from her home community, and her family would no longer be able to visit her regularly.

When Mary saw Ms. Thomas, she was shocked at the change in her. She seemed to have aged rapidly in the months she had been away. Her speech was slower and more hesitant, and she no longer had the "spunk" she was known for. Mary was concerned about how long Ms. Thomas could continue to live in her small house, even though she shares it with an unmarried daughter, the daughter's boyfriend, and their two small children.

Mary decided that she would like to make a home visit to meet with the entire family and assess the adequacy of the supports for continued home care. The family is quite concerned about the problem and is eager to meet with Mary. Ms. Thomas had been providing child care for her grandchildren before her stroke but can no longer manage this. Her daughter is willing to take the children to the local child-care center and would like to keep her mother at home. However, they all agree that someone must be home with her during the day when the adults are at work.

In looking for the best way to help Ms. Thomas and her family, Mary phones a number of agencies. She finds that there is no adult day-care center or other suitable program in the community. Ms. Thomas cannot stay at the senior center all day, since this facility is geared to providing group activities for the well elderly. Within a few months she will become housebound and decide to enter a residential care facility.

Transportation

Charles Evans, a sixty-five-year-old man, has been alcoholic for much of his adult life. He has been in a mental hospital for some years but was released five years ago. Since then he has lived in a community-care facility, a nonmedical facility for those needing care and supervision in the activities of everyday living. Although he is younger than most of the residents in this privately owned home that houses several other elderly people, he suffers from more severe mental disabilities than the other residents.

Mary knows about Mr. Evans because she meets once a month with a group of operators who run the "board-and-care homes" in the community. The meetings were initiated by workers representing various agencies such as mental health, health, social services, and recreation. These meetings are a rather forward-looking attempt to serve the population in community-care facilities and at the same time help to educate the operators in how to deal with residents in the best way possible.

Mr. Evans needs some rather extensive dental work and is unable to manage public transportation without getting disoriented or lost. The operator of the home is technically responsible for seeing that he gets where he needs to go. However, she is also responsible for providing supervision at all times for the other residents, and she feels she cannot afford to hire another person to assist her.

The issue of transportation for those unable to drive or use the limited public transit system has long been a difficult one for the elderly in this community. Mary decides that she needs to set both an immediate and long-term goal in this situation. As no transportation is presently available except a subsidized ambulance service for medical emergencies, she will need to patch something together immediately. She is able to arrange for the Red Cross to take Mr. Evans for his appointments, using a volunteer driver. However, this is almost a personal favor, since their major function is to serve the military population.

Many of the elderly who are too poor or too ill to drive a car could still use public transportation if it were both accessible and safe. Older people in suburban or rural areas often lack buses to take them to distant shopping or medical appointments. For the inner-city older person, public transit may be available but unsafe, since the high crime rate particularly penalizes the elderly rider. Many of these transportation problems are shared by handicapped people of all ages, and the two groups have joined forces at the state and national level to demand greater access to public transportation.

However, there remains a group of people like Mr. Evans, who would need alternative transportation even if fixed-route buses and streetcars were available. Some cannot walk several blocks to get a bus, some cannot keep their balance while standing on a moving bus, and others lack the capacity to hear, see, or understand transit directions. Perhaps the most practical alternative for this group is the subsidized taxi service.

Summary of Cases

In summarizing these case examples, we find that human needs are interrelated and so services to the elderly must be coordinated. Health care services cannot be used without access to transportation to medical appointments. The suitability of housing for the frail elderly often depends on whether the necessary personal services or household help are available—or affordable. Few communities in the United States offer a coordinated network of services to the elderly. At best, they provide discrete services to some portion of the needy elderly.

The elderly represent a heterogeneous population with diverse needs. Despite the current emphasis on enabling the elderly to remain in their own homes, there will always be some people who need good institutional care, either because their families can no longer bear the burden and community-based supportive services are lacking, or because their own coping capacities have diminished to the point where independent living has become a terrible burden. The remedy for poor nursing home care is to improve the quality of that care. The remedy for premature institutionalization is to offer a comprehensive range of community services to deal with a wide range of disabilities. For example, some housing programs include a range of options for residents: independent apartments, apartments that include meal services and housekeeping assistance, day-care facilities, and a nursing-care unit.

Throughout this text we have referred to both the changing nature of the American family and the extent to which it continues its traditional functions of caring for its members. We need coordinated government policies that will assist the family with some of these functions while recognizing that in some situations family care is neither available nor desirable.

The issue of *independence versus dependence* has been another theme throughout the text. There is a biologically based dependence at certain periods in the life span, such as in infancy. We have also shown how societies tend to socialize their members so as to produce the characteristics valued by that society. Our society places a particularly high premium on independence and individual autonomy. We do not accept a renewed dependency in old age easily. Such dependency is often seen as a sign of weakness rather than as a biological imperative. When severe health problems cause older people to become more dependent, they are sometimes described as becoming "like a child again"—a position of very low status.

If aging is to become fully accepted as a normal developmental phase of life, we must learn to accept adult dependence as well as independence. Our model of successful aging need not be a person who retains all the capacities of middle age. Instead, we should be prepared to provide opportunities for people to fulfill their physical, mental, and emotional potential at this last stage of life while maintaining the maximum amount of autonomy possible. In the last analysis, the care that we offer our aged population is a reflection of the organization of our society and the hierarchy of values that it expresses. As our economic and social institutions change, so do we change the way in which we care for our dependent populations.

SUMMARY

Definite physical, intellectual, and psychological problems occur in old age, but the extent to which older people suffer from impairment of abilities varies widely. Many individuals remain active and healthy throughout their lifetimes. However, social workers tend to see the most impaired, who need supportive services or long-term care.

Our retirement system defines sixty five as the start of old age, although sixty-five-year-olds are generally not very different than they were five years earlier. The percentage of the elderly in the population is increasing, and this trend is expected to continue. Women live longer than men and are more frequently widowed. Women, nonwhites, and people over seventy five years old suffer most frequently from poverty when they are old. By the year 2000, 44 percent of the elderly are expected to be seventy five years old or older.

The percentage of people over sixty five in the labor force has decreased. When adequate pensions are available, many workers look forward to retirement. However, involuntary retirement because of age discrimination or health problems can have a devastating effect on the individual.

Women are more apt to live alone than men because over half the women over sixty five are widowed. The elderly maintain contact with their children and other relatives, but some have only fragile connections with persons they can turn to in time of crisis. Although the institutionalized elderly constitute only about 5 percent of the aged population, they account for 20 percent of the population eighty five years old and older.

The physical changes of aging include a decline in hearing and vision and decreased functional ability of the heart and other muscles. Defects may result from inherited or environmental factors. Some health problems are remediable and others are not, and a person who is experiencing difficulties in one area may function extremely well in another.

Old age is characterized by an increase in chronic diseases such as arthritis, rheumatism, heart conditions, and high blood pressure. Higher rates of illness are found among the poor and the nonwhite. Those who have some form of chronic impairment may differ greatly in both the extent of their disability and in their psychological capacity to cope with it.

While only a small percentage of the elderly suffer severe restrictions due to chronic conditions, the elderly account for nearly one-third of the nation's health expenditures and are the major users of long-term care facilities. Chronic health problems often require long-term care, which may be offered through community services or in institutions. Adequate resources must be allocated for home-care services, and the quality of our institutions must also be improved. Ideally, communities should provide a range of supportive services, including housing that accommodates several levels of disability, home helpers, meal programs, and transportation. The United States spends much less on home helpers than many European countries.

Some of the elderly now in private boarding homes and nursing homes were previously in mental hospitals or suffer from organic brain syndrome. We lack adequate programs to serve this group and often fail to differentiate between older persons who show mental symptoms because they are overmedicated, those who are in poor physical health, and those who are depressed because of recent losses or stresses.

Age itself is not a reliable index of cognitive performance. Although we see some slowing of performance and memory loss, a person's overall cognitive functioning is most closely related to his or her education and previous levels of performance. Individuals vary in their ability to compensate for cognitive deficits.

The pattern of adjustment to the changes brought about by aging is highly related to previous personality and life style. Some people look forward to retirement and a gradual disengagement from society. Others find continued involvement and activity most satisfying. Whether an individual reacts well or poorly to retirement depends on his or health, income, personal history, and whether the retirement was chosen or voluntary.

Loss of spouse or other close relationships is another major stress affecting the aged population. Grieving over loss is part of the adjustment process. Social workers use individual and group counseling to help individuals deal with loss. The social isolate and the potential suicide are among the groups not usually served by social agencies.

Successful aging involves both a life-review process and a coming to terms with the meaning of one's life and the inevitability of death. There is increasing interest in finding ways for medical care to include a concern for the psychosocial needs of the patient. Terminally ill patients may want more control over their treatment and a lessened emphasis on continued artificial prolongation of life.

The case illustrations point to the need for a wide range of coordinated services to serve the needs of the elderly. We now lack many of the services that might prevent premature institutionalization.

SUGGESTED READINGS

Atchley, R. *The Social Forces in Later Life.* Belmont, Calif.: Wadsworth, 1977. This is an excellent introduction to the problems of aging, approached from a multi-disciplinary viewpoint. The major focus is on the individual's relationship to society, and the field of social gerontology receives special emphasis.

Brody, E. *Long-Term Care of Older People: A Practical Guide.* New York: Human Services, 1977. Of special interest to social workers, this book describes the components of good long-term care for the elderly, with special emphasis on the role of individual and group services to residents and their families. Practical advice is given about intake procedures, record keeping, and other areas.

Butler, R.N., and Lewis, M.I. *Aging and Mental Health: Positive Psychosocial Approaches.* St. Louis: C.V. Mosby, 1977. A thorough summary of the nature of physical and emotional problems in old age, along with a discussion of appropriate treatment and prevention.

Coles, R. *The Old Ones of New Mexico.* Garden City, N.Y.: Anchor/Doubleday, 1975. Through his interviews and observations of aged Indians in the Southwest, Coles portrays a society in which the elderly are able to maintain both dignity and self-respect.

De Beauvoir, S. *The Coming of Age.* Patrick O'Brian, trans. New York: Putnam's, 1972. This is an attack on society's age prejudices by a prominent French writer. De Beauvoir also has a concern for the special problems faced by women today.

Silverstone, B., and Hyman, H.K. *You and Your Aging Parent: The Modern Family's Guide to Emotional, Physical, and Financial Problems.* Random House, 1976. This very practical guide for the general public as well as the professional provides extensive coverage of the problems families face. There is an equally comprehensive guide to available social services and other community resources for the elderly.

GLOSSARY

Activity theory A theory that adjustment to old age is maximized if individuals remain active and involved with others.

Aging Biological development beyond the point of optimal maturity.

Aggressive behavior Hostile actions with the intent to injure, as distinct from assertive behavior. (Sometimes used in a broader sense that includes assertive behavior.)

Alleles A pair of genes, found on corresponding chromosomes, that affect the same trait.

Amniocentesis A test given pregnant women in order to detect chromosomal abnormalities by analysis of fluid from the membrane enclosing the fetus.

Anal period Freud's second psychosexual stage, in which the child gives up some control over the sensual pleasures of the processes of bodily elimination in order to gain parental approval.

Androgynous personality A sex-role identity that incorporates some positive aspects of both male and female traditional behavior.

Assertive behavior Direct acts that further one's interest but do not harm others. See *aggressive behavior.*

Attachment The close emotional relationship between child and long-term caregiver. The first significant attachment occurs during the child's first year.

Behavior modification Programs that use principles of operant conditioning to shape behaviors for therapeutic goals.

Casework The social work method by which individuals and families are helped on a case by case basis to deal with problems affecting their interpersonal functioning.

Causality The relationship between a cause and its effect. See *correlation.*

Chromosome A chainlike structure in the nucleus of the cell that carries the basic transmitters of hereditary traits. See *genes.*

Chronic brain syndrome Mental disorders in the aged caused by irreversible physical deterioration of the brain.

Classical conditioning (Also known as *respondent conditioning.*) A type of learning in which a neutral stimulus (a bell) becomes the conditioned stimulus for a response (salivation) through repeated pairings with an unconditioned stimulus (food).

Climacteric Interrelated physical and emotional symptoms accompanying hormonal changes in middle-aged men and women.

Cognitive development The development of mental capacities, including the capacity to receive, process, and give meaning to information.

Cohabitation An arrangement in which a man and woman live together without being legally married.

Cohort sequential analysis A research method that studies selected age groups over a staggered time period, correcting the bias inherent in the logitudinal study.

Community organization Methods of intervention used by social workers to help people plan collective action to deal with social problems.

Competence motivation Being moved to acquire skills in order to achieve a feeling of satisfaction.

Concrete operations Piaget's third stage of cognitive development in which children begin to think more logically and realistically about relationships between objects in their environment.

Conservation of matter The cognitive ability that allows the child to judge changes in amount based on logical thought rather than mere appearances. It is central to Piaget's concept of the concrete operational stage.

Correlation A relationship between two or more variables that does not necessarily imply that one variable causes the other.

Criterion-reference test A test that measures an individual's performance in terms of specified skills or objectives. See *norm-referenced test.*

Critical period The *only* time when prenatal development can be influenced by a particular environmental factor. See *optimal period.*

Cross-sectional study A method of studying child development in which a comparison is made between samples of individuals representing different age populations.

Crystallized intelligence The area of intelligence that includes verbal reasoning, vocabulary, comprehension, and aspects of spatial perception.

Defense mechanisms The Freudian term for techniques that individuals use to reduce anxiety due to emotional conflicts.

Denial A defense mechanism in which a person refuses to admit the existence of the anxiety-producing situation.

Dependent variable The variable in an experimental research design that changes as a result of manipulating an independent variable.

Desensitization A technique in behavior therapy that gradually reduces an individual's anxiety about a specific object or situation.

Development Changes in the structure, thought, and behavior of a person over time.

Discrepancy hypothesis The theory that infants experience stranger and separation anxieties as a result of their recently acquired ability to differentiate between the familiar and the unfamiliar.

Disengagement theory A theory of adjustment in old age that considers a gradual withdrawal from society as natural.

Displacement A defense mechanism in which a less threatening person or object is substituted for the real source of anger or anxiety.

DNA (Deoxyribonucleic acid) A large, complex molecule composed of carbon, hydrogen, oxygen, nitrogen, and phosphorus. It contains the genetic code that regulates the functioning and development of the organism.

Down's Syndrome (Mongolism) A genetic abnormality in which the presence of an extra chromosome causes improper physical and mental development.

Dream, The   Levinson's term for the youthful ideal that is gradually molded into an attainable goal.

Ego identity   Erikson's term for the integrated, consistent self-image that develops as the adolescent becomes more emotionally independent from parental controls.

Electra complex   The Freudian term for the unconscious sexual attraction girls have toward their fathers, which they renounce in the course of normal development.

Embryonic period   The prenatal period that begins approximately five days after conception and lasts about seven weeks. During this time, the major structures and organs of the embryo are formed.

Erogenous zones   The Freudian term for parts of the body that give sexual pleasure when stimulated. The earliest erogenous zone is the mouth, as the infant derives pleasure from the act of sucking.

Euthanasia   The practice of easing the suffering of the hopelessly ill by either actively hastening death by means of drugs or passively withholding life-sustaining procedures.

Extrinsic motivation   Motivation that comes from an outside source—for example, the desire to win a prize or please a parent.

Feedback   Evaluative or corrective information about one's behavior that comes from oneself or others.

Fetoscope   A long hollow needle equipped with a light and a lens to enable a doctor to observe the fetus in the uterus.

Fetus   The prenatal human from three months after conception until birth.

Fixated   A Freudian term referring to an inappropriate focus on the gratifications of an earlier psychosexual stage that prevents the individual from achieving full emotional maturity.

Fluid intelligence   An area of intelligence that is based mainly on the effectiveness of neurological and physiological factors, including motor speed and memory.

Formal operations   The last of Piaget's cognitive stages, that begins in adolescence and is characterized by the ability to critically examine and evaluate one's own thought processes and behavior.

Genes   The chromosomal units that are composed of DNA and control the transmission of inherited characteristics.

Genetic code   The biochemical basis of heredity contained in DNA molecules.

Genital stage   In psychoanalytic theory, the last stage of sexual development that begins after the onset of puberty and is characterized by heterosexual behavior.

Genotype   The genetic makeup of an individual or group.

Gerontology   The study of aging and the problems of the aged.

Gestation   The period from conception to birth—an average of 266 days in humans.

Group work   A social work method in which groups are the medium through which social work objectives are achieved.

Growth Progressive development of the individual to the point of optimal maturity.

Hospice A residence for the terminally ill that focuses on relief from pain and meeting the emotional needs of the dying person.

Hyperactivity A characteristic of children considered to be excessively active and who often have impaired coordination and a short attention span.

Hypothesis A tentative assumption about relationships that can be proved or disproved.

Identification Incorporating within oneself the behavior and qualities of a person one respects and wants to emulate.

Imprinting The instinctual process by which newly hatched birds form a rapid and relatively permanent bond with the parent.

Independent variable The variable that experimenters introduce in order to observe the resulting outcome. See *dependent variable.*

Innate drives In Freudian theory, powerful instinctual forces that are expressed in different ways as the individual matures.

Intelligence Quotient (IQ) The ratio between an individual's mental age and chronological age, multiplied by 100.

Intrinsic motivation Motivation related to the pleasure the activity causes the individual, in contrast to external rewards or punishments.

Latency A term used by Freudians to describe the period from about five years to the onset of puberty, during which sexual urges are relatively dormant.

Learning The developmental process by which behavior changes in response to experience.

Learning disability Extreme difficulty in academic learning, with no detectable physiological abnormality. The term is used to describe a wide variety of problems.

Living will A document informing others of the signer's wish to avoid use of heroic measures to maintain life in the event of terminal illness.

Long-term care Residential care or community-based health and social services for the aged who can no longer manage their daily routines unassisted.

Long-term memory A term used by information theorists to refer to storage of information for periods up to a lifetime. See *short-term memory.*

Longitudinal study A research study in which changes in the same subjects are observed over a period of time.

Maturation The unfolding of the inherited potential of the individual.

Meiosis The process of cell division in reproductive cells, in which the chromosomes are reduced to half the number present in other cells. See *mitosis.*

Menarche The time of the first menstrual period.

Menopause The permanent ending of menstruation.

Mentor A sympathetic counselor or guide who instills self-confidence and helps advance the career of a younger adult.

Minimal brain dysfunction Minor brain damage that may be difficult to detect but is considered responsible for some learning disabilities.

Mitosis The process of ordinary cell division that results in two cells identical to the parent cell. See *meiosis*.

Modeling A learning process in which individuals copy the behavior of others. See *identification*.

Neonate The newborn baby from birth to the end of the first month.

Norm-referenced test A test that compares an individual's performance with that of others in the same age group.

Oedipus complex The emotional conflict that Freudians believe to be based on the unconscious sexual attraction between boys and their mothers. See *Electra complex*.

Object permanence Piaget's term for the infant's realization that objects continue to exist even when they are out of sight or touch.

Open education An educational approach that emphasizes flexible and individualized instruction within the heterogeneous classroom. Goals are based on each child's needs, interests, and readiness to learn.

Operant conditioning Conditioning that occurs when rewards or reinforcements are offered to support the continued performance of a voluntary action.

Operational definition A definition that is useful to researchers because it uses precise and measurable terms.

Optimal period The period during which a particular environmental factor will have a heightened effect on development.

Oral stage Freud's first psychosexual period, during which the infant's sensual pleasure is focused around the mouth.

Organic disorder Term used to refer to mental illness in the elderly caused by temporary or permanent damage to brain tissue.

Ovulation The release of the ovum into one of the two Fallopian tubes. It occurs in humans about fourteen days after menstruation.

Ovum The female reproductive cell (the egg or gamete).

Peer group A formal or informal group whose members are about the same age. They often are also similar in social status.

Perinatology A branch of medicine that deals with the child's development from conception through infancy.

Phallic stage Freud's third stage of psychosexual development (ages three to five) during which the child's sensual pleasure focuses on the genitals.

Phenotype The visible properties of an organism. See *genotype*.

Pituitary gland An endocrine organ attached to the brain. It produces secretions that directly or indirectly affect most basic body functions.

Positive regard Term describing the totally accepting attitude of the therapist toward the client. This is a crucial aspect of Rogerian therapy.

Preoperational period Piaget's second stage of cognitive development, during which children begin to use language and other symbols. Their thinking tends to be concrete and egocentric at this time.

Primary group A small group that is relatively stable, whose members closely interact with one another and have common norms governing behavior.

Probability The chance that a given event will occur, expressed in mathematical terms.

Projection A defense mechanism in which one attributes one's own undesirable thoughts and actions to another.

Prosocial behavior Helping, sharing, and other actions that are intended to benefit others.

Punishment A penalty imposed for a fault or misbehavior—for example, spanking, scolding, isolation, or withholding of privileges.

Rationalization A defense mechanism in which an individual invents acceptable and rational reasons to explain unacceptable thoughts or behavior.

Reaction formation A defense mechanism in which individuals unconsciously mask their unacceptable thoughts or desires by behaving at an opposite extreme.

Readiness The time when an individual has matured enough to benefit from a particular learning experience.

Recall The ability to retrieve information from the short- or long-term memory.

Recognition The knowledge or feeling that something one observes has been seen before.

Regression A defense mechanism in which anxiety is dealt with by reverting to earlier, less mature behavior.

Reliability The extent to which an experiment or observation will produce the same results each time it is repeated.

Repression A process by which unacceptable desires or impulses are excluded from consciousness but continue to operate in the unconscious.

Respondent conditioning See *classical conditioning.*

Reward Something that is offered in return for a desired behavior with the aim of encouraging its repetition.

RNA (ribonucleic acid) A nucleic acid that is associated with the control of cellular chemical activities.

Roles Standards of behavior that apply to certain categories of persons.

Role-exit theory A theory that old age is characterized by the loss of familiar roles and the need to learn new ones.

Scheme Piaget's term for mental structures that allow information to be processed and understood if it "fits" the structure.

Sensitive periods All those times when an individual is particularly responsive to certain environmental influences.

Sensorimotor period Piaget's first cognitive stage, in which the infant integrates perceptions and motions and becomes aware of the independent existence of objects.

Sensory register The term information theorists use for the mental structure that records all information briefly, before any information enters conscious awareness.

Separation or stranger anxiety An infant's fear of separation from the caregiver and fear of strangers. It is related to the newly acquired ability to distinguish differences.

Sex-role stereotypes   Rigid ideas about what is appropriate masculine or feminine behavior.

Short-term memory   The working memory, consisting of information a person is consciously aware of at a particular time.

Socialization   The lifelong process by which an individual acquires the beliefs, attitudes, customs, and expectations of a culture or social group.

Social cognition   Thought processes and understandings of the social world.

Social work methods   The three major specializations in social work practice—casework, group work, and community organization.

Sociobiology   A discipline that seeks to integrate theories about our biological nature with theories about our cultural organization.

Sperm   The male reproductive cell (or gamete).

Status offenses   Actions that are only illegal for minors.

Sublimanation   The diversion of an instinctual desire so that it is expressed in a more socially acceptable form.

Symbolic representation   The use of words and images to represent events or experiences.

Teratology   The study of agents that cause abnormal prenatal development. Literally, "the study of monsters."

Triggering   The release of particular behaviors in response to the presence of specific stimuli.

Type A personality   The type of personality considered most prone to heart attacks—tense, achievement-oriented, and highly competitive.

Type B personality   The type of personality considered least prone to heart attacks—relaxed, patient, and nonaggressive.

Ultrasound   A technique using sound waves to produce a picture of the fetus in the uterus.

Validity   The degree to which a test actually measures what it sets out to study.

Variable   A factor that may be adjusted to assume different values. For example, age, income, and social class are variables.

Verbal mediation   The use of language to help solve a problem.

Withdrawal   A defense mechanism in which the individual runs away or mentally withdraws from unpleasant situations.

Zygote   A fertilized ovum.

REFERENCES

Abbott, J.W. Hospice. *Aging*, 1978, 5(3), 38–40.

Abramovitch, R., & Grusec, J.E. Peer Imitation in a Natural Setting. *Child Development*, 1978, 49, 60–65.

Aelfand, D., Hartmann, D., Cramer, C., Smith, C., & Page, B. The Effects of Instructional Prompts and Praise on Children's Donation Rates. *Child Development*, 1975, 46, 980–983.

Ainsworth, M.D.S. *Infancy in Uganda: Infant Care and the Growth of Love.* Baltimore: Johns Hopkins University Press, 1967.

Ainsworth, M.D.S. The Development of Infant-Mother Attachment. In B.M. Caldwell & H.N. Ricciuti (Eds.), *Review of Child Development Research* (Vol. 3). Chicago: University of Chicago Press, 1973.

Almo, J.S. Without Benefit of Clergy: Cohabitation as a Non-Institutionalized Marriage Role. In K. Knafl & H. Grace (Eds.), *Families Across the Life Cycle: Studies from Nursing.* Boston: Little, Brown, 1978.

Ananth, T. Side Effects on Fetus and Infant of Psychotropic Drug Use During Pregnancy. *International Pharmaco-Psychiatry*, 1976, 11(4), 246–260.

Anastasi, A. Heredity, Environment, and the Question of "How?" *Psychological Review*, 1958, 65, 197–208.

Anderson, E.S. *Register Variation in Young Childrens' Role-Playing Speech.* Paper presented at the Communicative Competence, Language Use and Role-Playing Symposium, Society for Research and Child Development, March 1979.

Aronfreed, T. *Conduct and Conscience: The Socialization of Internalized Control Over Behavior.* New York: Academic Press, 1968.

Astin, A.W. *Four Critical Years.* San Francisco: Jossey-Bass, 1977.

Atchley, R. *The Social Forces in Later Life.* Belmont, Calif.: Wadsworth, 1977.

Atkinson, R.C., & Shiffrin, R.M. The Control of Short-term Memory. *Scientific American*, 1971, 225(2), 82–90.

Authier, K. Defining the Child in Child Care, *Social Work*, November 1979, 24:6.

Babson, S.G., & Benson, R.C. *Primer on Prematurity and High-Risk Pregnancy.* St. Louis: C.V. Mosby, 1966.

Baldwin, A.L. The Effect of Home Environment on Nursery School Behavior. *Child Development*, 1949, 20, 49–61.

Bandura, A. *Principles of Behavior Modification.* New York: Holt, Rinehart & Winston, 1969.

Bandura, A. *Social Learning Theory.* Englewood Cliffs, N.J.: Prentice-Hall, 1977.

Bandura, A., Ross, D., & Ross, S.A. A Comparative Test of the Status Envy, Social Power, and Secondary Reinforcement Theories of Identificatory Learning. *Journal of Abnormal and Social Psychology*, 1963, 67, 527–534.

Bandura, A., & Walters, R.H. *Adolescent Aggression.* New York: Ronald Press, 1959.

Baratz, J.C. Teaching Reading in an Urban Negro School System. In F. Williams (Ed.), *Language and Poverty.* Chicago: Markham, 1970.

Barker, R.G., Dembo, T., & Lewin, K. Frustration and Regression. In R.G. Barker, J.S. Kovnin & H.F. Wright (Eds.), *Child Behavior and Development.* New York: McGraw-Hill, 1943.

Barnett, M. Who Can Deliver a Baby? *Nation,* July 2, 1977, 225, 10–12.

Bartlett, H.M. *The Common Base of Social Work Practice.* New York: National Association of Social Workers, 1970.

Baumgartner, L. Health and Ethnic Minorities in the Sixties. *American Journal of Public Health,* 1965, 55, 495–498.

Baumrind, D. Socialization and Instrumental Competence in Young Children. In W.W. Hartup (Ed.), *The Young Child: Reviews of Research* (Vol. 2). Washington, D.C.: National Association for the Education of Young Children, 1972.

Baumrind, D. A Dialectical Materialist's Perspective on Knowing Social Reality. *New Directions for Child Development,* 1978, 2.

Bayley, N. Consistency and Variability in the Growth of Intelligence from Birth to Eighteen Years. *Journal of Genetic Psychology,* 1949, 75, 165–196.

Beach, F.A. Introduction, *Human Sexuality in Four Perspectives.* Baltimore: Johns Hopkins University Press, 1976.

Becker, W.C. Consequences of Different Kinds of Parental Discipline. In M.L. Hoffman (Ed.), *Review of Child Developmental Research* (Vol. 1). New York: Russell Sage Foundation, 1964.

Bell, A.P., & Weinberg, M.S. *Homosexualities: A Study of Diversity Among Men and Women.* New York: Simon & Schuster, 1978.

Bell, S.M., & Ainsworth, M.D.S. Infant Crying and Maternal Responsiveness. *Child Development,* 1972, 43, 1171–1190.

Beller, E.K. Dependency and Independence in Young Children. *Journal of Genetic Psychology,* 1955, 87, 25–35.

Belsky, J., & Steinberg, L.D. The Effects of Day Care: A Critical Review. *Child Development,* 1978, 49, 929–949.

Bem, S.L. Androgyny vs. The Tight Little Lives of Fluffy Women and Chesty Men. *Psychology Today,* 1975, 9(4), 59–62.

Bem, S.L., Martyna, N., & Watson, C. Sex Typing and Androgyny: Further Explorations of the Expressive Domain. *Journal of Personality and Social Psychology,* 1976, 34(5), 1016–1023.

Benedek, T. Parenthood During the Life Cycle. In E.J. Anthony & T. Benedek (Eds.), *Parenthood: Its Psychology and Psychopathology.* Boston: Little, Brown, 1970.

Berger, B., et al. Child-Rearing Practices in the Communal Family. In A. Skolnick & J.H. Skolnick, *Intimacy, Family, and Society.* Boston: Little, Brown, 1974.

Bernstein, B. Elaborated and Restricted Codes: Their Social Origins and Some Consequences. In A.G. Smith (Ed.), *Communication and Culture.* New York: Holt, Rinehart & Winston, 1966.

Bettelheim, B. *The Uses of Enchantment: The Meaning and Importance of Fairy Tales.* New York: Random House, 1976.

Billingsley, A. *Black Families in White America.* Englewood Cliffs, N.J.: Prentice-Hall, 1968.

Billingsley, A. Illegitimacy and the Black Community. In *Illegitimacy: Changing Services for Changing Times.* New York: National Council on Illegitimacy, 1970, pp. 70–85.

Binet, A., & Simon, T. Méthodes Nouvelles Pour le Diagnostic du Niveau Intellectual des Anormaux. *L'Année Psychologique,* 1905, 11, 191–244.

Binet, A., & Simon, T. [*The Development of Intelligence in Children*] (E.S. Kite, trans.) Baltimore: Williams & Wilkins, 1916.

Birch, H.G. Malnutrition, Learning and Intelligence. *American Journal of Public Health,* 1972, 62(6), 773–784.

Birch H.G., & Gussow, J.D. *Disadvantaged Children: Health, Nutrition, and School Failure.* New York: Harcourt Brace Jovanovich, 1970.

Birren, J.E., (Ed.). *Handbook of Aging and the Individual.* Chicago: University of Chicago Press, 1959.

Bischof, L.J. *Adult Psychology.* New York: Harper & Row, 1969.

Blanchard, E. Social Work Practice with American Indians. In *Cultural Awareness in the Human Services.* Seattle: School of Social Work, University of Washington, 1979.

Blanton, R. History of Classification of Mental Retardation. In N. Hobbs (Ed.), *Issues in the Classification of Children.* San Francisco: Jossey-Bass, 1975.

Blau, Z.S. *Old Age in a Changing Society.* New York: New Viewpoints, 1973.

Bloom, B.S., & Krathwohl, D.R. *Taxonomy of Educational Objectives. Handbook I: The Cognitive Domain.* New York: D. McKay, 1956.

Bloom, L. *Language Development: Form and Function in Emerging Grammars.* Cambridge: M.I.T. Press, 1970.

Botwinick, J. Intellectual Abilities. In J. Birren and K.W. Schaie (Eds.), *Handbook of the Psychology of Aging.* New York: Van Nostrand Reinhold, 1977.

Boulette, T.T. The Spanish Speaking/Surnamed Poor. In *Child Welfare Strategy in the Coming Years.* Washington, D.C.: H.E.W. Publication No. (OHDS) 78–30158, 1978.

Bower, T.G.R. The Object in the World of the Infant. *Scientific American,* October 1971, pp. 30–38.

Bowlby, J. Separation Anxiety. *International Journal of Psychoanalysis,* 1960, 41, 89–113.

Bowlby, J. *Attachment.* New York: Basic Books, 1969.

Boyd, G.F. The Levels of Aspiration of White and Negro Children in a Non-Segregated Elementary School. *Journal of Social Psychology,* 1952, 36, 191–196.

Brazelton, T.B. *Infants and Mothers: Differences in Development.* New York: Dell, 1969.

Brody, E. Aging. In *Encyclopedia of Social Work.* Washington, D.C.: National Association of Social Workers, 1977.

Brody, J. Exercising to Turn Back the Years. *The New York Times,* June 6, 1979, pp. C 18–19.

Bronfenbrenner, U. *Two Worlds of Childhood: U.S. and U.S.S.R.* New York: Russell Sage, 1970.

Bronfenbrenner, U. *A Report on Longitudinal Evaluation of Preschool Programs* (Vol. 2). Washington, D.C.: H.E.W. Publication No. (OHD), 1974.

Bronfenbrenner, U. *The Ecology of Human Development.* Cambridge, Mass.: Harvard University, 1979.

Bruner, J.S. *The Relevance of Education.* New York: W.W. Norton and Co., 1971.

Bruner, J.S. *Beyond the Information Given: Studies in the Psychology of Knowing.* New York: W.W. Norton and Co., 1973.

Bruner, J.S., Oliver, R.R., & Greenfield, P.M. *Studies in Cognitive Growth.* New York: John Wiley, 1966.

Bühler, C., & Massarik, F., (Eds.), *The Course of Human Life: A Study of Goals in the Humanistic Perspective.* New York: Springer, 1968.

Burnham, A.S. The Heroin Babies are Going Cold Turkey. *New York Times Magazine,* January 9, 1972, p. 18.

Burnside, I.M. Sensory and Cognitive Functioning in Later Life. In I. Burnside, P. Ebersole & H.E. Monea (Eds.), *Psychosocial Caring Throughout the Life Span.* New York: McGraw-Hill, 1979. (a)

Burnside, I.M. The Later Decades of Life: Researches and Reflections. In I.M. Burnside, P. Ebersole & H.E. Monea (Eds.), *Psychosocial Caring Throughout the Life Span.* New York: McGraw-Hill, 1979. (b)

Butler, R.N. Successful Aging. *Mental Hygiene,* 1974, 58, 6–12.

Butler, R.N. *Why Survive? Being Old in America.* New York: Harper & Row, 1975.

Cain, G.G. Labor Force. In *Encyclopedia of Social Work.* Washington, D.C.: National Association of Social Workers, 1977.

Calder, R. Food Supplementation for Prevention of Malnutrition in the Pre-school Child. In National Research Council, *Pre-school Child Malnutrition: Primary Deterrent to Human Progress.* Washington, D.C.: National Academy of Sciences, 1966.

Carmichael, L. The Onset and Early Development of Behavior. In P.H. Mussen (Ed.), *Carmichael's Manual of Child Psychology* (3rd ed., Vol. 1). New York: John Wiley, 1970.

Caudill, W., & Weinstein, H. Maternal Care and Infant Behavior in Japan and America. *Psychiatry,* 1969, 32, 12–43.

Chess, S. Temperament in the Normal Infant. In J. Hellmuth (Ed.), *The Exceptional Infant* (Vol. 1). Seattle: Special Child Publications, 1967.

Chiancola, S. The Process of Separation and Divorce: A New Approach. *Social Casework,* October 1978, 59, 494–500.

Child, I.W. *Humanistic Psychology and the Research Tradition.* New York: John Wiley, 1973.

Chilman, C. *Adolescent Sexuality in a Changing American Society: Social and Psychological Perspectives.* Washington, D.C.: U.S. Department of Health, Education and Welfare, 1978.

Chilman, C.S. Teenage Pregnancy: A Research Review. *Social Work,* November 1979, 24(6), 492–497 (b).

Chomsky, N. (Review of *Verbal Behavior* by B.F. Skinner). *Language,* 1959, 35, 26–58.

Church, J., (Ed.). *Three Babies: Biographies of Cognitive Development.* New York: Random House, 1966.

Clark, K.B. Educational Stimulation of Racially Disadvantaged Children. In A.H. Passow (Ed.), *Education in Depressed Areas.* New York: Teacher's College, Columbia University, 1963.

Clark, K.B., & Clark, M.P. Racial Identification and Preference in Negro Children. In T.M. Newcomb & E.L. Hartley (Eds.), *Readings in Social Psychology.* New York: Holt, Rinehart & Winston, 1947.

Clarke-Stewart, K.A. And Daddy Makes Three: The Father's Impact on Mother and Young Child. *Child Development,* 1978, 49, 466–478.

Clausen, J.A. The Social Meaning of Differential Physical and Sexual Maturation. In S.E. Dragastin & G.H. Elder, Sr. (Eds.), *Adolescence in the Life Cycle.* New York: John Wiley, 1975.

Cloward, R.A., & Ohlin, L.E. *Delinquency and Opportunity.* Glencoe, Ill.: Free Press, 1961.

Cochran, M.A. A Comparison of Group Day Care and Family Childrearing Patterns in Sweden. *Child Development,* 1977, 48, 702–707.

Cohen, A.K. *Delinquent Boys: The Culture of the Gang.* Glencoe, Ill.: Free Press, 1955.

Cohen, L.B., & Gelber, E.R. Infant Visual Memory. In L.B. Cohen & P. Salapatek (Eds.), *Infant Perception: From Sensation to Cognition* (Vol. I). New York: Academic Press, 1975.

Collard, R.R. Exploratory and Play Behaviors of Infants Reared in an Institution and in Lower- and Middle-Class Homes. *Child Development,* 1971, 42, 1003–1015.

Comer, J.P., & Poussaint, A.F. *Black Child Care.* New York: Simon & Schuster, 1975.

Consumers Union. *Licit and Illicit Drugs.* E.M. Breacher (Ed.). Boston: Little, Brown, 1972.

Cooley, C.H. *Social Organization.* New York: Scribner's, 1909.

Coster, G. *Scientific American.* November, 1962, p. 44.

Coursin, D.B. *Nutrition and Brain Development in Infants.* Merrill-Palmer Quarterly, 1972, 18, 177–202.

Cowan, P.A., & Walters, R.H. Studies of Reinforcement of Aggression: I. Effects of Scheduling. *Child Development,* 1963, 34, 543–551.

Cowgill, D.O. Aging in American Society. In D.O. Cowgill & L.D. Holmes (Eds.), *Aging and Modernization.* New York: Appleton-Century-Crofts, 1972.

Cowgill, D.O. Aging and Modernization: A Revision of the Theory. In J.F. Gubrium (Ed.), *Late Life: Communities and Environmental Policy.* Springfield, Ill.: Chas. C Thomas, 1974.

Cox, H., & Bhak, A. Symbolic Interaction and Retirement Adjustment: An Empirical Asset. *International Journal of Aging and Human Development,* 1979, 9(3), 279–286.

Craig, G.J., & Garney, P. *Attachment and Separation Behavior in the Second and Third Years.* Unpublished manuscript, University of Massachusetts, 1972.

Craik, F. Psychopathology and Social Pathology. In J. Birrens et al. (Eds.), *Handbook of the Psychology of Aging.* Princeton: Van Nostrand Reinhold, 1977.

Cratty, B.J. *Perceptual and Motor Development in Infants and Children.* New York: Macmillan, 1970.

Cravioto, J., & Robles, B. Evolution of Adaptive and Motor Behavior During Rehabilitation from Kwashiorkor. *American Journal of Orthopsychiatry,* 1965, 35, 449–464.

Cromwell, R. et al. Criteria for Classification Systems. In N. Hobbs (Ed.), *Issues in the Classification of Children.* San Francisco: Jossey-Bass, 1975.

Cross, H.J., & Pruyn, E.L. Youth and the Counterculture. In J.F. Adams (Ed.), *Understanding Adolescence* (2nd ed.), Boston: Allyn & Bacon, 1973.

Cruickshank, W.M. Myths and Realities in Learning Disabilities. *Learning Disabilities,* 1977, 10(1), 57–64.

Cumming, E., & Henry, W.E. *Growing Old: The Process of Disengagement.* New York: Basic Books, 1961.

Curley, N.L., & Skerrett, K. The First Year of Marriage: Adjustments and Negotiations. In K. Knafl & H. Grace (Eds.), *Families Across the Life Cycle: Studies from Nursing.* Boston: Little, Brown, 1978.

Datan, N., & Ginsberg, L. (Eds.). *Life-span Developmental Psychology.* New York: Academic Press, 1975.

Davenport, W.H. Sex in Cross-Cultural Perspective. In F. Beach (Ed.), *Human Sexuality in Four Perspectives.* Baltimore: Johns Hopkins University Press, 1976.

De Avila, E.A., & Havassy, B.E. Piagetian Alternative to IQ: Mexican American Study. In N. Hobbs (Ed.), *Issues in the Classification of Children.* San Francisco: Jossey-Bass, 1975.

Dennis, W. *Children of the Creche.* Englewood Cliffs, N.J.: Prentice-Hall, 1973.

Dennis, W., & Najarian, P. Infant Development Under Environmental Handicap. *Psychological Monographs,* 1957, 717 (Whole No. 436).

Deutsch, M. Minority Group and Class Status as Related to Social and Personality Factors in Scholastic Achievement. *Monograph of the Society of Applied Anthropology,* 1960, No. 2.

Deutscher, I. Socialization for Postparental Life. In A. Rose (Ed.), *Human Behavior and Social Processes.* Boston: Houghton Mifflin, 1972.

Dewey, J. *Democracy and Education.* New York: Macmillan, 1916.

Diamond, M. Human Sexual Development: Biological Foundations for Social Development. In F.A. Beach (Ed.), *Human Sexuality in Four Perspectives.* Baltimore: John Hopkins University Press, 1976.

Dick-Read, G. *Childbirth Without Fear.* New York: Harper & Row, 1953.

Dieppa, I., & Montiel, M. *Hispanic Families: An Exploration.* Washington, D.C.: National Coalition of Hispanic Mental Health and Human Service Organizations, 1978.

Dollard, J., Doob, L.W., Miller, N.E., Mowrer, O.H., & Sears, R.R. *Frustration and Aggression.* New Haven: Yale University Press, 1939.

Dollard, J., & Miller, N.E. *Personality and Psychotherapy: An Analysis in Terms of Learning, Thinking and Culture.* New York: McGraw-Hill, 1950.

Dougherty, S.A. Single Adoptive Mothers and Their Children. *Social Work,* July 1978, Vol. 23(4).

Douvan, E., & Gold, M. Model Patterns in American Adolescence. In L.W. Hoffman and M.L. Hoffman (Eds.), *Review of Child Development Research* (Vol. 2). New York: Russell Sage Foundation, 1966.

Dovan, E., & Adelson, J.B. *The Adolescent Experience.* New York: John Wiley, 1966.

Dryer, P.H. Sex, Sex Roles, and Marriage Among Youth in the 1970's. In R.J. Havighurst & P.H. Dreyer (Eds.), *Youth: 74th Yearbook of the NSSE.* Chicago: University of Chicago Press, 1975.

Duberman, L. *Marriage and Other Alternatives.* New York: Holt, Rinehart & Winston, 1977.

Dunn, J.F. Mother-Infant Relations: Continuities and Discontinuities Over the First 14 Months. *Journal of Psychsomatic Research,* 1976, 20, 273–277.

Dwyer, J., & Mayer, J. Psychological Effects of Variations in Physical Appearance During Adolescence. *Adolescence,* 1968–69, 3, 353–380.

Ebersole, P. The Vital Vehicle: The Body. In I.M. Burnside, P. Ebersole & H.E. Monea (Eds.), *Psychosocial Caring Throughout the Life Span.* New York: McGraw-Hill, 1979.

Eckland, B.K. Theories of Mate Selection. *Eugenics Quarterly* (now *Social Biology*), 1968, 15, 17–23.

Eimas, P.D. Speech Perception in Early Infancy. In L.B. Cohen & P. Salapatek (Eds.), *Infant Perception: From Sensation to Cognition* (Vol. II). New York: Academic Press, 1975.

Elkind, D. Erik Erikson's Eight Ages of Man. *New York Times Magazine,* April 5, 1970.

Elkind, D. Recent Research on Cognitive Development in Adolescence. In S.E. Dragastin & G.H. Elder, Sr. (Eds.), *Adolescence in the Life Cycle.* New York: John Wiley, 1975.

Ellison, R. *Invisible Man.* New York: Random House, 1947.

Erikson, E.H. The Problem of Ego Identity. *Journal of the American Psychoanalytic Association,* 1956, IV(1), 58–121.

Erikson, E.H. Identity and the Life Cycle. *Psychological Issues,* 1959, 1, 1–71.

Erikson, E.H. *Childhood and Society* (Rev. ed.). New York: W.W. Norton and Co., 1963.

Erikson, E.H. *Identity, Youth and Crisis.* New York: W.W. Norton and Co., 1968.

Fagot, B.I. The Influence of Sex of Child on Parental Reactions to Toddler Children. *Child Development,* 1978, 49, 459–465.

Fauran, D., & Ramey, C.T. Infant Day Care and Attachment Behaviors Toward Mothers and Teachers. *Child Development,* 1977, 48, 1112–1116.

Fein, G.G., Johnson, D., Kossan, N., Stork, L., & Wasserman, L. Sex Stereotypes and Preferences in the Toy Choices of 20-Month-Old Boys and Girls. *Developmental Psychology,* 1975, 2(4), 527–528.

Feldman, C., & Shen, M. *Some Language-Related Cognitive Advantages of Bilingual Five-Year-Olds.* Paper presented at the meeting of the Society for Research in Child Development, Santa Monica, Calif., March 1969.

Feshbach, S., & Singer, R.D. *Television and Aggression: An Experimental Field Study.* San Francisco: Jossey-Bass, 1971.

Field, T. Effects of Early Separation, Interactive Deficits, and Experimental Manipulations on Infant-Mother Face-to-Face Interaction. *Child Development,* 1977, 48, 763–771.

Field, T. Interaction Behaviors of Primary vs. Secondary Caretaker Fathers. *Developmental Psychology,* 1978, 14(2), 183–184.

Fischer, D.H. *Growing Old in America.* New York: Oxford University Press, 1978.

Fischer, J., & Gochros, H. *Handbook of Behavior Therapy with Sexual Problems.* New York: Pergamon Press, 1975, 1976.

Fiske, M. *Middle Age: The Prime of Life?* London: Harper & Row, 1979.

Flavell, J.H. *Cognitive Development.* Englewood Cliffs, N.J.: Prentice-Hall, 1977.

Fleming, E.S., & Anttonen, R.G. Teacher Expectancy as Related to the Academic and Personal Growth of Primary-age Children. *Monographs of the Society for Research in Child Development,* 1971, 36 (5, Serial No. 145).

Forbes, D. Recent Research on Children's Social Cognition: A Brief Review. *New Directions for Child Development,* 1978, Vol. 1.

Forman, G.T. *The Early Growth of Logic in Children: Influences from the Bilateral Symmetry of Human Anatomy.* Papers presented at the conference of the Society for Research in Child Development, Philadelphia, April 1972.

Fraiberg, S.H. *The Magic Years.* New York: Scribner's, 1959.

Fraiberg, S.H. Blind Infants and Their Mothers: An Examination of the Sign System. In M. Lewis & L. Rosenblum (Eds.), *The Effects of the Infant on its Caregiver.* New York: John Wiley, 1974.

Fraiberg, S.H. *Every Child's Birthright: In Defense of Mothering.* New York: Basic Books, 1977.

Frankenburg, W.K., & Dodds, J.B. The Denver Developmental Screening Test. *Journal of Pediatrics,* 1967, 71, 181–191.

Frazier, A., & Lisonbee, L.K. Adolescent Concerns with Physique. *School Review,* 1950, 58, 397–405.

Frenkel-Brunswick, E. A Study of Prejudice in Children. *Human Relations,* 1948, 1(3), 295–306.

Freud, A. *The Ego and the Mechanisms of Defense.* New York: International Universities Press, 1946.

Freud, A. Adolescence as a Developmental Disturbance. In G. Caplan & S. Lebovici (Eds.), *Adolescence: Psychological Perspectives.* New York: Basic Books, 1969.

Freud, A., & Burlingham, D.T. *The Freud, Burlingham Reports, Foster Parents' Plan for War Children,* October 1943.

Fried, B. *The Middle-Age Crisis.* New York: Harper & Row, 1967.

Friedenberg, E.Z. Adolescence as a Social Problem. In H.S. Becker (Ed.), *Social Problems.* New York: John Wiley, 1966.

Friedrich, L.K., & Stein, A.H. Aggressive and Prosocial Television Programs and the Natural Behavior of Preschool Children. *Monographs of the Society for Research in Child Development,* 1973, 38 (4, Serial No. 151).

Furth, H.G. *Thinking Without Language.* New York: Free Press, 1966.

Gagnon, J.H. *Human Sexualities,* Glenview, Ill.: Scott, Foresman, 1977.

Gallagher, J. McC. Cognitive Development and Learning in the Adolescent. In J.F. Adams (Ed.), *Understanding Adolescence* (2nd ed.). Boston: Allyn & Bacon, 1973.

Gallegos, J.S., & Valdez, T.A. The Chicano Familia. In *Cultural Awareness in the Human Services.* Seattle: School of Social Work, University of Washington, 1979.

Gardner, H. *The Quest for Mind: Piaget, Lévi-Strauss, and the Structuralist Movement.* New York: Random House, 1973.

Gardner, W. *Children with Learning and Behavior Problems: A Behavior Management Approach.* Boston: Allyn & Bacon, 1974.

Garrett, D.N. The Needs of the Seriously Ill and Their Families: The Haven Concept. *Aging,* 1978, 6(1), 12–19.

Garrison, K.C. Psychological Development. In J.F. Adams (Ed.), *Understanding Adolescence* (2nd ed.). Boston: Allyn & Bacon, 1973.

Gelman, R. Cognitive Development. *Annual Review of Psychology,* 29, 1978.

Gerbner, G. Violence in Television Drama: Trends and Symbolic Functions. In G.A. Comstock & E.A. Rubinstein (Eds.), *Television and Social Behavior* (Vol. 1). Washington, D.C.: U.S. Government Printing Office, 1972.

Gesell, A. *The First Five Years of Life: The Preschool Years.* New York: Harper & Row, 1940.

Gesell, A., & Ilg, F.L. *The Child from Five to Ten.* New York: Harper & Row, 1946.

Gesell, A., Ilg, F.L., & Ames, L.B. *Youth: The Years from Ten to Sixteen.* New York: Harper & Row, 1956.

Getzels, J.W. On the Transformation of Values: A Decade after Port Huron. *School Review,* 1972, 80, 505–518.

Getzels, J.W., & Jackson, P.W. The Highly Intelligent and the Highly Creative Adolescent: A Summary of Some Research Findings. In C.W. Taylor (Ed.), *The Third (1959) University of Utah Research Conference on the Identification of Creative Scientific Talent.* Salt Lake City: University of Utah Press, 1959.

Gewirtz, J.L., & Boyd, E. Mother Infant Interaction and its Study. In W.W. Reese (Ed.), *Advances in Child Development and Behavior* (Vol. 9). New York: Academic Press, 1976.

Gilbert, N., Miller, H., & Specht, H. *An Introduction to Social Work Practice.* Englewood Cliffs, N.J.: Prentice-Hall, 1980.

Gilbert, N., & Specht, H. *The Emergence of Social Welfare and Social Work.* Itasca, Ill.: F.E. Peacock, 1976.

Ginzberg, E. Youth Unemployment. *Scientific American,* May 1980.

Glaser, R. Instructional Technology and the Measurement of Learning Outcomes: Some Questions. *American Psychologist,* 1963, 18, 519–521.

Glick, P.C., & Norton, A.J. Perspectives on the Recent Upturn in Divorce and Remarriage. *Demography,* 1973, pp. 301–314.

Glick, P.C., & Norton, A.J. Marrying, Divorcing, and Living Together in the United States Today. *Population Bulletin,* October 1977, 32, 6.

Glidewell, J.C., Kantor, M.B., Smith, L.M., & Stringer, L.A. Socialization and Social Structure in the Classroom. In L.W. Hoffman & M.L. Hoffman (Eds.), *Review of Child Development Research* (Vol. 2). New York: Russell Sage Foundation, 1966.

Glock, C.Y., & Bellah, R.N. (Eds.). *The New Religious Consciousness.* Berkeley: University of California, 1976.

Gochros, H.L. Human Sexuality. In *Encyclopedia of Social Work.* Washington, D.C.: National Association of Social Workers, 1977.

Goldberg, S. Infant Care and Growth in Urban Zambia. *Human Development,* 1972, 15, 77–89.

Goldberg, S., & Lewis, M. Play Behavior in the Year-old Infant: Early Sex Differences. *Child Development,* 1969, 40, 21–31.

Goode, W.J. Family Disorganization. In R.K. Merton & R. Nisbet (Eds.), *Contemporary Social Problems* (4th ed.). New York: Harcourt Brace Jovanovich, 1976.

Goodman, M.E. *Race Awareness in Young Children.* Cambridge, Mass.: Addison-Wesley, 1952.

Gordon, I. Improving Parent Skills. In E. Corfman (Ed.), *Families Today: A Research Sampler on Families and Children.* Washington, D.C.: HEW Publication No. (ADM) 79–815, 1979.

Gordon, M., & Shankweiler, P.J. Different Equals Less: Female Sexuality in Recent Marriage Manuals. *Journal of Marriage and the Family.* August 1971, pp. 459–465.

Goslin, D.A., (Ed.). *Handbook of Socialization Theory and Research.* Chicago: Rand McNally, 1969.

Gould, R.L. *Transformations, Growth and Change in Adult Life.* New York: Simon & Schuster, 1978.

Gratch, G. A Study of the Relative Dominance of Vision and Touch in Six-Month-Old Infants. *Child Development,* 1972, 43, 615–623.

Gratch, G., & Landers, W.F. Stage IV of Piaget's Theory of Infant Object Concepts: A Longitudinal Study. *Child Development,* 1971, 42, 359–372.

Greenwood, E. Attributes of a Profession. *Social Work,* July 1957, 2(3), 45–55.

Grimm, E.R. Psychological and Social Factors in Pregnancy, Delivery, and Outcome. In S.A. Richardson & A.F. Guttmacher (Eds.), *Childbearing: Its Social and Psychological Aspects.* Baltimore: Williams & Wilkins, 1967.

Gutmann, D.L. An Exploration of Ego Configurations in Middle and Later Life. In B.L. Neugarten, *Personality in Middle and Late Life: Empirical Studies.* New York: Atherton Press, 1964.

Gutmann, D.L. Parenthood: Key to the Comparative Psychology of the Life Cycle? In N. Daton & L. Ginsberg (Eds.), *Life Span Developmental Psychology.* New York: Academic Press, 1975.

Guttmacher, A. *Pregnancy, Birth, and Family Planning.* New York: Viking, 1973.

Hagan, J.W., Longeward, R.H., Jr., & Kail, R.V., Jr. Cognitive Perspectives on the Development of Memory. In H.W. Reese (Ed.), *Advances in Child Development and Behavior* (Vol. 10). New York: Academic Press, 1975.

Hale, B.J. Gestalt Techniques in Marriage Counseling. *Social Casework,* July 1978, 59(7), 428–433.

Hamachek, D.E. Development and Dynamics of the Adolescent Self. In J.F. Adams (Ed.), *Understanding Adolescence* (2nd ed.). Boston: Allyn & Bacon, 1973.

Hamilton, G. *Theory and Practice of Social Casework.* New York: Columbia University Press, 1951.

Hampshire, S. The Illusion of Sociobiology. *New York Review of Books,* 1978, 25, 15ff.

Hannan, M.T., et al. Income and Marital Events: Evidence from an Income Maintenance Experiment. *American Journal of Sociology,* May 1977, pp. 1186–1210.

Harlow, H.F. Love in Infant Monkeys. *Scientific American,* June 1959, pp. 68–74.

Harlow, H.F., & Harlow, M.K. Social Deprivation in Monkeys. *Scientific American,* November 1962, pp. 137–146.

Harris, Lewis, & Associates, Inc. Myths and Realities of Life for Older Americans. In R. Gross, B. Gross, & S. Seidman (Eds.), *The New Old: Struggling for Decent Aging.* Garden City, N.Y.: Doubleday-Anchor 1978 (originally published in 1975).

Hartford, M.E. *Groups in Social Work.* New York: Columbia University Press, 1971.

Hartup, W.W. Peer Interaction and Social Organization. In P.H. Mussen (Ed.), *Carmichael's Manual of Child Psychology* (3rd ed., Vol. 2). New York: John Wiley, 1970. (a)

Hartup, W.W. Peer Relations. In T.D. Spencer & N. Kass (Eds.), *Perspectives in Child Psychology: Research and Review.* New York: McGraw-Hill, 1970. (b)

Havighurst, R.J. *Human Development and Education.* New York: Longman, 1953.

Hayes, D.S. Cognitive Bases for Liking and Disliking Among Preschool Children. *Child Development,* 1978, 49, 906–909.

Healy, W., & Bronner, A.F. *Delinquents and Criminals, Their Making and Unmaking: Studies in Two American Cities.* New York: Macmillan, 1926.

Heath, P.J., & Somers, G.G. Labor Force: Entry. In *Encyclopedia of Social Work.* Washington, D.C.: National Association of Social Workers, 1977.

Heathers, G. Emotional Dependence and Independence in Nursery School Play. *Journal of Genetic Psychology,* 1955, 87, 37–57.

Hebb, D.O. *A Textbook of Psychology.* Philadelphia: Saunders, 1966.

Heiner, D.C., Wilson, J.F., & Lahey, M.E. Sensitivity to Cow's Milk. *Journal of American Medical Association,* 1964, 189, 563–567.

Hertzig, M.E., Birch, H.G., Thomas, A., & Mendez, O.A. Class and Ethnic Differences in the Responsiveness of Preschool Children to Cognitive Demands. *Monograph of the Society for Research in Child Development,* 1968, 33 (1, Serial No. 117).

Hess, E.H. Ethology and Developmental Psychology. In P.H. Mussen (Ed.), *Carmichael's Manual of Child Psychology* (3rd ed., Vol. 1). New York: John Wiley, 1970.

Hess, E.H. "Imprinting" in a Natural Laboratory. *Scientific American,* August 1972, pp. 24–31.

Hindley, C.B., Filliozat, A.M., Klackenberg, G., Nicolet-Meister, D., & Sand, E.A. Differences in Age of Walking in Five European Longitudinal Samples. *Human Biology,* 1966, 38(4), 364–379.

Hite, S. *The Hite Report.* New York: Macmillan, 1976.

Hoffman, M.L. Moral Development. In P.H. Mussen (Ed.), *Carmichael's Manual of Child Psychology* (3rd ed., Vol. 2). New York: John Wiley, 1970.

Hoffman, M.L. Homosexuality. In F. Beach (Ed.), *Human Sexuality in Four Perspectives.* Baltimore: Johns Hopkins University Press, 1976.

Hoffman, M.L. Sex Differences in Empathy and Related Behaviors. *Psychological Bulletin,* 1977, 84(4), 712–722.

Holt, J. *How Children Fail.* New York: Dell, 1964.

Hooper, F.H., & Sheehan, N.W. Logical Concept Attainment During the Aging Years. In W.F. Overton & J.M. Gallagher (Eds.), *Knowledge and Development. Vol. 1: Advances in Research and Theory.* New York: Plenum Press, 1977.

Horn, J.L. Organization of Data on Life-span Development of Human Abilities. In L.R. Goulet & P.B. Baltes (Eds.), *Life-span Developmental Psychology: Research and Theory.* New York: Academic Press, 1970.

Horton, D.L., & Turnage, T.W. *Human Learning.* Englewood Cliffs, N.J.: Prentice-Hall, 1976.

Hsu, F.L.K., et al. Culture Pattern and Adolescent Behavior. *International Journal of Social Psychiatry,* 1961, 7, 33–53.

Hunt, M. *Sexual Behavior in the 1970's.* New York: Dell, 1974.

Hunter, M., Schucman, H., & Friedlander G. *The Retarded Child from Birth to Five.* New York: Harper & Row, 1972.

Hutcheson, R.H., Jr. Iron Deficiency Anemia in Tennessee Among Rural Poor Children. *Public Health Reports,* 1968, 83, 939–943.

Hutt, C. Sex Differences in Human Development. *Human Development,* 1972, 15, 153–170.

Isaacs, S. *Intellectual Growth in Young Children.* London: Routledge & Kegan Paul, 1930.

Janis, L., & Wheeler, D. Thinking About Career Choices. *Psychology Today,* May 1978, pp. 67ff.

Jencks, C. *Inequality: A Reassessment of the Effect of Family and Schooling in America.* New York: Basis Books, 1972.

Jenkins, S. The Ethnic Agency Defined. *Social Service Review,* June 1980, 54(2), 249ff.

Jensen, A.R. How Much Can We Boost IQ and Scholastic Achievement? *Harvard Educational Review,* 1969, 39, 1–123.

Jones, B. The Dynamics of Marriage and Motherhood. In R. Morgan (Ed.), *Sisterhood Is Powerful.* New York: Vintage, 1970.

Jones, E. *The Life and Work of Sigmund Freud* (Vol. 3). New York: Basic Books, 1957.

Jung, C.G. The Stages of Life. In *Modern Man in Search of Soul* (W.S. Dell & C.F. Baynes, trans.). New York: Harcourt Brace Jovanovich, 1961 (originally published 1933).

Kadushin, A. Child Welfare: Adoption and Foster Care. In *Encyclopedia of Social Work.* Washington, D.C.: National Association of Social Workers, 1977.

Kadushin, A. *Child Welfare Strategy in the Coming Years.* U.S. Dept. of H.E.W. Publication No. (OHDS) 78–30158, 1978.

Kagan, J. Inadequate Evidence and Illogical Conclusions. *Harvard Educational Review,* 1969, 39, 274–277.

Kagan, J. The I.Q. Puzzle: What Are We Measuring? *Inequality in Education,* July 1973.

Kagan, J. The Psychology of Sex Differences. In F.A. Beach (Ed.), *Human Sexuality in Four Perspectives.* Baltimore: Johns Hopkins University Press, 1976.

Kagan, J., Kearsley, R.B., & Zelazo, P.R. *Infancy: Its Place in Human Development.* Cambridge, Mass.: Harvard University Press, 1978.

Kamii, C., & Radin, N. Class Differences in the Socialization Practices of Negro Mothers. *Journal of Marriage and the Family,* May 1967, 29(2).

Karlson, A.L. *A Naturalistic Method for Assessing Cognitive Acquisition of Young Children Participating in Preschool Programs.* Unpublished doctoral dissertation, University of Chicago, 1972.

Kaufman, A. Social Policy and Long-term Care of the Aged. *Social Work,* March 1980, 25, 133–138.

Keister, M.E. *The Good Life for Infants and Toddlers.* New York: Harper & Row, 1970.

Keller, S. Does the Family Have a Future? *Journal of Comparative Family Studies,* Spring 1971.

Kendler, T.S. Development of Mediating Responses in Children. In J.C. Wright and J. Kagan (Eds.), Basic Cognitive Processes in Children. *Monographs of the Society for Research in Child Development,* 1963, 28 (2, Serial No. 86).

Keniston, K. Social Change and Youth in America. In E.H. Erikson (Ed.), *Youth, Change and Challenge.* New York: Basic Books, 1963.

Keniston, K. Youth as a Stage of Life. In R.J. Havighurst & P.H. Dreyer (Eds.), *Youth: 74th Yearbook of the NSSE.* Chicago: University of Chicago Press, 1975.

Keniston, K., & The Carnegie Council on Children. *All Our Children: The American Family Under Pressure.* New York: Carnegie Corporation, 1977.

Kennell, T.H., Trause, M.A., & Klaus, M. Evidence for a Sensitive Period in the Human Mother. In CIBA Foundation Symposium, 33 (new series), *Parent-Infant Interaction.* Amsterdam: Associated Scientific Publishers, 1975.

Kephart, W.M. The Oneida Community. In W.M. Kephart (Ed.), *The Family, Society, and the Individual* (2nd ed.). Boston: Houghton Mifflin, 1966.

Kimmel, D.C. *Adulthood and Aging: An Interdisciplinary, Developmental View.* New York: John Wiley, 1974.

Kingston, M.H. *The Woman Warrior.* New York: Knopf, 1977.

Klineberg, O. *Negro Intelligence and Selective Integration.* New York: Columbia University Press, 1935.

Kluckhohn, C., & Murray, H.A. *Personality, Nature, Society, and Culture.* New York: Knopf, 1948.

Knox, A. *Adult Development and Learning: A Handbook on Individual Growth and Competence in the Adult Years for Education and the Helping Professions.* San Francisco: Jossey-Bass, 1977.

Koch, H.L. Sibling Influence on Children's Speech. *Journal of Speech Disabilities,* 1956, 21, 322–328.

Kohl, H. *36 Children.* New York: W.W. Norton & Co., 1968.

Kohlberg, L. The Development of Children's Orientations Toward a Moral Order. I: Sequence in the Development of Moral Thought. *Vita Humana,* 1963, 6, 13–35 (S.Karger, Basel, 1963).

Kohlberg, L. Moral Education in the Schools: A Developmental View. *School Review,* 1966, 74, 1–30.

Kohlberg, L. Revisions in the Theory and Practice of Moral Development. *New Directions for Child Development,* 2, 1978.

Komarovsky, M. Cultural Contradictions and Sex Roles: The Masculine Case. *The American Journal of Sociology,* January 1973, 873–874.

Konopka, G. Requirements for Healthy Development of Adolescent Youth. *Adolescence,* 1973, 8(31), 291–316.

Konopka, G. *Young Girls: A Portrait of Adolescence.* Englewood Cliffs, N.J.: Prentice-Hall, 1976.

Kozol, J. *Death at an Early Age.* New York: Bantam Books, 1970.

Kramer, M., Taube, L., & Redick, R. Patterns of Use of Psychiatric Facilities by the Aged. In C. Eisendorfer & M.P. Lawton (Eds.), *The Psychology of Adult Development and Aging.* Washington, D.C.: American Psychological Association, 1973.

Kreps, J., & Clark, R. *Sex, Age, and Work.* Baltimore: Johns Hopkins, 1975.

Kübler-Ross, E. *On Death and Dying.* New York: Macmillan, 1969.

Kübler-Ross, E. *Death: The Final Stage of Growth.* Englewood Cliffs, N.J.: Prentice-Hall, 1975.

Kulys, R., & Tubin, S. Older People and Their "Responsible Others." *Social Work,* March 1980, pp. 138–147.

Labov, W. The Logic of Nonstandard English. In F. Williams (Ed.), *Language and Poverty.* Chicago: Markham, 1970.

Lamaze, F. *Painless Childbirth: The Lamaze Method.* Chicago: Regnery, 1970.

Lamb, M., & Lamb, J. The Nature and Importance of the Father-Infant Relationship. *The Family Coordinator,* 1976, 4(25), 379–386.

Lansburgh, T.W. Child Welfare: Day Care of Children. In *Encyclopedia of Social Work.* Washington, D.C.: National Association of Social Workers, 1977.

Lasch, C. *Haven in a Heartless World.* New York: Basic Books, 1977.

Leboyer, F. *Birth Without Violence.* New York: Knopf, 1976.

Leifer, A.D., & Roberts, D.F. Children's Responses to Television Violence. In J.P. Murray, E.A. Rubenstein & G.A. Comstock (Eds.), *Television and Social Behavior* (Vol. 2). Washington, D.C.: U.S. Government Printing Office, 1972.

Leigh, J.W., & Green, J.W. The Black Family and Social Work. In *Cultural Awareness in the Human Services.* Seattle: School of Social Work, University of Washington, 1979.

Levinson, D.J. *The Seasons of a Man's Life.* New York: Knopf, 1978.

Levy, S.M. Temporal Experience in the Aged. Body Integrity and Social Milieu. *International Journal of Aging and Human Development,* 1978, 9(4), 319–343.

Lewis, M., & Rosenblum, L. (Eds.). *The Effect of the Infant on its Caregiver.* New York: John Wiley, 1974.

Lidz, T. The Adolescent and His Family. In G. Caplan & S. Lebovici (Eds.), *Adolescence: Psychological Perspectives.* New York: Basic Books, 1969.

Liebert, R.M., Neal, J.M., & Davidson, E.S. *The Early Window: Effects of Television on Children and Youth.* New York: Pergamon Press, 1973.

Lindemann, C. *Birth Control and Unmarried Young Women.* New York: Springer Publishing Co., 1974.

Lisina, M.I., & Neverovich, Y.Z. Development of Movements and Formation of Motor Habits. In A.Z. Zaporozlets & D.B. Elkonin (Eds.), *The Psychology of Preschool Children.* Cambridge, Mass.: M.I.T. Press, 1971.

Little, V.C. Open Care for the Aged: Swedish Model. *Social Work,* July 1978, pp. 282–288.

Loevinger, J. *Ego Development: Conceptions and Theories.* San Francisco: Jossey-Bass, 1976.

Lopata, H.Z. Widowhood: Societal Factors in Life-Span Disruptions and Alterations. In N. Datan & L.H. Ginsberg (Eds.), *Life-Span Developmental Psychology: Normative Life Crises.* New York: Academic Press, 1975.

Lorenz, K.Z. *King Solomon's Ring.* New York: Crowell, 1952.

Lorenz, K.Z. *On Aggression.* New York: Bantam Books, 1967.

Lott, B.E. Who Wants the Children? In A. Skolnick & J.H. Skolnick (Eds.), *Intimacy, Family, and Society.* Boston: Little, Brown, 1974.

Lovass, O.I. Effect of Exposure to Symbolic Aggression on Aggressive Behavior. *Child Development,* 1961, 32, 37–44.

Lowenthal, M.F., et al. *Aging and Mental Disorder in San Francisco.* San Francisco: Jossey-Bass, 1967.

Lowenthal, M.F., Thurnher, M., Chiriboga, D., & Associates. *Four Stages of Life: A Comparative Study of Women and Men Facing Transitions.* San Francisco: Jossey-Bass, 1975.

Luria, A.R. *The Role of Speech in the Regulation of Normal and Abnormal Behavior.* New York: Liveright, 1961.

Lyman, H. *Test Scores and What They Mean.* Englewood Cliffs, N.J.: Prentice-Hall, 1978.

Maccoby, E.E. *Parent-Child Interaction.* Paper presented at biennial meeting of Society for Research in Child Development, March 15, 1979.

Maccoby, E.E., & Feldman, S.S. Mother-Attachments and Stranger-Reactions in the Third Year of Life. *Monographs of the Society for Research in Child Development,* 1972, 37 (1, Serial No. 146).

Maccoby, E.E., & Jacklin, C.N. What We Know and Don't Know About Sex Differences. *Psychology Today,* December 1974, pp. 109–112.

Macklin, E.D. Heterosexual Cohabitation Among Unmarried College Students. *The Family Coordinator,* October 1972, pp. 463–471.

Mahler, M., Pine, F., & Bergman, A. *The Psychological Birth of the Human Infant: Symbiosis and Individuation.* New York: Basic Books, 1975.

Mandelbaum, A. Mental Health and Retardation. In *Encyclopedia of Social Work.* Washington, D.C.: National Association of Social Workers, 1977.

Manney, J.D. *Aging in American Society.* Ann Arbor: University of Michigan, 1975.

Martin, B. Parent-Child Relations. In F.O. Horowitz (Ed.), *Review of Child Development Research* (Vol. 4). Chicago: University of Chicago Press, 1975.

Maslow, A.H. *Motivation and Personality.* New York: Harper & Row, 1954.

Maslow, A.H. *Toward a Psychology of Being* (2nd Ed.). Princeton: Van Nostrand Reinhold, 1968.

Masters, W.H. Repairing the Conjugal Bed. *Time Magazine,* May 25, 1970, p. 49ff.

Masters, W.H., & Johnson, V.E. *Human Sexual Response.* Boston: Little, Brown, 1966.

Masters, W.H., & Johnson, V.E. *Human Sexual Inadequacy.* Boston: Little, Brown, 1970.

Masters, W.H., & Johnson, V.E. Emotional Poverty: A Marriage Crisis of the Middle Years. In *National Congress on the Quality of Life: The Middle Years.* Acton, Mass.: American Medical Association, Publishing Sciences Group, 1974.

Matas, L., Arend, R.A., & Sroufe, L.A. Continuity of Adaptation in the Second Year: The Relationship Between Quality of Attachment and Later Competence. *Child Development,* 1978, 49, 547–556.

McArthur, C. Personalities of First and Second Children. *Psychiatry,* 1956, 19, 47–54.

McBride, A.B. *The Growth and Development of Mothers.* New York: Harper & Row, 1973.

McCary, J.L. *Human Sexuality* (3rd ed.). Princeton: Van Nostrand Reinhold, 1978.

McCord, W., Mc Cord, J., & Zola, I.K. *Origins of Crime.* New York: Columbia University Press, 1959.

McGraw, M. *Growth: A Study of Johnny and Timmy.* New York: Appleton-Century, 1935.

Mead, M. Introduction, Sex and Temperament in Three Primitive Societies. In *From the South Seas.* New York: Morrow, 1939.

Mead, M., & Calas, E. Child-training Ideals in a Postrevolutionary Context: Soviet Russia. In M. Mead & M. Wolfenstein (Eds.), *Childhood in Contemporary Cultures.* Chicago: University of Chicago Press, 1955.

Mead, M., & Newton, N. Cultural Patterning of Perinatal Behavior. In S.A. Richardson & A.F. Guttmacher (Eds.), *Childbearing: Its Social and Psychological Aspects.* Baltimore: Williams & Wilkins, 1967.

Meadow, K.P. The Development of Deaf Children. In E.M. Hetherington (Ed.), *Review of Child Development Research* (Vol. 5). Chicago: University of Chicago Press, 1975.

Melges, F.T., & Hamburg, D.A. Hormonal Changes in Women. In F.A. Beach (Ed.), *Human Sexuality in Four Perspectives.* Baltimore: Johns Hopkins University Press, 1976.

Mercer, J.R. Psychological Assessment and the Rights of Children. In N. Hobbs (Ed.), *Issues in the Classification of Children.* San Francisco: Jossey-Bass, 1975.

Miller, D. The Native American Family: The Urban Way. In E. Corfman (Ed.), *Families Today: A Research Sampler on Families and Children* (Vol. 1). Washington, D.C.: H.E.W. Publication No. (ADM) 79–815, 1979.

Miller, D.R., & Swanson, G.E. *Inner Conflict and Defense.* New York: Schocken, 1966.

Miller, W.B. Lower Class Culture as a Generating Milieu of Gang Delinquency. *Social Issues,* 1958, 14(3), 5–19.

Millet, K. *Sexual Politics.* New York: Doubleday, 1969.

Monk, A. Family Supports in Social Work. *Social Work,* November 1979, 533ff.

Montada, L., & Filipp, S. Implications of Life Span Developmental Psychology for Childhood Education. In W. Reese (Ed.), *Advances in Child Development and Behavior* (Vol. 9). New York: Academic Press, 1976.

Montagu, M.F.A. Constitutional and Prenatal Factors in Infant and Child Health. In M.J. Senn (Ed.), *Symposium on the Healthy Personality,* Josiah Macy Jr. Foundation, 1950.

Moore, W.E. Occupational Socialization. In D.A. Goslin (Ed.), *Handbook of Socialization Theory and Research.* Chicago: Rand McNally, 1969.

Morison, P., & Gardner, H. Dragons and Dinosaurs: The Child's Capacity to Differentiate Fantasy from Reality. *Child Development,* 1978, 48, 642–648.

Mowbray, C.T., & Luria, Z. Effects of Labeling on Children's Visual Imagery. *Developmental Psychology,* 1973, 9, 1–8.

Murphy, J., & Florio, C. Older Americans: Facts and Potential. In R. Gross, B. Gross, & S. Seidman (Eds.), *The New Old: Struggling for Decent Aging.* Garden City, N.Y.: Doubleday-Anchor, 1978.

Murphy, L.B. *The Widening World of Childhood: Paths Toward Mastery.* New York: Basic Books, 1962.

Mussen, P.H., & Eisenberg-Berg, N. *Roots of Caring, Sharing, and Helping: The Development of Prosocial Behavior.* San Francisco: W.H. Freeman, 1977.

Mussen, P.H., & Jones, M.C. Self-conceptions, Motivations, and Interpersonal Attitudes of Late- and Early-Maturing Boys. *Child Development,* 1957, 28, 243–256.

Myers, N.A., & Perlmutter, M. Memory in the Years from Two to Five. In P. Ornstein (Ed.), *Memory Development in Children.* Hillsdale, N.J. Lawrence Erlbaum Association, 1978.

National Center for Health Statistics. *100 Years of Marriage and Divorce Statistics,* 1973, Series 21, No. 24, 10. (a)

National Center for Health Statistics. *Divorces: Analysis of Change,* 1973, Series 21, No. 22. (b)

National Center for Health Statistics. U.S. Department of Health, Education and Welfare, *Monthly Vital Statistics of the U.S. 1974.*

National Center for Health Statistics. *Monthly Vital Statistics Report,* 1975, Vol. 24(4).

National Center for Health Statistics. U.S. Department of Health, Education and Welfare, *Monthly Vital Statistics Reports,* 1976.

National Center for Health Statistics. *Monthly Vital Statistics Report* (Series 26, No. 10), March 1978.

National Council on Aging. *Fact Book on Aging.* Washington, D.C., 1978.

National Institute on Drug Abuse. *National Survey on Drug Abuse: 1977 (Vol. 1): Main Findings.* Washington, D.C.: U.S. Government Printing Office, 1977.

Neimark, E.D. Intellectual Development During Adolescence. In F.D. Horowitz (Ed.), *Review of Child Development* (Vol. 4). Chicago: University of Chicago Press, 1975.

Neugarten, B.L. Adult Personality: Toward a Psychology of the Life Cycle. In B.L. Neugarten (Ed), *Middle Age and Aging.* Chicago: University of Chicago Press, 1968. (a)

Neugarten, B.L. The Awareness of Middle Age. In B.L. Neugarten (Ed.), *Middle Age and Aging.* Chicago: University of Chicago Press, 1968. (b)

Neugarten, B.L. Continuities and Discontinuities of Psychological Issues Into Adult Life. *Human Development,* 1969, 12, 121–130.

Neugarten, B.L. Personality Change in Late Life: A Developmental Perspective. In C. Eisdorfer and M.P. Lawton (Eds.), *The Psychology of Adult Development and Aging.* Washington, D.C.: American Psychological Association, 1973, pp. 311–388.

Neugarten, B.L. *The Psychology of Aging: An Overview.* APA Master Lectures. Washington, D.C. American Psychological Association, 1976.

Neugarten, B.L. Personality and Aging. In J. Birren & K.W. Schaie (Eds.), *Handbook of the Psychology of Aging.* New York: Van Nostrand, 1977.

Neugarten, B.L., & Hagestad. In J.E. Birren (Ed.), *Handbook of Aging and the Social Services.* Princeton: Van Nostrand Reinhold, 1976.

Neugarten, B.L., & Moore, J.W. The Changing Age-status System. In B.L. Neugarten (Ed.), *Middle Age and Aging.* Chicago: University of Chicago Press, 1968.

Neugarten, B.L., Wood, V., Kraines, R., & Loomis, B. Women's Attitudes Toward the Menopause. In B.L. Neugarten (Ed.), *Middle Age and Aging.* Chicago: University of Chicago Press, 1968.

NICHHD (National Institute for Child Health & Human Development). Registry for Amniocentesis Study Group. *Journal of the American Medical Association,* 1976, 236, 1471ff.

O'Connell, V., & O'Connell, A. *Choice and Change: An Introduction to the Psychology of Growth.* Englewood Cliffs, N.J.: Prentice-Hall, 1974.

Offer, D., & Offer, J.B. *From Teenage to Young Manhood: A Psychological Study.* New York: Basic Books, 1975.

Olim, E.G., Hess, R.D., & Shipman, V.C. Maternal Language Styles and Their Implications for Children's Cognitive Development. In *The Effect of Maternal Be-*

havior on Cognitive Development and Impulsivity. Symposium presented at the meeting of the American Psychological Association, Chicago, September 1965. (a)

Olim, E.G., Hess, R.D., & Shipman, V.C. *Relationships Between Mothers' Abstract Language Style and Abstraction Styles of Urban Preschool Children.* Paper presented at the meeting of the Midwestern Psychological Association, Chicago, March 1965. (b)

Olim, E.G., Hess, R.D., & Shipman, V.C. Role of Mothers' Language Styles in Mediating their Preschool Children's Cognitive Development. *School Review,* 1967, 75, 414–424.

Opie, I., & Opie, P. *The Lore and Language of School Children.* London: Oxford University Press, 1959.

Pabon, E. Changes in Juvenile Justice: Evolution or Reform. *Social Work,* November 1978, 23(6), 492.

Palermo, D.S. Racial Comparisons and Additional Normative Data on the Children's Manifest Anxiety Scale. *Child Development,* 1959, 30, 53–57.

Parad, H.J. Crisis Intervention. In *Encyclopedia of Social Work.* Washington, D.C.: National Association of Social Workers, 1977.

Parke, R.D. Some Effects of Punishment on Children's Behavior. In W.W. Hartup (Ed.), *The Young Child: Reviews of Research* (Vol. 2). Washington, D.C.: National Association for the Education of Young Children, 1972.

Parke, R.D., & Collmer, C. Child Abuse: An Interdisciplinary Analysis. In E.M. Hetherington (Ed.), *Review of Child Development Research* (Vol. 5). Chicago: University of Chicago Press, 1975.

Paulby, S.T. Imitative Interaction. In H.R. Schaffer (Ed.), *Studies of Mother-Infant Interaction.* London: Academic Press, 1977.

Pavlov, I.P. [*Lectures on Conditional Reflexes*] (W.H. Gantt, trans.). New York: International Publishers, 1928.

Peck, R.C. Psychological Developments in the Second Half of Life. In B.L. Neugarten (Ed.), *Middle Age and Aging.* Chicago: University of Chicago Press, 1968.

Peck, R.F., & Berkowitz, H. Personality and Adjustment in Middle Age. In B.L. Neugarten (Ed.), *Personality in Middle and Late Life: Empirical Studies.* New York: Atherton Press, 1964.

Perkins, S.A. Malnutrition and Mental Development. *Exceptional Children,* 1977, 43(4), 214–219.

Phillips, J.L., Jr. *The Origins of Intellect: Piaget's Theory.* San Francisco: W.H. Freeman & Company Publishers, 1969.

Piaget, J. [*The Moral Judgment of the Child*] (M. Gabain, trans.). New York: Free Press, 1965. (Originally published 1932.)

Piaget, J. [*The Origins of Intelligence in Children*] (M. Cook, trans.). New York: International Universities Press, 1952. (Originally published 1936.)

Piaget, J. [*The Psychology of Intelligence*] (M. Percy & D.E. Berlyne, trans.). New York: Harcourt Brace Jovanovich 1950.

Piaget, J. *Play, Dreams and Imitation in Childhood.* New York: W.W. Norton & Co., 1951.

Piaget, J. [*The Construction of Reality in the Child*] (M. Cook, trans.). New York: Basic Books, 1954.

Piaget, J. *La Psycholoqie et L'epistemologie de la Fonction.* Paris: Presses Universitaires, 1968.

Piaget, J. *Genetic Epistomology,* New York: Columbia University Press, 1970.

Piaget, J. Intellectual Evolution from Adolescence to Adulthood. *Human Development,* 1972, 15, 1–12.

Pincus, A., & Wood, V. Retirement. In *Encyclopedia of Social Work.* Washington, D.C.: National Association of Social Workers, 1977.

Power, C., & Reimer, J. Moral Atmosphere: An Educational Bridge Between Moral Judgment and Action. *New Directions for Child Development,* 1978, 2.

Proshansky, H.M. The Development of Intergroup Attitudes. In L.W. Hoffman & M.C. Hoffman (Eds.), *Review of Child Development Research* (Vol. 2). New York: Russell Sage Foundation, 1966.

Provence, S., & Lipton, R. *Infants in Institutions.* New York: International University, 1962.

Radbill, S. A History of Child Abuse and Infanticide. In R. Helfer & C. Kempe (Eds.), *The Battered Child.* Chicago: University of Chicago Press, 1974.

Radke, M.J., Trager, H.G., & Davis, H. Social Perceptions and Attitudes of Children. *Genetic Psychology Monographs,* 1949, 40, 327–447.

Rainwater, L. *And the Poor Get Children.* Chicago: Quadrangle, 1960.

Rainwater, L. Crucible of Identity: The Negro Lower-Class Family. *Daedalus,* 1966, 95, 172–216.

Rank, O. *The Trauma of Birth.* New York: London: Routledge & Kegan Paul, 1929.

Read, K.H. *The Nursery School: A Human Relationships Laboratory* (5th Ed.). Philadelphia: Saunders, 1971.

Rector, M.G. Crime and Delinquency. In *Encyclopedia of Social Work.* Washington, D.C.: National Association of Social Workers, 1977.

Reilly, P. *Genetics, Law, and Social Policy.* Cambridge, Mass.: Harvard University, 1977.

Reinhold, R. Census Finds Unmarried Couples Have Doubled from 1970 to 1978. *The New York Times,* June 27, 1979, pp. A1, B5.

Restak, R.M. Birth Defects and Behavior. A New Study Suggests a Link. *The New York Times,* January 21, 1979, p. C7.

Rheingold, H.L., Hay, D.F., & West, M.T. Sharing in the Second Year of Life. *Child Development,* 1976, 47, 1148–1158.

Rice, R.M. *American Family Policy: Content and Context.* New York: Family Service Association of America, 1977.

Riley, M.W., & Waring, J. Most of the Problems of Aging Are Not Biological, But Social. In R. Gross, B. Gross, & S. Seidman (Eds.), *The New Old: Struggling for Decent Aging.* Garden City, N.Y.: Doubleday-Anchor, 1978.

Roff, M., & Sells, S.B. Relations Between Intelligence and Sociometric Status in Groups Differing in Sex and Socio-economic Background. *Psychological Reports,* 1965, 16, 511–516.

Rogers, C.R. *On Becoming a Person.* New York: Houghton Mifflin, 1961.

Rogers, D. *The Psychology of Adolescence* (3rd ed.). Englewood Cliffs, N.J.: Prentice-Hall, 1977.

Rogers, C.R., & Stevens, B. *Person to Person: The Problem of Being Human.* Lafayette, Calif.: Real People Press, 1967.

Rollin, B. Motherhood, Who Needs It? *Look,* September 22, 1970, 15–17.

Rosenfeld, A. Starve the Child, Famish the Future. *Saturday Review,* March 23, 1974, p. 59.

Rosenham, D. Preface. In H. Chauncey (Ed.), *Soviet Preschool Education* (Vol. 2). New York: Holt, Rinehart & Winston, 1969.

Rosenman, R.H. The Role of Behavioral Patterns and Neurogenic Factors on the Pathogenesis of Coronary Heart Disease. In R.S. Eliot (Ed.), *Stress and the Heart.* New York: Futura, 1974.

Rosenthal, R., & Jacobson, L. *Pygmalion in the Classroom: Teacher Expectation and Pupil's Intellectual Development.* New York: Harper & Row, 1968.

Ross, A.O. *Learning Disability, the Unrealized Potential.* New York: McGraw-Hill, 1977.

Ross, H., & Sawhill, I. *Time of Transition: The Growth of Families Headed by Women.* Washington, D.C.: Urban Institute, 1975.

Rossi, A.S. Transition to Parenthood. *Journal of Marriage and the Family,* 1968, 30, 26–39.

Rossi, A.S. A Biological Perspective in Parenting. *Daedalus,* Spring 1977.

Ruebsaat, H.J., & Hull, R. *The Male Climacteric.* New York: Hawthorn Books, 1975.

Rugh, R., & Shettles, L.B. *From Conception to Birth: The Drama of Life's Beginnings.* New York: Harper & Row, 1971.

Rushton, T.P. Socialization and the Altruistic Behavior of Children. *Psychological Bulletin,* 1976, 83(5), 898–912.

Ryan, P. Training Foster Parents. In E. Corfman (Ed.), *Families Today: A Research Sampler on Families and Children.* Washington, D.C.: H.E.W. Publication No. (ADM) 79–815, 1979.

Sapir, S.G., & Wilson, B. *A Professional Guide to Working with the Learning Disabled Child.* New York: Brunner, Mazel, 1978.

Sarason, S.B. *Work, Aging, and Social Change.* New York: Free Press, 1977.

Sarason, S.B., & Doris, J. *Psychological Problems in Mental Deficiency.* New York: Harper & Row, 1953.

Sarri, R. Adolescent Status Offenders: A National Problem. In *Child Welfare Strategy in the Coming Years.* Washington, D.C.: H.E.W. Publication No. (OHDS) 78–30158, 1978.

Scanzoni, J.H. *The Black Family in Modern Society.* Boston: Allyn & Bacon, 1971.

Scanzoni, L., & Scanzoni, J. *Men, Women and Change: A Sociology of Marriage and Family.* New York: McGraw-Hill, 1976.

Schachter, F.F., Shore, E., Hodapp, R., Chalfin, S., & Bundy, C. Do Girls Talk Earlier?: Mean Length of Utterance in Toddlers. *Developmental Psychology,* 1978, 14(4), 388–392.

Schaffer, H.R. *Studies in Mother-Infant Interaction.* London: Academic Press, 1977.

Schaie, K.W. A Reinterpretation of Age Related Changes in Cognitive Structure and Functioning. In L.R. Goulet & P.B. Baltes (Eds.), *Life-Span Developmental Psychology: Research and Theory.* New York: Academic Press, 1970.

Schaie, K.W., & Parham, I.A. Cohort-Sequential Analyses of Adult Intellectual Development. *Developmental Psychology,* 1977, 13(6), 649–653.

Schantz, C. The Development of Social Cognition. In E.M. Hetherington (Ed.), *Review of Child Development* (Vol. 5). Chicago: University of Chicago Press, 1975.

Schild, S. Social Work With Genetic Problems. *Health and Social Workers,* February 1977, 2(1).

Schock, N. Biological Theories of Aging. In J. Birren & K.W. Schaie (Eds.), *Handbook of the Psychology of Aging.* New York: Van Nostrand Reinhold, 1977.

Schwartz, B. Unwed Parents. In *Encyclopedia of Social Work.* Washington, D.C.: National Association of Social Workers, 1977.

Sears, R.R. Dependency Motivation. In M.R. Jones (Ed.), *The Nebraska Symposium on Motivation* (Vol. II). Lincoln: University of Nebraska Press, 1963.

Sears, R.R., Rau, I., & Alpert, R. *Identification and Child Rearing.* Stanford: Stanford University Press, 1965.

Segal, D.J. Smoking, Drinking, and Your Baby's Health. *Mental Retardation Bulletin,* 1973–1974, 2(2), 64–67.

Sena-Rivera, J. La Familia Chicana. In *Families Today* (Vol. 1), Washington, D.C.: National Institute of Mental Health, H.E.W. Publication No. (ADM) 79–815, 1979.

Severin, F.T. What Humanistic Psychology is About. *Newsletter Feature Supplement.* San Francisco: Association for Humanistic Psychology, July 1974.

Shaffer, J.B.P. *Humanistic Psychology.* Englewood Cliffs, N.J.: Prentice-Hall, 1978.

Shanas, E., et al. *Older People in Three Industrial Societies.* New York: Atherton, 1968.

Shanas, E., et al. The Family as a Social Support System in Old Age. *Gerontologist,* April 1979, pp. 169–174.

Shapiro, M. Legal Rights of the Terminally Ill. *Aging,* 1978, 5(3), 23–27.

Sherif, M., Harvey, O.J., White, B.J., Hood, W.B., & Sherif, C.W. *Intergroup Conflict and Cooperation: The Robber's Cave Experiment.* Norman: University of Oklahoma Press, 1961.

Sherif, M., & Sherif, C.W. *Groups in Harmony and Tension.* New York: Harper & Row, 1953.

Simon, W., & Gagnon, J.H. On Psychosexual Development. In D.A. Goslin (Ed.), *Handbook of Socialization Theory and Research.* Chicago: Rand McNally, 1969.

Simon, W., & Gagnon, J.H. Psychosexual Development. In A. Skolnick & J.H. Skolnick (Eds.), *Intimacy, Family, and Society.* Boston: Little, Brown, 1974.

Simpson, W.J. A Preliminary Report on Cigarette Smoking and the Incidence of Prematurity. *American Journal of Obstetrics and Gynecology*, 1957, 73, 805–815.

Siporin, M. *Introduction to Social Work Practice.* New York: Macmillan, 1975.

Skinner, B.F. *The Technology of Teaching.* New York: Prentice-Hall, 1968.

Skinner, B.F. *Beyond Freedom and Dignity.* New York: Knopf, 1971.

Skolnick, A., & Skolnick, J.H. (Eds.). Introduction, *Intimacy, Family, and Society.* Boston: Little, Brown, 1974.

Slobin, D.I. They Learn the Same Way All Around the World. *Psychology Today,* July 1972, pp. 71–74.

Smart, M.S., & Smart, R.C. *Infants: Development and Relationships.* New York: Macmillan, 1973.

Smith, S.E. Drugs and Pregnancy. *Nursing Times,* December 4, 1975, pp. 1948–1949.

Sorensen, R.C. *Adolescent Sexuality in Contemporary America: Personal Values and Sexual Behavior, Ages 13–19.* New York: Collins Publishers, 1973.

Specht, H., & Vickery, A. *Integrating Social Work Methods.* London: George Allen & Unwin, Ltd., 1977.

Spencer, W.A., Mitchell, M.B., & Salhoot, J.T. Disability and Physical Handicap: Services for the Chronically Ill. In *Encyclopedia of Social Work.* Washington, D.C.: National Association of Social Workers, 1977.

Spiker, C.C. Behaviorism, Cognitive Psychology, and the Active Organism. In N. Paton & H.W. Reese (Eds.), *Life-Span Developmental Psychology: Dialectical Perspectives on Experimental Research.* New York: Academic Press, 1977.

Spiro, M.E. *Children of the Kibbutz: A Study in Child Training and Personality.* New York: Schocken Books, 1965.

Spitz, R.A., & Cobliner, W.G. *The First Year of Life.* New York: International Universities Press, 1966.

Spock, B. Baby and Childcare. 1957.

Sroufe, L.A. Wariness of Strangers and the Study of Infant Development. *Child Development,* 1977, 48, 731–746.

Stack, C. *All Our Kin: Strategies for Survival in A Black Community.* New York: Harper & Row, 1974.

Stein, A.H., & Friedrich, L.K. Impact of Television on Children and Youth. In E.M. Hetherington (Ed.), *Review of Child Development* (Vol. 5). Chicago: University of Chicago Press, 1975.

Stein, P.J. *Single.* Englewood Cliffs, N.J.: Prentice-Hall, 1976.

Sternglass, E.J. Cancer: Relation of Prenatal Radiation to the Development of Disease in Childhood. *Science,* 1963, 140, 1102–1104.

Stone, J.G. *Play and Playgrounds,* Washington, D.C.: National Association for the Education of Young Children, 1970.

Stone, L.J., Smith, H.T., & Murphy, L.B. (Eds.). *The Competent Infant: Research and Commentary.* New York: Basic Books, 1973.

Strayer, F.F., & Strayer, J. An Ethnological Analysis of Social Agonism and Dominance Relations Among Preschool Children. *Child Development.* 1976, 47(4) 980–989.

Sutton-Smith, B.A. Formal Analysis of Game Meaning. *Western Folklore,* 1958, 13–24.

Sutton-Smith, B.A., & Rosenberg, B.G. *The Sibling.* New York: Holt, Rinehart & Winston, 1970.

Sykes, G.M., & Matza, D. Techniques of Neutralization: A Theory of Delinquency. *American Sociological Review,* 1957, Vol. 22.

Taft, L.I., & Cohen, H.J. Neonatal and Infant Reflexology. In J. Hellmuth (Ed.), *The Exceptional Infant* (Vol. 1). Seattle: Special Child Publications, 1967.

Tanner, J.M. Sequence, Tempo, and Individual Variation in the Growth and Development of Boys and Girls Aged Twelve to Sixteen. *Daedalus,* 1971, 100, 907–930.

Taussig, H.G. The Thalidomide Syndrome. *Scientific American,* August 1962, pp. 29–35.

Thornberg, A.D., & Grinder, R.E. Children of Aztlan: The Mexican-American Experience. In R.J. Havighurst & P.H. Dryer (Eds.), *Youth: The 74th Yearbook of the N.S.S.E.* Chicago: The University of Chicago Press, 1975.

Thrasher, F.M. *The Gang.* Chicago: University of Chicago Press, 1927.

Timiras, P.S. *Developmental Physiology and Aging.* New York: Macmillan, 1972.

Timiras, P.S. Biological Perspectives on Aging. *American Scientist,* 1978, 66, 605–613.

Tonna, E.A. Aging of Skeletal and Dental Systems and Supporting Tissue. In C.E. Finch & L. Hayflick (Eds.), *Handbook of the Biology of Aging.* New York: D. Van Nostrand, 1977.

Troll, L.W. *Early and Middle Adulthood.* Monterey, Calif.: Brooks/Cole Publishing Co., 1975.

U.S. Bureau of the Census. *Current Population Reports,* 1974, P-23, No. 46, p. 45.

U.S. Bureau of the Census. *Money Income of Families and Persons in the U.S.,* 1976, p. 127.

U.S. Bureau of the Census. *Statistical Abstract of the United States: 1978.* Washington, D.C.: U.S. Government Printing Office, 1978. (a)

U.S. Bureau of the Census. *Households and Families by Type,* March 1978. (b)

U.S. Department of Labor. Dual Careers (Vol. 2). Manpower Research Monograph, 1973, No. 21.

U.S. Federal Bureau of Investigation. 1977.

Vaillant, G. The Climb to Maturity: How the Best and Brightest Come of Age. *Psychology Today,* September 1977, p. 34ff.

Veevers, J.E. Voluntary Childless Wives: An Exploratory Study. *Sociology and Social Research,* 1973, 57, 356–366.

Walker, D., Grimwade, J., & Wood, C. Intrauterine Noise: A Component of the Fetal Environment. *American Journal of Obstetrics and Gynecology,* 1971, 109(1), 91–95.

Wallerstein, J.S., & Kelly, J.B. *Surviving the Breakup: How Children and Parents Cope with Divorce.* New York: Basic Books, 1980.

Warner, R., & Rosett, H.C. The Effects of Drinking on Offspring. *Journal of Studies on Alcohol,* 1975, 36(11), 1395–1419.

Watkins, E.L., & Johnson, A.E. (Eds.). *Removing Cultural and Ethnic Barriers to Health Care.* Chapel Hill: University of North Carolina, 1979.

Watson, G. Some Personality Differences in Children Related to Strict or Permissive Parental Discipline. *Journal of Psychology,* 1957, 44, 227–249.

Watson, J.B., & Raynor, R. Conditioned Emotional Reactions, *Journal of Experimental Psychology,* 1920, 3, 1–14.

Wattenberg, E., & Reinhardt, H. Female-Headed Families: Trends and Implications, *Social Work,* November 1979, 24(6).

Wender, P.H. *Minimal Brain Dysfunction in Children.* New York: John Wiley, 1971.

Wheeler, S. Delinquency and Crime. In H.S. Becker (Ed.), *Social Problems.* New York: John Wiley, 1967.

White, B.L., & Watts, J.C. *Experience and Environment: Major Influences on the Development of the Young Child* (Vol. 1). Englewood Cliffs, N.J.: Prentice-Hall, 1973.

White, R.W. Motivation Reconsidered: The Concept of Competence. *Psychological Review,* 1959, 66, 297–333.

Williams, J.E., Bennett, S.M., & Best, D. Awareness and Expression of Sex Stereotypes in Young Children. *Developmental Psychology,* 1975, 5(2), 635–642.

Williams, R.L. The Silent Mugging of the Black Community. *Psychology Today,* May 1974, pp. 32–34.

Williams, R., & Wirth, C. *Lives Through the Years.* New York: Atherton, 1965.

Wilson, A.B. Social Stratification and Academic Achievement. In A.H. Passow (Ed.), *Education in Depressed Areas.* New York: Teacher's College, Columbia University, 1963.

Wilson, A.B. Educational Consequences of Segregation in a California Community. In *U.S. Commission on Civil Rights, Racial Isolation in the Public Schools* (Vol. 2). Washington, D.C.: U.S. Government Printing Office, 1967.

Wilson, E.O. *Sociobiology: The New Synthesis.* Cambridge, Mass.: Belknap Press, 1975.

Winchester, A.M. *Human Genetics.* Columbus: Chas. E. Merrill, 1979.

Winick, M., & Brasel, J.A. Early Malnutrition and Subsequent Brain Development. *Annals New York Academy of Sciences,* 1977, 300, 280–282.

Wood, K.M. Casework Effectiveness: A New Look at the Research Evidence. *Social Work,* November 1978, 23(6), 437–458.

Woodcock, L.P. *The Life and Ways of the Two-Year-Old.* New York: Basic Books, 1941.

Wuthnow, R. The New Religions in Social Context. In C.Y. Glock & R.N. Bellah (Eds.), *The New Religious Consciousness.* Berkeley: University of California, 1976.

Wyden, B. Growth: 45 Crucial Months. *Life,* December 17, 1971, p. 93ff.

Yankelovich, D. The New Psychological Contracts at Work. *Psychology Today,* May 1978, pp. 46–50.

Yarrow, L.J. Separation from Parents During Early Childhood. In Hoffman & Hoffman (Eds.), *Review of Child Development Research*. New York: Russell Sage Foundation, 1964.

Yarrow, L.J., Rubenstein, J.L., Pedersen, F.A., & Jankowski, J.J. Dimensions of Early Stimulation and their Differential Effects on Infant Development. *Merrill-Palmer Quarterly*, 1972, 18, 205–218.

Yendovitskaya, T.V. Development of Memory. In A.V. Zaporozlets & D.B. Elkonin (Eds.), *The Psychology of Preschool Children*. Cambridge: M.I.T. Press, 1971.

Zabin, L.S., Kantner, J., & Zelnick, M. The Risk of Adolescent Pregnancy in the First Months of Intercourse. *Family Planning Perspectives*, July 1979, 11, 215–222.

Zaporozlets, A.Z., & Elkonin, D.B. (Eds.). *The Psychology of Preschool Children*. Cambridge: M.I.T. Press, 1971.

Zelnik, M., & Kantner, J. Sexual and Contraceptive Experiences of Young Women in the United States, 1971–1976. *Family Planning Perspectives*, March-April 1977.

Zeskind, P.S., & Ramey, C.T. Fetal Malnutrition: An Experimental Study of its Consequences on Infant Development in Two Caregiving Environments. *Child Development*, 1978, 49, 1155–1162.

Zilbergeld, B., & Evans, M. The Inadequacy of Masters and Johnson. *Psychology Today*, August 1980.

NAME INDEX

Chess, S., 44
Chiancola, S., 274
Child, I. W., 273
Chilman, C. S., 196, 198, 199, 200
Chomsky, N., 106, 107
Chukovsky, K., 139
Church, J., 57
Clark, K. B., 156, 176
Clark, M. P., 176
Clark, R., 82, 271
Clarke-Stewart, K. A., 83
Clausen, J. A., 189
Cloward, R. A., 205
Cobliner, W. G., 78
Cochran, M. A., 83
Cohen, A. K., 205, 213
Cohen, H. J., 43
Cohen, L. B., 63
Coles, J. F., 162
Coles, R., 181, 318
Collard, R. R., 66
Collmer, C., 131
Comer, J. P., 176
Cooley, C. H., 173
Coster, G., 77
Coursin, D. B., 64
Cowan, P. A., 126
Cowgill, D. O., 281
Cox, H., 301
Craig, G. J., 129
Craik, F., 297
Cratty, B. J., 102
Cravioto, J., 64
Cromwell, R., 159
Cross, H. J., 242
Cruikshank, W. M., 160
Cumming, E., 298
Curley, N. L., 238

Datan, N., 219
Davenport, W. H., 234
Davidson, E. S., 128
Davis, H., 175
Davitz, J., 277
Davitz, L., 277
DeAvila, E. A., 111

deBeauvoir, S., 318
Dembo, T., 125
Denney, R., 251
Dennis, W., 66, 78
Deutsch, M., 175
Deutscher, I., 267
Dewey, J., 155
Diamond, M., 188
Dick-Read, G., 40, 51
Dieppa, I., 109
Dodds, J. B., 57
Dollard, J., 125
Doris, J., 30
Dougherty, S. A., 245, 247
Douvan, E., 197, 201
Dryer, P. H., 197
Duberman, L., 237, 245, 251
Dunn, J. F., 70
Durkheim, E., 204
Dwyer, J., 189

Ebersole, P., 259, 264
Eckland, B. K., 238
Eimas, P. D., 58
Eisenberg-Berg, N., 124, 127
Eisendorfer, 265
Elkind, D., 191, 256
Elkonin, D. B., 104
Ellison, R., 201
Erikson, E. H., 85, 86, 96, 130, 171, 194, 198, 213, 219, 237, 256, 257, 305
Evans, M., 236

Fagot, B. I., 134
Fauren, D., 82
Fein, G. G., 63
Feldman, C., 110
Feldman, S. S., 76
Feshbach, S., 127
Field, T., 71, 72, 84
Filipp, S., 6
Fischer, D. H., 282
Fischer, J., 236
Fiske, M., 266, 267, 277

Wilson, J. F., 65
Winchester, A. M., 28, 37
Wineman, D., 181
Winick, M., 64
Wirth, C., 299
Wood, C., 27
Wood, K. M., 12
Wood, V., 284, 285, 300
Woodcock, L. P., 102
Wuthnow, R., 194
Wyden, B., 64

Yankelovich, D., 231
Yarrow, L. J., 66, 80
Yendovitskaya, T. V., 148

Zabin, L. S., 199
Zaporozlets, A. Z., 104
Zelazo, P. R., 82
Zelnick, M., 198, 199
Zeskind, P. S., 47
Zilbergeld, B., 236
Zola, I. K., 168

SUBJECT INDEX

Abortion:
  and chromosomal abnormality,
    32–33
  funding of, 27
  spontaneous, 26
  and Supreme Court, 27
Achievement:
  of firstborn or only child, 171–72
  educational, 152–57
Activity theory, 298
Adjustment:
  to aging, 297–306
  to death, 306–8
  to middle age, 257–58
  to pregnancy, 23–24
  to retirement, 299–301
Adolescence:
  cognitive development, 190–94
  cultural context, 185–86, 193–94
  definition of, 185
  delinquency and crime, 203–9
  disengagement from family, 195–96
  drug use, 206–7
  ego identity, 194–95
  friendships, 196, 197, 200–201
  moral development, 191–94
  motherhood in, 199–200
  physical growth, 186–87
  and prejudice, 201
  self-esteem in, 189–90

sexual behavior, 196–200
sexual maturation, 186, 187–90
social roles, 200–201
status offenders, 207–9
and unemployment, 202-3
youth culture, 193–94
Adoption (*see also* Placement):
  and adolescent parents,
    199–200
  and birth records, 49
  of handicapped children, 81
  of infants, 80–81, 84
  and infertility, 25
  single parent, 248
Adulthood (*see* Aged; Aging; Middle
    age; Young adulthood)
Africa:
  childrearing patterns, 88
Aged (*see also* Aging):
  chronic illness, 291–92
  death of spouse, 303–5
  defined, 281
  dying, 306–10
  families of, 267, 286–88
  health problems of, 290–91
  income of, 283–84
  institutionalization and alternatives,
    287
  isolated, 287
  long-term care of, 291–92